The Scottish Contribution to Modern Economic Thought

AUP titles of related interest

LABOUR MARKET EFFICIENCY
R J Elliott

INVESTMENT IN THE ENVIRONMENT
Eric Gillett

THE COMMERCIAL LOBBYISTS
Grant Jordan

DAVID HUME PAPERS
THE SMALL ENTREPRENEURIAL FIRM
Gavin C Reid and Lowell R Jacobsen

AGATHOTOPIA
The Economics of Partnership
James E Meade

THE ECONOMICS OF PARTNERSHIP
Sam Brittan

ECONOMICS OF COMMERCIAL TELEVISION
Gordon Hughes and Daniel Vines

The Scottish
Contribution
to Modern
Economic Thought

edited by
DOUGLAS MAIR

ABERDEEN UNIVERSITY PRESS
Member of Maxwell Macmillan Pergamon Publishing Corporation

First published 1990
Aberdeen University Press

© Aberdeen University Press for the collected works 1990

British Library Cataloguing in Publication Data

The Scottish contribution to modern economic thought.
1. Economics. Theories
I. Mair, Douglas
330.1

ISBN 0 08 037723 8

Typeset and Printed by AUP Aberdeen—a member of BPCC Ltd

Contents

Acknowledgements

Aberdeen University Press acknowledges permission to publish from the following:

Scottish Economic Society
> A L Macfie, 'The Scottish Tradition in Economic Thought'
> D P O'Brien, 'The Longevity of Adam Smith's Vision: Paradigms, Research Programmes and Falsifiability in the History of Economic Thought'
> Sheila C Dow, 'The Scottish Political Economy Tradition'

American Economic Association
> Horst C Recktenwald, 'An Adam Smith Renaissance *anno,* 1976? The Bicentenary Output—A Reappraisal of his Scholarship'

Basil Blackwell
> Terence Hutchison, *Before Adam Smith: The Emergence of Political Economy 1662–1776* (1988) Chapters 11, 19 and 20

Cambridge University Press
> John Gray, 'Hayek, the Scottish School and Contemporary Economics', in *The Boundaries of Economics* (1988)

The David Hume Institute and Verlagsgruppe Handelsblatt, Düsseldorf
> Sir Alan Peacock, 'Foreword to David Hume's Political Discourses' and Andrew S Skinner, 'Adam Smith and Economic Liberalism'

John Donald
> Andrew S Skinner, 'Sir James Steuart, Economic Theory and Policy' in *Philosophy and Science in the Scottish Enlightenment* (1989)

Macmillan, London and Basingstoke
> Walter Eltis, 'Sir James Steuart's Corporate State', in *Ideas in Economics* (1986)

Routledge
> Ronald L Meek, 'The Rehabilitation of Sir James Steuart', in *Economics, Ideology and other Essays* (1967)

University of Toronto Press
> R W James, 'Rae on Political Economy', in *John Rae, Political Economist* Vol 1 (1965)

Introduction

Douglas Mair

The purpose of this volume is twofold. First, it is to demonstrate that there exists a uniquely Scottish mode of thought in economics and, second, to show that this Scottish mode is having an important influence on the development of late-twentieth-century economic thought. Indeed, as Dr S Dow argues in her essay 'The Scottish Political Economy Tradition', a number of the new research programmes in economics not only owe their inspiration to the Scottish economists of the eighteenth and nineteenth century but also the historical, philosophical and sociological approach that is starting to re-emerge in much of the new thinking in Europe and in North America is distinctively Scottish. The aim of this volume of essays is not so much to assert Scottish intellectual 'property rights' over certain aspects of the new thinking that is emerging, but to remind us Scots ourselves of the pre-eminent position that Scottish political economy once enjoyed and could again attain. There is an irony that at a time when the Scottish tradition is beginning to reappear in other parts of the world, the financial pressures that have been exerted in recent years on the Scottish universities have to a considerable degree eroded their ability to teach and research in the traditional Scottish way. For those of us who believe that the Scottish political economy tradition has pedagogic merit, there exists a real danger that this tradition will founder on the rock of financial exigency. And there is a further irony in that the government which is making it more difficult for the Scottish political economy tradition to survive professes to be doing so in the name of the economic liberalism of Adam Smith.

This volume is structured around two central essays. The first is Professor A L Macfie's classic paper 'The Scottish Tradition in Economic Thought', which first appeared in the *Scottish Journal of Political Economy* in 1955 and the more recent 1987 essay by Dr S Dow 'The Scottish Political Economy Tradition' also in the *Scottish Journal*. As long ago as 1955 Macfie was calling for a return to the philosophical (or sociological) method of the Scottish school, arguing that a Scottish revival was overdue. The rather sorry state of economics in the mid 1950s provided what Macfie saw as an opening for Scottish thinkers. Unfortunately, no Scot has risen to the challenge and the new thrust in economics has come from furth of Scotland, although drawing heavily on Scottish method and practice. Many economists now see their discipline as being in a state of 'crisis'—although this is not necessarily any bad thing because if we view the progress of science from a Kuhnian standpoint, periodic 'scientific revolutions' are the hallmark of a mature and progressive discipline. A resurgence of interest in political economy as the Scots developed the subject is one way in which economics is attempting to address the perceived shortcomings of its current orthodoxy. Or, if we wish to think of the progress of economics as Lakatos presents it as a series of interrelated research programmes, then, to an increasing extent, economists are beginning to realise that it may be rational to switch from what is perceived to be a degenerating neoclassical research programme to a progressive political economy research programme. But lest any reader interpret this volume as an appeal for a return to a peculiarly Scottish and xenophobic form of economics, it should be remembered that the Scottish political economists whose ideas are presented in this volume—Adam Smith, David Hume, Sir James Steuart and John Rae—were all widely travelled, drawing on and contributing to a much wider European or North American intellectual tradition.

Although this volume includes the three chapters from Professor T Hutchison's magisterial *Before Adam Smith: The Emergence of Political Economy 1662–1776* which deal primarily with the development of seventeenth- and eighteenth-century thought in Scotland by Scottish philosophers and political economists, it is important to remember that at the same time important new ideas were emerging in France, in Italy and in England. There was a two-way flow of ideas between Scotland and Europe and what Hutchison does superbly well is to put the Scottish tradition into its European context. He presents the names of Hume, Steuart and Hutcheson alongside Petty, Locke, Boisguilbert, Mandeville, Cantillon, Galiani and Quesnay as gems in a row of 'superb, scintillating beads' who together made up what Louis Salleron has described as 'the most brilliant period in the history of economics'. As Dow writes in her essay, the intellectual links between Scotland and the Continent were an important factor in shaping the particular form taken by the Scottish Enlightenment. In her view, much of the new and interesting work in political economy is being done in Europe (and in North America among those with strong links with continental Europe.) To the very substantial extent that the Scots influenced the growth of that European tradition, then the Scottish connection is an important dimension of this new European and North American thinking.

The influence of the Scots has endured. In his essay on David Hume, Sir Alan Peacock writes that before setting up the recently established David Hume Institute in Edinburgh, he approached a number of prominent economists and lawyers asking them if they would be willing to associate themselves with the Institute. They all accepted Peacock's invitation and three of them wrote tributes to Hume as one of the major influences on their thinking. The three who wrote—Friedrich Hayek, George Stigler and James Buchanan (an Austrian and two Americans)—share the distinction of being Nobel laureates in economics. Hayek has always acknowledged his indebtedness to the thinkers of the Scottish school and in particular to Hume and Smith. As Gray points out in his essay, Hayek has gone so far as to distinguish two divergent and opposed intellectual traditions—that of the French Enlightenment which he sees as inspired ultimately by a variation of Cartesian rationalism, and that of the Scottish Enlightenment, with its roots in a Christian and sceptical recognition of the limits of human understanding. Hayek identifies himself explicitly with the Scottish tradition although, as Gray goes on to argue, the Scottish tradition is only one strand in Hayek's complex intellectual make up. The important point, however, is that the Scottish tradition, although maturing and interacting along with other European cultures in the eighteenth century, had then and has retained through to the present day its own distinctive characteristics.

Hume and Smith were close personal friends and each held the other in high esteem. While Hume is remembered primarily for his outstanding influence as a philosopher, the enduring importance of Smith as a political economist is unquestioned. The essay on Smith by Recktenwald has been selected for inclusion in this volume principally because it brings together such a wide range of material that has been and is still being written on Smith. In the essay by O'Brien a number of the reasons for the longevity of Smith's paradigm are discussed. O'Brien rates Smith along with Keynes as one of the two most influential economists the world has ever known. In trying to find an explanation for the longevity of Smith's paradigm and its remarkable powers of resilience, O'Brien is of the opinion that Lakatos' method of scientific research programmes provides vastly more illumination of Smith's grand design than alternative explanations offered by Popper or Kuhn. While O'Brien has reservations about how strictly it may be possible to interpret Smith within a Lakatosian framework, it is his judgement, nevertheless, that the Smithian research programme is still a progressive one, even after more than two centuries.

While the international and enduring fame of Hume and Smith are well-established, the significance of the other two Scottish political economists—Sir James Steuart and John Rae—selected for inclusion in this volume may not be so obvious. They share the distinction that their principal works—Sir James Steuart's *An Inquiry into the Principles of Political OEconomy* and John Rae's *New Principles*—'fell deadborn from the presses' to use a phrase of Hume to describe his own lack of literary success. But Steuart and Rae are are now seen as much more influential and perceptive figures than their contemporaries gave them credit for. Until recently, history has not treated either Steuart or Rae kindly. But, as Meek points out in his essay, Steuart is now seen as a man writing perhaps as much as two centuries ahead of his time. Although Steuart's literary style leaves much to be desired, he clearly set out the principles of the corporate state and Eltis in his essay argues that advocates of orthodox Keynesianism find much more inspiration in Steuart than they do in Smith.

This highlights one of the many apparent contradictions of the Scottish tradition. If we accept O'Brien's judgement that Smith and Keynes were the two most influential economists ever to have lived, then we might expect to find much of Smith in Keynes. In fact, the opposite is the case. As Recktenwald points out, much of the post-war assessment of Smith is coloured by Schumpeter's opinion that Smith's *Wealth of Nations* does not contain any entirely new analytical ideas, principles or method. From this verdict, Recktenwald observes, it is only a small step to the supercilious judgement that Smith as a theorist was unoriginal and that his methods were eclectic, fuzzy or turbid. This view of Smith (which incidentally Recktenwald does not share) has been compounded by Keynes' criticism of *laissez-faire* based on what Recktenwald considers was a mistaken interpretation by Keynes of Smith's system. The Scottish influence on Keynes is, therefore, not Smith but rather Steuart. Yet Smith effectively ignored Steuart's *Principles of Political OEconomy*. In his wellknown letter to William Pulteney, Smith wrote: 'Without once mentioning it (Steuart's *Principles*), I flatter myself that every false principle in it will meet with a clear and distinct confutation in mine.' Following the Scottish tradition, therefore, does not lead us along a clearly defined path from the eighteenth century to the present day. Even such a grand design as Smith's cannot encompass present day Keynesianism and its post-Keynesian development. Steuart, rather than Smith, is the Scot who has inspired that particular tradition.

Rae's *New Principles* also has been much misunderstood and misrepresented since its original publication in 1834, although its originality has been recognised by such great names as John Stuart Mill, Eugen Bohm-Bawerk and Irving Fisher. Schumpeter, who has a rather negative opinion of Smith, holds Rae in high esteem and wrote thus of Rae's *New Principles*, '. . . We must see in his work another *Wealth of Nations* or, more correctly, something that with ten additional years of quiet work, graced by an adequate income could have grown into another and more profound *Wealth of Nations*.' But Schumpeter sees Rae as much more than just a rather pathetic and neglected figure in the history of economic thought. As I argue elsewhere (Mair, 'John Rae: Ugly Duckling or Black Swan?' *Scottish Journal of Political Economy*, forthcoming), Rae had a significant influence on the development of Schumpeter's own thinking on the theory of economic development and in his *Theory of Economic Development*, Schumpeter pays tribute to the 'powerful penetration and originality of [Rae's] work.' There is now a great deal of interest among economists in Schumpeter, particularly in his work on business cycles and innovation. Economists such as Nelson and Winter in their book *An Evolutionary Theory of Economic Change* have drawn heavily on Schumpeter and by extension on Rae. But Rae has also been a source of inspiration for both Austrian and Institutional economics. Bohm-Bawerk, one of the principal architects of the Austrian School, rewrote Volume 1 on the history and critique of interest theories of his well known *Capital and Interest* specifically to acknowledge the influence of Rae, of whom he had been unaware at the time he had written the first edition. Of Rae, Bohm-Bawerk wrote: 'It was on the subject of the theory of capital . . . that Rae held a number of exceedingly original and remarkable views, and those views exhibit unmistakable similarity to views which were developed about half a century later by Jevons and myself.' Rae is also recognised as having been an important influence on the thinking of the founding father of Institutionalist economics, Thorstein

Veblen, and this influence is explicitly acknowledged by the great Institutionalist, W C Mitchell.

As we have seen above, Smith's economic liberalism and Steuart's corporatism have led to radically different present-day perspectives on economics. Rae, too, had profound differences with Smith. In his essay, R W James quotes the passage from Rae in which Rae makes his dissent trenchantly clear: '. . . in my opinion the disciples and followers of Adam Smith, in claiming for the speculations contained in the *Wealth of Nations*, and for the doctrines they have founded on them, the rank of an experimental science, the conclusions of which are entitled to the same credence with other experimental sciences, act injudiciously, and by insisting on pretensions which are unfounded, injure the cause of that philosopher (Adam Smith) and conceal his real merits.' In Rae's view, Smith's philosophical system of the *Wealth of Nations* can only lead the mind 'farther and farther away from truth and reality, into the barren and wearisome regions of mere verbal abstractions'. Rae's fundamental disagreement with Smith was over the issue of whether or not individual and national interests are identical. Rae argued that there is a fundamental distinction between the factors governing the wealth of individuals and the factors governing the wealth of nations. Smith argued that these would be reconciled by the operation of the Invisible Hand, whereas Rae argued that individuals could only become rich by increasing their share of individual wealth, while nations were constrained to create new wealth before they could become richer. Nations could only grow richer with the help of what Rae called the 'inventive faculty'. In his essay on Rae, Dr A Brewer shows that Rae has a coherent view of the determinants of output, employment and economic growth in which the role of invention is central as compared to its peripheral status in Smith's *Wealth of Nations*. Brewer presents Rae's growth model in modern terms which highlight the emphasis placed by Rae on the importance of technical change. As with Smith vs Steuart, so, too with Smith vs Rae—following the Scottish tradition takes us down entirely different roads.

So what is this Scottish tradition? For Macfie, it is best described as a philosophical or sociological approach to social issues. It is a tradition which grew out of the Scottish soil and truly reflected the Scottish atmosphere. That Scottish atmosphere had been created by outstanding scholars like Carmichael, Hutcheson, Hume and Smith who had put the social sciences on a par with the natural sciences. As Hutchison observes in his essay on moral philosophy and political economy in Scotland, the canvas on which the Scots were working comprised a very large area of moral philosophy. In modern terms one might think of it as a kind of comprehensive theory of society, concerned with how ethics, attitudes and sentiments are formed, as well as with the economic life of society, the principles of economic policy and the principles of law and jurisprudence. The comparatively recent reintegration of law and economics which has been taking place, particularly in North America, may be seen as an example of a return to the Scottish tradition. The economic approach to the law is deductive, that is, it makes assumptions about human behaviour and seeks to deduce the implications of these assumptions for specific circumstances. The prestigious *Journal of Law and Economics* and the growing body of literature in this area are symptomatic of how this essentially Scottish approach is emerging as a new area of interest for economists.

Scottish political economy draws on philosophy, history and law as its tributaries. Dow identifies a number of its essential characteristics. These include—an acceptance of the limitations of theory; a concern with practical issues; a preference for arguing from first principles; and a preference for a breadth of understanding achieved by drawing on a number of disciplines in an integrated way. Mathematics has a relatively unimportant role to play in the Scottish schema. This is partly because that with their traditional modesty the Scottish political economists made no claims to a monopoly of the absolute truth on the grounds that arguments cannot be settled solely by virtue of the internal logic of formal theories. Mathematics does not sit easily with the Scottish interest in historical and institutional relationships.

The Scottish tradition dominated British and even European political economy for the best part of a century from the middle decades of the eighteenth century to about the middle of the nineteenth century. Why did it go into decline from around 1850 to 1860? Part of the reason is that after John Stuart Mill there were simply no Scots of the stature of the heroes of this volume to carry on the tradition. John Rae, who lived on until 1872, was a peripatetic figure earning his living variously as a teacher, doctor and administrator in California, Central America and Hawaii. He was never a member of the 'invisible college' of British mid-nineteenth-century economists and economics in North America did not really begin to assert itself until around the turn of the century. The spirit of the times of the 1870s witnessed the emergence of Benthamite Utilitarianism and the eclipse of the Scottish tradition. The method of analysis which emerged after 1870 was the technique of static equilibrium which, of course, was there in the *Wealth of Nations* but only in Part. 1 thereof. Marshall, the great architect of Victorian and early-twentieth-century economics, for all his professed eclecticism chose to build his positive economic theory on the 'mechanistic' ethical or psychological assumptions of utilitarianism. But as economics has found to its cost over the last century or so, static equilibrium theory is not well equipped to handle disequilibrium. Change and innovation are features of economic life which neoclassical economics has been unable to address adequately.

In a remarkably prescient passage in his essay, Macfie allows himself the indulgence of a bit of historical speculation. Let us ask, he writes, what might have happened if Benthamism had not captured the dynastic succession? Is it possible that the spirit and outlook of Rae might have gained command? Would economics have given more weight to the importance of invention, novelty and new arrangements in history? If economics from around 1870 had gone down the road indicated by Rae, it is Macfie's judgement that economic theory would certainly be better balanced, more realistic and more practical than it is today and much more capable of resolving the main economic problem of unpredictable growth or decay, inevitably away from equilibrium. In the thirty-five years since Macfie wrote his essay, economists have become increasingly aware of the limitations of much of their theoretical armoury. New ideas and new thinking which are very much in the Scottish tradition are starting to gain ground. To paraphrase the well known remark made by Professor George Stigler on the occasion of the bicentenary of the publication of the *Wealth of Nations*: 'It is not only in Chicago that Adam Smith is alive and well!'

CHAPTER ONE

The Scottish Tradition in Economic Thought

A L Macfie

Scot. Jnl. of Pol. Econ. June 1955

I

This essay must start with a confession. In undertaking, some months ago, to submit an article on some subject as 'The Scottish Tradition in Economic Thought', I was, it is now clear, in a state of not very creditable ignorance. I had then a rather vague idea that one could in an article say something directly significant on this subject. I had, of course, at various times read the Scots classics in a rather haphazard way; but the effect of reading them all straight through in their proper sequence, in the hope of tracing the individual Scottish thread running through them—the effect of this has been radical. For it has forced the conviction that there is a quite specific doctrine and method in Scots economic thinking, especially clear and influential between roughly 1730 and 1870, and still alive, if not on top. As it shows some of the greatest names— Hume, Smith, the Mills—and also some considerable satellites—Hutcheson, Lauderdale, Rae, McCulloch—it at once appears that a mere article will not do. If there is a Scottish line inspiring these great writings, then only a volume could do it justice. The kind of thesis one would like to examine is the view that between Hutcheson and John Stuart Mill it was that Scottish mode of approach that formed the atmosphere of British economic thought. But this starts many other hares, and the most we can do here is to chase some of them conscientiously.

Our general theme must then be that there is a characteristic Scottish attitude and method which is important in the history of economic thought. It may be called the philsophical approach, though many may prefer to call it, equally aptly, the sociological approach. This is not the dominant approach today in academic teaching—the scientific or analytical method holds that place every-where—but in Scotland the traditional approach is still alive and influential.

It should then be our business to show that this Scottish method and interpretation grew in a definitely historical setting. It grew out of the Scottish soil and reflected truly the Scottish atmosphere. To establish this one would need to describe at least four influences which nourished it. First, there is the place of Scots social thinking in the stream of European culture and history. The Scots gave it their own typical turn but their thought is in the broad Stoic stream. It was brought to its highest pitch by Hutcheson, Hume and Smith. Rather more speculatively, it was alive and dominant in the Mills. Then this Scottish method has its simple everyday reflection in the teaching and curricula of the Scots universities, especially Glasgow in the period between Carmichael and Smith, and later Edinburgh. This we need to prove the persistence, the natural roots of the method. It has formed the seed-bed of Scots students and teaching—all of them in all our Scottish universities—right back to link up with the Middle Ages. This in turn reflects the character and interests of the Scottish people, and they again have their special contacts and friendships with the Continent, practical contacts shaping the education of the people who provided the leaders in Scotland till after the 1745 rebellion.

It will then be necessary to show how this approach and method were at work in the classical sequence up to and including the Mills. It was indeed working in Marshall, though more as a climate than as the guiding line. Is this not the way in which his faithfulness to the classic line, on which he so insisted, took effect? Certainly Jevons was the more typical English exact scientist. But we must not digress. An equally strong claimant as a fact is the decline of the philosophic method from its dominant position, or from being a pervading atmosphere, after about 1870. Along with this we have to note the relative decline from eminence of Scots economic thinkers. After the Mills no Scot reaches the heights in economic theory, and after Marshall there are no more 'three-deckers', no comprehensive philosophic surveys of economic theory. Whether this is because the Scot can be great only when he may also philosophise is a matter for speculation.

Then finally one 'lone star' influence that demands notice is the fact of Smith's genius. Genius can have strange indirect effects. Its brilliance often extinguishes other valuable, though lesser lights. This is not due to any lack of sources in Smith's work; they are all there. But successors cannot continue on the level of genius. One aspect of the great man, probably that which suits later conditions, is chosen, much of the rest probably rejected. The section of Smith's work which was so chosen and developed till it became supreme was the first two books of the *Wealth of Nations*. The theory of static equilibrium there so carefully sketched has grown into an analytic system and method which has for long dominated English-speaking universities, and our universities today control our theory as never before in modern times. It is a paradox of history that the analytics of Book I, in which Smith took his own line, should have eclipsed the philosophic and historical methods in which he so revelled and which showed his Scots character. Book I of the *Wealth of Nations* is now a part of world thought, as is the *Origin of Species*, or *Principia Mathematica*. But even so we cannot speak for the future. The positive analytic method is a mere stripling. An immense future stretches ahead; and the past certainly shows that each phase of social development produces its own philosophy and method in all the social disciplines. Do those signs of today which spell out the future show any special call for the sociological method? If so, a Scottish revival is due. An opportunity is opening for Scottish thinkers.

II

We begin then with the thesis that there is a unique Scots method, or approach, or interpretation of social issues, as individual as any personal approach, and that it can be described as philosophic or sociological. It rises to maturity in the eighteenth century, especially through the work of Hutcheson, Hume and Adam Smith. They gave it its unique bite and flavour, though the flavour depends on the Scottish soil and cultivation in the propensities and institutions of the people. This is seen in the course of writings taken as their normal education by all the members of this close-knit group—between Edinburgh and Glasgow. The course began with Natural Theology (including some Natural Philosophy), went on to Moral Philosophy, and thence to Justice and Law. It was under the law of contract and private property, with its social aspects, that the broad descriptive and critical comments on political economy arose (the kind of discursive comment *ambulando* which the philosophic method naturally and richly inspires). This accepted sequence is found in all the writers—in Gershom Carmichael, Adam Ferguson and Dugald Stewart as much as in the great trinity. It also dominates the method and point of view of Lauderdale and Rae, though after Smith the more specialised treatment of economics inevitably begins. Each writer may give his work a special slant towards his own special interest: Hutcheson towards morals, Hume towards metaphysical scepticism and also history, Ferguson towards sociology and Smith towards economics. Smith, however, like Hume, adds the crown of genius, and genius is apt to confuse the inevitabilities of logic. It also shapes history in a way which may obscure the roots and setting of the writer. Thus, just because Smith is a world figure, we are apt to ignore his completely Scottish character. We cannot begin to understand him, especially what are often thought of as his weaknesses, if we thus ignore his roots, for the Scottish method was more concerned with giving a broad well balanced comprehensive picture seen from different points of view than with logical rigour. In fact, Smith was, like the others, a philosophic writer, modelled on Hutcheson, whom W R Scott truly called the 'preacher-philosopher'. His aim was to present all the relevant facts critically. Modern writers start from a totally different angle. They found on the law of non-contradiction. They aim at isolating one aspect of experience and breaking it down by analysis into its logical components. Thus the older type of writer is often accused of 'inconsistencies', and certainly these are to be found, especially in Hutcheson, whose pupil here Smith certainly was. To the analyst such inconsistencies are anathema. To the modern method they represent failure. But to the philosopher they reflect the facts of our experience. It is part of wisdom to recognise, accept and be able to carry such inconsistencies. While we should of course try to reduce them, we should not insist on avoiding them in our critical descriptions, for then we omit the crux of our fate, and also the practical human problem.

This attitude is still very much alive in the Mills. James is the most sociological of the Benthamites and his valuable historical and psychological expansions are in the true synthetic tradition. The son of course is both the jack and master of all trades. If one reads through the *Logic,* the *Political Economy,* and the main ethical and political writings in one gulp, the sheer wide power, range and status of this mind cannot be missed. But the 'improvement' bacillus is always at work in it, inspiring and driving—the optimistic tough individual practical belief in wide human improvement reflected down from Hutcheson and Smith. The Utilitarian movement is itself, of course, a philosophy. But as a philosophy it is English rather than Scottish, especially in its positivism and its willingness to be dominated by facts. Bentham gave it these main characters; by contrast the Scottish qualities in the Mill writings are unmistakable.

But is the attitude and tradition still alive? Well, it has to be confessed, only in a rather negative way. Scots teachers and writers are today certainly primarily interested in the historical or the social and critical sides of economics. They of course teach the analytics, the perfected system of Marshall's *Principles*. But that is a world movement. They were themselves brought up in it. The writings of Scots economists are, however, still coloured by the traditional Scottish point of view. One hint, significant if slight, anyone immersing in this literature can hardly miss. In the Scots writings up to recent times there is hardly, so far as I can find, one serious example of the use of mathematics to develop analysis. (The Hutcheson example is well known. He removed the mathematical passage in the second edition of the *Inquiry concerning Beauty and Virtue*.) Some may contemplate this fact with relief. The whole Scots sequence cleaves to actual events, to historical and institutional relations growing through them, and to the individual experiences that support and develop the argument. But such individual factors do not lend themselves to mathematical or purely deductive logical treatment. It is not the case that there is any relative weakness in the Scot in mathematics. The facts certainly prove the opposite in the eighteenth and nineteenth centuries, in Glasgow and Edinburgh.[1] The obvious explanation is that the Scottish philosophical and the mathematical methods do not blend. The assumptions in the first are normative, in the second exact. For this very reason, mathematical processes are especially grateful to the English exact positive scientific approach in economics. It is no doubt a useful contrast of methods within our small island. Ideally, the one should stimulate the other.

It should be noticed here that this approach is reflected in the curricula of the Scots universities, and always has been. It has been bred into Scots thinking over all the generations, and is now steadily acquired as well as inherited. This can be illustrated by the curricula of the eighteenth century. The course was in Humanity and Greek, Philosophy (metaphysical and natural), Logic and Moral Philosophy, and, less securely though it was always there, Mathematics.[2] It is here interesting that in August 1695 'the Faculty at Glasgow appointed "Mr John Tran . . . to compose the Ethics, Oeconomics and Politics" for the general course in philosophy which the Parliamentary Commission of 1695 was seeking to arrange by agreement between the four Scots universities'. This was only a tidying operation, for the disciplines were already established in all the universities. Lively individual preferences, as might be expected, prevented any common course from ever reaching print, so Mr Tran's course is not available; but the fact stands out that as early as 1695 'Oeconomics and Politics' were established studies for the graduands.

We should never forget that Adam Smith grew from these roots; that his work is as influenced by them as any writer's could be; and that it could not have grown from any but just such an exactly and richly cultivated soil. This fact has been obscured by the unfortunate inadequacy of Scottish histories of the seventeenth century. Yet, as H W Meikle insisted in his Murray Lecture, the foundations for the future cultural growth were in fact largely laid in Scotland in the seventeenth century. Adam Smith was taught in a burgh school in Kirkcaldy, and later in the normal courses of a Scots university he built up the knowledge, methods and aims of his own thinking. He was not building on air or mere personal talent, as popular records are apt to suggest. We should remember such strategic events as these: The Advocates' Library began its modern career in 1682, and, as Dr Meikle insists, it was one of the vital vehicles of Scottish culture. Again, Stair's *Institutions of the Law of Scotland* appeared in 1681. This is the scientific genesis and inspiration of Scottish jurisprudence, and is itself a unique work by any standard. It was from such stems that Smith's genius was bred. The foundations remain to this day. No Scottish student in Arts can take a pass degree without a philosophy, and the Honours courses are based on the width of the pass degree, as knowledge of at least four subjects is required in it though modern specialisation has made some inroads. This training has no doubt encouraged a people more interested in a philosophic argument (and in persuading other people that he, the teacher, is right) than even in getting what one wants. (Does not the Englishman typically make exactly the opposite choice?) The Scots theological interests and relations should also be mentioned, but cross illustrations will grow as we proceed.

We note next that this local movement of thought was itself also a reflection, though as an original facet; a reflection of what was perhaps the major European stream. It is the great flow from Stoicism. But the Scottish inspiration came rather through the Roman glosses than from the Greek sources. Cicero, Marcus Aurelius, Seneca, Epictetus, these were Hutcheson's mentors (though Leechman mentions the way he encouraged Greek studies). Hume's references are to the same texts, and so it is for all of them. They did not—they were not trying to—dig so deep as the mighty Greeks. They were painting a broad practical sketch of society, expressing all the important balances, not exposing the roots. For these slightly superficial surveys the Roman texts were invaluable models. As an example, take Hutcheson dealing in their typical way, later followed by Hume and Smith, with the advantages of social life. He quotes Cicero (*De Finibus*) on the advantages of a population sufficient to allow of division of labour. The passage has his usual optimistic flavour. It does not appear in his treatment of economy, and it is interesting as showing the social origin of the Scottish treatment of division of labour rather than the more individualistic source described by Locke. But this so fruitful treatment of division of labour is still embedded in an ethical, political, legal argument.[3] It was Smith who was inspired to effect its transference, to form the premiss of a purely economic argument and so give a new science its task and direction.

The Stoic influence in Scottish thought is most apparent in the constant study of Law. Especially on the practical side of this philosophising, the argument was carried by discussions of property rights and origins, or by questions on contract, particularly in relation to land. This appears in the first teacher of the school, Gershom Carmichael, under whom Hutcheson studies and whose major work was the editing of the text of Puffendorf. So we are back to the broadest river in European culture, the Stoic-inspired Roman jurisprudence, carried practically throughout Europe on the broad currents of Roman and Canon Law. The richest contacts for Scotland came from France and Holland. (The French, like the Scots were more deeply versed and skilled in Latin than in Greek.) In our Glasgow school this comes through directly in the study of Puffendorf, and especially of Grotius, whom Smith read under Hutcheson. This tradition pervades the *Wealth of Nations*, but in a Scottish dress. It is optimistic, tolerant, always eager for social benefits between as well as within nations, very different from the nervous, individualist, critical, touchy excursions of the revolutionary French writers. This good temper the school owes at least as much to Hutcheson as to Smith. Leechman, who was a pupil of Hutcheson and later became Principal in Glasgow, has described Hutcheson's personal attitude in words which apply equally to Smith, and indeed to Hume and all the Edinburgh writers. In spirit, aim and conduct they were citizens of the world, and they behaved as such. The world was smaller then and more harmonious, but these sympathies and contacts still struggle to live in Scotland today.

These scrappy remarks are all that space allows here. The place of Scottish thought in the main stream of European jurisprudence is a subject that grows in subtlety and scope the more one learns about it. It would need a long chapter in any volume dealing with our subject. Its literature is as massive and difficult as any Europe's thought can show. But there is a more popular level of interpretation, and it may be useful to suggest in a footnote some simple writings that at least serve as introductions or summaries.[4]

The main faith which the Law of Nature and Stoicism inspired in Scotland was a faith in natural liberty in a natural society. Here certainly Smith was Hutcheson's faithful disciple. Of Hutcheson, Leechman tells us: 'As he had occasion every year in the course of his lectures to explain the origin of government, and compare the different forms of it, he took peculiar care, while on that subject, to inculcate the importance of civil and religious liberty to the happiness of mankind: as a warm lover of liberty, and manly zeal for promoting it, were ruling principles in his own breast; he always insisted on it at great length, and with the greatest strength of argument and earnestness of persuasion: and he had such success on this important point, that few, if any, of his pupils, whatever contrary prejudices they might bring along with them, ever left him without favourable notions of that side of the question which he espoused and defended.' Smith certainly was so influenced with the others. But our view of natural liberty in the *Wealth of Nations* has received a deceptive twist from history, from the individualism of the industrial developments, and the interpreters, apologists and critics, of the Industrial Revolution. This twist does not do balanced justice to Smith's own feeling about natural liberty: here he followed his teacher, and was in a broad way, at one with his fellow writers. The arguments were thrashed out in relation to the American colonists. On this, though earlier, Hutcheson was at least as liberal and decisive as Smith.[5] And the extent to which Smith's imagination could range is seen in his suggestions for federal government in a unified British family. Here again we have to make an effort of historical imagination to see what our classic fathers wanted and appreciated. We are so apt to read our own wants, especially in terms of some index number of the standard of living, into their more closely-knit social and cultural aspirations. Perhaps this quotation from Hume expresses their hopes as tersely and vividly as we have space for: 'The more these refined arts advance, the more sociable do men become; nor is it possible that, when enriched with science and possessed of a fund of conversation, they should be contented to remain in solitude, or live with their fellow-citizens in that distant manner which is peculiar to ignorant and barbarous nations. They flock into cities; love to receive and communicate knowledge; to show their wit or their breeding; their taste in conversation or living, in clothes or furniture. Curiosity allures the wise; vanity the foolish; and pleasure both. Particular clubs and societies are everywhere formed, both sexes meet in an easy and sociable manner, and the tempers of men, as well as their behaviour, refine apace. So that, besides the improvements which they receive from knowledge and the liberal arts, it is impossible but they must feel an increase of humanity from the very habit of conversing together and contributing to each other's pleasure and entertainment.' Natural liberty is a very different sentiment when inspired by the aim of 'an increase in humanity' from that pervading business specialisation. But it was this society as a glorified Athenaeum that these eighteenth-century Scotsmen desired, and indeed to a creditable, if limited, extent achieved.

It might here be convenient very briefly to recall some of the more influential factors in these Scottish contacts; especially with France and Holland. The natural enemy was England, and this lingered, so far as influences went, into the early eighteenth century. So the inevitable friends were found in the Low Countries and France. Professor Mackie remarks: 'There was much coming and going between Scotland and France, where until about 1670, the government accorded to the Huguenots the privileges promised by the Edict of Nantes in 1598, and it is obvious that in the world of western scholarship the man from Glasgow could fully hold his own.' That he did so can be gathered, on a popular level, from such a study as *The Scot Abroad* by John Hill Burton. The direct evidence is scattered over the memoirs of scholars, statesmen and fighting men in all the literatures of Europe. The Reformation paved the way for a possible partnership with England but the balance swung decisively only in the eighteenth century. We need merely mention the economic ties with the Low Countries. Only 1707 with its gradual opening of freer trade for Scotland, and the swing towards the west in commercial expansion, displaced these predominant links with the Continent. Of equal influence, especially in the sixteenth and seventeenth centuries, were the religious contacts. Scottish churchmen in their many see-saw evasions tended towards Holland, Geneva, even France, rather than towards England.

The evidence here is well known. What was important was the personal and social impact of these contacts. It is best realised through the diaries—again a formidable library. But four famous later ones can be recalled—those of

'Jupiter' Carlyle, Ramsay of Ochtertyre and Cockburn, and, most intriguing of all, the recent Boswell volumes. There is also a lesser known one, from which a passage seems worth quotation, because it reflects vividly a swing in Scottish social habit; it comes from *John Fergusson 1727–50 (An Ayrshire Family in the 'Forty-Five)* by James Fergusson. Lord Kilkerran, a Court of Session judge, is concerned about the education of his son, the subject of the biography. He wishes a legal training such as will suit him to care for the Ayrshire estate. 'John's education', we are told,[6] 'had advanced to the university stage when, in the autumn of 1743, his father decided that it should be completed in England. It was an unusual decision for those days. For generations past Scottish boys, especially students of law, had gone to the continent to seek such instruction as they could not get at home. This was partly because of the long wars with England and the traditions of continental alliances and friendships they left behind. Moreover, English universities were not open to Presbyterians, nor, if they had been, could the Roman Law, on which the Scottish legal system is founded, be studied there so well as in the Netherlands, where Lord Kilkerran himself had gone as a young man, and many of his contemporaries.' The boy was placed at Dr Dodderidge (dissenting) Academy at Northampton. In a letter to the reverend doctor the father says, 'The boy is seventeen since July last, and after being taught Latin and Greek at a publick school[7] with the assistance of a tutor, has been one year at the University with Mr Maclairn, Professor of Mathematicks, whose name will not be unknown to you. What his proficiency has been in the languages I shall not anticipate your judgment, and as they are of great use in life, especially the Latin, for the study of Roman law, to which I intend he shall apply himself, I hope it will not be out of your way to improve him in the knowledge of that language. The Greek I know you are more fond of in England than we are here, and for gentlemen educated for the church it is absolutely necessary, but otherwise I consider it only as a part of the belles lettres.'

This no doubt marks a social watershed. Thereafter, in growing volume the contacts are English. In the earlier diaries, however, we feel the strength of the personal influences. They are mainly centred round the Law and the Church. The leaders of Scotland depended on the management of their estates, or aimed to acquire estates. The law they must know was feudal and Roman, and the preeminent schools of such law were in Holland and France. Every man of property, intent on the education of his heirs, inevitably sent them on their Continental travels. In this regard, it is one of the smaller compensations of Boswell's swing to good behaviour that he turned (with such agonising) to Holland and the traditional road for Scottish finish, for one could desire no more complete short account of the type of studies young Scotsmen followed than that in *Boswell in Holland*, and the spice of genius is added, as ever with Boswell. Part of the genius brings us to the heart of the personal life for the many Scots who share in Boswell's gaieties. But they are all very serious also, as one would expect of the breed. We certainly feel their determination to master any knowledge which will help them to manage their Scottish affairs.. The same practical spirit and thoughtful comparative study of foreign institutions also flavours Sir James Steuart's volumes.

In their social gatherings the Church and the men-at-arms are the other main contributors. From the diaries we can sense the strength of the eclectic tradition. They are typically curious about people, men at work, about comparative institutions and what we would call 'social statistics'. They are not concerned with logical processes or sequences, or the framing of abstract hypotheses and their analysis to their utmost limits. They wish to build a truly balanced picture of social life as they found it and the forces which controlled it. Here it must be insisted Adam Smith is a true Scot of the eighteenth century. He had the common Latin Continental scholarly basis (how strange to find his library so full of Stoic texts, so almost entirely devoid of technical economic texts). He is not consciously concerned with building a logical model, or even with arguing in the merely logical mode. We should note his inconsistencies, but we should remember that they are the reflections of the method. Each aspect, the analytical, the historical, the contemporary-comparative (or sociological), is dealt with in turn. The inconsistencies arise out of these different aspects, and so out of real conditions. In Book I we have the analytics, and they bore such great issue that Book I has almost obliterated the rest in the world's estimate; but the rest is at least as characteristic of Smith as Book I. It is the *whole* book which represents his meaning.

Next in this family history come that unique father and son, James and John Stuart Mill. That this is fact some may contest; especially outside Scotland they may not be recognised as full-blooded Scots. Their effective lives were spent in the metropolitan circles of British culture, and they spent their lives in advocating a social theory and policy which are generally regarded as English, though they are more truly British. Certainly, we ought to accept the son's own words that *philosophically* he was no Utilitarian. One could spend an article on each of these issues; here we can only summarise. About James Mill there is really no question. To the end of his days he was as Scots as his native Angus (and the breed there is strong). Of his type he is really a very Scots Scotsman, so Scots that the parishioners who heard his early 'tasting' sermons could not thole him. No doubt a church is one of the few places in which a Scotsman submits to being told, but evidently the burning ardour to teach that was James Mill's enduring dynamic in life took intensities which even they were not prepared willingly to stomach.

His story is as typical a Scot success story as one could find. He had the special qualities and virtues of the Scottish approach, and he brought them from Scotland via Edinburgh University. He was interested in all social forces and structures. There are the usual exercises in comparative sociology in both the *Elements* and the *History of British India*. (In the latter there is an interesting reference to the work of John Millar in Glasgow; a direct link between the tradition's source and the modern classical sequence.)[8] And of course he shows the eclectic interests that are so Scottish, especially in his wide psychological insights. The simple clarity of his thought and style reflect his great Scottish predecessors (of the east rather than the west coast). Indeed his very clarity may explain why he has been so constantly underestimated. Obscurity is one way to temporary reputation. Ricardo's *Principles* is, to most non-specialists at least, unintelligible if they try to consider the book as a coherent system.[9] So it is probably Mill's translation of it in his *Elements* that in the earlier period carried the original work into the central consciousness of ordinary British thinking. For Mill's little book is entirely clear, though it is probably as near to what Ricardo meant as anyone is likely to get, which may not be very near. But further, here, and most distinctly, the economic theory is placed in its proper relation to the other social sciences, in the true Scottish manner. 'It is also,' he writes, 'in a peculiar manner, the business of those whose object it is to ascertain the means of raising human happiness to its greatest height, to consider, what is that class of men by whom the greatest happiness is enjoyed. It will not probably be disputed, that they who are raised above solicitude for the means of subsistence and respectability, without being exposed to the vices and follies of great riches, the men of middling fortunes, in short, the men to whom society is generally indebted for its greatest improvements, are the men, who, having their time at their own disposal, freed from the necessity of manual labour, subject to no man's authority, and engaged in the most delightful occupations, obtain, as a class, the greatest sum of human enjoyment. For the happiness, therefore, as well as the ornament of our nature, it is peculiarly desirable that a class of this description should form as large a proportion of each community as possible.' So even James Mill saw visions, and here what a prescient vision! For he foresaw the welfare state, in which we are all to be comfortably middle class. There is, further, no doubt that on its personal side Mill was the driving power of the whole movement. The tributes of George Grote[10] and of his own son, and his letters with Ricardo leave no doubt about this. Through him the Scottish tradition flows through the veins of the whole Utilitarian movement.

For the son, on the merely factual side, the case is less obviously strong. His mother was English, though she had little, if any, influence on his intellectual life. He lived in England through his formative and most active years. But was it England? Could anyone live under the direct guidance of James Mill without living rather intensely in Scotland? The famous, in some respects infamous, education was his father, and it is just a supreme example or excess of a peculiarly Scottish propensity. It formed Mill through and through. It produced a mind of unique power, speed and range. Reading over his major works—and one has to do this to sense his special power, for it is this extensive rather than intensive—one cannot miss the recognition that this is a weapon specially forged, made possible only by the conscious persistence of its maker. Evidence of a type which others may find inconclusive is the simple fact, that, in these two, any knowledgeable Scot will recognise his brothers; not in capacity, but rather in their fanaticisms and weak spots. Especially Scottish is their consuming desire to teach everyone they meet. If one were asked to find outstanding examples of this fanaticism, few could stand beside them. Perhaps the Ancient Mariner could. With that goes the typical elimination of the humorous point of view which is so generally accepted in the south as Scottish. The teaching Scot, like the ravening wolf, is too busy to be humorous. If his mind had been disengaged he could no doubt have seen the joke, perhaps as quickly as a Frenchman or a missionary. But he is not interested in the joke. He has to get his message across. It is not argued that this is necessarily a proper attitude. It is merely insisted that it is a Scots attitude, and that the Mills illustrate it pre-eminently. Then again, Mill's 'inconsistencies' are even more famous than Smith's and they arise out of the same method for the same reasons. There are other questions that arise with John Stuart Mill, especially perhaps in regard to his wife's responsibility for the social aspects of his writing, but these we must ignore. They do not alter the broad conclusion as to Mill's responsibility for the sociological emphasis throughout the *Principles*, and especially in the theory of distribution. Yet this is entirely what one would expect of one brought up by his father, who was in turn nourished by the Scots method and interests.

This brings us to about 1870, or indeed later, if we include Marshall. Marshall is the equivocal figure. If the Mills are typically Scots, Marshall is the proper English contrast. The *Principles* of Marshall is in the shape and spirit of the *Principles* of Mill, as Marshall delighted to insist. One wonders at times if he does not protest too much. Certainly the tone and wide sympathies, especially of Books III and VI, are in the tradition, but the footnotes and Books IV and V introduce the modern monographic, abstractly analytic method. The history passes down to the Appendices. Some gremlins have slipped into the cupboards and cellars of the venerable building. As we know, the footnotes and the appendices have grown to separate commands. They have sunk the 'three-deckers', which sail the seas of realistic speculation no more. Perhaps it was Jevons who launched the decisive attack, for he began the long line of modern positive scientific monographs, but the contributions of Marshall towards their ultimate victory are as subtle and deep as was Marshall himself.[11]

However this may be, the fact which stands out for us is clear. The specific Scots tradition ceases to dominate about the middle of the century (sharing rule with Ricardo). There are no great, or even highly placed, Scottish writers in economic theory after Mill, and after Marshall the tradition that Scots thinkers did so much to form, the eclectic, comparative, widely sociological tradition, has faded out. What is still very much alive is the analytic method, the technique of static equilibrium which finds its source, or a main source, in Book I of the *Wealth of Nations*. But this is no longer specifically Scottish. It is absorbed into the stream of world thought as truly as is the central theory of Darwinian evolution. In its modern, dominantly Marshallian perfection it has captured the Universities. All academic economists have spent their lives teaching it as the core of their subject. And the Universities today control the spirit of social theory far more exclusively than in the eighteenth or even the nineteenth century. Only Smith of our greater Scots economists was an academic, and he was so much more. This (perhaps temporary) eclipse of the Scottish method is then the last fact we must, rather dismally, record.

III

We turn from fact to fiction—here admittedly a distinction of degree. The effect of Smith's genius on the course of the Scottish tradition is a difficult speculation. Yet one cannot ignore it, for it was also Smith's genius which started the modern analytic method on its conquering course. Anyone who studies any pre-Smith Scottish economist (Sir James Steuart, say), then Ricardo, the Mills and Marshall in sequence, will accept this. Here then is the novel individual force that Smith himself contributed. But in his use of history and of broad sociological facts and comparisons to develop his argument and to demonstrate the need for considering all the influences together as seen in actual institutions—in this Smith was not original, he was simply Scottish. His aim was the Scottish, not the modern aim. If here also he shows genius, as he did, it lies in the richness, the apt relevance of his illustrations. It is a mistake here merely to lament the past. The old sociological thinkers of the Scottish school had weaknesses and gaps that to us are glaring. Especially, their view of what can pass as a fact fully deserved Dugald Stewart's inspired description, 'conjectural history'. With their equipment, based as it was on little more than travellers' tales, facts could hardly be more than conjecture. If the older method is ever to revive in economics, we must realise that the task will be much more difficult than it was in the eighteenth century. Then one mind could reasonably absorb all the writings on the social sciences, as a glance through Adam Smith's library will show. Today this is impossible. We are all so specialised that when we stray from our own disciplines the sense that we may be talking weak superficialities is an inadequacy that we must accept and face. May it not be mere arrogance for any of us to expect to survey all the know-ledge? Or has the delusion of Faust in reality captured our spirits? A due humility seems to require that we take the risk of these recognised inade-quacies. The eighteenth-century thinkers were not accustomed to speak with the assured dogmatism of our modern analysts. As we are, with our present one-line specialisms, we run the risk that nowhere will a balanced picture of the whole social adventure, or even sections of it, be drawn. Yet this should always be the crown of our endeavour. Are our trained thinkers then to leave this valuation to journalists and politicians, for it will inevitably be made by someone? It is neither fair nor right that they should be alone in making it. And it seems immensely dangerous to allow them to be alone.

It should not be laid to Smith's account that Benthamite Utilitarianism became the basis of orthodox economic thought. The opposite is the truth, on the ethical side; Smith there went much deeper than Utilitarianism. It is in fact just an accident of history—one of the many which underline the inadequacy of mechanistic interpretations—that the method of static equilibrium origin-ated in his Book I. The central assumptions of Benthamite Utilitarianism are themselves antithetic to the whole spirit of the Scottish social school. The main philosophic contrast is between a mechanistic psychology, which inevitably eliminates any truly moral theory, and the optimistic forward-looking assumptions of the Scottish school; or again it is seen in the fact that the Scots saw the central fact as a *growing* society, a creature quite different from any mere individual, whereas to Bentham any society was merely an aggregate of individuals. This broad contrast is of central importance for modern economics simply because Marshall accepted as the basis of his positive economic theory the mechanistic 'ethical' or psychological assumptions of Bentham.[12] The static equilibrium theory of 'normal' value is therefore itself inevitably mechanistic. It traces the run down, after disturbance, to a position of stable equilibrium. It has great heuristic value. But its practical inadequacy stands out; it is not equipped to deal with changes *away* from equilibrium. Yet these changes seem to dominate our economic fates.

In this context a historical speculation will perhaps be allowed. Suppose Benthamism had not captured the dynastic succession. Is it possible that then the spirit and outlook of Lauderdale and Rae might have gained command? We can at least imagine it. They were both critics of Smith, inevitably though admiringly, but they were both completely in the Scots manner and method. It is, however, the line of their criticism that is significant. They thought Smith's theory should give more weight to the importance of invention, novelty, new arrangements in history. Smith, of course, did much here, but to Lauderdale and Rae it is picked on as the core of economic growth, and this is suggested as the central issue in theory and practice.[13] One cannot say this of the *Wealth of Nations*. If their interpretation had developed, it would have had to do so through the Scottish type of procedure, by comparative and historical excursions. The analytic equilibrium theory in fact misses change. It cannot cope with the individual causes of change, just because it is analytical. This means that the method deals with laws and characters that are common to different economic situations. But change and innovation cannot be dealt with by such a method, simply because an innovation, an economic novelty or change away from equilibrium, is by definition a fact. It is therefore in the major sense unique, not common. If it is thus unique as history, it must then be dealt with, it can only be dealt with finally, by methods which are proper to the particular, to qualities as well as quantities. Such methods as the historical, the philosophical or the sociological, are in their turn complementary. The Bentham-Marshall analysis has given us keen cutting power where regularities can be traced, and this is invaluable, but the older method has faltered or been absorbed in the sands of specialisation. Yet the strong basis for its use, as Lauderdale and Rae saw it, still remains. Enterprise is its most positive pole. It is the individual improving or creative element that finds some place in *every* worker in his degree. This is the drive behind economic growth. There are ample sources for this, as for most lines of theory, in the *Wealth of Nations*. Had it grown, it is possible to imagine the type of theory that Schumpeter has so richly developed in our day, working in broadening circles through the whole range of economic experience over the last two centuries. If this had happened, our economic theory would certainly be a better balanced, a more realistic, more practical equipment than it is today. We might also be nearer control of our main economic evil, the problem of unpredictable growth or decay, inevitably away from economic equilibrium.

IV

If we try to account for the decline in the Scottish influence, we become even more speculative, and because, apart from its influence on the future (on which this article will end), the subject is of no special practical importance, only brief comment is attempted. We should perhaps first remember that the very brilliance of our eighteenth century throws our judgement out of balance. One would not expect the splendour of classical Athens from its modern representatives. The power of the Scottish influence on European thought is indeed surprising as coming from such a small and then rather remote people. That they realised their position is often evident in their remarks. It is taken for granted quite naturally in this letter from David Hume to Gilbert Elliot (1757): 'Is it not strange,' he writes, 'that at a time when we have lost our Princes, our Parliaments, our independent Governments, even the presence of our chief nobility, are unhappy in our Accent or Pronunciation, speak a very corrupt Dialect of the tongue, which we make use of: is it not strange, I say, that in these circumstances, we should really be the people most distinguished for Literature in Europe?' It is the strangeness, not the fact that excites his wonder. The fact was accepted, and Hume was certainly no boaster, and was in a position to judge. To ask why it happened is as hopeless of answer as questions about any broad movement of history.

On the more practical side, the cradle being mainly in Glasgow, there is real occasion for research into the economic setting there over the century, for it showed a vigorous outburst of energy, and opportunities made and taken, such as would stimulate and direct wider social enquiries. The eighteenth century rapidity at least must be rather unique. Later, Glasgow slowed down to the tempo and form of British industrial development in general. But the answers we can offer to 'Why the decline in Scots economists?' are at best negative. The one positive factor we have noted is that an antithetic movement of thought captured the leadership of social thinking, and Scotsmen, like Welshmen, or even Irishmen, have been absorbed into it. We in the Scottish Universities have done our due and proper part in teaching economic theory in the Bentham-Marshall tradition to a rich flow of students. The present article may at times have seemed critical of that tradition, but this is not intended. Any fair estimate must recognise the invaluable services to accuracy of definition, objective consistency and cutting edge that the more positive methods have built and sustained. When we remember the vague guesses of previous speculation we must insist that these disciplines of the experimental and scientific methods are at least an essential stage in the longer journey of knowledge. But are we sufficiently satisfied with their results to regard them as more than a stage, tool-making rather than directly ore-bearing?

However that may be, there is little doubt that Scotsmen, while acquiescent, have not been entirely comfortable and luxuriant in modern economic theorising, and it may well be that men so placed do not tend to excel there. The Scottish mood remains critical. The trend has been to teach the orthodox line, but to do one's special work rather in historical, social or semi-philosophical research. The two obvious Scots rebels should at least be mentioned—Ruskin and Carlyle. That their crusade was largely emotional is not in itself to its discredit. But here we deal with scientific thought, so we need only remark that their protests were typical of the Scottish tradition in that they were broadly social and moralistic. A more closely reasoned academic reaction is to be found in one who taught Marshall's system all his academic life yet came in the end to feel it was not enough. William Smart's *Second Thoughts of an Economist* puts the equilibrium theory of distribution entirely fairly (on the lines of his book on Distribution). He quietly insists that if you are teaching mere economics, you must in logic and common sense distribute according to 'economic worth'. Where he reacts, as he reflects on his work towards its close, is in the conviction that economic theory should itself be based on assumptions which are at once more realistic and more moralistic than those accepted in Marshall's footnote (on page 17). He agrees that the static equilibrium theory of prices follows logically from the assumption that a rising standard of living is a sufficient aim for economic science—but only, he correctly points out, if we think of the standard of living in merely quantitative terms. If exact logic is maintained, Benthamite assumptions can lead only to such conclusions. (Strict logic is not in fact maintained.) Yet, to this experienced business man who later turned to teaching and economic history, it was clear that the quantitative measure was incapable of dealing with the real emotions and forces which inspire business and working men. If pushed to the application we wish to reach, it gives false results. We wish, for workmen also, the economics of free enterprise in a growing society rather than what we have been given, the economics of free competition in a static society. This is the Scottish reaction still at work.

It is difficult to give a kenspeckle link in the tradition between Smart and John Stuart Mill, simply because there are then no kenspeckle Scots economists. In Glasgow the man who bridged these years was Edward Caird. He taught some economic theory in his Moral Philosophy course, but in the only set of notes available (made by a student in his class) the economic theory is slight;[14] it is typically illustrated from classical and Stoic sources, interlaced into their moral theories. He certainly regarded it as part of his duty, though a small part, to teach Political Economy, but when he felt the subject growing beyond his energy he gladly passed it on (in 1887) to William Smart. The following passage,[15] which concludes a public lecture by Caird, shows, however, how conscious he was of the wider social forms in economic life, and how typically Scots was his reaction to them: 'I do not think it will be possible henceforth to separate political economy from the general study of politics, or to discuss the laws of the production and distribution of wealth apart from the consideration of the relation of the distribution of wealth and the modes of distributing it to the other elements of social well-being. The abstraction of science will always be necessary for thorough knowledge of economy, as of everything else; but when we isolate part of *human* existence, it is more important than in relation to any other subject to remember that we *are* abstracting—i.e. that we are dealing with fragments of a whole, of which no final account can be given by anatomy. The practical value of the social science of the future will depend not only on the way in which we break up the complete problem of our existence into manageable parts, but as much and even more upon the way in which we are able to gather the elements together again, and to see how they act and react upon each other in the living movement of the social body.'

One might well ask, where has the Scots energy gone, if it has lacked the highest achievement in economics? Some questions merely raise others. After all, the abilities of a people can be spread over all its interests. To academic minds, Theology, Philosophy, the Law, Science, Medicine have always opened wide doors, and there the generations of Scottish scholars have found at once satisfaction and distinction. But more specifically, one may expect a people to follow its aptitudes. If so, Scots interested in sociological or normative processes would not find these very directly in modern analytical economics. Here it may be fair to note the numbers of distinguished Scots in the history of social anthropology. In the eighteenth century they shared almost an oligopoly with the French, but later we have Maine, J F McLennan, W Robertson Smith and Frazer. Closer to home and today, we note W R Scott, Sir Alexander Gray and Professor Hamilton in their contributions to economic history. And, in general, anyone who knows the Scots universities from the inside realises that the most natural approach of Scotsmen is either philosophical or historical, or severely applied in the sense that it confines itself to interpretation based on scientifically established fact. So it is with the students also. No-one who has taught Scots students can miss the special response when the philosophic aspect is raised. We cannot explain such tastes. It is just 'the nature of the beast'.

Finally, as to the future, will it be likely to offer new opportunities to Scotsmen to follow their bent? If it does, we may expect a more positive Scottish contribution. Whether Scots today maintain the qualities so impressive in their scholarly past is endlessly debatable because the limits of the argument cannot be fixed. Their interest in the speculative and in the normative type of knowledge is certainly as intense. It appears that the influence of the Church is not dominant as it certainly was in the eighteenth century. It was the Presbyterian structure that then most closely expressed the familial relations of the relatively small society which led the country.[16] This may have diminished, but mainly in form. If one were to add the intellectual impacts of the Church, the Universities, the Law, Medicine, the more scientific side of business, the Scots are certainly as intellectually inclined today as ever they have been. Then again, one might point to some watering of the warm family emotion which formed our earlier loyalties and institutions. Certainly the power of the larger kinship group has passed. But we remain a small tightly knit nation, keenly interested in each other as persons living together. That this still lives is expressed in our poetry, essentially a folk, a family literature. The talented editors of A Scots Anthology (stretching from the thirteenth to the twentieth century) remark: 'The main body of Scottish poetry is not in this heroic vein but springs from the normal day to day life of the people, a people who, until the end of the eighteenth-century, lived wholly in the country or in small towns where you had only to go down a wynd off the main street to reach the country. It was, too, a remarkably homogeneous people. Rich and poor lived pretty close together and the gap between the great folk and the common folk was not an unbridgeable gap; divisions between the classes did not obscure their common humanity. And so we find that a court poet like Dunbar could leave the lofty, artificial, allegoric strain and be not only familiar, but vulgar; that some of the best of our songs of peasant life and feeling are by writers of the landed and professional classes; that Scott—Sheriff of Selkirk, Laird of Abbotsford, and Baronet—could write of the life and feelings of common folk with an understanding and reverence equalled only by Wordsworth; and that, in our own time, *Fisher Jamie*—that delightful serio-comic elegy on a Tweed-side poacher—was composed by a highly cultured Scot who ended his life as Governor-General of Canada and Chancellor of the University of Edinburgh.' If one reads through these five hundred or so pages of living emotion, the continuing sense of personal individual life in a free community is manifest. We may still then feel assured that whether or not we are the size of our fathers, we remain the same kind.

The future, however, will open to us only if we give it what it wants. Are there any signs that there may be a renewed need for the Scottish approach in the social sciences? Here we can only consult our broad impressions. Are we satisfied that the methods of analytic economics are sufficient or indeed alone suitable as the theoretical approach to the economic issues now typical in industry? In the nineteenth century the practical effort was specialised as never before. It appeared reasonable to treat by a linear science what was then practised as a rather linear way of life in private business. Even within their own minds, it was customary for business men to keep somewhat separate the standards of business from their more speculative ethical and religious ideals, and a simple code of the economic man could have sufficient appearance of practical relevance, as well as afford a firm intellectual basis. Between them social biology, Freud, the joint-stock company, modern nationalism and wars, the inevitable state direction they foster, have altered the slant of our thought about man in society. The importance of groups as the setting of the individual, perhaps the central awareness of the eighteenth century in Scotland, this awareness is today again dominant; dominant in fact, and therefore to be dealt with by scientists; dominant in the kind of problem which practice proposes to thought, as in all the mixed issues of welfare and defence which make up the traffic of our political life. In this new world, the effort to see the different aspects together in their proper relations again becomes at least as important as the exact definition and analysis of each aspect. The two traditional methods, the analytic and the synoptic, are then seen to be complementary, mutually supporting and nourishing each other. We may well have to be patient with sociology. Its difficulties are immense. But if there is a future for sociological economics and politics—and if there is not we shall have to make it—then there is an opportunity for the resurgence of the Scottish tradition and the Scottish genius. May the opportunity make the men!

NOTES

1   For the seventeenth century *see* H W Meikle, *Some Aspects of the later seventeenth century in Scotland,* p 25.

2   The Chair of Mathematics in Glasgow dates from 1691 but it was not until 1826 that the subject was formally admitted to the curriculum for the degree of MA. This seems to have kept down the number taking the subject. But the record is creditable, especially in the great period. *Cf* Mackie, *The University of Glasgow,* p 216.

3   This passage occurs in Vol I, p 289, of *A System of Moral Philosophy*, in a discussion
     of 'the necessity of a social life'. It is quite separate, in place and subject, from his
     treatment of economic values which occurs in Vol II, Ch 12, embedded in his
     consideration of contracts.

4   *Legacy of the Middle Ages* (Meynial on Roman Law); *Cambridge Medieval
     History*, Vol V (Hazeltine, Roman and Canon Law); Vinogradoff, *Roman Law in
     Medieval Europe*; Bryce, *Studies in History and Jurisprudence, Holy Roman Empire*;
     James Macintosh, *Roman Law in Modern Practice*; and J N Figgis, *From Gerson to
     Grotius*.

5   *Cf. The William and Mary Quarterly*, Vol XI, No 2 (April 1954). For Hutcheson
     the article by Professor Caroline Robbins (a grateful name) is specially interesting.
     The whole number is very relevant.

6   *Op. cit.* p 25.

7   The High School of Edinburgh. The mathematician is Colin Maclaurin, of the
     Treatise on Fluxions.

8   Mill quotes Millar as an authority on three occasions: in important footnotes on
     the English constitution, slavery in primitive times and the position of women in
     North American tribes. Calling him 'that sagacious contemplator of the progress
     of society', he later remarks that 'the writings of Mr Millar remain about the only
     source from which the slightest information on the subject can be drawn', the
     subject being civilisation among the Hindus. I am indebted to Dr R L Meek for this
     reference.

9   Need it be said that no criticism of Ricardo is here intended? His contribution to
     economics is shining and accepted. But many will agree with Schumpeter's
     summary: 'Ricardo's *Principles* are the most difficult book on Economics ever
     written. It is difficult enough even to understand it, more difficult to interpret it,
     and most difficult to estimate it properly' (*Economic Doctrine and Method*, p 80).

10   G Grote, *Minor Works*, p 284.

11   This paragraph may seem to suggest that Marshall would have sympathised with
     the predominance of analytics and the specialised monograph. I believe this is the
     opposite of the truth. Marshall was essentially a perfectionist, seeking to reform the
     institutions and members of the *society* he knew, and wished us all to know. If so,
     he was nearer the early classics than the economic theorists of today.

12   *Principles*, p 17n.

13   For emphasis on the vital importance of what we can summarise as 'know-how',
     and the suggestion that Smith did not give it sufficient weight, see Lauderdale,
     Inquiry into the Nature and Origin of Public Wealth, pp 159–61, 176–7, 184–5, where
     Smith is criticised for missing the special productivity of capital, its own
     productivity as distinct from that of labour; *cf.* also p 287. For Rae this productivity
     of capital is the central theme. It inspires the whole of his remarkable *Sociological
     Theory of Capital*. Mill with his usual wisdom quoted fully from the outstanding
     passage (Mill's *Principles*, pp 165–72), but Rae's theme just is that economic
     progress depends on enterprise, so in turn on the existence of those social
     conditions which call it forth. Chapters IX, X and XIV are especially relevant.

14   There may be further sets of his notes in private hands. If so they would be
     welcomed by the Library of his University, if legible.

15   Edward Caird, *The Moral Aspect of the Economic Problem* (1888).

16   *Cf.* Mackie, *The University of Glasgow*, pp 186, 212.

CHAPTER TWO

The Scottish Political Economy Tradition

Sheila C Dow

Scot. Jnl. of Pol. Econ. Nov 1987

INTRODUCTION

Thirty-one years ago, Professor Macfie addressed the Scottish Economic Society on the subject of the Scottish Tradition in Economic Thought. In that address (Macfie, 1955), he made the case that the attitude and method which characterised early Scottish economic thought were distinctive, that they had had an important influence on the subsequent development of the discipline, and that they were still recognisable in the work of twentieth-century Scottish economists. Professor Macfie further argued that economics as generally practised had diverged unduly from the Scottish tradition; a Scottish revival was thus warranted.

Since then, there has indeed been a growing awareness of the shortcomings of orthodox economics, to such an extent that it is now conventional to describe economics as being in a state of 'crisis' (see for example Hicks, 1974, and Bell and Kristol, 1981). Along with this questioning has arisen a growing interest in political economy as an alternative approach, and in the figures of the Scottish Enlightenment as the founders of the political economy tradition (see Whynes, 1984, Campbell and Skinner, 1982 and Hont and Ignatieff, 1983).

The purpose of this paper is to return to Macfie's concern with the contemporary relevance of those aspects of political economy which are peculiarly Scottish, and to reassess the degree to which these aspects still survive in the 1980s. As such, we start with a policy question: what are the major deficiencies in contemporary orthodox economics? A discussion of these deficiencies follows, in terms of alternative approaches to theory appraisal. Much of non-orthodox economics which conforms to modern (Kuhnian) philosophy of science may be classified as political economy. But the methodological principles of political economy in this general sense tend not to be very fully specified. The distinctive features of the peculiarly Scottish political economy tradition are then outlined in the context of the intellectual climate within which they were originally formed. This tradition is interesting because it is fairly well-defined, and spawned many of the subsequent, diverse, forms of political economy. Finally, we consider how congenial the current climate in Scotland is to the survival of these distinctive features; the role of the system of university education is highlighted.

POLITICAL ECONOMY AS A RESPONSE TO CRISIS

The economics discipline is in a state of turbulence. This turbulence is evident at several levels. In terms of theory content, there has been a remarkable pace of change in what is regarded as conventional; the life cycle of the Philips curve is a case in point. Further, attempts to appraise these changes in theory content have caused a heightened awareness of the methodological issues behind theory appraisal: by what criteria do we judge new theories in relation to old? These issues have surfaced, too, at the popular level, as the general public attempt to assess the relative merits of the different policy stances implied by different theories. Indeed, much of the disquiet in the profession has been prompted by the general public's impatience with (if not contempt for) a profession which manifestly fails to resolve its own internal differences.

What economists themselves regard as the deficiencies of their discipline varies inevitably with their approach. There are two broad categories which reflect the approaches, respectively, of what we may call traditional and modern philosophy of science (although the roots of the modern approach predate the traditional approach). According to traditional philosophy of science, science is cumulative, adding to knowledge over time. Further, the justification of a theory is distinct from the context of its discovery. (See Hacking, 1981, pp 1–2.) Theory, according to this view, progresses more or less continuously. Thus, for example, both Friedman (1956) and Lucas (1980) regard Keynes' work as a stepping-stone to modern theory, but one which is now superseded. Since the context of discovery of a theory is irrelevant to its justification, all of Keynes' theory which is useful is already incorporated in modern theory.

Periods of turbulence are thus the result simply of particularly productive advances in economic theory, often requiring that economists learn new concepts, modelling techniques and technology. Turbulence is an indicator of notable progress; it is an indicator of deficiencies only insofar as economists persist in their old ways. The perceived deficiencies which have motivated the emergence both of rational expectations theory and of recent developments in pure general equilibrium theory referred to the microfoundations of macro-economics; progress consisted of building theoretical systems, extending from individual behaviour to macroeconomic aggregates, which are internally consistent.

Modern philosophy of science, as initiated by Popper (1959) and taken furthest by Kuhn (1962), rejects the notion of an inevitable progress in science, and places considerable importance in the context of scientific discovery. While Popper and Lakatos (1970) did suggest procedures for assessing theoretical developments as being progressive or regressive, Kuhn denies the feasibility of objective assessment. Theories are developed within what he calls paradigms, which are adopted by scientific communities; individual scientists in general accept the broad principles of the paradigm (its *Weltanschauung*) in order for them to communicate with each other, and to provide a basis on which 'normal science' may proceed. A crisis emerges, however, when the perception is generally held that enquiry within the dominant paradigm palpably fails to address important issues, or contradicts what is regarded (outside the paradigm) as an important fact. Then 'extraordinary science', which questions the principles underlying the dominant paradigm, may generate a scientific revolution, with the overthrow of the dominant paradigm in favour of an alternative. Criteria of appraisal are employed during the crisis by those defending one paradigm against another; any scientist must adopt such criteria, whether implicitly or explicitly. But there are no extra-paradigmatic criteria for appraisal.

For those economists whose approach corresponds to these principles of modern philosophy of science, the current turbulence in economics takes on a particular character. First, if science does not inevitably progress, economics is capable of wrong turnings. However, a turning is 'wrong' only by the criteria of particular paradigms. It is important, therefore, to delineate the boundaries of paradigms. Further, since paradigms are the outcome of the activities of communities of economists within particular historical environments, it is regarded as important to understand those economists and the nature of the communities.

Within economics, the dominant paradigm is one which adopts the traditionalist approach to philosophy of science. But there are several subsidiary paradigms which do not. (See Dow, 1985.) What their purveyors perceive as the deficiencies of mainstream economics will thus depend on the criteria inherent in their own paradigm. Thus, while there is a common perception of a crisis in orthodox economics, the nature of this crisis and the way in which it should be addressed are subject to diverse treatments. (See Bell and Kristol, 1981, and Whynes, 1984, for example.)

Whynes' book nevertheless draws together a diversity of alternatives to the orthodoxy under the umbrella of political economy. This suggests a common element in criticisms of the orthodoxy and in the general character of the alternative way in which we should proceed. Criticisms of the orthodoxy predominantly concern relevance to real-world issues, realism of assumptions and the degree to which theoretical developments are motivated by technical considerations internal to the theories themselves.

In particular, orthodox theory is governed by the logic of axiomatic systems, requiring both reductionism (so that all aspects of theory are derived from the same, universal axiomatic system) and dualism (whereby strict distinctions are drawn between exogenous and endogenous variables, between knowledge and ignorance, between rationality and irrationality, and so on). This type of theoretical structure is inevitably formalistic, and exclusive; further it is conducive to building on atomistic utilitarian foundations, to extending economic principles to cover (and thus endogenise) as many aspects of the economy as possible, but to imbuing those variables which remain exogenous with undue importance as the only feasible source of change in the system. The resulting depiction of the behaviour of individuals and societies is regarded as unrealistic by the critics of the orthodoxy. In turn, they argue that the orthodox system precludes consideration of the important issues of persistent unemployment, of struggles for income shares between classes, or of creative entrepreneurial behaviour.

Hahn (1977, 1981 and 1983), as one of the leading figures in the orthodoxy, accepts that these limitations exist, but nevertheless argues that this type of theoretical system is the only one which is acceptable on methodological grounds. But those who, in line with modern philosophy of science, allow for the simultaneous existence of internally valid, incommensurate paradigms are free to consider alternatives. The political economy alternative is put forward as being more able to deal with pressing policy issues, more realistic in its depiction of the behaviour of individuals and institutions, and more concerned that these features should be maintained than by technical considerations inherent in any one theoretical framework. Political economists thus start with policy issues rather than theoretical *curiosa*, they consider the historical background to these issues, they study institutional arrangements and they study the history of economic thought in order both to understand theory and to adapt it for application to particular contexts. The use of empirical material varies; some would classify themselves as political economists who shun econometrics in favour of a more casual empiricism, more in keeping with the limited information yielded by data series collected over time and thus changing economic, institutional and behavioural structures. Others would classify themselves also as political economists who rely almost exclusively on empirical work as a means of keeping close to 'the facts' and thus ensuring the relevance of their work.

The use of the term 'political economy' is in fact often imprecise and sometimes contradictory. This is at once its strength and its weakness. Modern philosophy of science, and the general political economy approach suggest tolerance in that they admit the (internal) validity of coexisting paradigms. Thus, within political economy, it is possible to have several paradigms based on different perceptions of what are relevant issues, and what is realistic. On the other hand, there is a danger of presuming a degree of synthesis which is not present. Certainly, the lack of synthesis between well-specified groups such as neo-Austrians and Marxians is readily apparent. Indeed the virtues of tolerance and pragmatism may be taken too far. Thus John Neville Keynes' (1891) classic treatise on 'The Scope and Method of Political Economy', written under Marshall's influence (see Skidelsky, 1983, Chapter 3) could be said to have papered over the cracks which divided deductivists from inductivists. As a result, he diverted attention from important methodological issues, while at the same time paving the way for the dominance of the marginalists over political economists (see Deane, 1983).

A similar effect may arise from a quite different quarter in our own times. Adopting a stance consistent with modern philosophy of science, McCloskey (1983) argues that it is persuasiveness which wins economic arguments, not methodological rectitude. It would be easy, from an orthodox perspective, to infer the conclusion (which others have reached from Kuhn's work) that 'anything goes'. Such a dualistic response is inherent in the orthodox approach. For those under the influence of, and yet critical of, the orthodox approach, the political economy alternative may similarly seem to offer a *carte blanche*.

It is for this reason that it is especially appealing to look back at the Scottish political economy tradition. Political economy, particularly in its Scottish roots, offers neither an axiomatic straitjacket, nor a *carte blanche*. Its unifying principles refer to something other than a formal theoretical system. The Scottish tradition allows us to consider one possible set of underlying principles within the context which generated them.

The Distinctiveness of Scottish Political Economy

The character of Scottish political economy stems from the environment which spawned it. Economic conditions in eighteenth-century Scotland played their part in determining the issues to be addressed: the conditions for economic growth, co-ordination within an economy with specialised production, income distribution, the role of government in the economy, and so on. But, as Professor Macfie (1955) pointed out, it is the attitude and method of the Scottish approach which are so distinctive. For these we must look beyond the strictly economic sphere.

Political economy emerged in the eighteenth century as a field of enquiry within the Scottish Enlightenment, which straddled the full range of intellectual endeavour in Scotland, drawing on the intellectual developments of the seventeenth century (see Cameron *et al.* 1981). Of the many factors underlying the Enlightenment, three have particular significance for political economy: the social and intellectual pervasiveness of religious issues, the nature of the education system and Scottish jurisprudence.

The eighteenth century saw an application of rationalism to religious questions as an alternative to the dogmatism of the seventeenth century (see Sutherland, 1982), within a society where religion played a very important part. The ensuing religious debates which such an approach opened up went hand in hand with questions about the religious significance of a rationalist approach to the natural sciences. Attempts at resolution of the fundamental issues involved in such debates, for Adam Smith (1795), led him to develop a position building on Humean ideas, closely resembling that set out two centuries later by Kuhn, and by Shackle (1967).[1] In other words, the modern philosophy of science adopted (in greater or lesser degree) by modern political economists in fact dates from the eighteenth century. Indeed, Smith provides a richer basis than Kuhn, with the originality of his development of epistemological principles and with his explicit recognition of the significance of persuasion.[2]

Scottish political economy thus developed from its earliest years in an environment which spawned a philosophy of science which denied any claims of theory to absolute truth (and, at the same time, put the social sciences on a par with the natural sciences). While the Scottish economists vigorously defended their theories on their own   grounds, inherent in the intellectual climate of the time (one which encouraged debate over arguments rather than dogmas) was *some* degree of acceptance that others might equally legitimately defend their theories on their own grounds. Tolerance in this context by no means precludes a forceful use of powers of persuasion. On the contrary, it implies that arguments cannot be settled by the internal logic of formal theories.[3]

This greater tendency to admit the possibility of legitimate alternatives applied too to debates over education, which also profoundly influenced the character of Scottish political economy.[4] First, a preference for studying Latin rather than Greek, Macfie argues, reinforced the tendency to focus on practical problems, and thus to opt for breadth rather than depth of understanding.[5] Second, this quest for breadth was reflected in the degree structure in Scottish universities, as formed in the seventeenth century. (See Cant, 1982 and Davie, 1961.) Students were admitted in their mid-teens benefiting those who might otherwise have been excluded by their limited access to good higher schooling. The degree proceeded by a set range of subjects which provided a broad education in the areas of language, philosophy and the exact sciences.[6] The most distinctive of this range of subjects were in the second category: moral philosophy and logic and metaphysics. The training provided in these classes set its stamp on the conduct of classes in all other disciplines. Further, since moral philosophy and logic and metaphysics were taught at a general level, it was arguments from first principles on issues of general interest which predominated over specialist topics internal to the disciplines. The importance of proficiency in argument from first principles was reinforced by the practice of examination by peer review. At a more general level, the propensity to argue from first principles was a direct product of the preoccupation with the application of rational argument to religious questions.

It was in the moral philosophy class at Glasgow University that Hutcheson and Smith raised political economy issues for general discussion. It is not surprising therefore that political economy should have developed as a moral science. Further the character of political economy was moulded by the cross-fertilisation of disciplines emerging at the same time, notably sociology, psychology and jurisprudence. History was already inherent in much of the Scottish general university education, reflecting the emphasis on first principles. Thus it was customary for the professors of physics and mathematics, for example, to teach the elements of their subjects, as being the most important part, and to do so by laying out the historical development of ideas. (See Davie, 1961, part II, chapter 1.) Indeed, it can be argued that the emergence of so many new ideas and disciplines within Scotland during and after the Enlightenment was in no small part due to the perspective represented by these features of the education system.

Finally, the moral principles of Scottish jurisprudence had a profound influence on the way in which political economists depicted human behaviour. Whatever the balance between the competing stances of civic humanism and civil jurisprudence (discussed by Pocock, 1983), man was not viewed as an isolated atom, but as a political being or a social being. (Again, this aspect of thought can be traced to the pervasive religious perspective on all issues, whether that perspective did or did not involve scepticism.) Thus Hume would refer to 'society' rather than individuals, and Smith would discuss the tempering effect of social pressures on individual greed. It was this view of individuals as members of society, rather than isolated atoms, which provided the basic principles underlying Scottish political economy, differentiating it from formal utilitarianism.

Further, the context of contemporary thought on jurisprudence was one of debate around the competing considerations of laws of natural justice on the one hand and moral sense, evolving by social convention, on the other. Smith's own work on the question of justice (as on the origins and practice of government) drew on the relativistic aspects of his moral philosophy, pointing to the importance of social conventions, which could not be explained by rationality. At the same time, he sought the common elements of convention as indications of principles which were independent of environment. (See Skinner, 1979a, chapter 3.) The resulting creative admixture of principle and convention is characteristic also of the method of Scottish political economy. (See the discussion of argument from first principles, below.)

To summarise, then, it is being suggested here that the new discipline of political economy absorbed in some measure the following features from its environment:

1 an acceptance of the limitations of theory
2 a recognition of the sociological and psychological aspects of theory appraisal
3 a concern with practical issues
4 a consequent preference for breadth of understanding of the background to these issues, over depth of isolated aspects
5 a preference for drawing on several disciplines in an integrated manner to provide that depth
6 a preference for arguing from first principles
7 a preference for approaching a subject's first principles by discussing their historical development
8 a specification of first principles in terms of a non-individualistic representation of human nature, with a consequent emphasis on conventional behaviour.

As always with such characterisations of bodies of thought, a degree of cohesion is implied which may be contradicted by studies of individuals. Emphasis so far has been placed on Smith as the archetypal Scottish political economist who most clearly conforms to the above characterisation. Although individuals within a scientific community might disagree, the concept of paradigm is a useful device for specifying those elements held more or less in common within that community, and which allow them to communicate. Indeed, the presence of argument is an indication of communication and thus of some commonality of view. (See Dow, 1985, chapters 1–3.) The relevant community of scholars here includes some who would disagree with some of the elements outlined above, and yet who contributed, through debate, to the development of a paradigm which we have identified here in an abstract form. This community included such people (in alphabetical order) as Anderson, Carmichael, Chalmers, Ferguson, Hume, Hutcheson, Lauderdale, Reid, Steuart, and Stewart. But it is Smith who represents the crystallisation of the Scottish approach to political economy.

One aspect of the characterisation of Scottish political economy which particularly requires further discussion is the propensity to argue from first principles. This aspect is emphasised by Macfie (1955), and reinforced by the (Newtonian) emphasis placed on logical purity, or well-foundedness, rather than the (Cartesian) criterion of efficiency (Davie, 1961, p 111) When combined with the common description of Enlightenment figures as 'rationalist', we would appear to be close to describing political economy as being based on an axiomatic system, like general equilibrium theory (and indeed that implication is drawn by those general equilibrium theorists who trace their roots to Adam Smith). Further, a 'first principles' approach might seem to detract from practical application.[7] Certainly Smith (1795) applauded the aesthetic appeal of theoretical systems. But, in order to understand the nature and role of such systems, it is useful to consider first the Scottish views on mathematics, which were aired fully in the debates on the design of the university system (*vis-à-vis* the English universities).

Those advocating the English system of retaining philosophy only as a specialist subject adopted the Platonic view that mathematics is a necessary training for philosophy. The Scottish tradition, however, adopted a tripartite approach whereby education proceeded in parallel in the three areas of language, philosophy and exact science (Davie, 1961, p 84). Mathematics thus entered the Scottish system, not as a vehicle for abstract reasoning for its own sake, but as a tool developed by active scientists. The emphasis on teaching mathematical foundations was seen as contributing to its adaptability to the solution of practical problems, avoiding 'the rival extremes of a crude empiricism and of a barren formalism' (Davie, 1961, p 132). And yet the limitations of mathematics were emphasised in a manner which finds a strong echo in Keynes' views of mathematics, and probability in particular. The following argument is attributed to George Jardine, a pupil of Adam Smith, and the chief formulator of Scottish educational ideals.

> Proficiency in mathematical reasoning . . . because of its being concerned with technical terms and necessary facts, did not . . . lead to proficiency in ordinary reasoning, since this latter process had to do with contingent facts expressed in colloquial terms.
>
> (Davie, 1961, p 170)

It is the combination of argument from first principles, with a consciousness of the impossibility of encompassing 'ordinary reasoning' in formal, or mathematical terms, which accounted for the eschewance of universally applicable, formal, axiomatic systems of thought. The interdisciplinary nature of enquiry into political economy problems at once allowed a further understanding of 'contingent facts' and yet further prevented any notion of employing a single formal system. The 'first principles' of Scottish political economy referred to man's nature as a social being:

> Its method was to start with the facts of human nature, with actual motives, with the influences of classes and groups—what bound them together and divided them, with the aesthetic and moral benefits derived from social life.

> (Macfie, 1967, p 17)

Such first principles (in contrast to the utility maximisation first principles of modern mainstream economics) are clearly not conducive to formalism, and quickly lead to chains of reasoning within different disciplines, each with their own method of analysis (some of which may be mathematical). In particular, this approach allows the combination of principle with convention (which was epitomised by Smith's work on justice), a combination precluded by formal, axiomatic systems of thought.

As a result, it appeared that many of Smith's arguments were inconsistent (see Campbell and Skinner, 1976, pp 59–60 and Macfie, 1955). Yet such a judgement is only a criticism within an all-encompassing axiomatic structure. Smith's arguments may be inconsistent according to one particular type of formalism. But, given the diversity of methods employed, his work has a unity derived from first principles.

> The real object for Smith was to produce a compendious system of thought . . . which would link together in the fancy . . . *all* those different movements and effects which are already in reality performed. In fulfilling this task, Smith provided a system of thought which was composed of a number of separate parts . . . organised in such a way as to provide the reader with an understanding of the linkages involved.

> (Skinner, 1979b, p 111)

Thus the holism of political economy referred to the first level of abstraction, i.e. the political economist's imagination, which held a systemic, or organic view of economic relationships within the history of society. This contrasts with the holism of modern orthodox theory which refers to the second level of abstraction, the formal analytical structure: unity is found in the analytical framework rather than the object of study.

The Desirability and Feasibility of a Revival of Scottish Political Economy

A strong case may be made for the relevance of Scottish political economy to current economic problems. Macfie's (1955) arguments are as valid now as they were thirty-one years ago. Political economy cannot provide precise answers to policy questions; but neither can any other approach to economics. (Formalistic approaches only allow precise answers to formal theoretical questions; see Coddington, 1975.) Where problems are identified with institutions (such as corporations and unions), with the psychology of economic agents in their formation of expectations in particularly unsettled economic conditions, where the differences between institutions in different countries within an increasingly interdependent world are of great importance to one's own economy, where, in general, economic principles must be readily adaptable to deal with rapidly changing conjunctures and institutional arrangements, a policy-oriented multi-disciplinary approach, which emphasises facts and history, seems to hold much promise. This is what I would classify as political economy in its most general sense.

But the Scottish tradition has additional features which are of great importance: the philosophical nature of its first principles and its emphasis on structure, in thought and in education, as in its characterisation of economics. To make the case for employing such a mode of thought (philosophical and structured) is a circular affair. How can one persuade others that their mode of thought is less useful than one's own when the case is made in terms of one's own mode of thought, but understood only in terms of the others' mode of thought? This is the essence of the problem posed by paradigmatic divisions. For those who already employ the political economy mode of thought I have been describing, it will inevitably seem a correct mode of thought; for others it is less likely to be seen as incorrect, so much as not understood. Adam Smith's concept of sympathy is very apt: readers feel sympathy with a set of arguments if they share the same language, attitude and mode of argument.

Nevertheless, there are two avenues for developing or propagating a paradigm. The first lies in articulating it clearly and persuasively to those who feel sympathy for the approach, but are unsure as to how to employ it, while the second lies with the process of education in general and in economics in particular. The Scottish political economy approach, being more structured than some other forms of political economy, should be more conducive to generalisation; the difficulty often in conveying the principles of political economy lies in its grounding in particular contexts. Given the relative demise of the Scottish type of political economy, however, much work still has to be done in articulating its principles in terms of the issues which currently face economists, and in drawing the attention of mainstream economists to the growing contemporary political economy literature which does exist.

The forces leading to the relative demise of the Scottish tradition themselves pose interesting questions. But the demise is by no means complete. The fact that so many of us still recognise and feel sympathy with earlier articulations of Scottish political economy is evidence that the tradition persists. Further, many of the new directions in economics, responding to the sense of crisis, are fully consistent with the Scottish tradition. The genealogy of these directions too is relevant. Much of the new interesting work in political economy is being done in continental Europe (and in North America among those with strong links with continental Europe). The intellectual links between Scotland and the continent were an important factor in the particular form taken by the Scottish Enlightenment. Thus many modern developments in political economy can be seen to have roots in common with the Scottish tradition.

But Professor Macfie's optimism about the continuity of the tradition stemmed from his view of the Scottish student *sui generis*, as having a 'philosophic bent' i.e. that the mode of thought characteristic of Scottish political economy is already habitual among our students. More generally, it is important for the future of the Scottish tradition whether the traditional style of reasoning is present in the current generation of economists emerging from Scottish universities (if indeed it was present in the 1950s) and whether this style of reasoning is necessary for perpetuating the Scottish political economy tradition. Kuhnian analysis would support the view that it is necessary (but not sufficient) for a scientific revolution that alternative paradigms be put forward. Cast of mind will determine receptivity towards, and indeed initial recognition of, such alternatives. Cast of mind determines what will, in Smith's terms, be 'psychologically satisfying'.

The conditions which created the cast of mind which formed the Scottish political economy tradition were very different from those of the present century. But one aspect of those conditions which can be singled out is the education system, something which Smith (1795, IV: 35) himself highlighted as a factor in the propagation (or shifting) of ideas.[8] Certainly, the education system of the eighteenth century was itself a product of its environment. But, as a central feature of any intellectual environment, the education system provides a focus for consideration of the present intellectual environment in Scotland. *If* the present education system promotes a cast of mind unsympathetic to the Scottish tradition in political economy, then a revival of that tradition would be difficult without changes in the education system. As a first step, therefore, the relative demise of the Scottish education system, since the nineteenth century, as the British system of education became more uniform. However, changes in the last thirty years have reflected a reassessment of educational philosophy in Britain, in times both of resource plenty and resource shortage; by no means all these changes have represented moves away from the Scottish tradition.

Just as the early Scottish education system can be said to have influenced the growth of political economy, then, its current form requires reassessment if we are concerned about the survival of political economy in Scotland. For those of us who regard the political economy approach as the most appropriate for addressing current problems, it seems important, therefore, to consider seriously the significance for economics of particular features of the traditional character of Scottish university education.

CONCLUSION

This paper raises more questions than it answers, and accordingly constitutes a statement of intent with a view to future work in this area. At one level, the relationship between degree structure (and the underlying philosophy of education) on the one hand, and the form and content of economics on the other, warrants serious investigation. At another level, the distinctiveness of Scottish political economy from other forms of political economy, and the implications of arguing from first principles in particular, require further consideration. In turn, the feasibility of such an approach in the modern context of specialisation must be considered. This leads to questions about the implications for political economy of the particular form this specialisation has taken not only in economics, but in related disciplines, such as history and economic history.[9] Traditional political economy was inter-disciplinary in the sense that the related disciplines were integrated in an organic way. It may be that modern disciplinary specialisation might limit political economy now to a multi-disciplinary approach.

The exercise of pursuing these enquiries itself accords with the principles of the Scottish political economy tradition. It is prompted by the policy question posed by the current state of unrest in economics. It requires an interdisciplinary approach, with a particular emphasis on history. It requires a philosophical grounding in those principles of theory formulation which also encompass the feasibility of several coexisting bodies of theory. Finally, it emphasises the importance of communities of scholars and informed lay-people in the formation and establishment of ideas and educational practice, rather than the role of isolated individuals.

REFERENCES

Anderson, R D (1983). *Education and Opportunity in Victorian Scotland* Oxford: Clarendon

Bell, D and Kristol, I (eds) (1981). *The Crisis in Economic Theory* New York: Basic Books

Cameron, J *et al.* (1981). Stair Tercentenary Papers. *The Juridical Review* (December), 102–76

Campbell, R H (1980). *The Rise and Fall of Scottish Industry* Edinburgh: John Donald

Campbell, R H and Skinner, A S. (eds) (1976). A Smith, *The Wealth of Nations*, Glasgow edition. Oxford: Oxford University Press

——(1982). *The Origins and Nature of the Scottish Enlightenment* Edinburgh: John Donald

Cant, R G (1982). Origins of the Enlightenment in Scotland: The Universities. In R H Campbell and A S Skinner, 1982, 42–64.

Coddington, A (1975). 'The Rationale of General Equilibrium Theory', *Economic Inquiry,* 13 (December), 539–58

Davie, G E (1961). *The Democratic Intellect: Scotland and her Universities in the Nineteenth Century* Edinburgh: Edinburgh University Press

——(1981). *The Scottish Enlightenment* London: The Historical Association

Deane, P (1983). 'The Scope and Method of Economic Science', *Economic Journal,* 93 (March) 1–12

Dow, S C (1985). *Macroeconomic Thought: A Methodological Approach* Oxford: Basil Blackwell

Friedman, M (1956). The Quantity Theory of Money: A Restatement. In M Friedman, *Studies in the Quantity Theory of Money* Chicago: Chicago University Press

Hacking, I (ed) (1981). *Scientific Revolutions* Oxford: Oxford University Press

Hahn, F H (1977). Keynesian Economics and General Equilibrium Theory: Reflections on some Current Debates. In G C Harcourt (ed) *The Microeconomics Foundations of Macroeconomics* London: Macmillan
——(1981). General Equilibrium Theory. In D Bell and I Kristol (eds) (1981)
——(1983). *Money and Inflation* Cambridge, Mass: MIT Press
Hicks, J R (1974). *The Crisis in Keynesian Economics* Oxford: Basil Blackwell
Hont, I and Ignatieff, M (eds) (1983). *Wealth and Virtue* Cambridge: Cambridge University Press
Keynes, J N (1981). *The Scope and Method of Political Economy* London: Macmillan
Kuhn, T S (1962). *The Structure of Scientific Revolutions* Chicago: Chicago University Press
Lakatos, I (1970). Falsification and the Methodology of Scientific Research Programmes. In I Lakatos and A Musgrave (eds) *Criticism and the Growth of Knowledge* Cambridge: Cambridge University Press
Lucas, R E Jr (1980). 'Methods and Problems in Business Cycle Theory', *Journal of Monetary Economics*, 5 (Supplement) 7–29
Macfie, A L (1955). 'The Scottish Tradition in Economic Thought', *Scottish Journal of Political Economy*, 2 (June), 81–103
——(1967). *The Individual in Society: Papers on Adam Smith* London: George Allen and Unwin
McCloskey, D N (1983). 'The Rhetoric of Economics', *Journal of Economic Literature*, 21 (June), 481–517
Pocock, J G A (1983). Cambridge Paradigms and Scotch Philosophers. In I Hont and M Ignatieff (eds) (1983)
Popper, K R (1959). *The Logic of Scientific Discovery* London: Hutchinson
Shackle, G L S (1967). *The Years of High Theory* Cambridge: Cambridge University Press
Skidelsky, R (1983). *John Maynard Keynes. Vol 1: Hopes Betrayed 1883–1920* London: Macmillan
Skinner, A S (1979a). *A System of Social Science: Papers Relating to Adam Smith* Oxford: Clarendon
——(1979b). 'Adam Smith: An Aspect of Modern Economics?' *Scottish Journal of Political Economy* 26 (June), 109–25
Smith, A (1795, 1980). History of Astronomy. In W P D Wightman (ed) *Essays on Philosophical Subjects* (Glasgow edition), Oxford: Clarendon
Sutherland, S R (1982). The Presbyterian Inheritance of Hume and Reid in R H Campbell and A S Skinner (eds) (1982), 131–49
Whynes, D K (ed) (1984). *What is Political Economy? Eight Perspectives* Oxford: Basil Blackwell

NOTES

1 The comparison is drawn by Skinner, 1979b, and by Raphael and Skinner in the general introduction to the Glasgow edition of Smith (1795), where Raphael also explores the influences on Smith's epistemological thinking. See Smith (1795, pp 15–21).

2 See Skinner (1979a, Ch 8, especially pp 207–8) for an example of Smith's use of the techniques of persuasion in his treatment of the colonial system.

3 It is a mistaken, dualistic, interpretation of the paradigmatic view that 'anything goes'. Rather than ending argument, the paradigmatic view elucidates the way in which arguments are conducted, depending on whether the participants are within the same, or differing paradigms.

4 The character and impact of Scottish educational tradition have been presented rather differently by Davie, 1961, and Anderson, 1983. But the fact that the arguments in favour of the Scottish system of education were put forward in the context of influence for change originating outside Scotland illustrates how Scottish Enlightenment thought was influenced by the change in political climate following the Treaty of Union. The educational argument was not conducted around an attack on alternative systems, but around a defence of the Scottish system.

5 The Roman/Stoic influence was also felt via the Scottish legal system, and issues in jurisprudence, touched on below.

6 This structured generalism is to be distinguished from the generalism which allows free choice of subjects, an educational approach which supports a different type of political economy from the Scottish tradition.

7 See Campbell, 1980, pp 30–7a, for a discussion of the role of the Scottish academic style of reasoning in promoting or inspiring the industrial revolution.

8 Here again Smith predates Kuhn (1962), who emphasises the significance of education for the continuance of dominant paradigms, and particularly the role of textbooks and exemplars in encouraging a particular method of addressing—and choosing—problems.

9 A question at issue is how far these disciplines, as specialisms, diverge from their eighteenth-century character, when employed now in an inter-disciplinary framework. See Campbell and Skinner, eds (1976, pp 50–60) on the distinctive historical approach of the eighteenth century.

CHAPTER THREE

Moral Philosophy and Political Economy in Scotland

Terence Hutchison

Before Adam Smith: The Emergence
of Political Economy 1662–1776
(Basil Blackwell, 1988)

I

The contribution of the Scottish Enlightenment to—what was to become—
political economy may be said to have begun with the lectures of Gershom
Carmichael and his edition of Pufendorf's *De officio hominis et civis* (1718,
revised 1724). It was Carmichael who introduced into Scotland the work of
Samuel Pufendorf and the ideas of the natural-law philosophers. As such, he
played a vital role in both the history of Scottish philosophy and the history of
economic thought. Sir William Hamilton stated that Carmichael 'may be
regarded, on good grounds, as the true founder of the Scottish school of
philosophy' (1872, vol I, 30n, quoted by Taylor, 1955, 253). More recently,
among historians of political economy, W L Taylor appears to have been the
first to have given Carmichael some of the attention he deserves.

Carmichael (1672–1729) studied at Edinburgh and taught philosophy, first,
very briefly, at St Andrews, and then, from 1694 to the end of his life, in
Glasgow. In 1727, two years before his death, he became the first occupant of
the celebrated chair of Moral Philosophy at Glasgow, subsequently adorned
by his pupil, Francis Hutcheson, and later by Adam Smith. Carmichael's
publications, all in Latin, comprised his *Introduction ad logicam* (1720), and the
Synopsis theologiae naturalis (1729), but probably his most important
achievement was his edition with notes of Pufendorf's *De officio hominis et civis*
(1718, revised ed 1724). Frances Hutcheson referred to this work by Pufendorf,
'which that worthy and ingenious man, the late Professor Gershom
Carmichael of Glasgow, by far the best commentator on that book, has so
supplied and corrected that the notes are of much more value than the text'
(1747, v).

The persistence of Carmichael's influence was emphasised by W R Scott
who, having noted that Adam Smith was reading Grotius (in Latin, of course)

at fifteen, added: 'At that time his teacher, Francis Hutcheson was using as one of his textbooks, the edition of Gershom Carmichael, his predecessor, of Pufendorf's *De officio hominis et civis*' (1937, 112). Scott further observed how Adam Smith himself, in his final course of lectures in Edinburgh (1751) 'returned to Carmichael's treatment of Pufendorf, making his course one of Jurisprudence (as it was continued in the *Glasgow Lectures*) within which there were large ethical and economic parts' (112). Thus, the general framework of Hutcheson's and Smith's conception and treatment of moral philosophy, political economy, and jurisprudence came from Pufendorf, via Carmichael. So also did their first treatments of the fundamental concepts of value and price.

In Pufendorf's manual, *De officio*, the important contribution, as regards basic economic theory, comes in chapter XIV 'De pretio'. To its nine brief pages Carmichael added ten brief notes, of which the longest summarises his analysis of price and value. Closely following Pufendorf, Carmichael noted that, in the first place, for a good or service to have a price it must possess a certain usefulness, or 'aptitude', either actual *or imagined*: 'Generally, the price of things depends on these two elements: *scarcity* and *the difficulty of acquiring* them. Moreover, scarcity can be derived from two things, the number of those demanding the good or service, and the "aptitude", or usefulness, *which they think it contains* and which can have use for human life, or confer some pleasure' (1724, 247n, some italics added).

Thus Carmichael, like Pufendorf, explicitly recognised as fundamental the subjective element in price and value, and he was followed on this point by Francis Hutcheson. Neither Pufendorf, Carmichael nor Hutcheson sought to employ the concept of 'real', objective usefulness which was to be introduced in the *Wealth of Nations*.

Carmichael also left unpublished manuscripts in Glasgow, and until these become available the full scope and details of his ideas cannot precisely be assessed. However, the examination of these documents, in the first instance by Professor Hans Medick (1973), has revealed another important feature of Carmichael's contribution, that is, his exposition of the ideas of John Locke, in particular regarding the labour theory of property, from the second of the *Two Treatises of Government* (1690, ch v). This theory sought to explain and justify the private occupation of land and the original acquisition of property in a previously unoccupied world: every man's labour is his own property, and so are also the things to which he has applied his labour, or worked on, notably the land which a man has occupied and cultivated (see Moore and Silverthorne, 1983, 82). But although Locke combined, in the second of his treatises of government, a labour theory of property with a labour theory of value, neither theory logically entails the other. Obviously one can hold a labour theory of value and reject a labour theory of property (as Marxists presumably do) and vice versa. So it would seem at least premature to suggest that Carmichael upheld a labour theory of *value*, or that the labour element, or emphasis, in Adam Smith's theorising on value and price should be traced back to Carmichael's exposition of Locke, important though this was. In fact, if Hutcheson faithfully followed his teacher Carmichael, then Carmichael expounded a labour theory of property, based on Locke's theory, but not a labour theory of value.

II

On Carmichael's death in 1729 he was succeeded in the chair of moral philosophy at Glasgow by his pupil Francis Hutcheson (1694–1746), of whom it has been said that, by general agreement, he was 'the personality most responsible for the new spirit of enlightenment in the Scottish universities' (Bryson, 1945, 8). Hutcheson was born in Northern Ireland, of Scottish descent, and had studied the classics, philosophy and theology at Glasgow. He had then opened his own school in Dublin, before returning to Glasgow, to succeed his old teacher. 'The never-to-be-forgotten' Hutcheson, as his pupil Adam Smith described him, was evidently a most impressive teacher and lecturer. In the general coverage and conception of his courses he followed the lines laid down by Pufendorf and Carmichael, though introducing his own new directions at some points. Among his earlier writings was a severe criticism of Mandeville. Hutcheson's main doctrines were presented in two works, both published posthumously, more briefly in *A Short Introduction to Moral Philosophy* (1747) (an English translation of an earlier Latin version), and, in comprehensive form, in his three-volume *System of Moral Philosophy* (1755).

Each of these works has a chapter on 'value and price' which follow Pufendorf's corresponding chapters fairly closely, indeed almost word for word at some points. but Hutcheson covered several economic topics such as taxation and foreign trade, not discussed by the earlier writers of the natural-law school. His re-statement of the analysis of value and price may be taken from his *Short Introduction*:

> The ground of all price must be some *fitness* in the things to yield some use or pleasure in life; *without this they can be of no value.* But this being presupposed, the price of things will be in a composed proportion of the *demand* for them, and the *difficulty* in acquiring them. The demand will be in proportion to the numbers who are wanting them, or their necessity of life. The *difficulty* may be occasioned many ways; if the quantities of them in the world be small; if any accidents make the quantity less than ordinary; if much toil is required in producing them, or much ingenuity, or a more elegant genius in the artists; if the persons employed about them according to the custom of the country are men in high account, and live in a more splendid manner; for the expense of this must be defrayed by the higher profits of their labours and few can be thus maintained.

> (1747, 199, italics added)

Perhaps even more clearly than Pufendorf, Hutcheson was presenting a demand-and-supply theory of value and price. Like both Pufendorf and Carmichael, and unlike Adam Smith in a crucial passage in the *Wealth of Nations*, Hutcheson explicitly emphasised not only that without providing some use or pleasure a thing could not have value, but also that value was subjective:

By the use causing a demand we mean not only a natural subserviency to our support, or to some natural pleasure, but any tendency to give satisfaction, by prevailing custom or fancy, as a matter of ornament or distinction, in the more eminent status; for this will cause a demand as well as the natural use. In like manner, by difficulty of acquiring, we do not only mean great labour or toil, but all other circumstances which prevent a great plenty of the goods or performances demanded. Thus the price is increased by the rarity or scarcity of the materials in nature.

(1755, vol II, 54–5)

The word 'rarity' is of some significance in view of its subsequent use in French by Auguste and Léon Walras. On value, Hutcheson concluded: 'When there is no demand there is no price were the difficulty never so great; and were there no difficulty or labour requisite to acquire, the most universal demand will not cause a price; as we see in fresh water in these climates' (II, 54; see also Taylor, 1965, 66).

Hutcheson thus followed very closely the natural-law theory of value and price as developed by Pufendorf and Gershom Carmichael, in terms of scarcity, demand and supply, rather than a labour theory. But he supported the Lockean labour theory *of property,* as expounded in Glasgow by Carmichael. Hutcheson insisted on

. . . the right of property each one has in the fruits of his own labour; that is, we must approve the securing to him, where no public interest requires the contrary, and must condemn as cruel, unsociable, and oppressive, all depriving men of the use and free disposal of what they have thus occupied and cultivated, according to any innocent inclination of their hearts.

(II, 320)

Hutcheson argued strongly that this occupancy-cum-labour principle of property was profoundly beneficial to society. For the great motive force of an economy must be the individual's hopes of future wealth from his labours, for himself or his family:

Nay the most extensive affections could scarce engage a wise man to industry, if no property ensued upon it. He must see that universal diligence is necessary. Diligence will never be universal, unless men's own necessities, and the love of families and friends, excite them. Such as are capable of labour and yet decline it, should find no support in the labours of others. If the goods procured, or improved, by the industrious lie in common for the use of all, the worst of men have the generous and industrious for their slaves.

(II, 321)

Of course, if some constitution could be devised which could *compel* all men to labour, and then ensure the distribution of the product in accordance with need or merit, then the right of the individual to property in the fruits of his labour would not be necessary. But this was politically Utopian:

Such constant vigilance . . . of magistrates, and such nice discernment of merit, as could ensure both an universal diligence, and a just and humane distribution, is not to be expected. Nay, no confidence of a wise distribution by magistrates can ever make any given quantity of labour be endured with such pleasure and hearty good-will, as when each man is the distributor of what he has acquired among those he loves . . . And what plan of polity will ever satisfy men sufficiently as to the just treatment to be given themselves, and all who are peculiarly dear to them, out of the common stock, if all is to depend on the pleasure of magistrates, and no private person allowed any exercise of his own wisdom or discretion in some of the most honourable and delightful offices of life? Must all men in private stations ever be treated as children or fools?

(II, 323)

Hutcheson recognised some limitations to the occupancy-and-labour principle of property. Occupancy of land did not bestow property rights if the land was not, or could not be, worked by the occupier. But he rejected fundamentally and explicitly the socialist, Utopian notions of Plato and Sir Thomas More. He described the former's ideas as 'too arrogant', and presented the occupation-and-labour principle of property as a justification for economic individualism and free enterprise.

Hutcheson then passed from the subject of the values and prices of goods and services to that of the means, or medium, of exchange, and the qualities of an effective medium:

In setting the values of goods for commerce they must be reduced to some common measure on both sides . . . The qualities requisite to the most perfect standard are these; it must be something generally desired so that men are willing to take it in exchange. The very making any goods the standard will of itself give them this quality. It must be portable; which will often be the case if it is rare, so that small quantities are of great value. It must be divisible without loss into small parts, so as to be suited to the values of all sorts of goods; and it must be durable, not easily wearing by use, or perishing in its nature.

(II, 55-6; Taylor, 1965, 73-4)

Hutcheson emphasised that nominal changes in coins cannot affect 'real' values: 'If the legal names of our crown pieces were doubled so that the ounce of silver were called 10 shillings, the nominal prices of all goods would rise as much . . . 'Tis a fundamental maxim about coin, that "its value in commerce cannot be varied by names" ' (II, 59-60).

On a number of other important points Hutcheson anticipated the views of Adam Smith. For example, he emphasised the advantages of large scale and specialisation, and of the division of labour:

Nay 'tis well known that the produce of the labours of any given number, twenty, for instance, in providing the necessaries or conveniences of life, shall be much greater by assigning to one, a certain sort of work of one kind, in which he will soon acquire skill and dexterity, and to another assigning work of a different kind, than if each of the twenty were obliged to employ himself, by turns, in all the different sorts of labour requisite for his subsistence, without sufficient dexterity in any . . .

Larger associations may further enlarge our means of enjoyment, and give more extensive and delightful exercise to our powers of every kind. The inventions, experience, and arts of multitudes are communicated; knowledge is increased, and social affections more diffused.

(II, 288-9; Taylor, 1965, 58)

Today, of course, 'small is beautiful' may seem to be a more attractive maxim. Indeed, Adam Smith was to emphasise the stultifying and alienating effects of intense specialisation and division of labour associated with large-scale production. But size and scale are relative and must be understood in relation to the conditions of the day.

Also in Hutcheson's remarks on taxation there may appear to be a suggestion of Smith's maxims when he emphasised proportionality: 'Above all a just proportion to the wealth of the people should be observed in whatever is raised from them' (II, 341).

He championed strongly the 'natural' freedom of the individual, as a prerequisite for his happiness, but, regarding the major policy principle of freedom of trade his views were markedly opposed to those of Smith. For Hutcheson was something of a mercantilist in maintaining that a surplus of exports over imports would bring a country an increase in wealth: 'Industry is the natural mine of wealth, the fund of all stores for exportation, by the surplus of which, beyond the value of what a nation imports, it must increase in wealth and power' (II, 318). In fact, in the field of foreign trade, Hutcheson supported an active role for government and most of the usual mercantilist measures:

> Foreign materials should be imported and even premiums given, when necessary, that all our hands may be employed; and that by exporting them again manufactured, we may obtain from abroad the price of our labours . . .
>   Foreign manufactures and products ready for consumption, should be made dear to the consumer by high duties, if we cannot altogether prohibit the consumption; that they may never be used by the lower and more numerous orders of the people, whose consumption would be far greater than those of the few who are wealthy.

(II, 318-19; and Taylor, 1965, 119-21)

Moreover, industrious foreigners should be welcomed to settle, and the shipping industry should be assisted. Hutcheson also supported the doctrine of low real wages to maintain the supply of labour (in contrast to Adam Smith): 'If a people have not acquired an habit of industry, the cheapness of all necessaries of life rather encourages sloth' (II, 318).

We have noticed above the fundamental point regarding the subjectivity of utility, or use, on which Hutcheson and Smith (at one crucial point in the *Wealth of Nations*) diverged. But there was another argument, fundamental to what subsequently came to be called 'macroeconomics', on which Hutcheson pointed the way, and which Smith, following his teacher, eventually made a cornerstone of the classical model. The original point arose out of Hutcheson's opposition to Mandeville's doctrines on luxury.

Hutcheson's criticism of Mandeville was one of the earliest and perhaps the most important, since it was based not only on forthright moral opposition (as was Berkeley's), but also on fundamentally diverging economic assumptions. In opposition to Hobbes and Mandeville, Hutcheson believed that man was not exclusively selfish and incapable of genuinely altruistic choices. He therefore also believed that expenditure on necessities and serious conveniences, and on helping the poor, not only should, but *would* come before frivolous luxuries, going on to maintain, in a vital leap from normative moral principles to a positive economic assumption that income not spent in one way *would*, if not squandered on luxuries, get spent in another way, either on prudent, useful conveniences, or on necessities for the poor. Until everyone in the world had been supplied with all the necessities of life, demand could be, and, it was assumed, would tend to be, maintained at an adequate level, without luxury expenditure. Hutcheson did not emphasise the beneficial possibilities of investment expenditure, which saving would make room for, but his prudent propositions led on, in the work of his great pupil, to what Schumpeter called 'the Turgot-Smith theory' of saving and investing, to the effect that all savings passed smoothly—and even 'immediately'—into investment.

Hutcheson's criticism of Mandeville came first in his *Remarks upon the Fable of the Bees* (1725-7), before he took up the Glasgow chair. His argument was: 'Unless therefore all mankind are fully provided not only with all necessaries, but all innocent conveniences and pleasures of life, it is still possible, without any vice, by an honest care of families, relations, or some worthy persons in distress, to make the greatest consumption' (1727, 63).

Hutcheson then turned this possibility into an actuality, when he seized upon Mandeville's far-fetched example which purported to show that thieves were good for trade and the economy, because they stimulated the production and employment for locksmiths:

> Who needs be surprised that luxury or pride are made necessary to public good, when even theft and robbery are supposed by the same author to be subservient to it, by employing locksmiths? Were there no occasion for locks, had all children and servants discretion never to go into chambers unseasonably, this would make no diminution of manufactures; the money saved to the housekeeper would afford either better dress, or other conveniences to a family, which would equally support artificers.
>
> (64-5)

Here Hutcheson was adumbrating what Keynes was to call the 'classical' assumption that all income not spent in one way would be spent in another. He made no suggestion that government spending, income redistribution, or even monetary policy, might ever be necessary to maintain expenditure and demand. Hutcheson, therefore, made an important contribution to the process by which Becher's 'Principle', that one man's spending was another man's income, was transformed into Smith's 'Principle' that one man's *saving* was also another man's income. On this point, though he shared his moral condemnation of Mandeville, Hutcheson differed from Berkeley, who supported government expenditure, income redistribution, and monetary and banking reform, to maintain demand. There was also, as we shall discuss below, some divergence, on this fundamental issue, between Hutcheson (and Smith), on the one hand, and David Hume, on the other.

Francis Hutcheson had been described as the 'father' of the Scottish Enlightenment, since he was 'a major and often very personal influence on the two most important eighteenth-century Scottish philosophers' (see Campbell, 1982, 167). This is not to be denied regarding some central and fundamental principles of moral philosophy. But regarding economic ideas, there are important divergences between this great triumvirate. David Hume developed vital theories of money, interest and the balance of payments which were new, as far as Scotland was concerned, and not shared by Hutcheson or Smith, and which certainly ran basically counter to Hutcheson's mercantilistic tendencies. Adam Smith started from, and retained *some* of his heritage from Pufendorf, Carmichael and Hutcheson, but later went in for certain new departures, derived more from Petty and Locke.

III

The University of Glasgow was one of the first and most important of the founts and origins of the Scottish Philosophical Enlightenment, and especially of its contribution to political economy. But, in this great, meteoric intellectual movement, outstandingly the most brilliant and original thinker and writer— or 'by far the most illustrious philosopher *and historian* of the present age', as Adam Smith called him (1976, vol III, 790, italics added) was neither a Glaswegian nor an academic. Though, as a boy, he studied for a time at Edinburgh University, David Hume never obtained a degree. Subsequently, hardly to the credit of those celebrated institutions, he failed to obtain either of the chairs he sought, one at Edinburgh in 1744–5, and one at Glasgow in 1751.

Though Hume proclaimed himself, in his autobiography, as 'of a good family both by father and mother' (see Mossner, 1980, 6), the Humes were not at all wealthy. David Hume, following family tradition, made an early attempt to enter the legal profession, and then tried commerce in Bristol. Both were swiftly abandoned, though subsequently he performed highly successfully on various diplomatic missions, notably in Paris in 1763, when he was fêted by French intellectual society. He later vigorously contested what he described as 'the ancient prejudice' that 'a man of genius is unfit for business'. But, as a young man, Hume saved himself—as his first biographer put it—from 'falling into that gulf in which many of the world's greatest geniuses lie buried— professional eminence' (Burton, 1895, vol 1, 28).

For Hume started life with a consuming passion for learning and philosophy. With no settled career prospects in front of him, at the age of twenty-three he showed what he was made of:

> I went over to France, with a view to prosecuting my studies in a country retreat: and there I laid that plan of life which I have steadily and successfully pursued. I resolved to make a very rigid frugality supply my deficiency of fortune, to maintain unimpaired my independency and to regard every object as contemptible except the improvement of my talents in literature.

Surely no-one among the great thinkers was more thoroughly his own man. He settled near Rheims for about three years and wrote *A Treatise of Human Nature*, which he later described as having been 'planned before I was one and twenty, and composed before twenty five' (Hume, 1932, vol II, 158). He called this great work a failure which 'fell dead born from the press'. But it was the presentation only, not the substance, that he recast in subsequent writings. In the twentieth century his *Treatise* came to be 'recognized as Hume's supreme philosophical effort' (Mossner, 1980, 117).

He proceeded in the 1740s and 1750s to redevelop and extend his ideas in volumes of essays, inquiries, and discourses. His work on political economy was concentrated in some nine essays which appeared in *Political Discourses* (1752). Together these pieces would add up to a single short volume, but were collected with many others on philosophical, political and literary topics. His aim was to discuss the main, broad policy issues of the day, and to correct what he regarded as prevailing fallacies. He made no attempt at a systematic view of an independent   subject. He wrote almost nothing on value and price, for example. Hume's group of essays did, however, make some contribution to the identification of a separate field of study, and, though he does not appear to have used the term 'political economy', there was an element of systematisation in the method he applied.

Hume's economic essays fall into two or three groups. First came those 'Of Commerce' and 'Of Refinement in the Arts', which were concerned with the longer-run effects, highly beneficent as Hume saw them, of the commercial and economic progress which he was convinced was going forward. This kind of longer-run historical process was always one of his main interests: What were its social effects? Would it last? Would, or could, poorer countries catch up and surpass the richer or more advanced? These were the historical and developmental questions to which Hume sought answers, and he broached them in the first two of his economic essays.

Then came the four essays best known to economists: 'On Money', 'On Interest', 'On the Balance of Trade', and 'On the Jealousy of Trade'—this last piece added in 1758. There were also two essays on public finance ('Of Taxes' and 'Of Public Credit') *plus*, finally, the longer work, 'Of the Populousness of Ancient Nations', which is of particular interest in relation to classical political economy.

The subtitle of Hume's great *Treatise* had been 'an attempt to introduce the experimental method of reasoning into moral subjects'. In his Introduction, Hume wrote:

> . . . as the science of man is the only solid foundation for the other sciences, so, the only solid foundation we can give to this science itself must be laid on experience and observation . . .
>   . . . None of them [these sciences] can go beyond experience or establish any principles which are not founded on that authority.

> (1739 [1911], vol I, 5–7)

The interpretation of just 'what Hume really meant' by this 'attempt', has so far taken up many shelves of literature, comment and interpretation. We may, however, begin here with what Hume said in his brief methodological introduction to the first of his economic essays, that 'Of Commerce'. Here he was concerned with the respective roles in the study of mankind, of, on the one hand, general principles, or 'reasonings', and on the other hand, of particular historical considerations, or circumstances. He first asserted that 'it is certain, that general principles, if just and sound, must always prevail in the general course of things' (1955, 4). Indeed, in his claims for the method of deduction from general principles, Hume was, at some points, highly enthusiastic about the possibility of reaching 'consequences almost as general and certain as any which the mathematical sciences afford us'. He soon, however, restored the balance by emphasising on the next page, the variability of human opinions, manners and conduct, which would render attemps to establish generalisations either dangerous or impossible: 'Man is a very variable being, and susceptible of many different opinions, principles, and rules of conduct. What may be true, while he adheres to one way of thinking, will be found false, when he has embraced an opposite set of manners and opinions' (1955, 5).

In his essay 'Of Civil Liberty' Hume began by conceding:

> I am apt, however, to entertain a suspicion, that the world is still too young to fix many general truths in politics, which will remain true to the latest posterity. We have not as yet had experience of three thousand years; so that not only the art of reasoning is still imperfect in this science, as in all others, but we even want sufficient materials upon which we can reason. It is not fully known what degree of refine-ment, either in virtue or vice, human nature is susceptible of, nor what may be expected of mankind from any great revolution in their education, customs, or principles.
>
> (1752, [1800], vol 1, 62)

Hume always sought to maintain an intellectual balance, and may be found inclining first one way and then the other, between an optimistic confidence in general principles and in the conclusions they yield, and, on the other hand, a sceptical caution, based on historical relativism and a recognition of human variety and variability. In his essays, he repeatedly demonstrated his concern to balance reliance on general principles with a rich supply of historical evidence, illustrations, and qualifications; so that he might well be regarded as a pioneer of the historical method in political economy. In his essay 'Of the Study of History', Hume emphasised how history was,

> not only a valuable part of knowledge, but opens the door to many other parts, and affords materials to most of the sciences . . . we should be for ever children in understanding, were it not for this invention, which extends our experience to all past ages, and to the most distant nations; making them contribute as much to our improvement in wisdom, as if they had actually lain under observation.
>
> (398)

IV

The general principle which Hume sought to establish in his essay 'Of Commerce' was that of the beneficence of economic progress and its complementarity with the increase of happiness and freedom, regarding which he was highly confident (much more so than Adam Smith). Moreover, the interests of government and people (or 'state') were complementary: 'Thus the greatness of the sovereign and the happiness of the state are, in great measure, united with regard to trade and manufacturers' (1955, 12).

Hume optimistically maintained that, in his day, a régime such as that of ancient Sparta, where the standard of living of the people was kept down and all luxury suppressed so as to enhance the military power of the government, 'appears to me almost impossible' (8). He supported the development of manufacturers and 'mechanic arts', both for the employment they afforded, and for the stimulus they gave to agricultural production by providing commodities and luxuries to be worked for by the agricultural sector. The development of foreign commerce also encouraged new tastes, new manufactures, and technical progress: 'Thus men become acquainted with the pleasures of luxury and the profits of commerce; and their delicacy and industry, being once awakened, carry them on to farther improvements, in every branch of domestic as well as foreign trade' (14).

Hume wanted growing wealth to be widely distributed, and introduced the argument from diminishing utility:

> Every person, if possible, ought to enjoy the fruits of his labour, in a full possession of all the necessaries, and many of the conveniences of life. No one can doubt but such an equality is most suitable to human nature, *and diminishes much less from the happiness of the rich man than it adds to that of the poor*. It also augments the power of the state, and makes any extraordinary taxes or impositions be paid with more cheerfulness.
>
> (15, italics added)

He recognised the disadvantage of high wages in foreign trade, though he rejected the low-wage doctrine of many 'mercantilists', and maintained that there was a strong complementary relationship between wealth, widely diffused among 'the common people', and political liberty.

The essay 'Of Refinement in the Arts' developed further the arguments of the preceding essay in examining the effects of luxury. Hume was here concerned with the issue raised so provocatively by Mandeville, and so warmly debated, from the other side, by Hutcheson, and Berkeley. Here, as so often, he is to be found taking up a balanced, middle position, protesting against 'those preposterous opinions' entertained on the subject of luxury, at the one extreme by 'men of libertine principles', and, at the other, by 'men of severe morals' (20). Hume rejected both these extremes and maintained that 'ages of refinement are both the happiest and the most virtuous'. Moreover, he believed that activity and employment were beneficial for their own sake.

> In times when industry and the arts flourish, men are kept in perpetual occupation, and enjoy, as their reward, the occupation itself, as well as those pleasures which are the fruit of their labour. The mind acquires new vigour; enlarges its powers and faculties; and by an assiduity in honest industry, both satisfies its natural appetites, and prevents the growth of unnatural ones, which commonly spring up, when nourished by ease or idleness.
>
> (21)

Industry and knowledge developed in a complementary relationship. Hume rejected the example of Ancient Rome, the decline of which had been so often attributed to the growth of luxury. For this fall had been brought about, not by luxury, but by 'an ill-modelled government, and the unlimited extent of conquests'. Luxury stimulated industry.

Finally, and most important, progress in the arts was favourable to liberty and 'has a natural tendency to pressure, if not produce a free government' (28). This was because such progress fostered the emergence of 'that middling rank of men, who are the best and firmest basis of public liberty' (28).

Certainly Hume to *some* extent agreed with Francis Hutcheson that unemployment was not *inevitably* the alternative to luxury. But he was more inclined to share Mandeville's sceptical view of human nature:

> To say, that, without a vicious luxury, the labour would not have been employed at all, is only to say, that there is some other defect in human nature, such as indolence, selfishness, inattention to others, for which luxury, in some measure, provides a remedy; as one poison may be an antidote to another . . . By banishing vicious luxury, without curing sloth and an indifference to others, you only diminish industry in the state, and add nothing to men's charity or their generosity.
>
> (30–1)

Hume's conclusion was: 'Luxury, when excessive, is the source of many ills; but is in general preferable to sloth and idleness, which would commonly succeed in its place' (32). Thus, his contribution to the luxury debate provided an excellent example of a Humean balancing act. Having begun by taking up the anti-Mandeville line of argument of Francis Hutcheson, Hume then went on to accept what amounted to a moderately pro-Mandeville conclusion.

V

Much the best-known to economists of Hume's essays are those 'Of Money', 'Of Interest', and 'Of the Balance of Trade'. In each he was concerned with refuting a major current fallacy: (a) that it was important for a country to possess a large quantity of money; (b) that a large quantity of money made for a low rate of interest; and (c) that a deficit on the balance of trade was most damaging to a country, and must be actively prevented at almost any cost.

Hume was far from being the first critic of so-called 'mercantilist' doctrines on money. But he stated with great clarity and cogency what came to be regarded as the classical refutation of excessive concern with an increasing money supply. Money was 'only the instrument which men have agreed upon to facilitate the exchange of one commodity for another' (33). In fact, a greater quantity of money may be disadvantageous, as contrasted with a greater quantity of the real factors: 'The greater number of people and their greater industry are serviceable in all cases; at home and abroad, in private and in public. But the greater plenty of money, is very limited in its use, and may even sometimes be a loss to a nation in its commerce with foreigners' (34). For there were corrective processes at work which would remedy the situation: 'There seems to be a happy concurrence of causes in human affairs, which checks the growth of trade and riches, and hinders them from being confined entirely to one people; as might naturally at first be dreaded from the advantages of an established commerce' (34). For in the rich, established countries, the greater quantity of money would keep prices and costs high: 'And, in general, we may observe, that the dearness of everything, from plenty of money, is a disadvantage, which attends an established commerce, and sets bounds to it in every country, by enabling the poorer states to undersell the richer in all foreign markets' (35). Hence, Hume's doubts, about the advantages of paper credit and schemes such as John Law's, which would tend to raise prices.

Hume sought to establish two 'observations'. The first was that the absolute quantity of money was of no significance, but that an increasing quantity should be a most important objective of policy. Thus Hume was seeking to show that the frequently posed question as to what was the 'right' quantity of money for a country was, in the long run, meaningless (but only in the very abstract case of the long run):

> It is indeed evident, that money is nothing but the representation of labour and commodities, and serves only as a method of rating or estimating them. Where coin is in greater plenty; as a greater quantity of it is required to represent the same quantity of goods; it can have no effect, either good or bad, taking a nation within itself; any more than it would make an alteration on a merchant's books, if, instead of the Arabian method of notation, which requires a few characters, he should make use of the Roman, which requires a great many.
>
> (37)

But Hume then passed at once from this static proposition to emphasise the highly stimulating immediate effects of an increasing quantity of money, clearly assuming the existence of unemployed resources:

> ... it is certain that, since the discovery of the mines in America, industry has increased in all the nations of Europe, except in the possessors of those mines; and this may justly be ascribed, amongst other reasons, to the increase of gold and silver. Accordingly we find, that in *every* kingdom, into which money begins to flow in greater abundance than formerly, everything takes a new face: labour and industry gain life; the merchant becomes more enterprising, the manufacturer becomes more diligent and skilful, and even the farmer follows his plough with greater alacrity and attention.
>
> (378, italics added)

Hume then traced out the channels and the dynamic process, through which the increase in the money supply took effect. Certainly the initial effects seemed highly beneficent. For prices did not rise immediately. But he warned: 'In my opinion, it is only in this interval or intermediate situation, between the acquisition of money and rise of prices, that the increasing quantity of gold and silver is favourable to industry' (38).

In his conclusion, however, in spite of all his previous proto-classical views Hume came out with a statement of what might be regarded as the essence of the mercantilist position on monetary policy:

. . . it is of no consequence, with regard to the domestic happiness of a state, whether money be in a greater or less quantity. *The good policy of the magistrate consists only in keeping it, if possible, still increasing; because, by that means, he keeps alive a spirit of industry in the nation, and increases the stock of labour, in which consists all real power and riches.*

(39, italics added)

Hume certainly seemed to be describing solid, lasting gains, and not simply some fleeting, temporary advantages. It may be noticed also that he stated that 'the magistrate' should 'keep' ('if possible') the money supply 'still increasing', not merely temporarily raise it in conditions of unemployment. Of course, he was assuming growth potential in the economy, but he said nothing of possible inflationary dangers, or of the limits set by full employment. As many mecantilists would have enthusiastically agreed, Hume then followed up by emphasising the disadvantages of a *decreasing* money supply, 'A nation, whose money decreases, is actually, at that time, weaker and more miserable than another nation, which possesses no more money but is on the increasing hand' (40).

The transitional maladjustments could be very damaging and quite long-lasting: 'The workman has not the same employment from the manufacturer and merchant; though he pays the same price for everything in the market. The farmer cannot dispose of his corn and cattle; though he must pay the same rent to his landlord. The poverty, and beggary, and sloth, which must ensue, are easily foreseen' (40).

The second 'observation' which Hume sought to establish was a counterpart of the first, in that he denied the significance, or ill effects, of a 'scarcity of money'. For he insisted that a depression should be described as flowing from a 'decrease' of money, and not from a 'scarcity', and that the real cause of the difficulties was 'the manners and customs of the people'—who should (apparently) be expected to adjust more flexibly to vagaries in the money supply.

Hume then put forward a broad, if not very precise, restatement of the quantity theory: 'It seems a maxim almost self-evident, that the prices of every thing depend on the proportion between commodities and money, and that any considerable alteration on either has the same effect, either of heightening or lowering the price. Increase the commodities, they become cheaper; increase the money they rise in their value' (41). He asserted that with economic progress and an unchanging quantity of money prices would fall (43), but did not envisage possible maladjustments. He concluded, once again, that 'the want of money can never injure any state within itself', but that a 'general increase' in the money supply was important. There was not necessarily a definite contradiction here, but there does appear to be some contrast, which could usefully have been clarified by some explanation and reconciliation.

The fallacy which Hume was concerned to refute in his essay 'Of Interest' was that interest could be lowered by expanding the money supply; that is, he was rejecting what Heckscher described as the mercantilist idea of money as a kind of factor of production (1955, vol II, 200). Hume sought to relate interest to the rate of profit, and to the 'real' return on investment, or the productivity of capital—as Joseph Massie had recently done in his *Natural Rate of Interest* of 1750 (see chapter 13, V). It was emphasised by Hume that it was not a scarcity of money, but 'real' factors, three in particular, which made for a high rate of interest: 'a great demand for borrowing; little riches to supply that demand; and great profits arising from commerce' (49). He thus put forward a supply and demand theory. He added that interest fell with economic progress, which he saw as encouraging frugality, while the competition of capitals (as Smith was to argue) depressed the rate of profit in the longer term.

In the essay 'Of the Balance of Trade', Hume was concerned to deny 'this apprehension of the wrong balance of trade'. Here he introduced his well-known assumption of four-fifths of all the money in Great Britain being annihilated in one night (or, alternatively, of all the money being multiplied five-fold in one night). No difficulties of adjustment were discussed. In fact, it was suggested that the transition, and any problems it might bring, would be of the briefest. If four-fifths of the money was lost, 'must not the price of all labour and commodities sink in proportion?' (1955, 63). No nation could then compete with Britain in foreign markets: '*In how little time*, therefore, must this bring back the money which we had lost, and raise us to the level of all neighbouring nations?' (63, italics added).

Hume certainly seems to have been referring here not to a longer-term, secular process of the rise or decline of rich and poor countries, but to a comparatively much shorter process of adjustment between countries, usually, of a similar level of wealth and development. He then proceeded to introduce the subsequently familiar comparison with how the force of gravity equalised out water levels: 'Now it is evident that the same causes, which would correct these exorbitant inequalities, were they to happen miraculously, must prevent their happening in the common course of nature, and must for ever, in all neighbouring nations preserve money nearly proportionable to the art and industry in each nation. All water, wherever it communicates, remains always at a level' (63).

Hume compared international imbalances in trade with inter-regional imbalances, as, for example, between London and Yorkshire, which gave rise to no 'gloomy reflections'. He reasserted his old suspicions about paper money, and suggested—in direct opposition to Benjamin Franklin—that paper money was quite unnecessary in the colonies, and that, if the paper were abolished, sufficient gold and silver would return—as had been available before the introduction of paper.

He reasserted, rather than denied, however, the common mercantilist doctrine of the destructiveness of hoarding, especially (as Petty had observed) by the government, and the beneficence and importance of 'circulation'. Hoarding, which Hume presumably regarded as attaining significant dimensions, was 'a practice which we should all exclaim against as destructive, namely, the gathering of large sums into a public treasure, locking them up, and absolutely preventing their circulation' (72). But he then soon proceeded to balance this proposition by asserting, on the next page, that, in the case of the massive hoarding by Henry VII, it was not 'probable that the diminution of circulating money was ever sensibly felt by the people, or ever did them any prejudice. The sinking of the prices of all commodities would *immediately* replace it, by giving England the advantage in its commerce with the neighbouring kingdoms' (73, italics added). Hume went on to make a considerable concession to 'mercantilist' doctrines regarding import duties. He did not support the wholesale removal of tariffs: 'All taxes, however, upon foreign commodities are not to be regarded as prejudicial or useless . . . A tax on German linen encourages home manufactures, and thereby multiplies our people and industry. A tax on brandy increases the sale of rum, and supports our southern colonies' (76).

Hume's conclusion, however, *seemed* to be emphatic and unqualified: 'In short, a government has great reason to preserve with care its people and its manufactures. Its money it may safely trust to the course of human affairs, without fear of jealousy.' This statement, if left unqualified, might have appeared to justify an attitude of 'money doesn't matter', or of monetarist *laissez-faire*, implying that the economy should be expected to adjust rapidly to *any* vagaries of the money supply. Such suggestions were to appear, at some points, in the *Wealth of Nations*. However, Hume added a further final sentence as to the duty of government: 'If it ever give attention to this latter circumstance [sc. the money supply], it ought only to be so far as it affects the former [i.e. people and manufactures]'(77). But if the money supply, or alternatives thereof, might often and seriously affect 'people and manufactures'—and therefore require governmental attention—how much was left of the pronouncement that government might safely trust its money 'to the course of human affairs'?

VI

The essay 'Of the Jealousy of Trade', added in 1758, expressed more thorough-going free-trade views, based on an international harmony of interests. Hume was here concerned to demolish the mercantilist conception of international trade as a zero-sum, your-win-my-loss game, and had been anticipated, in these views, by Carl, Gervaise and Vanderlint:

> I will venture to assert, that the increase of riches and commerce in any one nation, instead of hurting, commonly promotes the riches and commerce of all its neighbours; and that a state can scarcely carry its trade and industry very far, where all the surrounding states are buried in ignorance, sloth, and barbarism . . . I go farther, and observe, that where an open communication is preserved among nations, it is impossible but the domestic industry of every one must receive an increase from the improvements of the others.
>
> (78)

These were sweeping statements. Hume continued by maintaining that foreign trade, as in the case of Britain, gave an impetus to technical advance. Moreover: 'Nature, by giving a diversity of geniuses, climates, and soils, to different nations, has secured their mutual intercourse and commerce, as long as they all remain industrious and civilized' (79). The increase of industry among a country's neighbours, increased the consumption of that country's goods. With diversification and adaptability no country need fear the consequences of losing a market for one or other of its products. These optimistic views culminated in Hume's famous proclamation: 'Not only as a man, but as a British subject. I pray for the flourishing commerce of Germany, Spain, Italy, and even France itself' (82).

When discussing adjustments in international trade, Hume seems some-times to have been referring to relations between rich and poor countries in terms of longer-run development and progress, and sometimes to relations between countries, at a similar level of wealth, in terms of shorter-run processes. In fact, in Hume's writings, and in interpretations of them, the distinctions were not always clear as between shorter-term disequilibria, and the much longer-run secular, historical processes of the economic rise, or relative decline, of nations, such as Spain in the seventeenth (and Britain in the twentieth) century. As with George Berkeley, Richard Cantillon, and other writers of this period, the familiar modern distinction was seldom to be found between longer-term processes of growth (or decline), and shorter-run, or cyclical, increases or decreases in employment and production. Hume seems to have seen the process of adjustment to balance-of-payments disturbances as taking place in 'little time' and he actually used the word 'immediately'. But the decline of 'old' industries, and of whole economies, surely had to be envisaged as much longer-run processes. However, as in Cantillon's account of balance-of-trade adjustments, these distinctions were not always clearly observed in the writings of Hume.

These distinctions, or, at some points, the disregard of them, are significant in interpreting the exchanges between Hume and Josiah Tucker, or what has come to be called 'the rich country–poor country' debate. As we have seen, Hume had expressed considerable optimism regarding economic progress, which, however, he soon qualified, or, as so often, balanced. For he had also suggested that all human things have the seeds of decay. On the other hand, the more unreservedly optimistic Dean Tucker contended that economic progress generally, for an advanced country, had no limits, or no *ne plus ultra*. The debate between the two (for some reason transacted through Lord Kames) was begun by Hume's letter of 4 March 1758, with some warm compliments on Tucker's 'profound knowledge of the theory of commerce, joined to an enlarged acquaintance with its practice'. In fact, each of the participants had been fully prepared in advance to accept most of the other's arguments. As Hume stated: 'All the advantages which the author insists upon as belonging to a nation of extensive commerce are undoubtedly real: great capital, extensive correspondence, skilful expedients of facilitating labour, dexterity, industry, etc, these circumstances give them an undisputed superiority over poor nations, who are ignorant and inexperienced' (200). He proceeded to formulate the issue as follows:

> The question is, whether these advantages can go on, increasing trade *in infinitum*, or whether they do not at least come to a *ne plus ultra*, and check themselves, by begetting disadvantages, which at first retard, and at last finally stop their progress.

Among these disadvantages, we may reckon the dear price of provisions and labour, which enables the poorer country to rival them, first in the coarser manufactures, and then in those which are more elaborate. Were it otherwise, commerce, if not dissipated by violent conquests, would go on perpetually increasing, and one spot of the globe would engross the art of industry of the whole.

(200)

Hume would probably have accepted Tucker's point, but he countered the Dean's optimism, which was supported by 'the goodness of Providence', as follows: 'It was never surely the intention of Providence that any one nation should be a monopolizer of wealth: and the growth of all bodies, artificial as well as natural, is stopped by internal causes, derived from their enormous size and greatness. Great empires, great cities, great commerce, all of them receive a check, not from accidental events, but necessary principles' (201).

Tucker, of course, protested that he did not envisage any inevitable tendency to a national monopoly, and claimed subsequently to have influenced Hume towards his own line of thinking. But though Hume's later essay 'Of the Jealousy of Trade', showed, as we have noted, some move towards rather more unqualified free-trade sentiments, as compared with his previous essays, this may not have been due to his debate with Tucker. Anyhow, Hume concluded his letter by proclaiming his intention to launch a further attack on 'the narrow malignity and envy of nations' and he emphasised his pleasure in having the Dean as an ally (202).

VII

Two of Hume's economic essays are concerned with public finance, those 'Of Taxes' and 'Of Public Credit'.

On taxes, Hume began with an attack on the 'prevailing maxim' that each increase in taxation 'increases proportionately the industry of the people' (83). He recognised the great dangers of this notion, but maintained that it had a considerable element of truth, and he proceeded to bring to bear much historical evidence and analysis. But then—not untypically—he went on promptly to reassert the proposition in more qualified and precise terms. It depended on historical circumstances:

When a tax is laid upon commodities, which are consumed by the common people, the necessary consequence may seem to be, either that the poor must retrench something from their way of living, or raise their wages, so as to make the burden of the tax fall entirely upon the rich. But there is a third consequence, which often follows upon taxes, namely that the poor increase their industry, perform more work, without demanding more for their labour. Where taxes are moderate, are laid on gradually, and affect not the necessaries of life, this consequence naturally follows; and it is certain, that such difficulties often serve to excite the industry of a people, and render them more opulent and laborious, than others, who enjoy the greatest advantages.

(83)

It may be noted that Hume was referring to what 'often' happens, not to what always, or even generally happens. But what is most obvious is that, with regard to the vital subject of wages, Hume certainly entertained no such general theory as that of the 'natural' wage, as defined in the more hard-line versions of the Malthusian doctrine. In fact, Hume could almost be said to out-Giffen Giffen: in times of scarcity and high prices, not only did the poor apparently consume more of the basic foodstufs, but they lived better into the bargain: ''Tis *always* observed in years of scarcity, if it be not extreme, that the poor labour more, and really live better, than in years of great plenty, when they indulge themselves in idleness and riot' (83n).

In conclusion, Hume denied the physiocratic doctrine that all taxes fall ultimately on land, and maintained that the best taxes are those on luxury consumption goods.

In his discussion of public credit, Hume was concerned to emphasise the great disadvantages and dangers of large and mounting public debts. He refuted the idea that because they only involved a transfer, from a right pocket to a left pocket, public debts were no burden. Listing the kinds of damage and burdens such debts could bring, Hume mentioned first how London had 'already arrived at such an enormous size, and seems still increasing' (95). He emphasised that, as a form of paper credit, public debts had 'all the disadvantages attending that species of money'. Furthermore, the taxes necessary to service the debt would oppress the poor, or raise the price of labour. It could also be damaging if the debt passed, as it often did, into foreign hands, or into the hands of the idle. He warned that Great Britain was already some way down this perilous road. But, Hume explained, 'so great dupes are the generality of mankind', that the same disastrous course was followed over and over again: 'Mankind are, in all ages caught by the same baits. The same tricks, played over and over again, still trepan them. The heights of popularity and patriotism are still the beaten road to power and tyranny' (104).

In his main philosophical works, other important insights of Hume are to be found concerning the principles of economic policy. In discussing the origin of civil government he gave an excellent explanation of the role of government in providing public goods:

Two neighbours may agree to drain a meadow, which they possess in common: because it is easy for them to know each other's mind; and each must perceive that the immediate consequence of his failing in this part, is the abandoning the whole project. But it is very difficult, and indeed impossible, that a thousand persons should agree in any such action; it being difficult for them to concert so complicated a design, and still more difficult for them to execute it, while each seeks a pretext to free himself of the trouble and expense, and would lay the whole burden on others. Political society easily remedies both these inconveniences . . . Thus, bridges are built, harbours opened, ramparts raised, canals formed, fleets equipped, and armies disciplined, everywhere, by the care of government; . . . though composed of men subject to all human infirmities.

(1739 [1911], vol II, 239)

Significant, also for the political principles underlying Hume's attitude to economic policy, was his theory of property. He had little place for labour in explaining property, which he regarded as derived, fundamentally, from the prevalence of scarcity (see section III, 'Of Justice', in his *Inquiry Concerning the Principles of Morals*). He began with the proposition 'that public utility is the *sole* origin of justice' (1751 [1800], vol II, 231), and went on to explain how, with scarcity lifted, in a Utopian condition of 'profuse abundance of all external conveniences', there would be no need for private property, or for government protection for it. Again, in another kind of Utopia, where everyone was so perfectly generous and altruistic, 'the whole human race would form only one family where all would lie in common, and be used freely, without regard to property' (233).

On the other hand, at the opposite extreme, in situations such as those of a shipwreck, or a besieged city, 'the strict laws of justice', and of property rights, might be suspended (234).

The usual condition of mankind, however, was very different:

> The common situation of society is a medium amidst all these extremes. We are naturally partial to ourselves, and to our friends; but are capable of learning the advantage resulting from a more equitable conduct. Few enjoyments are given us from the open and liberal hand of nature; but by art, labour, and industry, we can extract them in great abundance. Hence the ideas of property become necessary in all civil society: hence justice derives its usefulness to the public: and hence alone arises its merit and moral obligation.
>
> (236–7)

The question arose of the distribution of property. 'In a perfect theocracy, where a being, infinitely intelligent, governs by particular volitions', the principle of distribution would be, 'to assign the largest possession to the most extensive virtue, and give everyone the power of doing good, proportioned to his inclination' (241). But Hume dismissed such Utopian speculations with scathing indignation, insisting, 'that a rule which, in speculation, may seem the most advantageous to society, may yet be found, in practice, totally pernicious and destructive' (241). Though he supported the reduction of some inequalities, he went on to a comprehensive attack on egalitarianism:

> . . . however specious these ideas of *perfect* equality may seem, they are really, at bottom, *impracticable*; and were they not so, would be extremely pernicious to human society. Render possessions ever so equal, men's different degrees of art, care, and industry will immediately break that equality. Or if you check these virtues, you reduce society to the most extreme indigence; and, instead of preventing want and beggary in a few, render it unavoidable to the whole community. The most rigorous inquisition too is requisite to watch every inequality on its first appearance; and the most severe jurisdiction, to punish and redress it. But besides, that so much authority must soon degenerate into tyranny, and be exerted with great partialities . . .
>
> Who sees not, for instance, that whatever is produced or improved by a man's art or industry ought, for ever, to be secured to him, in order to give encouragement to such useful habits and accomplishments?
>
> (243)

Mention should also be made of the essay 'Of the Populousness of Ancient Nations', an historical study very learned with regard to the ancient world, but rather more concerned with politics than economics. Hume opposed the thesis, put forward by Montesquieu (in his *Esprit des lois*, book XXIII) that population had declined from the level attained by 'the ancient nations'. This question was, at the time, strange as it may seem today, one of considerable ideological importance. It bore on the question of the advance and progress represented by the contemporary, mid-eighteenth-century world, and Hume described it as 'the most curious and important of all questions of erudition' (see Mossner, 1980, 264).

He suggested that the advances of the modern over the ancient world must have encouraged population increase:

> All our later improvements and refinements, have they done nothing towards the easy subsistence of men, and consequently towards their propagation and increase? Our superior skill in mechanics; the discovery of new worlds, by which commerce has been so much enlarged; the establishment of posts; and the use of bills of exchange: these seem all extremely useful to the encouragement of art, industry, and populousness. Were we to strike off these, what a check should we give to every kind of business and labour, and what multitudes of families would immediately perish from want and hunger?
>
> (1955, xc and 146)

North-western Europe was, perhaps naturally enough, the centre of the world for Hume:

> Choose Dover or Calais for a center: draw a circle of two hundred miles radius: you comprehend London, Paris, the Netherlands, the United Provinces, and some of the best cultivated parts of France and England. It may safely, I think, be affirmed, that no spot of ground can be found, in antiquity, of equal extent, which contained nearly so many great and populous cities, and was so stocked with riches and inhabitants.
>
> (170)

On the other hand, he threw out a number of somewhat Malthusian observations:

> How fast do mankind multiply in every colony or new settlement; where it is an easy matter to provide for a family; and where men are nowise straitened or confined, as in long established governments?
>
> (111)

> The prolific virtue of men, were it to act in its full extent, without that restraint which poverty and necessity imposes on it, would double the number every generation.
>
> (128)

But Hume, as we have seen from his treatment of wages, was some way from believing either in what became the classical population doctrine, or in hard-line Malthusianism, as a general theory.

VIII

We have several times noted the element of balance in Hume's views and theories. His intellectual optimism about the study of what he called 'moral subjects' was balanced by an underlying element of scepticism and agnosticism. His search for general principles was balanced by an emphasis on human variety and the diversity of particular historical cases and conditions. In fact, Hume's methodological balance was struck at a point distinctly more inclined towards the historical view than it was by his successors, even more so than by Adam Smith—who, for his part was *far* more concerned with the historical dimension than were most of his fellow classicals. Again, in his discussion of luxury, Hume's criticism of Mandeville was balanced by qualifications which conceded a large part of the Mandevillian argument. In fact, in much of his economic writing Hume was concerned to restate recent and contemporary ideas with suitable qualifications and improved elegance and precision.

Sometimes Hume has been listed with the English classical economists, and certainly the inclusion of such a brilliant and outstanding philosopher would enhance the prestige of the classical school. Doubtless he was an early exponent of classical ideas on several important topics, though his were hardly the first statements of the new theories. As regards money and international trade, he was anticipated by Gervaise, Vanderlint and Cantillon, and to some extent by Carl. Nor was he by any means the first to attack 'mercantilist' doctrines on money. Moreover, Hume rejected other classical doctrines, as we have seen with regard to population and wages, and also regarding the unconditional beneficence of frugality. Nevertheless, the force and cogency of his arguments and his great philosophical reputation gave an important impetus to some of the doctrines subsequently incorporated into the classical system.

On the other hand, to describe Hume as 'transitional' might be taken as implying a failure on his part to push his ideas to their logical or valid conclusions. But Hume, quite deliberately, did not go the whole way, and usually insisted, in the last analysis, on a qualified balance. He was too deeply committed to historical relativism and empiricism to accept a single model, without very serious qualifications. Having described Locke as having one foot in the classical world, Keynes described Hume as having a 'foot and a half in the classical world. For Hume began the practice among economists of stressing the importance of the equilibrium position as compared with the ever-shifting transition toward it, though he was still enough of a mercantilist not to overlook the fact that it is in the transition that we actually have our being' (1936, 343n). Apart from the inadequacy and ambiguity of the 'mercantilist' category—and of the 'classical' concept too—this description of Hume as three-quarters 'classical' goes too far. For Hume brought to bear on controversial issues a philosophical balance and perspective. He was the archetypal two-handed economist, and none the worse for that. For surely it is perfectly valid and intellectually respectable for a philosopher to have two hands, in so far as 'two-handedness' is the attribute of one who is appropriately cautious in his generalisations because of the breadth of his views and his awareness of historical and institutional variety and variability. It is not for philosophers to make up politicians' minds for them: they have other, in the long run, more valuable, intellectual objectives to pursue.

IX

The contribution of the Scottish Enlightenment to the development of political economy was obviously one of its most important aspects and achievements. If, in our period, this contribution is taken as lasting from Carmichael's edition of Pufendorf (1718) down to the *Wealth of Nations*, it covered fifty-eight years. David Hume's *Essays* came just past half-way, fifteen years before Sir James Steuart's *Principles*, and just on a quarter of a century before the culminating achievement of Adam Smith. In 1737, at about the time that Hume was completing his masterpiece, *A Treatise of Human Nature*, the fourteen-year-old Smith was entering the Moral Philosophy class of Francis Hutcheson who was then in the middle of his Glasgow career. According to W R Scott, fourteen was, at that period, late, not early, for a boy to enter Glasgow University, eleven or twelve being the usual age (1937, 28). One can only speculate as to how far Smith's late entry was connected with his being an only son, in delicate health, whose father had died before he was born. Nevertheless, he was already well advanced in Latin, which must have helped considerably his progress at the university, where he obtained as sound an educational foundation for what was to be his lifework as could have been obtained anywhere else in the world at that time, as he himself was later to maintain (in his letter to William Cullen on 20 September 1774):

> In the present state of the Scotch universities, I do most sincerely look upon them as, in spite of all their faults, without exception the best seminaries of learning that are to be found anywhere in Europe. They are, perhaps, upon the whole, as unexceptionable as any public institutions of that kind, which all contain in their very nature the seeds and causes of negligence and corruption, have ever been, or are ever likely to be.
>
> (Thomson, 1859, vol I, 473)

Grotius, together with Carmichael's edition of Pufendorf, supplemented by ideas from John Locke, on the labour theory of property (but not of value, the whole elaborated so eloquently by 'the never-to-be-forgotten' professor: this was the basis of the course of studies out of which Smith's great work was eventually to emerge.

After less than three years at Glasgow, Smith, in July 1740, went on to Oxford, where between the ages of seventeen and twenty-three, he spent six years at Balliol College. W R Scott patriotically asserted that 'the Oxford of his time gave little, if any, help towards what was to be his lifework' (1937, 40). Certainly Smith's denunciation of the teaching—or, rather, non-teaching—of the Oxford of his day is well known. Probably, also, he found the Jacobite sympathies current in Oxford, and in his own college, in particular, at least distasteful. Nevertheless, Oxford perhaps provided Smith, given his own remarkable original talents and dedication, with what he may then have needed most (even though he was unaware of this): that was, good libraries and leisure—(or σχολή, the means to scholarship)—plus the freedom to read and think his own thoughts. Anyhow, Sir George Clark has mentioned 'the remarkable coincidence between the books referred to in the footnotes to the *Wealth of Nations* and the books which are known to have been in the college library when its future author was in residence' (1932, 73).

Moreover, the young Smith's six years in England may have been invaluable, from the point of view of his future interests in the wealth of nations, as providing first-hand acquaintance with English social, political and economic institutions, to which he was to pay significant tributes in his masterpiece. For though England was, at this juncture, philosophically somewhat in the shade compared with Scotland and France, she was approaching a supremely significant phase in her, and the world's economic history. The observant Smith might well have found stimulating comparisons between the economic life and institutions of an economically rather more advanced country, as contrasted with his native land; and the *Wealth of Nations* may, eventually, have been enriched by its author's first-hand experience and impressions of English life and society at that juncture.

Smith returned to Scotland from Oxford in August 1746, and early in 1751 he got a chair at Glasgow. It hardly seems that he could have seriously wasted his time at Oxford, from the point of view of his subsequent work and interests, if, within less than five years of his return north, he was equipped to soar to such eminence. If the vast ignorance as to how Smith spent his six years at Oxford is highly regrettable, the scraps of rather haphazard and, apparently, not entirely reliable information about his subsequent four years or so, after his return, are tantalising in the extreme. One fact, however, that seems certainly, though not precisely, to be established, is that sometime in these years came his first meeting, and the beginning of his friendship, with his fellow-bachelor David Hume.

Smith was well connected through his mother and through his friends, and it was apparently thanks to Lord Kames that he obtained the job—unconnected with the university—of delivering public lectures in Edinburgh, then apparently a fashionable medium of enlightenment. These lectures seem to have dealt with a wide range of subjects, including rhetoric, languages and *belles lettres*. But the final course, in 1748–9, was apparently devoted to civil law and jurisprudence, and included some discussion of what was to be a main theme of the *Wealth of Nations*. In his memoir of Smith, Dugald Stewart quoted, as apparently extracted from these lectures, the now well-known anticipation of what was to be called 'the simple system of natural liberty':

> Man is generally considered by statesmen and projectors as the materials of a sort of political mechanics. Projectors disturb nature in the course of her operations in human affairs; and it requires no more than to let her alone and give her fair play in the pursuit of her ends that she may establish her own designs . . .
>   Little else is requisite to carry a state to the highest degree of opulence from the lowest barbarism, but peace, easy taxes and a tolerable administration of justice; all the rest being brought about by the natural course of things. All governments

which thwart this natural course, which force things into another channel, or which endeavour to arrest the progress of society at a particular point are unnatural and to support themselves are obliged to be oppressive and tyrannical.

(Stewart, 1811, 100; also Scott, 1973, 54)

Furthermore, according to Scott, it 'can be stated with a fair degree of certainty' that book III of the *Wealth of Nations*, on 'the different progress of opulence in different nations' can be traced back to the Edinburgh period (1937, 56). But, more recently, it has been denied, with reference to other claims regarding manuscripts in which the division of labour is discussed, that they date back as far as this (see Meek and Skinner, 1973, 1094 ff). It certainly seems, however, very probable that Smith had arrived at the basic notions of his 'simple system' in those Edinburgh years. But just how far he had got, and how his ideas compared with those already published in England by, among others, North, Martyn, Gervaise, Vanderlint and Tucker, must remain debatable.

These vital years in the young Smith's career coincided with what we have called the 'mid-century efflorescence', which extended, as we have seen, both over most of Western Europe, as well as over a full range of philosophical and 'scientific' interests, and of which developments in what was to be called 'political economy' were only a small part. As regards works devoted in part (in some cases, in small part) to political economy there may be noted those of Montesquieu (1748), Tucker (1749 and 1751-2), Postelthwayt (1749 and 1751), and Galiani (1751)—this latter probably for some time unknown in Britain. Finally, of course, there was David Hume's *Political Discourses* (1752). This was part of the background of intellectual efflorescence against which the young Smith's ideas were developing at this important stage of his life and work.

Two vacancies, in November 1750, and in 1751, opened the way for Smith's occupancy at Glasgow, first, briefly of the chair of Logic, and then, on the death of Professor Craigie, of the celebrated chair of Moral Philosophy, of which Carmichael and Hutcheson had been the first and second holders respectively, and of which the young Smith became the fourth. He was to remain in this chair in Glasgow twelve-and-a-quarter years, until in January 1764 he departed for London and France as tutor to the Duke of Buccleuch.

Just when Smith's plans for his lifework began to take shape cannot be known. Doubtless they grew and changed. But it was on settling into the chair of Moral Philosophy at Glasgow that he was able to launch effectively whatever plans he had by then formed, and through his lecture courses he was able to build up his grasp of the fields which he had set out to master. As he himself later put it:

To impose on any man the necessity of teaching, year after year, any particular branch of science, seems in reality, to be the most effectual method of rendering him completely master of it himself. On being obliged to go every year over the same ground, if he is good for anything, he necessarily becomes, in a few years, well acquainted with every part of it. If upon any particular point he should form too hasty an opinion one year, when he comes in the course of his lectures to reconsider the same subject the year thereafter, he is very likely to correct it.

(1976, 812; see Hutchison, 1978, 4)

'The particular branch of science' with which Smith was concerned comprised a very large area of moral philosophy, in fact, in modern terminology, a kind of comprehensive theory of society, covering how ethical views, attitudes, or sentiments, were formed, as well as the economic life of society, the principles of economic policy, and the principles of law and jurisprudence.

It is of interest to speculate as to what might have happened to Smith's career and achievements as a moral philosopher and political economist, if his immediate predecessor Craigie had lived ten years longer, and Smith had missed the decade or more of learning by teaching in respect of this great subject area. Would his *magnum opus* have been, perhaps, in another field, possibly in one of those broached in his essays? Anyhow, before we break off, one feature of his Glasgow environment may be noted which must have considerably stimulated and fed an interest in political economy. This was the contact Smith had with the merchants of the city—which was particularly important in imbuing the *Wealth of Nations* with its vitally realistic, practical, concrete power. For, as John Rae remarked: 'It was amid the thickening problems of the rising trade of the Clyde, and the daily discussions they occasioned among the enterprising and intelligent merchants of the town, that he grew into a great economist' (1895, 87).

In these years of the early 1750s, however, important new departures were on the way in most or all of the leading countries, not only (though pre-eminently) in Scotland. Even in England, further down the west coast of Britain, in another rapidly rising port, a Welsh-born clergyman was vigorously expounding the practical principles of economic freedom.

REFERENCES

I

Carmichael, G (1724). Annotations, in revised ed of *De officio hominis et civis* by S Pufendorf

Hume, D (1739). *A Treatise of Human Nature* Everyman ed, 1911, 2 vols

—— (1751). 'An Inquiry concerning the Principles of Morals', in *Essays and Treatises on Several Subjects* vol II, 1800, 213ff

—— (1752). 'Of Civil Liberty', in *Essays and Treatises on Several Subjects* vol I, 1800, 91ff

—— (1932). *Letters of David Hume* (ed) J Y Greig, 2 vols

—— (1955). *Writings on Economics* (ed) E Rotwein

Hutcheson, F (1725-7). *Remarks upon the Fable of the Bees*

—— (1747). *A Short Introduction to Moral Philosophy*

—— (1755). *A System of Moral Philosophy* 3 vols

Smith, A (1976). *The Wealth of Nations* 3rd ed, 1784 (ed) R H Campbell, A S Skinner and W B Todd

—— (1978). *Lectures on Jurisprudence* (ed) R L Meek, D D Raphael and P G Stein

II

Arkin, M (1956). 'The Economic Writings of David Hume, a Reassessment', *South African Journal of Economics* **24** (3), 204ff.

Bagehot, W (1879). 'Adam Smith and Our Modern Economy', in *Economic Studies* (ed) R H Hutton, new ed 1895, 125ff

—— (1881). 'Adam Smith as a Person', in *Biographical Studies* (ed) R H Hutton, 247ff.

Bonar, J (1922). *Philosophy and Political Economy*

Bryson, G (1945). *Man and Society: the Scottish Inquiry of the Eighteenth Century*

Burton, J H (1895). *Life and Correspondence of David Hume* 2 vols

Campbell, T D (1982). 'Francis Hutcheson' in *The Origin and Nature of the Scottish Enlightenment* (ed) R H Campbell and A S Skinner

Clark, G N (1932). 'The Study of Economic History', in *The Study of Economic History* (ed) N B Harte, 1971.

Duke, M I (1979). 'David Hume and Monetary Adjustment', *History of Political Economy* **11**, 572ff.

Forbes, D (1954). 'Scientific Whiggism: Adam Smith and John Millar', *Cambridge Journal* **7** (11), 643ff

—— (1975) *Hume's Philosophical Politics*

Hamilton, W (1872). Introduction to *Works of Thomas Reid* 2nd ed

Heckscher, E (1955). *Mercantilism* 2 vols, 2nd ed

Hill, J B (1846). *Life and Correspondence of David Hume*

Hont, I (1983). 'The Rich-Country-Poor-Country Debate in Scottish Classical Political Economy', in *Wealth and Virtue* (ed) I Hont and M Ignatieff, 271ff

Hutchison, T W (1953). 'Berkeley's *Querist* and its Place in the Economic Thought of the Eighteenth Century', *British Journal for the Philosophy of Science* **4**, 13

—— (1978). *Revolutions and Progress in Economic Knowledge*

Johnson, E A J (1937). *Predecessors of Adam Smith*

Keynes, J M (1936). *General Theory of Employment, Interest and Money*

Low, J M (1952). 'An Eighteenth-Century Controversy in the Theory of Economic Progress', *Manchester School* **20**, 311ff

Medick, H (1973). *Naturzustand und Naturgeschichte der bürgerlichen Gessellschaft*

Meek, R L and Skinner, A S (1973). 'The Development of Adam Smith's Ideas on the Division of Labour', *Economic Journal* **83**, 1094ff

Moore, J and Silverthorne, M (1983). 'Gershom Carmichael and Natural Jurisprudence', in *Wealth and Virtue* (ed) I Hont and M Ignatieff, 73ff

Mossner, E C (1980). *Life of David Hume*

Perlman, M (1987). 'Of a Controversial Passage in Hume', *Journal of Political Economy* **95**, 274ff

Rae, J (1895). *Life of Adam Smith*

Robbins, L C (1952). *The Theory of Economic Policy in English Classical Political Economy*

Schatz, A (1902). *L'O Euvre économique de David Hume*

Scott, W R (1900). *Francis Hutcheson*

—— (1937). *Adam Smith as Student and Professor*

Semmel, B (1965). 'The Hume-Tucker Debate and Pitt's Trade Proposals', *Economic Journal* **75**, 759ff

Stewart, D (1811). *Memoir of Adam Smith*

Taylor, W L (1955). 'Gershom Carmichael: a Neglected Figure in British Political Economy', *South African Journal of Economics* **23,** 251ff

—— (1965). *Francis Hutcheson and David Hume as Predecessors of Adam Smith*

Thomson, J (1859). *An Account of the Life, Lectures and Writings of William Cullen M. D.* 2 vols

Vickers, D (1959). *Studies in the Theory of Money, 1690–1776*

CHAPTER FOUR

History and Political Economy in Scotland: Alternative 'Inquiries' and Scottish Ascendancy

Terence Hutchison

Before Adam Smith: The Emergence
of Political Economy 1662–1776
(Basil Blackwell, 1988)

I

David Hume, in his own day more famous as an historian than as a philosopher, is reported to have stated: 'I believe this to be the historical age and this the historical nation' (see Bryson, 1945, 78). Certainly, in the middle decades of the eighteenth century, in much of western Europe, a remarkable surge of interest in history and historical inquiry took place. Vico and Montesquieu were the inspiring pioneers, with Montesquieu's work much the better known. The *Esprit des lois* was translated into English in 1750 and had probably its most powerful effect in Scotland. Earlier, the natural-law system of moral philosophy, as developed in Glasgow by Carmichael and Hutcheson, had not provided much scope for the historical method, though Adam Smith, from an early stage of his work, had shown an interest in an historical approach (see Skinner, 1965, 3). In the second half of the century Hume's claim that Scotland was 'the historical nation' acquired much justification, and it was pre-eminently Hume himself who led the way by providing the philosophical foundations, and by demonstrating the possibilities in moral philosophy, or in the moral or social sciences, of the historical method, a method and approach closely linked with his empirical principles. Indeed, Albert Schatz went so far as to claim that Wilhelm Roscher's manifesto of the German Historical school, in 1843, had been fully anticipated in Scotland a century previously in so far as David Hume 'had done more than formulate it, he had applied it' (1902, 61). Certainly, as regards political economy, one of the first and most important, if small-scale, applications of an historical method and approach is to be found in Hume's economic and political essays. The full-scale application, however, of history to political economy, came with the two great, contrasting Scottish *Inquiries*, that of Sir James Steuart into the principles of political economy, and that of Adam Smith into the nature and causes of the wealth of nations.

Before we turn to these major applications of an historical approach, a few brief remarks about the historical method, and about two lesser, but highly interesting Scottish exponents, may be appropriate. Together with its interest in historical records and research, the Scottish concern with history focused on two sets of questions, or processes: on the one hand on origins, and, on the other hand, on empirically observed processes of the development and progress of nations and peoples, the historical treatment of which included their economics, politics, law and sociology, in a comprehensive theory of society. As Professor Lehmann, in his distinguished study of the Scottish Enlightenment, writes regarding the 'historical-mindedness' of Scottish thought at this juncture:

> We use this term with a threefold implication: first, there is the more obvious meaning of an interest in recorded history, historical research and historical interpretation; next is implied an interest in origins, in continuities through time in the development of social and political institutions, present, of course, also in the first meaning but viewed now on certain theoretical assumptions that can best be indicated by such terms as 'natural history,' 'evolution,' the 'idea of progress'; and finally there is implied an empirical approach to socio-historical reality that attempts to see any subject under study—be it political, economic, literary, any particular custom, institution or what not—in the concreteness of a particular time and place, in an organic relation to other phenomena whether past or present.
>
> (1960, 98)

Two interesting Scottish exponents of the historical method, who have both been described as pioneers of sociology, and who were both very well known to Adam Smith, were Adam Ferguson (1723–1816) and John Millar (1735–1801). Ferguson, before becoming, in 1759, a professor at Edinburgh, where he occupied a succession of chairs, had been an army chaplain with the Black Watch regiment (thus providing a parallel with Süssmilch, the Prussian army chaplain and great pioneer of demography). Ferguson began his *History of Civil Society* (1767), his most important work, with a strongly social or sociological—rather than individualist—methodological emphasis: 'Mankind are to be taken in groups, as they have always subsisted. The history of the individual is but a detail of the sentiments and thoughts he has entertained in the view of his species: and every experiment relative to this subject should be made with entire societies, not with single men' (1767, 6). Ferguson continued with a quotation from Montesquieu: 'Man is born in society, and there he remains' (24). Ferguson subsequently went on to stress the beneficence of spontaneous, unplanned processes, as contrasted with the effects of deliberate governmental regulations (and has been approvingly quoted by Hayek on this point). Ferguson described how,

> ... nations stumble upon establishments which are indeed the result of human action but not the result of human design.
>
> (187)

> The forms of society are derived from an obscure and distant origin; they arise, long before the date of philosophy, from the instincts, not from the speculations of man

... We ascribe to a previous design, what came to be known only by experience, what no human wisdom could foresee, and what, without the concurring humour and disposition of his age, no authority could enable an individual to execute.

(188, quoted by Hayek, 1949, 7)

The anti-governmental implications of these ideas, and how little government regulations and planning could achieve, were emphasised by Ferguson:

A people intent on freedom, find for themselves a condition in which they may follow the propensities of nature with a more signal effect than they which the councils of state could devise. When sovereigns, or projectors, are the supposed masters of this subject, the best they can do is to be cautious of hurting any interest they cannot greatly promote, and of making breaches they cannot repair.

(215)

Ferguson summarised his individualistic and libertarian economic philosophy as follows: 'Secure to the workman the fruit of his labour, give him the prospects of independence or freedom, and the public has found a faithful steward in hoarding what he has gained . . . Commerce . . . is the branch in which men committed to the effects of their own experience, are least apt to go wrong' (219). With regard to national wealth:

The great object of policy . . . is to secure to the family its subsistence and settlement; to protect the industrious in the pursuit of his occupation; to reconcile the restrictions of police and the social affections of mankind, with their separate and interested pursuits . . . When the refined politician would lend an active hand, he only multiplies interruptions and grounds of complaints.

(220)

Ferguson described the advantages of the divisions of labour, and how 'the subdivision of arts and professions tends to improve the practice of them, and to promote their ends' (353). But, as noted by Marx, he emphasised the damaging and stultifying effects of the specialisation of labour even more forcefully than Adam Smith:

Many mechanical arts indeed, require no capacity; they succeed best under a total suppression of sentiment and reason; and ignorance is the mother of industry as well as superstition. Reflection and fancy are subject to err; but a habit of moving the hand or foot, is independent of either. Manufactures, accordingly, prosper most where the mind is least consulted and where the workshop may, without any great effort of the imagination, be considered as an engine, the parts of which are men.

(280, quoted and discussed by Skinner, 1965, 17)

By including a mention at this point of John Millar and his work, we are jumping a little ahead chronologically. For Millar was a pupil, perhaps the most distinguished, of Adam Smith, who had attended Smith's Edinburgh lectures and his first classes at Glasgow. Subsequently Millar was Professor of Civil Law at Glasgow from 1761 until 1801. He was described by Adam Smith's biographer, John Rae, as 'the most effective and influential apostle of Liberalism in Scotland in that age' (1895, 53–4). Rae's judgement, while apparently, in one important respect, putting the pupil above the master, should be compared and contrasted with Millar's criticisms of Smith's forthright views on the freedom of markets.

Millar summed up his historical approach in the Introduction to his most important work, *Observations concerning the Origin of the Distinction of Ranks in Society* (1771). According to Millar, in order to know what is the best form of government, we have to study the past. But really to understand the past we must know the circumstances which produce certain social forms. Millar has been interpreted as an anticipator of the historical materialism of Marx, though it seems unlikely that Millar's writing exercised any influence, directly or indirectly, on German thought. But the Scottish historical school of the eighteenth century were certainly, on some important points, anticipators: Ferguson of Carl Menger and Hayek and Millar of Marx. In some of its manifestations, however, the Scottish historical movement took on some objectionable and pretentious historicist features, most notably in James Mills' *History of India* (1818)—which was so enthusiastically received by Ricardo. As Roy Pascal noted in his seminal article: 'It is very remarkable how this whole historical school becomes lost in the nineteenth century' (1938, 177). According to Professor D C Coleman, most of the blame for the distortion and 'bowdlerization' of the role of history in political economy should be ascribed to the 'two southbound Scots', James Mill and McCulloch (1987, 20).

It remains immensely regrettable that in nineteenth-century political economy in England, dominated by the abstract deductivism of Ricardo and Senior, the historical dimension of the subject was so long and so thoroughly neglected. Apart from the efforts of a few such isolated figures as Richard Jones, historical economics was largely abandoned to the Germans, though it was to Scotland that its origins and two of its earliest outstanding achievements were due. The title, proudly but justifiably claimed by Hume, of being 'the historical nation', passed, in the nineteenth-century, from Scotland to Germany. Only after the decline and fall of the English classical school, around 1870, was the historical method of Hume, Steuart and Smith cultivated widely again in Britain.

II

Sir James Steuart (1713–80) came of a family eminent in law and politics, with its country seat near Edinburgh, where, at the university, he studied history and law, the former subject under the first professor of history to be appointed at that ancient institution. He took his bar examination in 1735, but never practised law. Most of the next five years were spent in travelling in Western Europe, first in Holland, then in Spain, where a famine in Andalusia may first have aroused his interest in political economy. Later he was in the south of France and Rome. By this time Steuart was committing himself to the Jacobite cause, in support of the claims to the English throne of 'the Old Pretender', the would-be James III, whom Steuart met in Rome.

In 1745, on the outbreak of the rebellion, Steuart was sent to Paris to become Prince Charles' ambassador and to seek French support. But after the battle of Culloden (1746), when the Jacobites were routed, Steuart faced a long exile as a rebel, spending the next seventeen years in various parts of Western Europe.

Just when Steuart first developed his interest in political economy is not clear. But according to the closing words of his great *Inquiry*, he began its composition in 1749, eighteen years before its publication. As we discuss later, both his political allegiance, and his long residence abroad in diverse countries, may have helped to shape his approach to economic problems. In 1754 he was in Paris, where he probably met Montesquieu and perhaps Mirabeau. Then he spent four years (1757–61) in the small, but delightful university town of Tübingen in Württemberg, where he made much progress with the composition of the *Inquiry*. At this time he also wrote his *Dissertation upon the Doctrine and Principles of Money applied to the German Coin* (1761). Subsequently, at the end of 1762, he was at last allowed by the English government to return home to Scotland, though he was not finally pardoned by King George III until 1771 (see Skinner, 1966, xliii).

In the meantime, Steuart had completed and published his *magnum opus*, his *Inquiry into the Principles of Political Economy: being an Essay on the Science of Domestic Policy in Free Nations, in which are particularly considered, Population, Agriculture, Trade, Industry, Money, Coin, Interest, Circulation, Banks, Exchange, Public Credit, and Taxes* (1767). These subjects, in the order given, were dealt with in five books. For some years the *Inquiry* met with modest, if qualified, approval. David Hume, who had helped Steuart obtain his royal pardon, was pleased with the work, though critical of its style. In 1772, Steuart's advice was sought by the East India Company, and he produced a report on the *Principles of Money Applied to the State of the Coin in Bengal.* In 1776, however, with the appearance of the *Wealth of Nations,* Steuart's work suffered, in Britain, an almost total eclipse. What Professor Andrew Skinner describes as Smith's 'curious omission', of any reference whatsoever to Steuart in the *Wealth of Nations,* on any subject, not even that of money and banking, proved to be a thoroughly successful controversial tactic.

Of the roughly twenty-eight years, from when (aet. 22) Steuart had departed on his five-year grand tour until, in 1763 (aet. 50), he returned home from exile, he had spent about twenty-two years in various European countries. His material, ideas and 'vision' were thus derived from a very wide and varied range of economic, social and political conditions, and, to a large extent from economies not then as advanced in economic and industrial development as Britain. In particular, Steuart may have been specially apprehensive regarding the dangerous and disadvantageous possibilities for his countrymen, of the merger of their smaller, weaker, and more remote, economy, with that of their much larger, more powerful, and rapidly growing, southern neighbour.

Certainly, Steuart's wide and varied experiences were intellectually reinforced by the influence on him of Montesquieu's *L'Esprit des Lois* (1748), with its message of historical-institutional relativism. Professor Skinner suggests that, in view of his knowledge of Italian, Steuart may also have been acquainted with the even more radical historical relativism of Vico. It also seems probable that, in his years in Tübingen, when writing his *Inquiry*, Steuart might have got to know the ideas of the cameralists, such as Becher or Justi, though he made no explicit references to German writers. Among works referred to, always politely, by Steuart, were those of Cantillon, Child, Davenant, Law, Locke, Melon, Mirabeau and Petty. Finally, there was the important influence of David Hume, who had deployed a historical-relativist approach to problems of political economy, though on a much smaller scale, in his *Essays*. Steuart was concerned with a much larger and more systematic treatise, for the title of which he very appropriately reintroduced from the French, the term 'political economy'—first used by Montchrétien, with not much significance, in 1615. This proved a timely stroke of nomenclature, as the subject moved towards its independence, for 'The Principles of Political Economy' remained a title very much in use during the next century. Moreover, Steuart was attempting a comprehensive treatment, similar to that of Ernst Ludwig Carl nearly half a century previously, but by no-one else since then, not even Cantillon, with regard to historical, political, and social factors.

III

The first sentence of the *Inquiry* proclaimed 'the greatest diffidence' with which Steuart put forward his theories and doctrines. Throughout, he set an example of caution and modesty. There could be no more extreme contrast—or, to some intellectual tastes, a more welcome one—with the dogmatic claims to self-evident certainty of the physiocrats. Such an example as that of Steuart carries a highly important and salutary message—though usually one that is unpopular and often disregarded. At the end of his preface, Steuart warned of the dangers of political disillusionment ensuing from overconfident, or pretentious, economic policy doctrines, based on economic theories of apodictic certainty: 'A people taught to expect from a statesman the execution of plans big with impossibility and contradiction, will remain discontented under the government of the best of Kings' (1966, 13).

Together with this general caution, Steuart committed himself to the pursuit of impartiality, though he was well aware of the impossibility of achieving perfection in this respect:

> Every writer values himself upon his impartiality; because he is not sensible of his fetters. The wandering and independent life I have led may naturally have set me free, in some measure, from strong attachments to popular opinions. This may be called impartiality. But as no man can be deemed impartial, who leans to any side whatever, I have been particularly on my guard against the consequences of this sort of negative impartiality . . .
>
> (10)
>
> . . . The speculative person, who, removed from the practice, extracts the principles of this science from *observation* and *reflection*, should divest himself, as far as possible, of every prejudice in favour of established opinions, however reasonable,

when examined relatively to particular nations; he must do his utmost to become a citizen of the world, comparing customs, examining minutely institutions which appear alike, when in different countries they are found to produce different effects . . .

(17)

Steuart was constantly concerned with the dangers of oversimplification—a concern which may have inclined him towards the excessive prolixity and ambiguity with which he has been charged. His warnings against a narrow systematisation, or 'conceits', as he called them, ran along similar lines to those of Condillac's castigation of *a priorist*, deductive systems:

> The great danger of running into error upon particular points relating to this subject, proceeds from our viewing them in a light too confined, and to our not attending to the influence of concomitant circumstances, which render general rules of little use. Men of parts and knowledge seldom fail to reason consequentially on every subject; but when inquiries are made concerning the complicated interests of society, the vivacity of an author's genius is apt to prevent him from attending to the variety of circumstances which render uncertain every consequence, almost, which he can draw from his reasoning. To this I ascribe the habit of running into what the French call *Systèmes*. These are no more than a chain of contingent consequences, drawn from a few fundamental maxims, adopted, perhaps, rashly. Such systems are mere conceits; they mislead the understanding, and efface the path to truth.

(8)

In fact, in a version of his preface, written for his friend Lady Mary Wortley Montague, Steuart characterised, not unfairly, some aspects of the age of the Enlightenment as follows: 'The vice of our age seems to be a propensity to run into such conceits with an appearance of reason' (quoted in Chamley, 1965, 134).

Subsequently, Steuart confessed:

> I am not fond of condemning opinions; but I am very much for limiting general propositions. I have hardly ever escaped being led into error by every one I have laid down. Nothing is so systematical, nothing so pretty in a treatise as general maxims; they facilitate the distribution of our ideas, and I have never been able to dash them out but with a certain regret.

(Steuart, 1966, 67–8)

The quantity theory of money was, for Steuart, a major example of the danger of trying to lay down 'general propositions'. The limitations of such generalities had constantly to be kept in view, for they were 'only true or false as they understood to be accompanied with certain restrictions, applications and limitations' (358).

If economic theories should be stated with such careful qualifications and restrictions, then *a fortiori*, policy statements needed to be even more qualified, with regard to the political, social and institutional conditions of the people, or country, to which the policies were being applied. For Steuart, political economy was essentially a policy subject, both 'science' and 'art': 'The great art therefore of political economy is, first, to adapt the different operations of it to the spirit, manners, habits, and customs of the people; and afterwards to model those circumstances so, as to be able to introduce a set of new and more useful institutions' (16).

The variety of conditions and institutions, at different times and places, with which the economist was confronted, was immense:

> If one considers the variety which is found in different countries, in the distribution of property, subordination of classes, genius of people, proceeding from the variety of forms of government, laws, climate, and manners, one may conclude, that the political economy in each must necessarily be different, and that principles, however universally true, may become quite ineffectual in practice, without a sufficient preparation of the spirit of a people.
>
> (17)

Steuart put much emphasis on what he called 'The Spirit of a People'—the title of his second chapter. He thus provided an intellectual link between Montesquieu before him, and—as Professor Paul Chamley has shown—Hegel subsequently, with his concept of the '*Volksgeist*': 'There is no treating any point which regards the political economy of a nation, without accompanying the example with some supposition relative to the spirit of the people' (23).

'Theorists' had to be especially careful when they descended into the policy arena to discuss particular proposals:

> Let theorists, therefore, beware of trusting to their science when in matters of administration, they either advise those who are disposed blindly to follow them, or when they undertake to meddle in it themselves. An old practitioner feels difficulties which he cannot reduce to principles, nor render intelligible to every body; and the theorist who boldly undertakes to remedy every evil, and who foresees none on the opposite side, will most notably miscarry, and then give a very rational account for his ill success. A good theorist, therefore, may be excellent in deliberation, but without a long and confirmed practice, he will ever make a blundering statesman in practice.
>
> (1767 [1770], vol II, 73)

IV

Steuart opened volume I of his *Inquiry* with the subjects of population and agriculture, starting with a three-stage theory of economic development—as contrasted with the four-stage theory of Smith and Turgot. Steuart's theory involved the interaction of population growth and food supply. The first and most primitive stage was that of nomads, or savages, living off the fruit and meat supplied by nature—or from beaver and deer in Smith's 'early and rude state of society'. The second stage was that of agriculture, with the regular application of labour to land, which made possible a great increase in food supply and population. The agricultural surplus had a vital role, for, with the third stage there was a surplus of food which could be used to meet other than basic, subsistence needs, so that manufactures could develop; and with the greater variety of goods, and expansion of trade, there came the emergence of money and an exchange economy. At each of the three stages of the growth process it was vital to raise the aspirations of the population for a higher material standard of living, by developing additional wants for new and superior-quality goods. Such aspirations were a main motive force towards higher productivity and production (see Eagly, 1961). It was the denial of the existence, or possibility of thus raising aspirations, or the belief that the labouring classes were wedded to traditional, static living standards, that was behind the doctrine of low wages, and the belief that higher wages would simply be taken out in more leisure. Steuart perceived the great importance of inducing higher levels of agricultural production by encouraging higher material aspirations in agricultural and manufacturing workers alike: 'We may lay it down as a principle, that a farmer will not labour to produce a superfluity of grain relative to his own consumption, unless he finds some want which may be supplied by the means of that superfluity' (Steuart, 1966, 40). Conversely 'other industrious persons' will not work to supply the wants of the farmer except to procure subsistence. These, Steuart continued, were 'the reciprocal wants whcih the statesman must create, in order to bind society together' (40)—assuming that the society consists of free men and not of slaves.

Not much was made in Steuart's *Inquiry*, of the division of labour as a prime mover in promoting growth. In Steuart's account, two major principles, or drives, were at work: one was what he called 'the generative faculty', which operated as in Malthus' theory, in that it 'resembles a spring loaded with a weight, which always exerts itself in proportion to the diminution of resistance: when food has remained some time without augmentation or diminution, generation will carry numbers as high as possible; if then, food comes to be diminished, the spring is overpowered . . . Inhabitants will diminish, at least, in proportion to the overcharge' (32).

The second principle at work was that of 'self-love, or a desire of ease and happiness', which, fortified by the aspiration effect, promoted the growth of production, the striving after luxury, and the expansion of the market economy.

According to Steuart:

> The principal object of this science is to secure a certain fund of subsistence for all the inhabitants, to obviate every circumstances which may render it precarious; to provide everything necessary for supplying the wants of the society, and to employ the inhabitants (supposing them to be free-men) . . . so as to make their several interests lead them to supply one another with their reciprocal wants.
>
> (17)

Economic growth did not figure prominently in Steuart's statements of the aims of policy. In fact, security was given a more prominent place. But it is rather anachronistic, and not very profitable, to argue over whether he took a shorter- or a longer-term view of policy objectives—that is, more in terms of short-term employment or long-term growth. Such distinctions have been developed much more recently and were by no means so clear-cut in the eighteenth century when the fundamental concepts of modern 'growth' theory, such as productive capital investment, and technological progress, were only just beginning to emerge explicitly; and while even the possibilities of the division of labour were not stressed by most writers. As Professor Skinner states, Steuart 'did not emphasise the importance of capital' (lxx); nor, as we have noted, did he make very much, explicitly, of the division of labour as part of economic development; while the idea of technological progress, so central in the twentieth century, was omitted even from some of the leading classical models,—not to mention those of the pre-classicals, and mercantilists. Economic growth, for Steuart, as for most eighteenth-century writers, was seen mainly in terms of increasing the output of the economy by raising the level of employment, and by providing the stimulus of suitably expansive monetary conditions, within a competitive framework.

V

Steuart repeatedly emphasised the objective of a high level of employment:

> A statesman should make it his endeavour to employ as many of every class as possible, and when employment fails in the common run of affairs, to contrive new outlets for young people of every denomination . . . Such members of the society as remain unemployed, either from natural infirmities or misfortunes, and who thereby become a load upon others, are really a load upon the state . . . A state should provide retreats of all sorts, for the different conditions of her decayed inhabitants: humanity, good policy, and Christianity, require it.
>
> (73)

These problems were, of course, not much discussed by Adam Smith; nor was the following question, which Steuart considered to be of major importance for the statesman: 'How he keep the whole of his people constantly employed, and by what means he may promote an equable circulation of domestic wealth?' (276). For, as Steuart noted when discussing government revenues: 'The number of people, well employed, makes the prosperity of a state' (1767 [1770], vol II, 336). Moreover, he recognised as part of 'the contract of society', a 'right to work', and insisted that it was a duty of government to provide employment for those returning from war service (1966, 122).

For Smith, most or all of these problems of unemployment would have been regarded as soluble by the spontaneous, self-adjusting processes of 'the simple system of natural liberty'. But Steuart did not discern any such mechanisms at work as would automatically bring about high and stable employment and growth, while leaving the human pilot, or statesman, with comparatively little to do.

Again and again Steuart emphasised the importance of maintaining what he called 'the balance of work and demand', more often, apparently, employing the concept of 'balance' in an aggregate sense, though sometimes with reference to particular goods or industries. He explained that he preferred 'the word "work" to that of supply, because it is the interests of the workman which chiefly come under our consideration' (1767 [1770], vol II, 65). Steuart insisted: 'The greatest care must be taken, to support a perfect balance between the hands in work and the demand for their labour' (195).

This balance was important, 'not with a view to enrich the state, but in order to preserve every member of it in health and vigour' (236). Steuart described four harmful consequences of an imbalance: 'Every subversion, therefore of this balance, implies one of four inconveniences, either the industrious starve one another; or a part of their work provided lies upon hand; or their profits rise and consolidate; or a part of the demand made is not answered by them' (1767 [1770], vol II, 65).

Like many writers in the seventeenth and eighteenth centuries, Steuart was much concerned with maintaining 'circulation', and with emphasising the harm done by unused savings, hoarding, and stagnation. Like Boisguilbert, Steuart stressed the greater propensity of the rich to hoard: 'When large sums are locked up, they produce nothing; they are therefore locked up not to be useful while they remain secreted, but that they may be useful when brought out in order to be alienated. In a state, therefore, where there are a few very rich and many very poor, there must be much money locked up' (II, 28).

Fiscal policy could be used to counter stagnation:

> Every application of public money implies a want in the state; and every want supplied, implies an encouragement given to industry. In proportion, therefore, as taxes draw money into circulation, which otherwise would not have entered into it at that time, they encourage industry; not by taking the money from individuals, but by throwing it into the hands of the state, which spends it; and which thereby throws it directly into the hands of the industrious, or of the luxurious who employ them.
>
> (725)

Together with fiscal policy, monetary and debt policy should be applied. The statesman:

> . . . ought all times to maintain a just proportion between the produce of industry, and the quantity of circulating equivalent, in the hands of his subjects for the purchase of it; that by a steady and judicious administration, he may have it in his power at all time, either to check prodigality and hurtful luxury, or to extend industry and domestic consumption . . . For this purpose, he must examine the situation of his country, relatively to three objects, *viz.* the propensity of the rich to consume; the disposition of the poor to be industrious; and the proportion of circulating money, with respect to the one and the other.
>
> (323–4)

It may be desirable to introduce paper or other 'symbolical' money:

> It is, therefore, the business of a statesman, who intends to promote circulation, to be upon his guard against every cause of stagnation; and when he has it not in his power to remove these political obstructions, as I may call them, by drawing the coin of the country out of its repositories, he ought . . . to facilitate the introduction of symbolical money to supply its place . . . he must facilitate circulation, by

drawing into the hands of the public what coin there is in the country, in case he finds any part of it locked up; and he must supply the actual deficiency of the metals, by such a proportion of paper-credit, as may abundantly supply the deficiency.

(325–6)

But the 'balance' must not be upset in the opposite direction: 'A statesman who allows himself to be entirely taken up in promoting circulation, and the advancement of every species of luxurious consumption, may carry matters too far and destroy the industry he wishes to promote. This is the case when the consequence of domestic consumption raises prices, and thereby hurts exportation' (326).

VI

We discussed earlier Steuart's emphatic warnings against attempts to lay down general rules, or theories, in political economy, and we noticed that the quantity theory of money was, for him, a major example of such an oversimplification. Of the quantity theories of Montesquieu and Hume, Steuart remarked: 'The ideas they have broached are so pretty, and the theory they laid down for determining the rise and fall of prices so simple, and so extensive, that it is no wonder to see it adopted by almost every one who has written after them . . . ' However: 'I think I have discovered, that in this, as in every other part of the science of political economy, there is hardly such a thing as a general rule to be laid down' (339).

Steuart stated his case against a quantity theory as follows:

Let the specie of a country, therefore, be augmented or diminished, in ever so great a proportion, commodities will still rise and fall according to the principles of demand and competition; and these will constantly depend upon the inclinations of those who have *property* or any kind of *equivalent* whatsoever to give; but never upon the quantity of coin they are possessed of.
   Let the quantity of coin be ever so much increased, it is the desire of spending it alone which will raise prices. Let it be dimininished ever so low, while there is real property of any denomination in the country, and a competition to consume in those who possess it, prices will be high by the means of barter, symbolical money, mutual prestations, and a thousand other inventions. (345)

. . . if the specie be found above the proportion of the industry, it will have no effect in raising prices, nor will it enter into circulation: it will be hoarded up in treasures . . . The value of each particular species of . . . consumption is determined by a complication of circumstances at home and abroad; consequently, the proportion is not determined by the *quantity* of money actually in the country. (350)

Suppose the specie of Europe to continue increasing in quantity every year, until it amounts to ten times the present quantity, will prices rise in proportion? I answer, that such an augmentation might happen, without the smallest alteration upon prices, or that it might occasion a very great one according to circumstances.

(355)

Steuart put great stress on the velocity of circulation as an element of effective demand. The quantity of metallic money was a largely passive element:

> . . . The money of a country . . . bears no determinate proportion to circulation; it is the money circulating, multiplied by the number of transitions from hand to hand. Again, we have said that the prices of all things are determined by demand and competition. The meaning of this, as it concerns the present question, is, that in the proportion to the competition of those who appear with money, in order to acquire what comes to market, a larger or a smaller sum is brought to circulation.

> (715)

Certainly Lionel Robbins was well justified in his observation, or complaint, that Steuart provided 'a sort of compendium of all subsequent anti-quantitative theories of money' (1963, 209).

On the subject of interest, Steuart showed how the rate of interest would be settled in a market by lenders and borrowers. He therefore criticised Sir Josiah Child, because, believing that a low rate of interest is good for trade, 'he seems to think, that it is the power of a legislature, by statute, to bring interest down to that level which is most advantageous to trade' (455).

The intervention of government was, however, needed for what Steuart called 'striking out as much as possible, the competition of spendthrifts at the money-market', who drove up the interest rate. But the rate should not be fixed by statute, but rather by the government influencing 'the extent of credit and paper money in circulation' (462). It could hardly be said that on the question of the regulation of the rate of interest Steuart was less liberal than Adam Smith.

VII

Turning to the problem of value and price, Steuart rejected the notion of absolute value, and emphasised subjective estimation:

> Value is a relative term; there is no such thing as absolute value; that is to say, there are no two substances in the universe different in themselves which can be so proportioned in their parts, as to be permanently of the same value at all times . . . Value is the estimation mankind put upon things; and this estimation, depending upon a combination of their own wants, fancies, and even caprices, it is impossible it should be permanent. The measure of value, then, must be that which measures not the positive worth of any thing; but the relative worth of all things compared with one another.

> (*Works*, 1805, vol V, 175)

In his *Inquiry*, however, Steuart defined the 'real value' of a good as its cost of production, any excess over which, in the price received, represented profit (159). The level of demand determined how far price exceeded cost of production. Emphasising the importance of ignorance, he explained that demand and supply can only be estimated imprecisely and uncertainly, since it was 'next to impossible to discover it exactly', so that merchants 'can only regulate the prices they offer, by what they may reasonably expect to sell for again' (175). Steuart also understood demand in terms of a schedule, relative to prices: 'What I mean by *relative* is, that . . . demand is *great* or *small*, according to prices: there may be a great demand for grain at 35 shillings per quarter, and no demand at all for it at 40 shillings' (176).

Moreover, Steuart discerned the idea of elasticity of demand: 'Demand has not always the same effect in raising prices: we must therefore carefully attend to the differences between a demand for things for the first necessity for life, and for things indifferent' (153).

He defined the equilibrium price as follows:

> . . . When we say that the balance between work and demand is to be sustained *in equilibrio,* as far as possible, we mean, that the quantity supplied should be in proportion to the quantity *demanded,* that is, *wanted.* While the balance stands justly poised, prices are found in the adequate proportion of the real expense of making the goods, with a small addition for profit to the manufacturer and merchant.
>
> (189)

This justly poised balance came about in conditions of what Steuart called 'double competition', that is, with numerous competitors, buying and selling on both sides of the market. He regarded double competition as bringing about a beneficent equilibrium, or balance, by preventing the excessive rise or fall of prices; it is this which prevents their excessive fall. 'While *double competition* prevails, the balance is perfect, trade and industry flourish' (173).

But, unfortunately, beneficent double competition was liable to be eroded by barriers or privileges, or superseded by monopolies. In particular, it was not effective enough in the most important market of all, that for the people's basic foodstuff. In the eighteenth century, a vital test of an economist's stance regarding economic policy turned on his attitude regarding the market for grain. According to Steuart, the market for the people's subsistence did not operate sufficiently smoothly and beneficently to be left free:

> A statesman therefore, should be very attentive to put the inland trade in grain upon the best footing possible, to prevent the frauds of merchants, and to promote an equal distribution of food in all corners of the country: and by means of importation and exportation, according to plenty and scarcity, to regulate a just proportion between the general plenty of the year in Europe, and the price of subsistence; always observing to keep it somewhat lower at home, than it can be found in any nation rival in trade.
>
> (255)

In his *Dissertation on the Policy of Grain*, Steuart warned against the effects in lean years of panic buying by an ignorant public:

> Natural subsistence must be kept, as to its value, in as exact a proportion as may be to the plenty of the year. And in times of scarcity, all a statesman can do, is to prevent the fears and prejudices of mankind arising from their inadequate notions concerning the degrees of scarcity, from destroying this proportion.
>
> (From *A Dissertation on The Policy of Grain, Works,* 1805, vol V, 353)

Steuart put forward a rather elaborate scheme for a public granary. In the debate over government intervention in the grain market, there were also at various times in the eighteenth century, on the same side as Steuart, such important and not illiberal writers as Boisguilbert, Galiani and Jeremy Bentham.

Steuart also applied his analysis of demand and supply (or 'work') to the prices of labour of different types. He denied that the price of labour was generally determined by the price of subsistence, and insisted that the price of the products was the main determinant: 'Now the price of a manufacturer's wages is not regulated by the price of his subsistence, but by the price at which his manufacture sells in the market . . . It is therefore the rate of the market for labour and manufactures, and not the price of subsistence, which determines the standard of wages' (691).

Steuart described the movement of wages as follows:

> When workers can insist upon an augmentation of their wages, the demand of the market must be greater than the supply from their work . . . Let the demand of the market fall, the prices of labour will fall . . . The workmen will then enter into hurtful competition, and starve one another, as has often been observed . . . Let the demand of the market rise, manufacturers may raise their wages in proportion to the rise of the market; they may in the cheapest years enjoy the highest wages; drink one half of the week, and laugh at their employer, when he expects they should work for less, in order to swell his profits in the rising market.
>
> (694)

The conclusion was: 'The price of subsistence, whether it be influenced or not by the imposition of taxes, does not determine the price of labour. This is regulated by the demand for the work, and the competition among the workmen to be employed in producing it' (695).

The basic framework, therefore, of Steuart's analysis of value, price and distribution was on rather different lines, and had a rather different emphasis, from that which was to underlie much of English classical theorising. With his rejection of absolute standards of value, or of objective value, with his emphasis on relativity and subjective estimates, with the refinements which he added to the concept of demand, with his denial of a link between subsistence and a general wage, and on his insistence on relating wages to products, Steuart's theoretical framework approached more closely that of the Italian and French theories, and the subsequent neoclassical framework of value and distribution analysis, than the system which was to prevail among the English classicals.

VIII

Regarding, finally, Steuart's policy views, he certainly tended to approach policy issues from the viewpoint of an ever-active 'statesman'. He supported government intervention in the vital market for grain; in less advanced economies he supported protection for manufacturing; in more advanced economies he considered that policies to raise employment would be necessary. But it would be misleading to describe Steuart as a thoroughgoing totalitarian *dirigiste* or 'planner', just because he took seriously the problem of involuntary unemployment. Certainly at one point he stated that 'a government must be continually in action' (21). Nor did he recognise the workings of far-reaching, self-adjusting mechanisms as operating very widely and effectively in the various economies he had observed at first hand—which hardly included the English economy. So with regard to important sectors, at any rate, he did not consider that such mechanisms could generally be left without governmental attention. But Steuart again and again declared himself, in the most emphatic terms, on the side of liberty. In particular, he stressed the need for the statesman, or policy maker, to work with, and not against the grain of individual self-interest, in that he should,

> . . . by direct motives of self-interest, gently conduct free and independent men to concur in certain schemes ultimately calculated for their own proper benefit.
>
> (1767 [1770], vol I, 149)
>
> The principle of self-interest will serve as a general key to this inquiry; and it may, in one sense, be considered as the ruling principle of my subject, and may therefore be traced throughout the whole. This is the main spring, and only motive which a statesman should make use of, to engage a free people to concur in the plans which he lays down for their government . . . Were public spirit, instead of private utility, to become the spring of action in the individuals of a well-governed state, I apprehend, it would spoil all.
>
> (42–3)

Steuart could hardly have insisted more strongly than he did on the libertarian principles underlying his approach to economic policy: 'Any free people who invest a statesman with a power to control their most trivial actions, must be out of their wits and considered as submitting to a voluntary slavery of the worst nature, as it must be the most difficult to be shaken off' (278).

Such a statement is hardly that of a totalitarian planner. Steuart emphasised regarding the kind of policies he advocated, that when,

> . . . the legislative power is exerted in acquiring an influence only over the actions of individuals, in order to promote a scheme of political economy, uniform and consistent in all its parts, the consequence will be so far from introducing slavery among the people, that the execution of the plan will prove absolutely inconsistent with every arbitrary or irregular measure.
>
> (278)

Steuart indicated what he meant by liberty:

> By a people's being free, I understand no more than their being governed by general laws, well known, not depending upon the ambulatory will of any man, or any set of men, and established so as not to be changed, but in a regular and uniform way; for reasons which regard the body of society, and not through favour or particular classes.
>
> (206)

Free exchange of goods and services was the vital constituent of freedom: 'This communicates the idea of a free society; because it implies the circulation of a real equivalent for everything transferred, and for every service performed' (261). Steuart, moreover, saw 'the public good' as formed by 'the combination of every private interest' (143). Certainly he entertained no notions of democracy—nor, of course, did Adam Smith.

It is worth re-emphasising, at this point, Steuart's mistrust of general policy judgements, and his insistence that policies must be related to the particular stage of development of an economy, as well as to the traditions, institutions and circumstances of different countries and peoples. As Professor Skinner has observed regarding Steuart's views on trade policy; he 'cannot be linked with any particular policy recommendations. Policies such as freedom of trade or protection are to be applied wherever they are relevant; whether or not they are relevant depends in turn on the conditions of the particular case' (1966, lxxix).

Professor Skinner goes on to observe that Steuart was more concerned with the objective of economic welfare than with that of power. If power, or military might, was the objective, Steuart considered that the Spartan system of Lycurgus, with its agrarian egalitarianism, was 'the most perfect plan of political economy' (218)—which, however, he refused to take seriously for his own country in his own day, describing his interlude about Sparta as 'a farce between the acts of a serious opera' (227).

In some respects Steuart's approach to policy questions was closer to that of the German cameralists than to that of many of the mercantilists. Furthermore, from his observation and experience, both at home and in Scotland, and during his travels in Europe—where he had studied economic problems more closely than any other English or Scottish economist of his time—Steuart had come to view policy from the standpoint of smaller and less advanced economies, and to develop his ideas regarding policy for 'infant trades'—anticipating, to some extent, the ideas of Friedrich List some three-quarters of a century later. His main point was that the learning of skills took time, and that learners needed protection against the already adept;

> The new beginners are put among a number who are already perfect: all the instructions they get is, *do as you see others do before you.* This is an advantage which an established industry has over another newly set on foot . . . What loss must be first incurred! What numbers of aspiring geniuses overpowered by unsuccessful beginnings when a statesman does not concern himself in the operation! . . . The ruling principle, therefore, which ought to direct a statesman in promoting and improving the infant trade of his people is to encourage the manufacturing of every branch of natural productions by extending the home consumption of them; by excluding all competition from strangers; by permitting the rise of profits, so far as to promote dexterity and emulation in invention and improvement.
>
> (262-3)

When, however, an economy moves into the next stage, that of foreign trade, the protection of infants should be removed:

> When a people have taken a laborious turn, when sloth is despised, and dexterity carried to perfection, then the statesman must endeavour to remove the incumbrances . . . The scaffolding must be taken away when the fabric is completed. These incumbrances are high prices, at which he has been obliged to wink, while he was inspiring a taste for industry . . . but when he intends to supply foreign markets he must . . . bring down the price both of subsistence and work.
>
> (1767 [1770], vol II, 74)

There may seem, indeed, to be something over-optimistic, or even naïve, in the assumption that 'the statesman' will be willing and able to reverse his policy of supporting particular interests in the economy, just when historical changes may require such a reversal, in the interests of the people as a whole.

IX

It has been the versions of the victors—the victors, at any rate, for a particular time, in particular countries—which have become the dominant, and even orthodox, versions of the history of economic thought. The versions, or viewpoints of the losers are largely disregarded, and Sir James Steuart has been one of the most consummate, outstanding losers in the history and historiography of the subject. In England in the nineteenth century, while the régime of classical orthodoxy dominated in that country, Steuart and his work suffered almost total eclipse, punctuated by occasional expressions of contempt; and this in spite of some recognition from McCulloch that he was, indeed, the author of 'the first English work which had any pretensions to be considered as a systematic and complete view of the subject' (1845, 11). Pigeon-holed ignominiously as 'the last of the mercantilists', Steuart was relegated, by such an authoritative nineteenth-century pundit as Sir Leslie Stephen, to a position 'amongst the most tiresome individuals of the most tiresome of all literary species—the inferior political economist' (1876, vol II, 304).

To some extent, it is fair that the prolixity and lack of organisation in Steuart's sprawling *Inquiry* should take the blame for its eclipse—he himself confessed to 'needless repetitions'. But in a serious subject, as the decades went by, such defects should not have proved fatal. To some extent, Steuart's stylistic faults were brought about by his intellectual virtues, and by his more persistent resistance to oversimplification than that shown by his leading rivals and critics. It is easier to write clearly and engagingly when one has a 'simple system' to expound.

More serious and more controversial are the questions about Steuart's politics, which are ambiguously stated, and might well be regarded as combining a lack of realism with a normatively unacceptable paternalism. A lack of political realism might be regarded as proved by his reliance, in economic policy, on the knowledge and benevolence of the statesman.

It should, however, be emphasised that Steuart's views on policy followed from his inability to discern, and therefore his unwillingness to rely on, the sufficiently rapid operation of self-adjusting mechanisms in the economies of his day, especially with regard to money and aggregate demand. He regarded involuntary unemployment as a very serious problem. It is, moreover, unjustifiable to accuse Steuart of assuming that governments were always omniscient. What he asserted was that, for perfectly successful policies, either through government action or by individuals in free markets, perfect knowledge would be required, and the more accurate the knowledge of the statesman the greater was his power to achieve the results he aimed at. Steuart had warned emphatically about the difficulties of arriving at reliable general theories in economics. Unlike his 'enlightened' contemporaries, he was well aware how scarce a commodity useful, well-tested economic knowledge was.

There can be no doubt that Adam Smith's politics, compared with Steuart's, seem more realistic with regard to the knowledge and benevolence of governments (though some might maintain not invariably with regard to the working of market mechanisms). Normatively, moreover, Smith's individualism was more widely acceptable among those who, in the ensuing decades, wielded most influence on economic policy and economic doctrines.

What should be respected, however, are the quality and importance of Steuart's contributions on a number of central questions of economic theory and analysis, in particular with regard to demand analysis and monetary theory. His wise methodological caution and unpretentiousness also deserve recognition and, still more, his emphasis on the historical dimension, and historical–institutional relativism—an emphasis he shared with Adam Smith. To refuse to recognise such positive contributions, because of a distaste for Steuart political inclinations, is hardly today characteristic of a serious professional attitude. Steuart's technical contributions to economic theory and analysis were not as important as those of Quesnay, but they were substantial. As regards the political element in their economic writings, both Steuart and Quesnay may be seriously criticised. Quesnay's political and philosophical doctrines, however, contain clear suggestions of modern totalitarianism not present in Steuart's work, which inclines politically rather in the direction of a Keynesian or social-democratic concern with economic insecurity and unemployment (see Vickers, 1970).

REFERENCES

I

Ferguson, A (1767). *A History of Civil Society*
Hume, D (1742). *Essays Moral and Political*
Millar, J (1771). *Observations concerning the Distinction of Ranks in Society*
—— (1787). *An Historical View of the English Government*
Steuart, J (1767). *An Inquiry into the Principles of Political Economy* 1770, 3 vols
—— (1966). *An Inquiry into the Principles of Political Economy* (ed) A S Skinner
—— (1805). *Works,* 6 vols.

II

Akhtar, M A (1978). 'Sir J Steuart on Economic Growth', *Scottish Journal of Political Economy* **25,** 57ff

—— (1979). 'An Analytical Outline of Sir J Steuart's Macroeconomic Model', *Oxford Economic Papers* **26,** 283ff

Anderson, G M and Tollison, R D (1984). 'Sir James Steuart as the Apotheosis of Mercantilism', *Southern Economic Journal* **51,** 456ff

Bryson, G (1945). *Man and Society*

Chamley, P (1963a). 'Sir J Steuart: Inspirateur de la Théorie Générale de Lord Keynes', *Revue d'économie politique* vol 3

—— (1963b). *Économie politique et philosophie chez Steuart et Hegel*

—— (1965). *Documents relatifs à Sir J Steuart*

Coleman, D C (1987). *History and the Economic Past*

Davie, G E (1967). 'Anglophobe and Anglophil', *Scottish Journal of Political Economy* **14,** 291ff

Eagly, R V (1961). 'Sir J Steuart and the Aspiration Effect', *Economics* (NS) **18,** 53ff

Eltis, W (1986). 'Sir James Steuart's Corporate State', in *Ideas in Economics* (ed) R D C Black, 43ff

Hayek, F A (1949). *Individualism and Economic Order*

Lehmann, W C (1960). *John Millar of Glasgow*

McCulloch, J R (1845). *The Literature of Political Economy*

Pascal, R (1938). 'Property and Society: the Scottish Historical School of the 18th Century', *Modern Quarterly* **3,** 167ff

Perelman, M (1983). *Classical Political Economy*

Rae, J (1895). *Life of Adam Smith*

Robbins, L C (1963). *Politics and Economics*

Schatz, A (1902). *L'oeuvre économique de David Hume*

Sen, S R (1957). *The Economics of Sir J. Steuart*

Skinner, A (1962). 'Sir James Steuart: Economics and Politics', *Scottish Journal of Political Economy*, **9,** 17ff

—— (1965). 'Economics and History—the Scottish Enlightenment', *Scottish Journal of Political Economy*, **12,** 1ff

Stephen, L (1876). *A History of English Thought in the 18th Century* 2 vols

Vickers, D (1959). *Studies in the Theory of Money, 1690–1776*

—— (1970). Review Article of *The Works, Political Metaphysical and Chronological of Sir James Steuart. Journal of Economic Literature* **8,** 1190ff

CHAPTER FIVE

Adam Smith and *The Wealth of Nations*

Terence Hutchison

*Before Adam Smith: The Emergence
of Political Economy 1662–1776*
(Basil Blackwell, 1988)

I

The quantity of secondary literature about the economics and political
economy of Adam Smith—especially since the very weighty additions which
appeared in 1776—may well be greater than the total amount of literature
devoted to the economics of perhaps even a dozen, or more, of the writers so
far discussed in this book. Not aspiring to add appreciably to this vast Smithian
accumulation, we shall be drawing, for the most part, on a previous minuscule
contribution (Hutchison, 1978, chapter 1).[1]

The *Wealth of Nations* lies on the borderline of our period. In this chapter
we are more interested in this supreme work as the culminating achievement,
which brought to a close our formative period, than as the opening, keynote
work of a new era. We shall be concerned with what Smith made of his
predecessors' work, together with what he failed to make of it, either because
he did not know it (e.g. the writings of Galiani and Condillac) or because he
deliberately chose to ignore it (e.g. Steuart's *Inquiry*).

The twenty-eight-year-old Smith was in 1751 at a turning point in his career
when he was appointed to the chair of Logic at the University of Glasgow, from
which he moved a year later to the chair of Moral Philosophy. Smith taught in
Glasgow for twelve years and three months, building up his course in Moral
Philosophy, while presumably, until 1759, concentrating his creative thinking
on his social-psychological study of 'moral sentiments', his *Theory* of which
(1759) won for him a high reputation and much applause in France.

Smith's lecture course in Glasgow was extremely wide-ranging, including
ethics, law and jurisprudence, together with economic analysis and policy. The
lectures possessed some characteristics very different from any to be found in
college courses today. On the one hand, they covered a number of very complex
subjects for the grasp of which highly mature minds might seem to be required.

On the other hand, it was addressed to young teenagers, who were discouraged from taking notes, and whose textbooks were in Latin. Of the four main parts of the course, 'police', or political economy, came last. Smith had dealt with topics in political economy in his lectures in Edinburgh in 1748–50. Presumably, however, his main creative effort in this sector of his vast field of interests did not come until the 1760s, or perhaps until some time after he had left Glasgow. Anyhow, the notes taken from this section of his lectures in 1762–3 and 1763–4 (see Smith, 1978, pp 331–94 and 486–554) may provide some indications of Smith's main ideas on political economy around the time of his fortieth birthday, and of his departure from Glasgow some six months later. Some tentative conclusions may be suggested as to which of the main topics eventually discussed in the *Wealth of Nations*, had been broached by Smith in his Glasgow lectures, and as to which questions he first addressed or formulated after 1764, or when he got down to writing his book in 1766–7.

In broad terms, it seems that in his lectures Smith's treatment of value and price kept more closely to the lines laid down by Francis Hutcheson (even more closely, it would appear in 1762–3 than in 1763–4). In the lectures also there was relatively much more concern with market price than with natural price, as contrasted with the *Wealth of Nations*.[2] Though the distinction between market and natural price appeared in the lectures, the notes are hardly full or clear regarding the relations between the two. What is absent from the lecture notes was the prominent emphasis on labour, either in terms of a labour-commanded theory of the absolute measure of value (in spite of a fleeting reference, see 1978, 503); or in the form of a labour-embodied theory of the determination of value in the 'early and rude state of society'. Nor, in the section devoted to jurisprudence does Smith follow up at all closely Locke's labour theory of property, though at certain points (1978, 17, 20 and 338) there seems to be a significant indebtedness—identified by the editors—to Locke's *Second Treatise of Civil Government*, the major, though not the only, fount and origin of labour theories both of property and value. Professor Bowley certainly did not exaggerate when she maintained: 'In the *Lectures* it is notable that Adam Smith has no trace of a labour theory of value, while labour as a measure of value is mentioned only in passing' (1973, 110).

Moreover, also almost entirely absent from the lecture notes is the fundamental analysis, in Volume II of the *Wealth of Nations*, of saving, investing, capital and money, which was to become the central pillar of classical macro-economics.

II

In January 1764 Smith abandoned Glasgow and academic life for wider prospects; or, as Keynes put it, 'at the age of 41 (just at the right moment, neither too soon or too late)', he 'launched himself on the great world' (1938, 33). He took the plum job of private tutor to a young Duke and, for nearly three years, travelled with his pupil in France, Switzerland and Italy, ending up with about nine months in Paris in 1766. At that time interest in, and enthusiasm for physiocracy, and the 'economists', was at or near its peak, and Smith met and discussed political economy with Quesnay, Turgot and others—the most important and consequential intellectual encounters of his life outside Scotland. Early in 1767 he was back with his mother in his native Kirkcaldy, in which small coastal town, in what must have been considerable intellectual isolation, he spent some seven years producing what eventually was recognised as his masterpiece. This was surely a feat of single-minded dedication and concentration, indicative of an almost infinite capacity for taking pains. In 1773 Smith relaxed somewhat, coming south to London for three years of more convivial revision and consultation with friends and intellectual society in London.

III

No comprehensive account of, or 'reader's guide' to, the *Wealth of Nations* is provided here. We merely discuss selected topics which seem significant from our particular perspective, that of considering Smith's book as the final, culminating work of our period. Let us take first the subject of scope and method.[3]

It must be emphasised first that Smith would never, for one moment, have entertained or accepted—even in his later years, after 1776, when the *Wealth of Nations* was bringing him such resounding and rewarding success—an interpretation of his intellectual career as having been centred upon, or dominated by, political economy, even in the broadest sense of the term.

For Adam Smith was, in fact, and undoubtedly always considered himself to be, a philosopher, in a highly comprehensive sense, not as interested in epistemology as Locke, Berkeley and Hume, but penetrating much more deeply into social and legal philosophy and the psychology of ethics. Smith remained a philosopher from the beginning to the end of his life. He would never have regarded his work as a whole as primarily economic. He thought of economics, or political economy, as only one chapter, and not the most important chapter, in a broad study of society and human progress, which involved psychology and ethics (in social and individual terms), law, politics, and the development of the arts and sciences.[4] Smith did not merely start life with a youthful enthusiasm for philosophy, and then eventually narrow down his interests in his maturity to become an economist. Fortunately for our subject, as it turned out, he did devote a decade or so of his prime years to political economy (using up, perhaps, quite a lot more scarce time than he had originally intended in completing his work in that particular section of his vast field). But having finished the *Wealth of Nations* Smith moved on, or back, to the history and philosophy of law and to the progress of the arts and sciences. When he lamented in his last days that 'he had done so little', Smith did not, of course, mean that he had planned, but failed to complete, further volumes on political economy (as Alfred Marshall originally planned a multi-volume *Principles of Economics*, which very unfortunately for the subject in the twentieth century was never completed in the form originally intended). What

Smith, with excessive modesty, was lamenting was that he had not completed more than a small part of his original vast philosophical-historical plan.[5] Therefore, that the *Wealth of Nations* played such an important role in establishing political economy as an independent subject is one of those felicitous, unintended and quite unplanned outcomes to which Smith himself assigned such an important, and often beneficent, role in human affairs. In his own celebrated words Smith himself was 'led by an invisible hand to promote an end which was no part of his intention' (1976a, 456)—the end, that is, of establishing political economy as a separate autonomous discipline.

One of the most important themes of Smith's vast, uncompleted life-work, seems to have been centred around the idea of human progress, or the progress of society.[6] In fact, as Walter Bagehot, in his essay of 1876, illuminatingly observed regarding the *Wealth of Nations*:

> It was not the exclusive product of a lifelong study . . . It was in the mind of its author only one of many books, or rather a single part of a great book, which he intended to write . . . He spent his life accordingly, in studying the origin and progress of the sciences, the laws, the politics, and all the other aids and forces which have raised man from the savage to the civilised state . . .
>
> He investigated the progress of opulence as part of the growth and progress of all things . . .
>
> The last way in which he regarded Political Economy was as a separate and confined speciality; he came upon it as an inseparable part of the development of all things, and it was in that vast connection that he habitually considered it.

(1881, 248–50; and 1895, 129)

But what interest, it may well be asked, for economists today, have Smith's apparently vast intellectual ambitions regarding the intended scope of his life-work, and the somewhat limited and subordinate place of the *Wealth of Nations* in that intended work? Are Smith's comprehensive intellectual ambitions and concepts more than a rather magnificent, 'period', museum specimen of eighteenth-century intellectual design, which, in any case, Smith himself came nowhere near to completing, and which have become quite obsolete and irrelevant in scale for the tasks of today?

Of course it can be validly claimed that for nearly two centuries the concentration and specialisation carried through by successive generations, beginning with Ricardo and Senior, has largely paid off, in spite of objections advanced from time to time by Historical, Comteist, Marxist and Institutionalist critics. But this specialisation and concentration in political economy and economics has depended, to a large extent, on the assumption of a fairly stable social and political environment which would not too seriously or irregularly interfere with economic processes, which processes, therefore, could be studied more or less in isolation. This assumption of a stable social framework—or what Pigou (1929, 21), before the world depression, was describing as a 'stable general culture'—permitted the development of classical, neoclassical and Keynesian economics in Britain. Indeed, there may always be plenty of more narrowly and specifically economic questions which will not require the kind of comprehensive social and historical setting envisaged by Adam Smith. But to the extent that the assumption of a more or less stable social framework, and the kind of specialisation in economics which it permits, *may be* becoming significantly less valid than it used to be, there may well be reasons for regarding Smith's conceptions of the scope of the subject, and its close interrelationships and interpretation with other fields, especially that of law, not simply as an obsolete, impracticable, intellectually unfeasible irrelevance, of no more than period interest for economists today. What, at least, might be concluded is that Adam Smith would not have neglected, or underestimated, the legal, social and social-psychological factors in our contemporary economic problems (for example, the problem of inflation) just because such factors may be outside what have more recently come to be regarded as accepted 'professional' or departmental frontiers.

IV

Conceptions of the scope of the subject are naturally related to conceptions regarding methods, and in turn are related to the kind of conclusions regarding policy which are considered intellectually feasible or justified. The combination and balance of methods employed in the *Wealth of Nations* have been as rarely followed by subsequent economists as have Smith's comprehensive conceptions of the scope, and of the wide-ranging interdependencies of social and economic enquiry. There was surely some justification for the claim of the historical economist Thorold Rogers, at the centenary celebrations in 1876, that there was 'nothing more significant than the differences of the process by which Adam Smith collected his inferences, and that by which his followers or commentators have arrived at theirs'.[7]

In fact, following what may be described as the James Mill-Ricardo methodological revolution, the comprehensiveness and balance of methods deployed in the *Wealth of Nations* has hardly ever been regained in a general work on the subject of major stature. It is a tribute to the remarkable balance which Smith achieved that he has been both acclaimed and criticised from both or all sides in subsequent methodological debates. But there is certainly a most striking contrast with the Ricardian methods which later obtained such prestige.[8] For the bulk of the text of the *Wealth of Nations* consists of descriptive and historical material. As one of Smith's recent successors at Glasgow has noted:

> He was rather a rich inductive thinker than a rigidly logical system-builder . . . though he was both. He had the modesty and wisdom always to give true weight to the facts . . . [He had a] genius for choosing and using factual data. He was at home in facts. He enjoyed ferreting them out, and giving them their proper weights.
>
> (Macfie, 1967, 13 and 139)

Sixty years after the appearance of the *Wealth of Nations*, Nassau Senior, in formulating the viewpoint established by the Ricardian methodological revolution, was to complain of 'the undue importance which many economists have ascribed to the collection of facts' (1836, 6).

According to Senior, the science of political economy, apart from its multifarious applications, was not, '*avide de faits*'. *Adam Smith emphatically was 'avide de faits',* and overwhelmingly demonstrated his avidity, and the conception of the subject which this avidity implied, in the *Wealth of Nations*.

In his *Lectures on Rhetoric and Belles Lettres*, Smith is reported as referring to 'abstract and speculative reasonings, which perhaps tend very little to the bettering of our practice' (1983, 37).

In fact, in the *Wealth of Nations* 'abstract reasonings' are mostly kept on a very tight rein. Smith is certainly not one for taking off into the Ricardian stratosphere of 'strong cases' or extreme, arbitrary abstractions. Of course Smith employed a 'system', as he called it, by which he meant an abstract, deductive model. But he sharply denounced 'the man of system' who indulges in, what Viner called, 'over-attachment or an exaggeration of the applicability to concrete issues without qualification of abstract and therefore at its best partial and incomprehensive theorising'. Smith very much doubted that abstraction could provide either understanding of the real world or, by itself, safe guidance for the legislator or statesman (Viner, 1965, 32; and 1968, 327).[9]

When Smith wanted to use a simple case for its illustrative value he seldom invented an abstraction. He sought to go back in history and find a factual illustration in a simpler kind of economy, such as the hand-to-mouth hunting and fishing economy which is so frequently referred to from the first page onwards in the *Wealth of Nations*. How far Smith's history, or sometimes what has been called his 'conjectural history', or conjectural anthropology, was always accurate, is beside the point methodologically. Smith did not consider that students of society, or of the wealth of nations, could, or should seek to compensate very far for their inability to experiment by setting up abstract models.

Smith was methodologically comprehensive. Though sharing much of the intellectual confidence of his age, he realised that significant or useful social and philosophical truth, including economic truth, was always a *very* scarce commodity, and especially so in relation with the extravagant needs for it implicitly postulated by, though often not explicitly understood to be an essential prerequisite for, the plans and projects of reformers and revolutionaries. So the student of society, or of the economy, cannot afford to overlook *any* method by which some grain or crumb of truth, however insubstantial and fragmentary, may be picked up. As John Neville Keynes said of Smith: 'He rejected no method of enquiry that could in any way assist him in investigating the phenomena of wealth' (1917, 10).[10]

In fact, Smith employed methods which recently have been powerfully denounced by some philosophers and economists. For Smith was a historical economist not only in the sense that he was empirical, but in that the theme of *progress through natural stages of development* runs all through his *Inquiry into the Nature and Cause of the Wealth of Nations*. Smith, in fact, like Hume, Ferguson and Millar, belonged to 'the historical age' and 'the historical nation'. He did not claim to have discovered 'laws' of economic development, or indeed, *any* economic laws, and so might not be describable as a 'historicist' in the fullest sense. But, especially in the often rather neglected Volume III of the *Wealth of Nations*, 'Of the Natural Progress of Opulence', Smith seeks to lay down 'the natural course of things' or an 'order of things which necessity imposes in general', though he allowed that this natural course or order could be 'inverted' by misconceived government policies.

Of course, as with most methods (including, for example, quantitative methods) 'historicist' procedures, as Sir Karl Popper has demonstrated, have been grossly misused, and wildly exaggerated claims have been made on their behalf. But if one is interested in different kinds of economy, existing at different times and places, and their different actual and potential levels of development, then one cannot afford fastidiously to dismiss 'historicist' concepts, questions, and methods, however uncertain and unreliable. Though the economist should test and scrutinise results or predictions with the utmost feasible strictness, he cannot dismiss in advance *any* method which may yield some fragment of insight—and certainly not just because such a method is not employed in what are called the most 'mature' natural sciences such as physics.

Therefore, even more definitely than with regard to the scope of the subject, there may seem to be important lessons to be found in the methodological comprehensiveness and balance of Smith's *Inquiry*, which has, in this respect, virtually never been emulated in a book of general principles of major importance. Though Marshall discerned and wrestled with the problem of meshing history and analysis in an exposition of general principles, following the methodological revolution of James Mill and Ricardo, no-one has really been able to put it all together again with the balance and comprehensiveness achieved in the *Wealth of Nations*.[11]

V

Adam Smith's *Inquiry*, with its abundantly marshalled empirical and institutional data, evidence, and illustrations, with its sometimes extensive historical digressions (for example, on silver, or on the corn trade, or on the Bank of Amsterdam), and with its exhaustive surveys of institutions (for example, educational institutions), is all eventually held together, securely but flexibly, by the thread provided by a single *type* of model or 'system': what Smith called the 'simple system of natural liberty', or what we might call the freely competitive, self-adjusting, market model. The conditions for 'natural' values and prices, wages, profits and rents, having been analysed the model is applied generally—but not dogmatically, universally, or exclusively—both to domestic and foreign trade as well as to the allocation of particular resources and to their accumulation and employment in the aggregate. Moreover, Smith uses his simple system of natural liberty as a historically 'dynamic' model, in that it is concerned not only with a static criterion, or ideal condition, but with the *progress* of the economy—an essential part of Smith's central theme. What Smith's *Inquiry* is primarily about is how 'the simple system', starting from individual initiative, allocates, accumulates, and reallocates resources via free markets so as to release and stimulate, more effectively than any other 'system', the economic forces which make for progress. The essential unique contribution of 'the simple system' is this vital and attractive complementary between individual freedom and the economic progress of society.

This assertion of the simple 'system', or the free-market model, in such broad, general terms (but not universally or exclusively) provides one of the main grounds for maintaining that Smith's *Inquiry* marks an epoch in the history of economic thought, or even a revolution in the subject. For it was Adam Smith who really generalised the theory of market self-adjustment as operating effectively, by and large—though with several and, in some cases, important exceptions—throughout the economic cosmos, domestically and internationally, micro-economically and macro-economically. We have already discussed the works of many writers before Smith who had discerned self-adjusting forces at work in particular sectors, and had also sometimes urged that in some areas these forces should be allowed to work themselves out free of government intervention: for example, Gervaise and Hume for international trade, North, Mandeville, and Josiah Tucker for domestic markets, and with regard to labour or capital markets. But it was Smith who asserted the 'system', or model in general terms, as a general answer regarding most economic processes of a 'natural' or normal kind. It must also be emphasised that for Smith self-adjustment was not assumed as a hypothetical abstraction, but was asserted as an imprecise and qualified empirical theory, open, in principle, to refutation, regarding how particular market processes actually and usually worked out. Smith discerned and asserted that market processes worked out in general, given some reasonably simply specifiable, and practically feasible, conditions, in a very different way from that which had mostly been stated or implied in previous economic writings.

In the *Wealth of Nations* there are two great economic forces or processes making for economic progress, which depend, in their turn, on the psychological factor of the individual's striving to better his condition, and on a favourable legal framework (especially regarding property and land tenure). The first of these two great economic forces is the division of labour. It has been justifiably asserted that the initial and basic proposition of Smith's *Inquiry*, that the division of labour depends on the extent of the market, 'is one of the most illuminating generalizations which can be found anywhere in the whole literature of economics' (Young, 1928, 529)—though hardly new in the *Wealth of Nations*.

What might be called Smith's micro-economics and international economics are concerned with how free competitive markets allow the division of labour to contribute with its full power to economic progress. The second great force, or process, making for economic progress is individual frugality or parsimony; and Smith's 'macro-economics' shows how, under his simple system of natural liberty, individual frugality, or parsimony can be fully implemented in the progress of the economy.

Of course, as we have already emphasised, Smith does not, for the most part, assert the empirical validity of the 'simple system', or model, in dogmatic, unqualified, or universal terms. In the mass of historical evidence and illustration, which it is an essential part of Smith's method to bring to bear, and to assign its due weight, a variety of qualifications and exceptions are to be found, certainly in micro-economic and international applications of 'the simple system' or model.

In the first place Smith emphasises the basic preconditions to be satisfied, such as a favourable legal and property framework. It was laws and customs relating to land tenure which 'have perhaps contributed more to the present grandeur of England, than all their boasted regulations of commerce taken together' (1976a, 392).

Smith is, of course, also constantly emphasising (and denouncing) the striving after monopoly and the persistence of monopolies and restrictive practices, 'which may endure for many centuries', or 'for ages together', and which are based sometimes on 'particular accidents' and sometimes on 'natural causes', as well as government legislation (1976a, 76–9).

The important qualifications and exceptions, which Smith cites, to the beneficient working of his simple system are well known.[12] They include, notably, defence and shipping, justice, public works (a potentially capacious category), and building methods and standards. Smith is even prepared to allow the government to fix or limit the rate of interest (for which he was logically rebuked by Jeremy Bentham). As regards foreign trade, he was ready to support an export duty on wool and moderate import duties for the purposes of revenue and retaliation or bargaining.

VI

Smith once described his treatment of economic policy in the *Wealth of Nations* as a 'very violent attack upon the whole commercial system of Great Britain' (Scott, 1937, 283).

Moreover, when he delivered that attack it was from what was still a heretical or minority point of view. As Walter Bagehot said, a hundred years ago, 'It is difficult for a modern Englishman, to whom "Free Trade" is an accepted maxim of tedious orthodoxy, to remember sufficiently that a hundred years ago it was a heresy and a paradox. The whole commercial legislation of the world was formed on the doctrines of Protection' (1895, 128).

But if Smith could be 'violent' in denunciation, and revolutionary in policies and objectives, he tended to be moderate and gradualist regarding timing and methods. As an empirical and historical economist, and as something of a historical relativist, Smith does not resort to abstract, absolute optima and maxima in his criticisms and appraisals of economic institutions and policies— which highly abstract criteria can be and often are used by economists in such misleading and question-begging ways. In *The Theory of Moral Sentiments* Smith's approach to policy-making even bears a somewhat conservative cast, in that he urges 'the man whose public spirit is prompted altogether by humanity and benevolence' to be prepared to bear with the faults and injustices of the existing order of society:

> He will content himself with moderating, what he often cannot annihilate without violence. When he cannot conquer the rooted prejudices of the people by reason and persuasion, he will not attempt to subdue them by force . . . he will accommodate, as well as he can, his public arrangements to the confirmed habits and prejudices of the people; and will remedy, as well as he can, the inconveniences

which may flow from the want of those regulations which the people are averse to submit to. When he cannot establish the right, he will not disdain to ameliorate the wrong; but like Solon, when he cannot establish the best system of laws, he will endeavour to establish the best that the people can bear.

(1976b, 233)[13]

It was here that Smith's methodological approach implied an attitude to policy differing very significantly from the narrowly abstract, *a priori*, deductive, 'rigorous' *laissez-faire* of Quesnay—and Ricardo. For Smith accused Quesnay of irrelevantly and misleadingly applying the criteria of absolute or perfect optimality, in imagining that an economy and polity 'would thrive and prosper only under a certain precise regimen, the exact regimen of *perfect* liberty and *perfect* justice . . . If a nation could not prosper without the enjoyment of *perfect* liberty and *perfect* justice there is not in the world a nation which could ever have prospered' (1976a, 674). In his theory and advocacy of free markets Smith did not concern himself with the Utopian abstractions of perfect *maxima* and *optima*. [14]

One of the most powerfully persuasive aspects of the *Wealth of Nations* derived from Smith's ability, in the conditions of his day, plausibly and validly to make the complementarity of freedom and economic growth, or progress, one of his central themes, proclaiming that more of both of two great, highly valued *desiderata* were simultaneously obtainable, so that there was no need to sacrifice one of them to obtain more of the other. But there can be no doubt as to which of this happily complementary pair Smith would have chosen if he had been forced to do so.[15] Smith was doubtful and ambiguous about the value or significance of an increase in wealth as a value or objective.[16] While greater wealth for a society had a part in rendering it more civilised and more free, or was an indicator of social progress, at any rate regarding individuals he insisted: 'In case of body and peace of mind, all the different ranks of life are nearly upon a level, and the beggar, who suns himself by the highway, possesses that security which Kings are fighting for' (1976b, 185).

This belief perhaps partly explains why Smith does not seem to show much interest in policies concerned with the distribution of wealth or income, or with problems of poverty. Anyhow, Smith would always have put freedom first, and he valued economic freedoms not mainly or simply because he believed that they promoted a more rapid growth rate of GNP per head, but for their own sake, or because they were an essential component of civil freedom.

VII

The primary economic idea, or theme, of the *Wealth of Nations* was one which had been developed bit by bit, throughout our period, by a number of different writers—from North and Martyn, Nicole and Boisguilbert, Mandeville, Carl, and others, through to Tucker and Hume. This idea, which, from the first page, provided both theoretical and policy *leitmotiv* of Smith's work, was concerned with how an economy progressed via specialisation and the division of labour, with the drive of self-interest of its individual participants canalised into socially beneficient directions by competitive markets. Some writers—such as E L Carl—emphasised the specialisation of land and machinery, as well as labour. It may, however, be noted that Adam Smith almost completely excluded one main reason for the specialisation of labour which had been emphasised by most of his predecessors on the subject: that of taking advantage of human diversity, which he saw as, in the main, not so much the cause, as the effect of the division of labour. Smith's view is one that might be expected rather from a social engineer or egalitarian.[17]

With the emphasis on specialism and the division of labour as a main cause, or source, of economic progress came the policy message of freeing and opening up markets, so that this source of progress could be drawn on to the full. Of those writers who developed the analysis of the beneficent effects of the division of labour, only the German cameralist, Ernst Ludwig Carl, was generally on the side of a *dirigiste* paternalism, rather than that of the freeing of markets and the economic initiative of the individual. Widespread, beneficent, more-or-less automatic self-adjusting mechanisms were, however, more and more perceived and analysed with regard to particular markets. but what would today be called 'macro-economic' self-adjustment with regard to money, saving and investment, which would obviate the need for concern or for central regulation with regard to the money supply, was hardly discerned as a possibility. Anyhow, in expounding his central theme Smith, while largely, but not entirely following his predecessors, applied all the philosophical, psychological and political insight for which he is almost unrivalled in the history of the subject.

VIII

We focus now on two basic theoretical innovations, introduced in the *Wealth of Nations*, which owed comparatively little to previous writers. (For we consider somewhat misleading Schumpeter's statement that the *Wealth of Nations* 'does not contain a single *analytic* idea, principle, or method that was entirely new in 1776' (1954, 184).) Indeed, we would claim that, as developed by Smith, these two innovations seem sufficiently new and fundamental as to justify the adjective 'revolutionary', especially in the light of the very powerful influence which they exerted in Britain for the next century. One of these innovations was central to Smith's micro-economics and one to his macro-economics.

The first of Smith's fundamental innovations was his crucial alteration of the concept of 'value in use', or utility, at a vital point in Volume I, chapter 4. He introduced his treatment of price and value by maintaining that 'utility', which 'may be called "value in use" ', was *not* a necessary prerequisite for value in exchange. For goods 'which have the greatest value in exchange' may have *no* 'value in use' (1976a, 44). Smith thus confused the relations between utility, demand, and value, by maintaining that what should be meant by a good having 'value in use', was not what had, and has, been meant by the great majority of economists, before and since, that is, the quality of being expected to satisfy a want, of whatever kind, 'real' and objective, or fanciful and subjective. It has been explained that Smith must rather have been restricting the meaning of value-in-use to some kind of normative, 'real', objective usefulness (see Bowley, 1973, 110ff; and Hollander, 1973, 133ff).

Two comments may be offered regarding this explanation. First, Smith inherited from Frances Hutcheson a long tradition which went back through Pufendorf, the Salamancan school, and a majority of the scholastics, according to which a fundamental role was played by a comprehensive, basically subjective, positive concept of utility. As we have seen, Pufendorf defined a good as possessing 'use' 'not merely' when it 'truly' helped to preserve or make pleasurable our existence, but when it did so, 'in the sole opinion of certain men' (1660 [1931], 65).[18]

Second, Smith's concept of utility was fundamentally at variance with the libertarian, individualist message of which Smith otherwise, throughout the *Wealth of Nations* was such a determined and effective champion. The case for economic freedom requires, or is crucially assisted by, a value analysis which gives a full role to *subjective* utility and *individual* choice and demand. Smith's 'real', normative, biological, or 'moralistic' concept of utility contained implications from which Smith himself would have recoiled in horror: that is, that there are real objective 'utilities', which experts, of one sort or another, are qualified to instruct us, or direct us about, which ought to control our valuations, preferences or choices. It is not too much to maintain that a subjective concept of utility is essential and fundamental to the case for, and explanation of, a pluralist and free economy and society. Seeking to explain Smith's conception of value-in-use or utility as unnecessary for exchange value, Professor Bowley (a steadfast supporter, who described his usage as 'exceedingly awkward' and 'all very tiresome' for Adam Smith's students) posed the question: 'Who does not remember the "utility" goods in the last war?' (1973, 136). The parallel is all too precise. It seems, however, somewhat incongruous to have to resort to the usage of wartime, governmental rationing officials for an explanation as to how the supreme champion of individual economic freedom came to break with the tradition of such a long line of distinguished predecessors regarding utility.

Since he was excusably ignorant of their writings on this subject it would be quite unfair to blame Smith for not following the analysis of utility and demand put forward by Galiani and Turgot, which, as has been observed, left comparatively little for the neoclassicals to achieve in the field of utility and demand analysis, apart from terminological precision or the application of mathematics.[19] In breaking, however, with the treatment of Pufendorf and Hutcheson, Smith both diminished or excluded the element of subjectivity and confused the relationship between utility and demand. Alfred Marshall's judicious conclusion seems unavoidable: 'Adam Smith makes himself the judge of what is useful to other people and introduces unnecessary confusion' (1975, 125).

Nor can Smith be criticised for not having followed up Condillac's path-breaking analysis of subjectivity, uncertainty, and erroneous expectations in market decisions. Condillac's work did not appear until a month or two before the *Wealth of Nations*. Professor Hayek, however, has maintained 'that every important advance in economic theory during the last hundred years was a further step in the consistent application of subjectivism' (1952, 52). Anyone prepared to uphold the wisdom of this *aperçu*, and to extrapolate it back another hundred years, will probably have to conclude that, with regard to the utility concept, a fundamentally retrogressive step was taken in the *Wealth of Nations*.

Moreover, Smith's treatment of utility and demand was followed up by his theories of labour commanded as an absolute measure of value, and of labour embodied as a determinant of value in primitive economies, together with his general cost of production theory of value.

Labour theories of value hardly have a coherent history before the *Wealth of Nations* independently of the scarcity and utility theory. Petty—followed by the young Benjamin Franklin—had thrown out, in passing, the idea of labour embodied—or labour and land embodied—as a rough-and-ready method of assessing properties for tax purposes. Locke had leaned heavily in the direction of labour in the value analysis in his political treatise, but not in his economic writings.[20] It was the *Wealth of Nations* which opened up the divisions— regarded by some as of the most fundamental importance—between theories of value based on scarcity and utility and those based on labour and cost of production.[21] We would not, however, go so far as to say, with R L Meek, that Smith 'makes it perfectly clear' that 'demand has nothing to do with the determination of exchange value' (1973, 73). For, in spite of his fine chapter 'of the natural and market price of commodities', there are several important points with regard to demand value and value on which Smith hardly offers a 'perfectly clear' analysis.

As regards labour commanded as an absolute measure of value, most value theorists had abandoned the idea of an absolute measure of value long before the *Wealth of Nations*. Montanari and Galiani had rejected the very notion, as did Steuart. As Smith's fellow-classical Nassau Senior remarked: 'Aristotle's description of value as depending on demand . . . approaches much more nearly to perfect accuracy than Smith's who, by adopting labour as a measure of value, and talking of labour as never varying in its own value, has involved himself and his followers in inextricable confusion' (1978, Vol II, 45).

Smith made a number of valuable contributions to the theories of rent, wages and profits. His theory of distribution, however, was shaped by his treatment of utility and value, which approached the valuation of factors of production from the cost side rather than from that of their utility and scarcity, or the productive contribution rendered. Galiani, on the other hand, drawing on scholastic sources, had recognised the labour element in the value of goods and services but had subordinated this to his general scarcity-and-utility value analysis.

It is not the case, however, that Smith clearly and categorically put forward a general labour theory of exchange value. He did not. Nor did he entirely omit either the demand side, or the subjective element—(which may be present in his concept of 'toil and trouble' in his labour-commanded measure of value). But his unhappy, tiresome, and awkward treatment of value-in-use, together with his introduction of a labour element both in the measurement of value and in the simplest case of exchange value, had confusing consequences which were very important for the subsequent history of value theory. According to Professor Bowley: 'Adam Smith is traditionally regarded as having introduced a labour theory of value into *The Wealth of Nations*' (1973, 110). This tradition may be wrong. No doubt some of his leading classical successors, together with most Marxists, have misunderstood or misrepresented Smith's views. Smith himself, however, must take his share of the blame, if he has been misunderstood or misrepresented. If Smith's treatment of value was not—as Professor Donald Winch justifiably denies that his politics were—'an episode, however crucial, that occurred some way along a road which runs from Locke to Marx' then a less unhappy, tiresome, and awkward treatment of utility and value by Smith himself would have rendered such an interpretation impossible from the start. Smith's treatment of value, however, would have needed to remain more precisely faithful to his predecessors, Pufendorf and Hutcheson, and to have avoided such an apparently fundamental influence from Locke's political writings.

A deep-seated source of Smith's confusion may be traceable to his failure to apply, sufficiently consistently, the positive-normative distinction, which had been developed by Petty and others in the seventeenth century, and which had been explicitly and masterfully employed by Cantillon. Smith, on the other hand, not only made much play with the fundamentally ambiguous adjective 'natural', he also introduced a normative-positive ambiguity into the basic concept of value-in-use, by assigning it a normative quality, according to which goods *ought* to be valued or demanded, rather than confining himself strictly to the positive treatment of how, in fact, goods actually were valued and demanded by fallible, gullible human beings.[22]

The most accurate account of Smith on value seems to have come from Professor Denis O'Brien:

> Adam Smith laid the foundations for classical value theory. What he did, and the way he did it, were to prove extremely important because he seems deliberately and consciously to have rejected the value theory which he inherited. He inherited a subjective value theory: and instead of developing this he largely substituted for it a cost of production theory . . . The dismissal of utility as a determinant of value is justified by reference to the 'diamonds and water' paradox although, as we have seen, Smith solved this in his *Lectures*. It is interesting to see that Smith so far purges his analysis of the subjective elements as to redefine utility.
>
> (1975, 78ff)

IX

The second of Smith's fundamental and indeed revolutionary theoretical innovations was that of his classical macro-economics, including his analysis of saving, investment and the rate of interest, together with his treatment of money. Certainly Smith had here one major anticipator, Turgot, in section 101 of his *Reflections*, which appeared ten years before the *Wealth of Nations* and propounded what Schumpeter called the Turgot-Smith theory of saving and investment—or saving *is* investment. Smith, however, built up the implications of the theory, as regards money and government policy, much further than Turgot. Apart from Turgot's paragraph only a few faint suggestions of what came to be classical macro-economics appeared before the *Wealth of Nations*—for example, very briefly in the writings of Hutcheson and Tucker.

Certainly the stress on the role of saving, investment, and capital accumulation was one of the most important, and relatively very new, features of the *Wealth of Nations*. Smith's point, however, was not merely the importance for economic progress of capital accumulation, but how, within the simple system of natural liberty, individual frugality would, in free markets, almost inevitably be fully and smoothly implemented and converted into capital accumulation and economic progress, without the intervention or activity of governments.

It was the simple system which enabled the frugal or parsimonious man, concerned simply to better his own condition, to be a public benefactor. Throughout his macro-economics, in both his analysis of saving and investment, and in his treatment of money, Smith held to the logic of his 'simple system', and its implications for government policy, in an almost completely consistent manner—apart from his incongruous approval of a maximum rate of interest. The author of the *Wealth of Nations* was the major creator of classical macro-economics. The saving and investment analysis of Volume II, chapter 3 constituted the keystone, supporting the exclusion or denial of hoarding, the condemnation of luxury expenditure, and the emphasis on the unconditional beneficence of frugality, doctrines which broke fundamentally not simply with the ideas of 'mercantilists', but, at vital points, with those of Boisguilbert, Mandeville, Hume, Steuart and Quesnay. These doctrines on saving and hoarding fitted logically with Smith's treatment of money. Assuming a certain institutional framework—not very easily defined, set up, or maintained, via the political process—Smith went on to expound a policy of monetary, or macro-economic *laissez-faire*, including what came to be the Ricardo (or 'Treasury') view regarding public investment. There had, moreover, been only a few intimations previously of the new, unconditionally pro-saving model in the writings of one or two of Smith's predecessors—as for example, in Francis Hutcheson's notable denunciation of Mandeville's eulogy of luxury spending—until, of course, the statement of the saving-is-investing analysis in Turgot's *Réflexions*. [23]

We noted the flexibility and qualifications with which Smith applied his 'simple system' in the fields of micro-economics and international trade. His macro-economics, on the other hand, was the one major area where he applied this 'system' without sufficient regard to qualifications and exceptions, or to the necessary conditions, which very much needed specifying, with regard to the monetary and banking framework.

First, there was Smith's bald, unqualified assertion about saving and investing that: 'what is annually saved is as regularly consumed as what is annually spent, and nearly in the same time too.'

Consequently: 'Every prodigal appears to be a public enemy, and every frugal man a public benefactor' (1976a, 337–40).

Secondly, there was Smith's treatment of the money supply. He seemed at times to suggest that it was simply a crude fallacy of 'the mercantile system' to be concerned about the money supply any more than, say, the wine supply: *laissez-faire* applied equally to wine and money. 'We trust with perfect security that the freedom of trade, without any attention of government, will always supply us with the wine which we have occasion for; and we may trust with equal security that it will always supply us with all the gold and silver which we can afford to purchase or to employ, either in circulating our commodities, or in other uses . . .' (1976a, 435)

At some points it seems that Smith was implying that his 'simple system' of competitive freedom could and would always be so flexible as to adjust satisfactorily to any variations in the money supply. Elsewhere Smith seemed to recognise that a growing economy needed a growing money supply, while pointing out, in the 'Digression on Silver', that the world supply of precious metals, or international liquidity, might be extremely uncertain and unreliable. However, Smith seemed also to assume that, internally, if the quantity of gold and silver was not maintained in a country, then paper money would automatically be created to the appropriate amount, without giving rise to any serious problems of central regulation: 'Upon every account, therefore, the attention of government never was so unnecessarily employed, as when directed to watch over the preservation or increase of the quantity of money in any country' (1976a, 437).

The foregoing statement appears to suggest that the money supply doesn't matter, and this rather cavalier treatment generated a long-persistent over-optimism, first regarding the intellectual and practical difficulties of devising and implementing, through governments, a satisfactory framework of monetary and banking rules and institutions, and secondly regarding the seriousness of defects in these rules, or in their implementation, for economic stability. With regard to money and macro-economics, Smith did not adequately develop the conditions and qualifications for his simple system which had been suggested by the less 'revolutionary' but more perceptive insights on these subjects of his greatest friend, David Hume, and of his eclipsed rival Sir James Steuart—sometimes referred to as 'the last of the mercantilists'. In an illuminating article Professor Checkland concluded:

> The banking expression of Smith's system of natural liberty was a set of institutions composed of many enterprises, none capable of monopolistic power or even leadership, each guided by prudential rules, and all trading within an environment of law provided by the state. Acting in aggregate they would, Smith implied, provide an optimal money supply or an effective approximation to it. But in the light of banking conditions in the Scotland of Adam Smith's time, not to speak of the years to follow when matters approximated even less to his assumption, his view of banking omitted important aspects of reality which, if properly attended to, might have damaged his view of economic processes.

> (1976, 523; quoted by Hutchison, 1978, 144n)

The two fundamentally contrasting *Inquiries*, Steuart's of 1767 into the principles of political economy, and Smith's of 1776 into the wealth of nations, epitomised the two opposing macro-economic viewpoints and doctrines, 'classical' and 'anti-classical' (or mercantilist-Keynesian) of the ensuing two centuries. If one wishes to sum up the contrast in a single assumption or idea, one can find it in that of smooth, rapid, beneficent self-adjusting tendencies: their denial by one and their assertion by the other. It was this powerfully fascinating idea and assumption of general, beneficent self-adjustment and self-equilibration, not only micro-economic but monetary and macro-economic, which underlay the Smithian-classical orthodoxy. Regarding macro-economics Steuart had, as his editor puts it, 'no very clear model' (Steuart, 1966, Vol. I, lviii). This was just what Smith seemed to offer, micro-economically *and* macro-economically.

Smith's theory of saving, investing and money broke fundamentally with the ideas, not only of Steuart, but with those of Quesnay, Hume, and most of the writers of our period from Petty onwards. Regarding the doctrines of Smith's predecessors, Professor C H Wilson has commented:

> Much thought and policy was devoted to ensuring that a supply of precious metal was maintained adequate for a sound and plentiful currency. The anxiety lest 'a scarcity of coin' should slow down the volume of trade and bring about an economic depression affected writers repeatedly every time a crisis threatened. To Adam Smith such anxieties were absurd. Yet his sense of historical change was not strong and his own chapter on Metallic and Paper Money contained implications which he does not fully consider. If the growth of new methods of payment had been of such significance in the century before 1776, how had Mun and his contemporaries fared without these later devices of paper money, bank credit, etc. whose effects Adam Smith found so beneficial?
>
> (1958, 17)

In other words, while for many or most of Adam Smith's predecessors the money supply, or the dangers of its inadequacy or instability, were serious and pressing problems; Smith, in the *Wealth of Nations* encouraged the idea that money and the money supply did not present any very urgent problems for policy, at any rate no more serious problems than did wine and the wine supply.

Smithian or 'classical' macro-economics were to achieve an extraordinarily long domination. As Schumpeter put it, the Smithian theory.

> . . . proved almost unbelievably hardy. It is doubtful whether Alfred Marshall had advanced beyond it, certain that J S Mill had not . . .
> . . . Secondly, the theory was not only swallowed by the large majority of economists: it was swallowed hook, line and sinker. As if Law—and others—had never existed, one economist after another kept on repeating that only [voluntary] saving was capital creating . . . this came to mean that every decision to save coincides with a corresponding decision to invest so that saving is transformed into [real] capital practically without hitch and as a matter of course.
>
> (1954, 325)[24]

Sir John Hicks, noting the significance of the Smithian revolution in macro-economics, explains its triumph in terms of the power of the self-adjusting model, emphasising its neglect of uncertainty:

> I believe that it is to be explained—that the whole change is to be explained—if we attribute it to the power of a model . . .
> . . . It was because the model paid no attention to plans and expectations that it neglected uncertainty and liquidity; so that the bridge between real theory and monetary theory, of the possibility of which Hume had had some inkling, remained unbuilt. The only monetary theory which could match the static real theory was one which concentrated upon the more mechanical aspects of the monetary system; this is just what the 'classical' Quantity theory was. The responsibility for all this goes back to Adam Smith; it is the reverse side of his great achievement.
>
> (1965, 41)[25]

X

In the preceding sections of this chapter a number of critical judgements have been suggested regarding two of Smith's most fundamental, and relatively novel contributions in the *Wealth of Nations* (so a precautionary restatement of the obvious may be prudent to the effect that Smith's book is, without question, by far the greatest ever written on its subject). Needless to say, many economists (including, almost by definition, the main body of Smith's orthodox English classical successors) over the century following 1776 upheld the main approach of these two fundamental theories, although with modifications at some points, especially in the case of the Smithian theory of value and price. Certainly, after the 1870s, support for Smith's approach to the theory of utility, value and price fell away markedly. Outside its native country, however, this branch of English classical orthodoxy—the labour and/or cost-of-production theory of value—never dominated as it did for near a century on its home ground.

Writing of his achievement in the *Wealth of Nations*, Jacob Viner maintained that 'Smith gave to economics for the first time a definite trend toward a logically consistent synthesis of economic relationships' (1928, 116). Such processes of logically consistent synthesising, together with their accompanying processes of selecting, simplifying, and systematising, sometimes also combined with changes in interest and emphasis, may bring impressive gains in the form of enhanced analytical rigour or persuasive power. Such gains, however, may have to be bought at a significant price in terms of flexibility and breadth of relevance. Furthermore, as Professor Skinner notes, '*The Wealth of Nations* succeeded', because it was 'a publication for the present time', and also 'contained a stirring message' (Smith 1976a, 47). 'A publication for the present time which contained 'a stirring message', while representing 'a logically consistent synthesis' might certainly have had to forego a wide institutional applicability. (Keyne's *General Theory* is another obvious example.)

Moreover, what Viner called the 'definite trend toward a logically consistent synthesis' so powerfully initiated by the *Wealth of Nations* was pushed drastically, in the half-century after 1776, to the extent of excluding or seriously diminishing some of the most important and valuable aspects of the original Smithian synthesis in the *Wealth of Nations*, notably the historical–institutional methodological approach and its rich, mature, political and psychological component.

Regarding the losses involved in what we called 'the Smithian revolution', we concluded, in 1978:

> A 'revolution' in political economy or economics usually or inevitably involves, or consists of some drastically new selection and simplification, *either* with regard to the questions given priority, *or* possibly, with regard to important elements in the answers—or both. In the case of the Smithian revolution, questions and theories, to which economists before and since Smith have attached great importance, were submerged by its triumph, mainly questions and theories regarding employment, interest and money, but, possibly also regarding utility and value. Any intellectual cost-benefit analysis will, of course, inevitably involve subjective valuations. However, in the case of the Smithian 'revolution', . . . there would appear to have been an overwhelming consensus, supported by almost all schools of economists, as to the epoch-making intellectual gains represented by *The Wealth of Nations*.
>
> (Hutchison, 1978, 25)

I do not wish to deny the existence of this overwhelming consensus regarding 'the epoch-making gains represented by *The Wealth of Nations*'. A decade later, I would maintain that the losses and exclusions which ensued after 1776, with the subsequent transformation of the subject and the rise to dominance of English classical orthodoxy, were also immense. These losses need to be considered seriously, since they include a major part of the *gains* established in the pre-1776, pre-classical period which this book has reviewed.

NOTES

1 The chapter on Smith in my book of 1978 was first written as a bicentenary lecture. I do not want to alter the general emphasis of the judgements it contains. As a result, however, of having devoted much of a decade to the study of Smith's predecessors, I feel that a certain shift in the general balance is desirable.

2 See Lapidus (1986, 60ff).

3 For comprehensive accounts of the *Wealth of Nations*, see the general introduction by R H Campbell and A S Skinner to Smith (1976a); also Blaug (1985, Chapter 2), Hollander (1973), O'Brien (1975) and Schumpeter (1954, 181–94).

4 Many writers have recognised that Smith was primarily a social philosopher. For example, James Bonar: 'Adam Smith undoubtedly started with the purpose of giving to the world a complete social philosophy' (1922, 149); A L Macfie: 'He himself would not have regarded his work as primarily economic. For him it was broadly social, fitting into that title the political as well as the psychological and ethical aspects of individuals living in societies' (1967, 13–16); Glen Morrow on the *Wealth of Nations*: 'This an economic work? It is far more than that; it is a history and criticism of all European civilisation . . . a philosophical work' (1928, 157). As J R Lindgren has insisted: 'All who are familiar with Smith's life and writings

recognize that he was a philosopher by profession and that all his writings were conceived and executed as works of philosophy' (1973, ix).

5   See Smith's letter to the Duc de la Rochefoucauld (1895), and both the preliminary advertisement and the closing paragraph of *The Theory of Moral Sentiments* (1976b).

6   See Duncan Forbes (1954, 643–70). Though, as T D Campbell has observed (1971, 80n), the theme of progress is not so prominent in *The Theory of Moral Sentiments*, it is present there to a significant extent.

7   Political Economy Club (1876, 32). Thorold Rogers' successors as economic historians have also laid methodological claim to the *Wealth of Nations*. George Unwin: 'Adam Smith was the first great economic historian, and I do not scruple to add that he is still the greatest. There is scarcely a page of *The Wealth of Nations* where history and theory are sundered from each other' (1908). According to R H Tawny (1932, 39 and 91): 'It is a truism that the central theme of *The Wealth of Nations* is historical.' In his bicentennial tribute H M Robertson suggested that 'the reader himself has to be something of an economic historian fully to appreciate *The Wealth of Nations*, whilst *other economists, who are without a true historical bent, somehow truncate it in their own minds*' (1976, 383, italics added).

8   See H J Bitterman (1940, 504): 'Smith's work is not deductive in the sense that could be applied to, say, the major works of Ricardo and Senior. The bulk of Smith's text consists of descriptive, historical, and statistical data, with a few inferences from "conjectural history".' On the other hand the views of a distinguished dissenter should be recorded: 'Smith's frame of mind was on the whole essentially unhistorical . . . historical narration and inductive reasoning were with him subordinate to a deductive movement of thought' (Ashley, 1900, 310). The answer to Ashley is twofold: (a) whether 'subordinate' or not, the input of historical narration and inductive reasoning is incomparably larger and more important than in any other comprehensive treatment of economic principles by a classical economist; and (b) Smith himself maintained: 'The general maxims of morality are formed, like all other maxims, from experience and induction . . . by induction from experience, we establish those general rules' (*Theory of Moral Sentiments*, 1976b, 319).

9   On 'the man of system', see *Theory of Moral Sentiments* (1976b, 233):

> The man of system . . . is apt to be very wise in his own conceit; and is often so enamoured with the supposed beauty of his own ideal plan of government, that he cannot suffer the smallest deviation from any part of it. He goes on to establish it completely and in all its parts, without any regard either to the great interests, or to the strong prejudices which may oppose it.

10 Smith's readiness to use different methods was not accompanied by any pretentious professional over-confidence regarding results. On the question of quantitative methods, Schumpeter castigated Smith for remarking that he placed 'no great faith in political arithmetic', or in the exactness of its computations: 'It was the inspiring message, the suggestive programme which wilted in the wooden hands of the Scottish professor . . . A Smith took the safe side' (1954, 212). After the considerable over-confidence of 'the quantitative revolution' to be brought about by the methods of econometrics, which took place after Schumpeter was writing, with such marvellous results for economic policies, it may be possible to discern more intellectual merit in the sobering attitude of someone who was ready 'to take the safe side'. Without, however, placing great faith in their estimates, Smith made considerable use of the work of Gregory King and Fleetwood (see 1976a, 534; and Chapter 4 in this volume).

On the other hand, unlike Petty and the quantitative writers of the seventeenth century, and unlike Cantillon, Adam Smith, with his lavish use of the ambiguous adjective 'natural', did not assist the recognition of the vital distinction between the moral and the technical, or between normative and positive.

11 On the methodological revolution of James Mill, Ricardo and Senior, see Chapter 2 of Hutchison (1978).

12 See Viner's essay on 'Adam Smith and *Laissez-Faire*' (1928, 116ff).

13 Smith returned to the comparison with the laws of Solon in the *Wealth of Nations* on the vital controversial questions of the corn laws and the prohibition of wheat exports, when the price had risen to a certain level. Again there is some contrast with the views of Quesnay: 'With all its imperfections . . . we may perhaps say that [this law] though not the best in itself, it is the best which the interests, prejudices and temper of the times would admit of' (1976a, 543). As the editors note regarding this passage, Smith had observed:

> Some general, and even systematical, idea of the perfection of policy and law, may no doubt be necessary for directing the views of the statesman. But to insist upon establishing, and upon establishing all at once, and in spite of all opposition, every thing which that idea may seem to require, must often be the highest degree of arrogance. It is to erect his own judgement into the supreme standard of right and wrong (*Theory of Moral Sentiments*, 1976b, 234).

14 Smith did not employ the concept of *perfect* competition (see Richardson, 1976, 350–60). Smith explicitly took account of the pervasiveness of ignorance, for example with regard to the prime motivator: 'Profit is so very fluctuating, that the person who carries on a particular trade cannot always tell you what is the average of his annual profit' (1976a, 105).

15 'Smith may be understood as a writter who advocated capitalism for the sake of freedom, civil and ecclesiastical' (Cropsey, 1957, 95).

16 The point about Smith is well put by D A Reisman:

> On the one hand, he *appears* to have been a commodity-utilitarian concerned with free trade, economic growth, the ending of restrictive practices and other ways of providing 'a plentiful revenue or subsistence for the people': while on the other hand, he seems to have been determined to prove that higher material standards of living do not, except for the poor, represent a significant change in human happiness (1976, 102).

As Reisman shows, there is no contradiction here.

17 The difference of natural talents in different men, is in reality, much less than we are aware of; and the very different genius which appears to distinguish men of different professions, when grown up to maturity, is not upon many occasions so much the cause, as the effect of the division of labour. The difference between the most dissimilar characters, between a philosopher and a common street porter, for example, seems to arise not so much from nature, as from habit, custom, and education (1976a, 28).

Other writers, such as Tucker and Franklin make differences of natural talents a main reason for specialisation and the division of labour.

18 As Odd Langholm has observed (1979, 144):

> The success of the value theory which was to be developed in the line extending from Montanari through Galiani to the Italian and French economists of the eighteenth centuries is in no small part explained by its emphasis on utility as a psychological experience, playing down considerations of the properties in goods which cause men to desire them, a preoccupation which is sure to take theorists away from the main point.

Langholm remarks that the main medieval source of value theory in Italy was based on Buridan's version of the concept of *indigentia*, which comprised 'every desire which moves us to set store by things'.

19 See Dimitriev (1902, 182), quoted in Chapter 15.

20 According to R L Meek in his history of the subject, 'the most advanced statement of the labour theory of value prior to the publication of *The Wealth of Nations*' (1973, 42) appeared in the anonymous pamphlet by William Pulteney, *Some Thoughts on the Interest of Money in General, and Particularly in the Public Funds. With Reasons for Fixing the same at a lower rate . . .* (1738). Pulteney's statement of the labour theory does not seem to go very significantly further than the *obiter dicta* of Petty, to whom, probably, Pulteney was indebted. William Pulteney, Earl of Bath (1684–1764), an aristocratic Whig politician, was a fluent, prolific, and versatile pamphleteer. His writings on political economy were mainly concerned with problems of the national debt. See the reprint of Pulteney's pamphlet introduced by P D Groenewegen (1982). Another eighteenth-century pamphleteer who mentioned the labour theory of value was W Temple, in his *A Vindication of Commerce and the Arts* (1758). We have previously mentioned Benjamin Franklin's brief statement, which followed Petty very closely.

21 The alleged schism between two main lines of thought on value and price is the theme of Baranzini and Scazzieri (1986). Such a schism could hardly have been claimed to exist before the *Wealth of Nations*. According to R L Meek: 'It cannot be too strongly emphasised that any approach to the problem of the determination of value from the side of utility and demand (as opposed to that of cost and supply) would have been regarded by him [Smith] as quite alien to the general outlook of *The Wealth of Nations*' (1973, 73). From a non-Marxian point of view M L Myers claims that Smith 'will never let go of a labour theory of value' (1983, 117).

22 Though they make their point in rather categorical black-and-white terms, one can understand the conclusions of Schumpeter and De Roover. According to Schumpeter, Smith was 'far below' Galiani on the subject of value and price (1954, 188); while De Roover, the distinguished authority on scholastic economics, concluded: 'The Doctors, especially the members of the school of Salamanca, made one of their main contributions in developing a theory of value, based on utility and scarcity, which is more in line with modern thinking than that of Adam Smith' (1955, 186).

23 See Hutchison (1953b, 52ff; and 1958, 393ff).

24 There have been two forms of the doctrine that 'money doesn't matter': that of modern Keynesian opponents of the quantity theory, and that of Smithian-classical anti-mercantilists. On the latter, see Eagly (1974), who describes the doctrine 'the underlying theme of classical monetary economics'. Eagly also contrasts the monetary analysis of Hume with that of Smith, and maintains that 'Hume's analysis is not that of classical economics', but is 'worked out in an essentially mercantilist theoretical framework' (71).

25 In an earlier paper (of 1929) Schumpeter complained that 'the arguments of the classicals were much too inadequate to be reliable . . . they overshot the target and arrived at propositions which, in their full generality, were hardly more correct than the errors they were opposing' (1985, 229).

CHAPTER SIX

An Adam Smith Renaissance *anno* 1976?
The Bicentenary Output—A Reappraisal of His
Scholarship

Horst Claus Recktenwald

Jnl. of Econ. Lit. March 1978

No other work in economics has ever received more attention on its anniversaries than Adam Smith's the *Wealth of Nations*. Around the globe both academics and 'men of affairs' have celebrated this event in 1976 with numerous contributions in books, articles, lectures, symposia, and even films.

Prima facie, this host of activities might be regarded as rituals or the programmed results of editors, publishers, and media managers. But without the professionals' serious involvement and scientific curiosity (Smith's 'wonder') and without public interest, such anniversary projects are more or less bound to fail.

In the scholars' world, as compared with the sesquicentennial and centennial publications, a kind of Smith *renaissance* seems to be in process. In my view, this new era of Smithian studies has four main features:

(1) There is an emphasis on viewing Smith's work comprehensively, as an integrated *whole*. Celebrants regard Smith primarily as a philosopher in the broad eighteenth-century sense. Wilhelm Hasbach, Emanuel Leser, August Oncken, and Walther Eckstein, all German historical economists, were actually on the right track in denying the existence of 'Das Adam Smith-Problem', the latter being the antinomy or fundamental contradiction between the *Wealth* and *The Theory of Moral Sentiments*. They considered, albeit, inadequately, the ethical, economic, historical, political, and methodological aspects of Smith's *complete* work as a general entity.

(2) There is a presentation and vindication of Smith's purely economic theory in geometric form by such scholars as Paul A Samuelson and Samuel Hollander, who have most recently started to scrutinise strictly Smith's circular flow and growth theories. Thus, they observed the second requirement of Isaac Newton's 'experimental method', which Smith thought applicable to the *Geisteswissenschaften*, too. [1] They have formally confirmed both logical consistency and realism in Smith's work.

(3) There is a special interest in Smith's social and historical system as background for his economic theory. Without knowledge of essential ideas of the *Theory* and the *Lectures*, it is hard to understand what the *Wealth* really means; I venture to say no serious student can avoid relating Smith's economic theory and Smith's policy, at least, to the *Theory*.

(4) Finally, there is a new concern with the role of the state and socio-political institutions in Smith's dual or 'mixed economy'. Previous scholars have attempted (a) to interpret conjecturally Smith's *political* economy and (b) to reconstruct one part of his original, if youthful, plan; that is a theory and history of jurisprudence by reassessing the *Lecture Notes*.

Any attempt to read and survey critically even the scientific publications in and about this anniversary year is virtually an insurmountable task; for the mere number, range, and variety of the topics are encyclopaedic.[2] To organise my reflections after reading a vast literature, I shall concentrate *very* restrictively[3] on seven topics: The new Glasgow edition of Smith's complete works as well as the four central issues mentioned above. I begin this essay with the lasting appeal of Smith's ideas, and I shall close with my reappraisal of his scholarship.

THE 1976 REVIVAL AND THE LASTING RADIATION OF SMITH'S IDEAS

Initially I shall cautiously try to explain that most astonishing phenomenon that a work allegedly 'in many parts obsolete, and in all, imperfect' as John Stuart Mill thought [86, (1848) 1965, p 28]; which according to Joseph Schumpeter [130, 1954, p 184], 'does not contain a single *analytic* idea, principle, or method that was entirely new in 1776', has found such a resonant echo after so much progress, at least change, in the following two centuries both in the sciences concerned and in the economic and social life. Despite the high scholarly standards of modern economics and other social sciences and the change in perspectives (e.g. the Keynesian revolution), nearly all the contributors (even the most critical) in 1976 are significantly impressed by Smith's original performance and its current relevance. What are the reasons for both the remarkable revival of interest and the indestructible vitality of his unique work?

Surely the change in perspective to greater focus on growth and development is an important cause for extending interest, as R D C Black emphasises in his stimulating and scholarly survey [15, 1976, p 62].[4] But even more fundamental for lasting appeal and interest, I am inclined to think, are the following reasons:

(1) The very catholicity of Smith's life work inspires. It contains many (yet uncovered) perspectives and facets and a variety of methods.[5] Works are extremely rare in which logical clarity *and* synthesis are so closely related to patient, accurate, and keen observation of reality and to such depth of historical knowledge. Perhaps this is the key to the maturity of Smith's wisdom and our enduring fascination with his ideas.

(2) His subject matter is timeless, even biblical; man's activity in society is analysed from different standpoints and generally the results are integrated.

(3) The self-interest and not selfishness is the very foundation of his edifice of thought; it is the important driving force in *real* life, ethically positive and of social benefit under definite conditions. Self-interest is a matter of empirical observation and not of ideology or abstraction.

(4) Smith's goal seems to be congruent with the perennial tasks of economics, namely, to seek (a) *causes* ('the natural course of things'), (b) *order* ('of things which necessity imposes in general') in man's persistent drive for bettering his own condition in the community, and (c) *principles* or policies to protect or correct man's activity. These correspond to our contemporary notions of positive, normative, and prescriptive economics.[6]

(5) Then, there is Smith's realism; his respect for facts and for men as they are when he undertakes normative judgements.[7] He avers that man's nature remains basically the same in operation as well as in principle. His view of man seems more realistic and comprehensive than the comparable views of David Ricardo, Karl Marx, and modern authors. He preaches neither a higher moral standard nor seeks, in John Stuart Mill's manner, to realise it, as Milton Friedman points out [37, 1977, p 31]. Most men will find Smith's pattern of moral values congenial.

(6) His great capacity for model-building by systematic thinking and synthesising is most impressive, and it may be attractive and fruitful to modern scholars when they attempt to integrate or merely survey the results of the highly refined division of labour even for small areas of economics.

(7) A final reason is his personal integrity and his fresh yet disciplined style, the outcome of patience, painful diligence, and self-command.[8]

THE 1976 GLASGOW MEMORIAL TO SMITH—A LANDMARK ITSELF

The new Glasgow edition of Adam Smith's *Works and Correspondence* is indispensable equipment for scholars with different interests in various fields. It stimulates and makes integrative or interdisciplinary studies more feasible. This new edition, the outstanding and most valuable tribute of a sensitive and critical generation to the world-wide celebrations, is a landmark itself. Certainly it bridges an apparent gap and is comparable to the complete editions of other English Classics, e.g. that of *The Collected Writings of John Maynard Keynes* (edited by The Royal Economic Society) [69, 1971-3] or of Piero Sraffa's *The Works and Correspondence of David Ricardo* [115, 1951-73].

Indeed, this solid Glasgow publication (three of nine volumes are yet to be published) eclipses comparable editions and sets new scholarly standards. Its sumptuous format and fine printing would have surely pleased Smith himself ('I am a beau in nothing but my books' [107, John Rae, [1895] 1965, p 329]) or Keynes, who both admired fine editions. yet, it is the content and method that really matter more, and this Glasgow edition deserves the praise and thanks from all scholars.

Edwin Cannan's famous *Wealth* edition [139], *the* reference book since 1904, was pathbreaking in method, thoroughness, and competence, although its tone is sometimes censorious and patronising.[9] Cannan's work has been excelled by far by R H Campbell's, Andrew S Skinner's and W B Todd's new two volumes edition [145, 1976], though the latter has benefited from the former; they have retained Cannan's original index.

Todd has painstakingly established the text and avoided distortions of historical evidence. Well argued, the third and not, as might be expected, the fifth edition (the last published in Smith's lifetime) serves as the template. Forty-nine copies in seven libraries have been carefully collated and integrated with a reference code. There is more. As an example of the technical care, duplicate copies in each library were compared to confirm the textual congruence *within* each edition.

Most helpful for the average reader are the annotations and the critical apparatus providing (a) all the variations of six editions; (b) the numbering of paragraphs, as in the Biblical exegesis; (c) a comprehensive system of cross references to passages within the *Wealth* and to Smith's other writings, including the (as yet unpublished) Lecture Notes [149, forth; 150, forth] and *Correspondence* [147, 1977]; (d) Smith's own references or sources; and (e) comments and notes on historical facts for the benefit of contemporary readers. Useful, and particularly time-saving is the 'Table of Corresponding Passages', referring to Cannan's 1930 and (the widely used and inexpensive) 1937 editions.

Readers not familiar with the *Wealth* may initially have some difficulty with this technical apparatus. They may also miss the titles of chapters and parts at the top of the page. Others, more knowledgeable about Smith, might want still more annotation and quotation, especially after Book II. On the whole, however, the editors' pains result in a well-balanced work, fully reflecting the development of new scholarly standards for our generation. Indeed, this is likely to be the classic edition, at least for the near future.

D D Raphael's and A L Macfie's new edition of the *Theory of Moral Sentiments* is of comparable calibre [146, 1976]. Amazingly it is the first scholarly edition in English (although not in German) that systematically notes and analyses all variations through the sixth edition. It owes much, as the editors acknowledge, to Walther Eckstein's famous 1926 German translation and his competent and textual criticism in the commentary [140, 1926]. Although drawing on Eckstein's introduction and notes (just as the new *Wealth* edition draws on Cannan's work), the Raphael-Macfie standard edition goes well beyond Eckstein with regard to the Stoics' and David Hume's influence on the evolution and reception of the *Theory*. Evidently the textual notes and cross references are more numerous than those in Eckstein's edition. However, in some cases, Eckstein discusses the sources at greater length, even if more speculatively.

The new *Theory* deals at length with an old question. Could Smith have altered his religious faith at the end of his life? As in Eckstein's introduction [140, 1926, pp xlv–l], the Raphael-Macfie Appendix II interprets new passages, such as the suppressed paragraph in the sixth edition (about the doctrine of divine reward and punishment in an afterlife), as an indication that 'Smith does not now give unqualified support to the doctrine as preached by Christians' [146, 1976, p 400]. They further state: 'Certainly Smith never abandoned *natural* religion' [146, 1976, p 400]. [10]

There are no modern publications on Smith's life as yet. His main biographers remain Dugald Stewart, John Rae, and William R Scott. One might well wonder how Ian S Ross's announced *Life of Adam Smith* [123, forth] will biographically utilise or exploit the correspondence, the scattered new information since Scott's work was done, and the evolution of thinking about the relation of the *Theory* and *Wealth* to the Lecture Notes and the other works. Students of Smith's writings will be interested in how the new *Life of Adam Smith* [123, Ross, forth] and E C Mossner's and I S Ross's *Correspondence* [147, 1977] will contribute to an understanding of dubious sources[11] of biographical statements and anecdotes and to the clarification of certain puzzles and uncertainties in Smith's *curriculum vitae* and works. For example, consider his influence on politics as a professional 'adviser', or Smith's studies at the University of Oxford (July 1740 till August 1746) and his later activities as a 'post-graduate' at Kirkcaldy in the light of his spectacular rise to an admired lecturer at Edinburgh and a professor at a youthful age in Glasgow. What about Schumpeter's[12] dictum, that the life-long *bachelor's* understanding of human nature lacked some experience in life? Perhaps such questions and other intriguing ones can never be answered because important materials were destroyed by heirs, a point made and deplored by Black, Hutton, and Viner.[13] It seems certain that Smith's letters will hardly constitute a basis for the self-portrayal of an economist in the making as Léon Walras's correspondence[14] did because the contents of most of his available letters are already known, the rest, alas, being destroyed.

Collected and documented in one place [112, Recktenwald, 1976] for the first time are the portraits by James Tassie and John Kay, pictures of all etchings, gravures, paintings, busts, coins, some letter facsimiles, and other materials (including portraits of his mother, the Duke of Buccleuch, Smith's ancestors, Smith's contemporaries and successors).[15]

Viewing Smith's Lifework and Methods as a Whole

In his famous letter (*Correspondence* No 248) to the Duke of Rochefoucauld in 1785, Smith notes that he had 'two other great works upon the anvil; the one a sort of Philosophical History of all the different branches of Literature, of Philosophy, Poetry, and Eloquence; the other is a sort of theory and History of Law and Government. The materials of both are in a great measure collected, and some part of both is put into tolerable good order' [147, 1977, pp 286-7].

A mere torso, 'crystallised fragments', of the first work, although as wide-ranging (less aesthetic but more 'scientific') as Herder's, Spengler's, or Toynbee's histories of human culture, was posthumously published by Black and Hutton in 1795 as *Essays on Philosophical Subjects* [148, forth].

The second part of this youthful 'design', no less ambitious, which had been announced in the first edition of the *Theory* and mentioned again thirty years later in the sixth, actually was partially included as 'History of Law and Government' in the *Wealth* (Books III and V) and in the *Lectures on*

Jurisprudence. The *theoretical* core of 'this great work', involving the rules of justice and (other) rules of morality, seems to have been projected as a critical discussion and confluence of two controversial schools of thoughts: Montesquieu's ideas in his *De l'ésprit des lois* [88, 1748] and the Samuel Pufendorf [106, 1759] and Hugo Grotius [42, 1625] views on natural law. The critical analysis and synthesis was an immense mental task and no less daring and difficult than the one Smith had so successfully executed in his ethical theory, where he discussed and combined *opposing* ideas advanced by ancient philosophers and especially by the exponents of the Scottish Enlightenment into a single coherent system. (see page 121).

Smith himself regarded the different facets of his (unfinished) lifework as comprising a single system. Thus, to understand adequately his main doctrines an accurate grasp of (1) Smith's *methods of inquiry* and (2) the *common* features of his systems of thought is an essential prerequisite for all scholars.

(1) *Methods of Inquiry*. Viner's view that Smith's methodology was basically eclectic has dominated the literature until recently. New studies by H J Bittermann [14, 1940], Overton H Taylor [159, 1960], Herbert F Thompson [161, 1965], Thomas D Campbell [25, 1971], J Ralph Lindgren [73, 1973], Samuel Hollander [56, 1976], and Andrew S Skinner [134, 1974; 135, 1974; 136, 1976], oppose Viner's view and offer a more precise interpretation by carefully considering Smith's *complete* work. The conclusions remain controversial but, as such, offer the basis for further research.

We find the key to understanding Smith's methods, as used in his study of the 'social sciences' (the world of human actions), in his fragmentary *Essays*, especially in his essay on the *History of Astronomy* [148, forth] and in his *Lectures on Rhetoric* [149, forth] where he examines the motives and principles which 'lead and direct' philosophic enquiries (a question in which great thinkers from Aristotle to Einstein were so much interested). His technique to identify the natural system or order was to discover inductively and deductively, by the 'experimental method', a few basic and plausible 'principles', accounting for observed 'appearances'. Smith calls the way of thinking 'the Newtonian method,'[16] which he considered appropriate for 'Moral and Natural Philosophy'.

There is little explicit evidence in Smith's text as to how he actually applies Newton's method. As I understand Smith's methodological *practice*, not his intention, he explains verbally how a few basic and plausible principles are connected in a 'chain', thus building up a system or a Kuhnian paradigm. yet, contrary to Newton (and most modern writers), he does not use *mathematical* analysis (a) to deduce the implications[17] of his initial generalisations, which were inductively arrived at. But evidently Smith meets the two other requirements of the Newtonian method:[18] namely, (b) to determine a principle through *observation* (not through *experiment* as in the *Naturwissenschaften*[19]) and (c) to test empirically the explanation. Obviously Smith's empirical standards of confirmation or refutation frequently do not measure up to modern ones, yet his reference to historical and contemporary facts and his critical empiricism remain impressive.

Most astonishing, however, may be the positive results of some scholars, who recently employed current refined techniques to formalise (1) Smith's economic system (e.g. Paul A Samuelson [129, 1977], Samuel Hollander [56, 1976]; (2) his growth model (e.g. Haim Barkai [11, 1969], William O Thweatt [162, 1957], W A Eltis [34, 1975], and Ralph Anspach [6, 1976]; and (3) his labour value theory (e.g. Heinz D Durz [70, 1976]). Finding no or minor inconsistencies, they seem to confirm Jevons's view that Adam Smith was 'very wise. . . to expound his *mathematical* theory (for I hold that his reasoning was really mathematical[20] in nature) in conjunction with concrete applications and historical illustrations'[21] (italics added).

So Samuelson [129, 1977, pp 42–4], with careful reading, infers in the *Wealth* a complete and valuable theoretical model. Using mathematical methods like duality–theory and Leontief-Sraffa modelling and using Smithian functions never before written down explicitly, he finds that: (a) Smith's value-added accounting is valid and does not involve vicious circle reasoning (as Marx holds); (b) Smith's pluralistic supply-and-demand analysis in terms of all three components of wages, rents and profits is correct and not trivial or tautological; it anticipates general equilibrium modelling; and (c) his vision of transient growth from invention and capital accumulation (allowing for the stages in Smith's theory) is isomorphic with Ricardo's, Malthus's, and Marx's models some parts of Smith's model being more realistic.

Hats off to Adam Smith, the theorist—such is Samuelson's verdict. It is in a sharp contrast with the more widespread supercilious discounting of Smith's analytical abilities.

In addition, Hollander's pathbreaking and critical analysis in large measure tends to confirm Boulding's observation that 'The whole Walrasian, Marshallian, and Hicksian price theory . . . is clearly implicit in Adam Smith's concept of natural price. . . . Similarly, in the theory of economic development, one sometimes doubts whether all the modern refinements and mathematical models are much more than talmudic exercises on the fundamental insight of Adam Smith, regarding the division of labour, . . . the impact of accumulation, and the effects of rising knowledge' [18, 1971, p 229].

This methodological discussion offers new perspectives and could encourage further comparative studies using modern techniques to attempt ambitiously an integration of Smith's other subsystems. There is, however, a *caveat*. Surely Smith would not have been willing to accept a strictly rational test of consistency. Smith was ever cognisant of the shortcomings of applying *exclusively* a rational criterion of truth. I do not refer to his well-known skepticism related to 'political arithemetick',[22] but to his distrust (by no means a refusal) of pure reason or logic as used by *man* to explain *man*. (Smith's attitude was similar to Aquinas's.[23])

Another aspect of this *caveat* comes from economists who doubt the usefulness of refined and elegant models for explaining reality reasonably. I shall deal with this problem more concretely later. Obviously having a high degree of abstraction can guarantee logical consistency, but may cost a grasp of *all* essentials of reality (factors and movements) that ought to be explained. Commonly an excessively logical or rationalistic mind has a narcissistic trait,[24] which may become dangerously unrealistic *if* not controlled by a keen sense of facts and precise and extensive human experience. A recent analysis[25] based on interviews with economic advisers may illustrate the highly limited applicability of *some* modern model results.

From the latter perspective, I think we should proceed by using the principles of formal thought: to apply both popular modern techniques to the other parts of Smithian system and other, if older, tools of reason. Thus I consider Adolph Lowe's [75, 1975] and Joseph J Spengler's [151, 1959] brilliant expositions of Smith's growth paradigms as characteristically Smithian in tenor and logic and a valuable counterbalance to Hollander's, Samuelson's Barkai's, and Eltis's analyses.[26]

Campbell's and Skinner's 'General Introduction' [145, 1976, pp 50–60] provides a remarkable contribution to a better understanding of Smith's methods as a *historical* scholar. It confirms Smith's impressive achievement both as an orthodox historian and a philosopher of history. Smith was a practitioner of the principles of the '*histoire rasonnée*' (conjectural history). I find the discussion of Smith's methodological failures and errors of great interest in my re-evaluating and revising old and new charges of discordances, puzzles, and value-judgements. Therefore, I shall deal briefly with this subject.[27]

Occasionally when quoting from memory, Smith misattributed ideas (*cf.* Eckstein [140, *Wealth*, 1926, pp 284, 583]; *Theory* [146, 1976, p 11]; *Wealth* [145, 1976, Introduction, p 52]), or his use of authorities may be inaccurate. At times he neglects to quote the source, even unconsciously repeating phrases from his own or other writings. Viewed pedantically and perhaps unfairly compared with later criteria of transcription, such carelessness can be made to appear as a substantial fault or even plagiarism, a charge sometimes raised in the literature. But compared to Smith's mental power, his grandiose concept, and his own intellectual indebtedness, this charge seems to me to be merely 'beckmesserisch' (nit-picking).

More serious are such Smithian errors, as 'not unique among historians, of failing to distinguish between the intention' of a statute and its implementation, and of 'read[ing] into a source more serious evidence in support of a proposition' than was appropriate [145, *Wealth,* 1976, Introduction, pp 53–4]. These and the other defects mainly appear in his attacks on mercantilism, political interventions, or the 'corporate' or monopolistic 'spirit'. His value judgements, often shrewd, become apparent. He converts his scholarly chair into a throne of judgement for 'bestowed praise and blame' [130, Schumpeter, 1954, p 185], or in his own rhetoric: The 'heated' *emotio* comes to dominate for a moment the 'cool' *ratio*.

Yet considered rightly, such historical speculations and defects rarely touch the core of his analytical argument.[28]

Lastly I draw attention to two truly original contributions. The first is his concept of sympathy and the impartial spectator (see *Theory* [146, 1976, pp 82–97]; Raphael's introduction [146, 1976, pp 1–32]; Campbell [25, 1971, pp 94–103; 127–61]), which is a method for synthesising or reconciling individual judgements in concrete situations. Sympathy explains man's faculty of socialisation and is based on both subrational sentiments (located between reason and the elementary instincts) and the ideal and real spectator, the latter being a personification of the conscience.[29] Both are moral judgements of right and wrong according to the *reactions* of gratitude and resentment to benefit and harm, respectively, under full or restricted information. Luigi Bagolini [9, 1975, pp 100–13] believes Smith's sympathetic concept continues to be relevant for judicial evaluation as an original integration of rational and emotional elements. John Rawls [108, 1972] compares his 'justice as fairness' concept with Smith's approach.[30] Rawls holds that Smith's idea of the impartial spectator presupposes excessive benevolence; by contrast, Campbell concludes that it contains excessive self-interest.

The simplicity of Smith's second original idea equals its importance. Smith analyses the permanent process of opposing and contending forces toward and away from a balance or equilibrium within the individual *and* in society. Using this idea, he seeks to explain obstructions ('irregularities') and conflicts.[31] The elements of his concept are motives, means, and ends in man's pursuit of (a) 'necessaries', (b) (imagined) 'conveniences' of life, and (c) status ('respect of our equals, our credit and rank in the society we live in', i.e. in modern terms, his welfare function) [146, *Theory*, 1976, p 212]. His criteria for judgement are propriety and utility (in the sense of usefulness, rather than desirability), which are occasionally compatible as, for example, in his prudent or frugal man (as public benefactor).

My concluding thought on Smith's methods of inquiry is a reference to Denis P O'Brien's [100, 1976, pp 133–50] perceptive attempt to understand Smith's lasting influences on *economics* in the light of Popper's, Kuhn's, and Lakatos's theories of science. O'Brien justifies the Lakatosian Research Programme method as the best means of explanation.

(2) *Common Features of Smith's Systems.* As to *scope* and *content* of Smith's lifework, there are two characteristic lines taken in recent research. The first elucidates and delineates the subsystems scattered through his works, and the second searches for common traits and central interdependencies of essential parts. Yet, it may be possible with this approach to correct or confirm propositions of former studies (see J Ralph Lindgren [73, 1973] and E G West [172, 1977]) or to discover new and surprising perspectives (see R L Heilbroner [50, 1976], Nathan Rosenberg [122, 1976] and G J Stigler [157, 1976]) and errors. Such systematic work may also bring piecemeal interpretations, new or old, into sharper relief and focus.

Man's activity in society is the *common* subject of Smith's four major writings on (psychological) ethics, economics, jurisprudence, and history. And, these four aspects of his central theme seem closely connected.

Smith's *economic* system, consisting in a more modern sense of a static or 'circular flow' model, and a dynamic or growth analysis, may be regarded as linked to both the *historical* system in so far as it is based on the 'commercial society' and the exchange economy (the fourth stage of his development theory). It is also linked to the *ethical* system because it is grounded in his view of man laid down in the *Theory*. In the *Theory* he explains how the self-interested individual may control his passions and actions, among them his self-love, and how he finds necessary standards of conduct for building a society. Since these may not be sufficient to secure a minimum of justice, some kind of magistracy becomes necessary to enforce compliance with laws through coercive and punitive action. In his unfinished system, the fragmentary history of *jurisprudence*, Smith explains the connection of the organisation of law and government with political and social changes in his theory of economic development and with his ethical concepts *via* moral rules.

Campbell and Skinner elucidate further common features apparent in the branches of his general system of thought [145, 1976, p 4]: The typical hypotheses that (a) the principles of human nature are invariant, (b) 'social outcomes' are 'unintended', and (c) manners and institutions may change through time and vary in different communities at the same point in time.

Thus, these four elements or branches of his general system seem well established and integrated.[32] They build up Smith's contribution to the social sciences in a modern sense.

Let me round off my reflections on this topic. As far as I see, many errors and enigmas said to flaw Smith's work come under five headings: (1) a failure to see his works as a unitary whole, (2) an unfortunate mixing of parts of his models in his different works[33] and, as a corollary, a deliberate and unjustified shifting from one subsystem to another,[34] (3) a lacuna associated with the unfinished 'theory and history of law and government', (4) an excessive stress by his critics on historical illustrations and ingenious or curious value judgements (commonly unimportant for his argument or overstated by isolating), and (5) the anachronistic habit of interpreting his words and ideas in the light of later insights, and experience, or of methods Smith would not have accepted.

Furthermore, many caricatures[35] and *clichés*, alleged errors, or silly criticisms (Smith as the prototype of Manchester liberalism or as an advocate of 'bourgeois economics' and of selfish materialism, who deals inadequately with ethical values) are all popular in literature and textbooks (for two centuries the object of moralists' mockery). They stem from careless thinking, impatient reading, prejudice, or oversimplification.

CURRENT CORRECTIONS OF PAST MISUNDERSTANDINGS

It is now conventional wisdom[36] that the so-called 'Adam Smith Problem', the conflict between his perception of the many-faceted human personality in the *Theory* and the economic man in the *Wealth*, is *passé*. It was a pseudoproblem [37] based possibly on ignorance and surely on misunderstanding of the terms 'sympathy' and 'self-interest.' Raphael and Macfie refute convincingly, and vivaciously, Buckle's[38] and Skarzynski's contrary arguments in their introduction to the *Theory* [146, 1976, pp 20–25]. On the other side, there appears to be a new trend in the bicentennial literature treating the *Wealth* and the *Theory* as complementary. Further, some scholars start by analysing parts of Smith's economic theory in the light of his comprehensive social and historical views. They open new perspectives of much interest. A few instances will serve as evidence.

Meek's and Skinner's account of the evolution of the division of labour principle [84, 1973] and another of Meek's analyses [83, 1976] threw new light on Smith's *Lectures on Jurisprudence*.[39] Skinner's paper [136, 1976] on the development of Smith's economic system as a Kuhnian paradigm in the Glasgow edition is a further example. All three analyses are stimulating and extremely precise.

Wilson explores the ways in which sympathy or fellow-feeling, which *may* lead to sacrificing personal advantage, can imply interdependence in utility function within and outside Paretian welfare economics [173, 1976, pp 73-99].[40] He argues 'that moral judgements derived from sympathy can provide a basis not only for the welfare state, but also a firm foundation for consumers' sovereignty and, more generally, for a wide measure of freedom in the conduct of economic affairs' [173, 1976, p 77]. Wilson's contribution, as stimulating as it is speculative, concludes by considering the links between sympathy and permissiveness (the modern term for individualism).

Smith's analysis of the labour market is typical of his contribution to economics and is consistent *and* integrated into his social system. Smith identifies the long-run influence of market forces and the growth of supply (population) and demand (income and capital) on both the aggregate wage rate *and* the wage structure. He records the interplay of supply and demand as 'tendencies', often interrupted by obstruction and a good deal of conflict. And he introduces his sociological insights from the *Theory*, particularly his realistic view of human nature, by *extensive qualification* of these rigidities by means of custom and status, training and education, and bargaining power. Occasionally we find some irrelevant value judgements with hortatory asides. Yet as E H Phelps Brown [104, 1976, p 251] and L C Hunter [59, 1976, p 260] argue, Smith provides an analytic framework and a skeleton map of the labour market area, which remains today as 'an instructive guide to our own world of labour' [104, Phelps Brown, 1976, p 251], although inevitably altered in detail and illustrations.

A further example for such integrative studies is Heilbroner's [49, 1975] account of Smith's socioeconomic system and his historical scheme. Heilbroner believes he has detected 'a dark side', a new 'Paradox of Progress', 'the disconcerting prognosis of an evolutionary trend in which both [material] decline and [moral] decay attend' [49, 1975, p 524]—a very pessimistic prospect. His interpretation contrasts with Eltis's [34, 1975, pp 426-54] and West's [169, 1969, pp 1-23; 170, 1975, pp 540-52] more optimistic essays on growth and alienation. Again, the latter topic undergoing currently a perennial rediscovery, has become inexplicably 'modish'.

Coat's careful interpretation[41] of 'Adam Smith and the Mercantile System' [28, 1975, pp 218-36] is an example of disentangling the combination of Smith's subtle analysis, historical insight, and policy prescriptions. These closely inter-woven strands of thought we find also in some other parts of Smith's works. Coat's article opens interesting perspectives regarding Smith's theory of history and politics and Smith's view of economic development.[42]

Another example of this central topic of contemporary writers is a reappraisal of the market as an important, misunderstood, and inadequately appreciated *social* mechanism. These analyses draw attention to the pursuit of self-interest in the light of *communication, co-ordination,* and *control*; they suggest implications for production and exchange; and other scholars deal similarly with the institutions of competition and monopoly. Nicholas Kaldor's[43] and G B Richardson's [116, 1975, p 356] provocative arguments that Smith's conception of competition depends on increasing returns and there through leads to specialisation and inter-dependence rather than to market concentration or a 'world of monopolies' (Joan Robinson) are most striking. Later writers have apparently formalised and corrected deficiencies in Smith's vision of competition,[44] by employing increased analytical rigour and elegant techniques; but they have done so at the cost of ignoring the process (Smith's 'tendency') towards, as well as away from, equilibrium and have overlooked Smith's belief in the evolutionary function of competition (an impetus to structural and technological change). The concept '*Schlafmützen-wettbewerb*' (sluggish competition) in our static market theory, as a necessary requisite to demonstrating the minimum conditions for optimal resource allocation, has replaced, at very high opportunity costs,[45] Smith's and Schumpeter's dynamic competition, which depends on new brands and techniques. Smith's market equilibrium is continually threatened by free entry and substitutes. Even far more it is menaced with autonomous changes in technique, tastes, and newly discovered opportunities for the division of labour, while uncertainty is intensified by millions of spontaneous decisions in a free society (see Friedrich A Hayek [48, 1948]).

On the other side, monopoly—born of the 'corporation spirit'—seemed to Smith to be 'a simple injustice, resulting from a combination of human selfishness, unequal distribution of economic power, and inadequate legal restraints' [28, Coats, 1975, pp 233–4] (see also Terence W Hutchison [61, 1976, p 527]) and was not to be measured exclusively by the rate of monopolistic profit.

The general trend in the arguments of these commentators is to suggest that the inclusion of other motives and elements in the analysis even strengthens Smith's own and others' arguments for his economic system.[46] Apparently, Smith believed that the analysis of the appropriate institutional framework of the functioning of the market is a proper subject worthy of economists' systematic studies.[47]

THE ROLE OF THE STATE AND INSTITUTIONS IN SMITH'S MIXED ECONOMY

A significant and comprehensive reassessment of Smith's *political* economy, from a historical as well as a modern standpoint, characterises recent scholarly efforts. There are renewed attempts to reconstruct and interpret his system of jurisprudence, only *partly* completed in his *Wealth* and the Lecture Notes.[48] Smith himself refers to his political economy in the most general terms as the 'natural system of perfect liberty and justice' [145, *Wealth*, 1976, p 606] or 'the liberal plan of equality, liberty, and justice' [145, p 664].

The *Wealth* has until now rarely been considered to be *essentially* related to any justice[49] guaranteed by 'the public magistrate'. Is a new 'Adam Smith Problem' now being created at a time when the welfare state (or the widely recovered enlightenment in the 'great body of people') is a popular mode? What about the conflict between liberty and justice (instead of self-interest versus sympathy) or an antinomy between his economics (utility) and jurisprudence (propriety)?

Yet many bicentennial celebrants are apparently more interested in Smith's practical concern with the role of the state, particularly in our 'mixed economy'. One group of distinguished economists dealt extensively (at the 1976 Glasgow Conference) with the respective functions of the market and the state. Both Alec Cairncross [24, 1976] and Thomas Wilson [173, 1976] paint an impressive picture of Smith's contribution to our understanding of this crucial and eternal problem in our world where nearly one-third of the goods and services are publicly provisioned (although not as yet publicly produced).

While in Walras's analytic construct and in neoclassical models the state is ignored, Lindahl, Musgrave, and Samuelson integrate government activity in a dual economy analysis, formally and most elegantly, nonetheless, the fundamental weakness of such integration for practical purposes is evident. By way of contrast, Keynesian and monetarists' models deal too one-sidedly with the stabilisation function and neglect the efficiency and equity aspects essential to the role of the state. No wonder then that many scholars are returning to Smith with a fresh interest in both his economic *and* political insights.

Smith's definition of political economy seems *prima facie* to be ambiguous, if not misleading. The *narrow* coverage of his definition found in the introduction to the fourth Book is: 'Political Economy, considered as a branch of the science of a statesman or legislator, proposes two distinct objects; first, to provide a plentiful revenue or subsistence for the people, or more properly to enable them to provide such a revenue or subsistence for themselves; and secondly, to supply the state or commonwealth with a revenue sufficient for the publick services. It proposes to enrich both the people and the sovereign' [145, *Wealth,* 1976, p 428].

This notion emphasises the link to his natural jurisprudence and considers political economy as one of many branches of the system of civil government [145, *Wealth,* 1976, p 679; 146, *Theory,* 1976, pp 340–2]. We find unexpectedly the *wide* scope of another definition at the end of the fourth Book, where Smith, while discussing Quesnay's system, explains 'what is properly called Political economy' is the analysis of 'the nature and the causes of the wealth of nations' [145, *Wealth,* 1976, pp 678–9]. Readers acquainted with Smith's major works may easily discover in *both* definitions of 'economics' (to use Marshall's term) the three components plain to everybody in his *Wealth*: (a) the purely analytic part of the explanation of how economic systems work (how people 'provide such revenue'); (b) an economic policy ('to enable' people 'to provide such revenue or subsistence for themselves'); and (c) the provision and financing of 'public services'.

Walras mistakenly thought, as William Jaffé notes [62, 1977, pp 23–4] that part (b) (the applied economics) made up the whole of Smith's political economy. By the way, Schumpeter's interpretation is also wrong.[50] Other authors, like Lord Robbins [118, 1976, pp 2–3], also restrict the use of the term political economy to part (b), that is to prescriptions or public policy in the economic field. In recent years it has become customary to use the notion 'political economy' or 'public economics' to designate a mixture of all three elements including pure analysis and policy prescription in part (b) and part (c) (the traditional public finance sector). These writers generally recognise the scarcity of resources available for public objectives by often using a sort of cost-benefit analysis. Others using this term emphasise the institution or the process of political decision. Thus, expressions like the political economy of education, theatres, trade interventions, regulations, or fees are now common in the literature.

From the vast literature on Smith's thoughts on *specific topics relating to state actities*, I can select only a few examples. Although Smith obviously advocates limited government, he assigns definite functions to the state. Both the scope and kind of public goods and services varies widely with the state of economic development and sometimes with remarkable time lags.[51] They also depend greatly on the efficiency of their provision and financing. Smith also delineates and combines the respective roles of the government and the market.

Alan Peacock [102, 1975] and others argue that the shortcomings of modern positive economics in the field of public finance justify a reappraisal of Smith's ideas, particularly the public service function of government. Musgrave investigates thoroughly [94, 1976] the normative and positive aspects of redistribution via the state by referring both to the *Theory* and the *Wealth*— no small task. His solutions contrast with Wilson's. Milton Friedman [38, 1976] discusses Smith's views on external effects (transaction costs) and on economic federalism, while James Buchanan [20, 1976, pp 271–86] and others expound on the state failures as compared with market failures and on elements of the method of cost-benefit analysis in Smith's work.

Smith apparently neglected the implications of public activities for political organisation. He did not present explicitly a coherent analysis of political behaviour or public choice, although he dealt with constitutional structure (see West [171, 1976]), basic laws, and the principles of how institutions should organise and finance public goods. He did emphasise the problem of equity versus efficiency.

The criticism of contemporary and historical institutions running through nearly all Smith's works involves a *host* of interesting elements for those seeking to develop a long overdue theory of state failures (see Recktenwald [112, 1976, p 136]). I shall mention only his contention that wherever feasible we should (a) take account of the self-interested nature of man when we set the pay for an administrator, judge, or teacher, to avoid a conflict between his own interest and the general good and (b) link both the beneficiary and financier of a public service;[52] if we aim at efficient performance in case (a) above and an optimal provision in case (b).[53] Given human nature as it is, any system as a social institution (the market *and* the state) that has to work efficiently and justly must have built-in sufficient incentives and disincentives, i.e. rewards for success and penalties for failure. In Smith's words, public services are never better performed than when they are rewarded in relation to performance. The lack of such awarding and punitive mechanisms is the decisive reason for waste and injustice; therefore, it is a strong element of any new theory of state failures.

In the world of public administration, Smith's four important *controls* (see below) on man's self-interested quest to improve his pecuniary and nonpecuniary position, should be considered from the standpoint that the public agency is itself a *public* monopolist. One wonders how much he has presaged the modern discussion on X-inefficiency and satisfying behaviour in the presence of market power. I select one example only; it is obvious that a strong correlation exists between the (nonpecuniary) self-interest of a bureaucrat and the size of his function, that is, the expenditures of his office; yet, it is still professionally a largely unexplored field.

Smith's skcepticism[54] about public institutions stems from his belief that they can become functionally independent of their origins; that is, the civil 'servant' may become highly isolated from the preferences and aversions of the public service consumer.

Stigler draws attention to Smith's failure to apply his principle of self-interest *systematically* to *political* behaviour [156, 1975, pp 237–46]; Mancur Olson extends the discussion to the problem of organised interests [138, Skinner and Wilson, 1975, pp 111–12], a dilemma in Smith's concept. Smith himself is most skeptical both as to the outcome when politicians, motivated by self-interest or benevolence, decide on public matters as well as to the means of control.

Since decisive misinterpretations, complaisant or malevolent, of Smith's liberal system of political economy are rooted in the fact that the *basic conditions* for its functioning are disregarded (perhaps because they are scattered through his writings), I conclude this section by exploring the *set* of individual, social, and legal controls on man's self-interested feelings and actions. This constitutes also the frame of axioms in Smith's theory of an exchange economy.

Smith, unlike Mandeville, Francis Hutcheson, and many modern moralists, regards self-interested activities as an *ethically* positive driving force, the motor of economic progress. These self-regarding actions are socially beneficial provided that they are controlled by a set of countervailing forces and rules:

(1) The supposed 'spectator' (as conscience) and the real 'spectator' are able to judge impartially the merit or demerit of an action. This concept is based on man's moral faculty of fellow-feeling, his disposition to secure the 'approbation of his brethren' when acquiring the sources of pleasure *and* avoiding pain.

Yet these individual barriers seem to be too weak to restrain self-interest from becoming selfishness because (a) the actual spectator is sometimes not sufficiently informed on the motives and circumstances of an action, (b) the *emotio* ('eagerness of passion') dominates the *ratio* in some actions, and (c) man's self-love is a stronger passion than his fellow-feeling and benevolence.

(2) A further safeguard mechanism for social order against the 'arrogance of self-love' are the general rules of morality, or standards of accepted conduct which are '. . . formed, by finding from experience, that all actions of a certain

kind, or circumstanced in a certain manner, are approved or disapproved of' [146, *Theory,* 1976, p 159].

(3) For Smith, the realist, these sanctions of public disapproval or reward are not strong enough to restrain man: 'In the race for wealth, and honours, and preferments . . .' [146, 1976, p 83] when he violates 'fair play' by inflicting damage on his fellows as competitors. To prevent such violations of justice, a system of positive law is necessary. Injustice generates a feeling of resentment, which naturally condones punishment. And to administer these positive rules of justice and to enforce obedience, the office of a public magistrate with adequate power to punish is created.

(4) The institution of competition as a mechanism in controlling man's self-interested striving for bettering his economic condition *and* his 'place' in society is of critical importance. The actual and potential pressure of rivalry permanently, immediately, and effectively restrains the egoistic conduct within due bounds. It *protects the weak, serves as self-defence* [145, *Wealth,* 1976, p 164], *and punishes at once and effectively.* Since fellow-feeling and beneficence as opposing forces diminish when the scale of 'society' increases from family, friends, and from parish up to the nation and to world communities and the efficacy of the other safeguards becomes weaker in this more impersonal atmosphere, competition becomes the most important restraint. This phenomenon of *distance,* well known to Plato, has been stressed by Viner [166, (1928) 1968], Recktenwald [112, 1976], Wilson [173, 1976, p 80], Anspach [5, 1972, p 196], and Coase [27, 1977]. It seems to be most important for an understanding of Smith's view of institutions, which are less responsive to the moral sentiments.

Given these conditions, in a freely negotiated trade all sides guided by self-interest must benefit; otherwise no exchange would occur. The accepted exchange value is then socially beneficial. Both benefits and trade are the results of man's pursuit of private interest and his propensity to bargain;[55] they are matters of empirical *observation* and not of abstraction or *ideology.* This is the kernel of the idea behind the Invisible Hand and clearly not a myth (J Arrow judged it a 'poetic' metaphor).

Samuelson believes he has identified in his new Smithian economic model a valid element in the Invisible Hand doctrine—a society's production can be efficiently organised by self-interest under conditions of perfect competition. He neglected of course, the possibly inefficient and unjust effects of state activities, e.g. providing and financing public goods [129, 1977, p 47].

A Reappraisal of Smith's Scholarship

To end this *tour d'horizon,* I draw attention to (a) some bright spots on the bicentennial map and (b) to Smith's scholarship.

(a) Articles on Smith's works from Marxian and neo-Marxian writers seem to be excessively orthodox both in method and substance, dealing for the most part with atavisms like Smith's value and wage theory or his views on alienation. Alienation evidently is a phenomenon (like environmental effects) that is *principally* independent of the economic and social order in an industrialised society.[56] There is still a lack of thorough and *undogmatic* studies of Smith's actual influence, especially on the young Marx, including subjects such as the historical (stage) theory or Smith's 'determinism' as against Marx's dialectic in the light of new insights into Smith's complete work.[57] Studies of the relationship between Smith and Keynes may be stimulated by the next two centenaries in 1983, Keynes' birthday and Marx's date of death. For a pioneering analysis, consider Jaffé's careful bicentennial article where he attributes Walras's blindness to the elements he had in common with Smith at least partly to the Frenchman's 'anglophobia' [145, 1976, pp 50-1]. In similar studies Samuelson and Hollander [57, 1977] compare and reappraise critically Smith's impact on Ricardo, Malthus, and Marx. Their original conclusions are contrary to conventional wisdom.

There are yet other empty boxes, more interesting for historians of economic thought: How can we explain Schmoller's peculiar aversion to Smith and the positive influence of Smith's economic, ethical, and political theories on Walther Eucken and the 'Freiburger School' and on Ludwig Erhard's policy foundation, the idea of the 'Soziale Marktwirtschaft'.[58]

(b) Finally, I turn to Smith's scholarship. Each epoch in its own way has tended to view and evaluate anew Smith's scientific performance and, of course, relevance. In the post-Second World War period Smith's image as scholar has been broadly influenced by Schumpeter's often quoted yet unduly generalised dictum, i.e. that the *Wealth* does not contain any entirely new *analytical* idea, principle, or method [130, 1954, p 184].[59] It is only a small step from this verdict *isolated* from its context to the supercilious judgement that Adam Smith as a theorist was unoriginal and that his methods and topics were eclectic, fuzzy or turbid. This extremely skeptical reservation has been further intensified by Keynes' criticism of and neo-Marxian attacks upon *laissez-faire* (a mistaken interpretation of Smith's system) and by a widespread and growing disenchantment with some results of neoclassical theory.

A more sensitive and sensible generation of scholars, reading critically the complete Smith and judging it with modern analytical tools, seems impressed by Smith's realism and his penetrating perception of man's nature. Although he never treated Smith's works as a complete whole, Schumpeter himself, by way of contrast, repeatedly judges Smith's *analytic* achievements as excellent. His various approvals are scattered over his great *History*. For evidence and to correct some false views of Schumpeter's actual appreciation, widely held, I note as an example, one of his statements: '. . . A Smith's political principles and recipes [that is, his system of political economy[60]] . . . are but the cloak of a great *analytic* achievement' [130, 1954, p 38, italics added].[61]

Approximating current assessments of the originality of Smith's performance is Schumpeter's evaluation: '[Smith's] mental stature was up to mastering the unwieldy material that flowed from many sources and to subjecting it, with a strong hand, to the rule of a small number of coherent principles,' as 'a great architect' [130, p 185].[62]

Smith's originality and uniqueness stem from his competency to reconcile and integrate (false) alternatives into a single logical and *realistic* model. [63]

As closing evidence I choose Smith's moral or social system. He thoroughly answers in his *Theory* the two cardinal questions: 'first, wherein does virtue consist?. . . And, secondly, . . . how and by what means does it come to pass, that the mind prefers one tenour of conduct to another?' [146, 1976, p 265].

Then he implicitly tests his results with a critical survey of at least six groups of important theories: the systems of propriety, of prudence, and of benevolence relating to the first question, and the systems of self-love, of reason, and of sentiment concerning the second one. Smith thinks all these systems contain *parts* of the truth. And he modestly adds: 'We may learn from each of them something that is both valuable and peculiar' [146, 1976].

Thus everybody is in a position to test each element in order to see (1) whether if at all, or in what degree Smith borrowed from the ancient philosophers, the scholastic doctors, and his contemporaries and (2) how each principle *changes* its meaning in the reconciling process, thus becoming an integrated part (a *new* element) of Smith's final system, in my view most important, but too often neglected. As a typical test result, I cite Raphael's and Macfie's conclusion: 'Smith rejects or transforms Hume's ideas far more often than he follows them' [146, 1976, p 10]. And we should remember Hume is said to be the main source of influence. Indeed, Smith was neither Hume, Hutcheson, or Mandeville, nor was he Newton, Pufendorf, or Quesnay. He was mentally independent, nobody's pupil, no epigone.

Strict scrutinisation reveals even to the most skeptical, Smith's intellectual stature and the mental force behind his great scientific performance.

Smith ever kept an open mind to shifting and constant elements of experiences in human action. And he unorthodoxically applied the principles of formal thought to its interpretation and understanding.

It is, surely, very important to seek a formal method of describing and explaining economic and social appearances, which facilitates avoiding mistakes in logic. But by itself this is not enough for a meaningful and useful economic and political theory or even for revealing the 'objective truth'. No amount of mathematical technicality, however refined, can, as Ragnar Frisch rightly argues, ever replace this inexplicable intuition. This intellectual activity is in my view by far the most vital part of our science. And Schumpeter himself like Smith excelled herein.

And if we are less dogmatic in applying the tools of reason to an economic argument, we may judge with balance the usefulness of the more visionary or loosely connected models, too; *provided* they are based on an understanding of the observable facts and free of dogmatic conviction. [64]

Schumpeter's assessment of the profit theory of Ricardo, his economist's economist, that 'it is an excellent theory that can never be refuted and lacks nothing save sense' [130, 1954, p 473], could never be applied to Smith's central theories.

From these perspectives, Smith as an early pioneer and theorist certainly does not need any charity or censorious patronage of an 'advanced' successor. Quite the contrary: his works are a fundamental source of inspiration; they may serve as a foundation of modern theory and policy in various fields. Actually, 'Smith . . . stands on a pinnacle'[65] as Samuelson claimed some years ago in his presidential address.

A final and more methodological aspect of Smith's scholarship, namely his mode of inquiry, is still to be considered. Given Francis Bacon's definition of science as an *ars inveniendi,* one task for economists is to build a comprehensive system, the 'machine'. Or in Smith's world, to discover its functioning in reality. The other task is to construct single tools for our 'box of tools' (Joan Robinson). Both tasks seem legitimate, both limited. The well-known weakness of the former stems from its rather loose connections, empirically difficult to test; the limits of the latter are its often second-or-third-best solution nature. Smith undoubtedly prefers Newton's ideas and method; other writers (perhaps like Molière's Monsieur Jourdain speaking prose) favour Aristotle's.[66]

Yet, to be more precise: Smith seems to have had a distinctive sense for bridging over the two ways of thinking, or for what Albert Einstein[67] has expressed by this argument: 'There could be no fairer destiny for any . . . theory than that it should point the way to a *more comprehensive* theory in which it lives on, as a *limiting* case' (italics added).

Examples of Smith's unusual ability to recognise such links and to construct syntheses are numerous. I point only to his grandiose attempts to combine (Aquinas-like) such initially irreconcilable phenomena as propriety and utility in his frugal or prudent man, as tangibles and intangibles in his welfare function, as *emotio* and *ratio* in his 'spectator' concept, as his constant data (man's nature) and changing variables (manners and institutions), as his micro and macro 'economics', and as his positive and natural rules of justice.

This mode of inquiry is, evidently, not immune to conflicts. It is, however, in contrast to the dialectic method of Karl Marx, who considers conflict in the absolute[68] and makes it a destructive principle. And Smith, of course, never contemplated settling conflicts by inhuman means.

At this beginning of a new era of Smithian studies and of a renaissance of Smithian ideas I have come to believe, after surveying the recent vast literature, that informed economists will answer positively Boulding's paraphrased view: Even after Samuelson and Arrow, we need Adam Smith for a very long time both for inspiration and control. And in closing I add: even the most 'advanced' or sophisticated economists can be unreservedly proud of a fellow scholar who so decisively contributed (as later such scholars as Walras, Marx, Weber, Schumpeter, Keynes, Samuelson, Friedman, Popper and Arrow were to do), (a) to eliminate the secular prejudices of ancient, scholastic, and idealistic philosophers, who judged the *utilitarian* sciences (including economics) to be banal or trivial, and (b) to build political economy into a self-reliant discipline of some reputation even in a purely rationalistic world.

In fact, Adam Smith was an educated and cultured man, creative and original as a thinker, and unique as an architect of thoughts. The indestructable vitality of his natural system of liberty *and* justice (i.e. his political economy), rests on his realistic observations and cool assessment of man's nature—the individual's *self-interested* economic and political activity in *society*. This dependable system of political economy is permeable and flexible. It is lucid, plausible, and yet open to improvement. Despite its imperfections, it seems to continue to be the very basis of those modern theories that have the best chance to explain and correct the working of an efficient and just economy *and* community in the future.

REFERENCES

Alesina, I (1976). 'Učenie Adama Smita i sovremennyj kapitalizm' ['The teaching of Adam Smith and a Contemporary Capitalism'], *Mirovaia Ékonomika i Meždunarodnye Otnošenija* (7), pp 72–83.

Allen, William R (Spring 1977). 'Economics, Economists, and Economic Policy: Modern American Experiences', *Hist Polit Econ,* 9(1), pp 48–88

Anikin, Andrej V (1976). 'Adam Smit i russkaja ékonomičeskaja mysl' ['Adam Smith and the Russian Economic Thought'] *VoprosyÉkonomiki,* 3, pp 112–22

—— (1976). 'Adam Smit—Klassik političeskoj ekonomii' ['Adam Smith—A Classic of Political Economy'], *Vestnik Moskovskogo Universiteta* (3), pp 55–62

Anspach, Ralph (Spring 1972). 'The Implications of the *Theory of Moral Sentiments* for Adam Smith's Economic Thought', *Hist Polit Econ* 8(4), pp 176–206

—— (Winter 1976). 'Smith's Growth Paradigm', *Hist Polit Econ* 8(4), pp 494–514

Armour, Leslie (Dec 1976). 'Smith, Morality, and the Bankers', *Rev Soc Econ* 34(3), pp 359–71

Avila, Manuel (Dec 1976). 'Smith and Undeveloped Nations', *Rev Soc Econ* 34(3), pp 345–58

Bagolini, Luigi (138, 1975). 'The Topicality of Adam Smith's Notion of Sympathy and Judicial Evaluations', in Skinner and Wilson (eds), pp 100–13

Banke, Niels (1976). 'Gamle og nye vurderinger af Adam Smith's *Wealth of Nations* (1776)' ['Old and New Views on Adam Smith's Wealth of Nations (1776)'] *National-okonomisk Tidsskrift* 114(1), pp 5–25

Barkai, Haim (August 1969). 'A formal outline of a Smithian Growth Model', *Quart J Econ* 83(3), pp 396–414

Baudet, H (1976). 'Adam Smith and Glasgow, Accompanying the New Glasgow Edition of the *Wealth of Nations*', *De Econ* 124(4), pp 395–402

Billet, Leonard (Dec 1976). 'The Just Economy: The Moral Basis of the *Wealth of Nations*', *Rev Soc Econ* 34(3), pp 295–315

Bitterman, H J (Dec 1940). 'Adam Smith's Empiricism and the Law of Nature', *J Polit Econ* 48(4–5), pp 487–520, 703–34

Black, R D Collision (144, 1976). 'Smith's Contribution in Historical Perspective', in Smith, Adam, pp 42–63

Blaug, Mark (Winter 1975). 'Kuhn versus Lakatos, or Paradigms versus Research Programmes in the History of Economics', *Hist Polit Econ* 7(4), pp 399–433

Botha, D J J (Dec 1976). 'Adam Smith: Homage from Germany', *South African J Econ* 44(4), pp 412–16

Boulding, Kenneth E (Fall 1971). 'After Samuelson, Who Needs Adam Smith?' *Hist Polit Econ* 3(2), pp 225–337

Brown, A H (138, 1975). 'Adam Smith's First Russian Followers', in Skinner and Wilson (eds), pp 247–73

Buchanan, James M (Jan 1976). 'The Justice of Natural Liberty', *J Legal Stud* 5(1), pp 1–16

—— (144, 1976). 'Public Goods and Natural Liberty', in [Smith, Adam], pp 271–86

Buckle, Henry T (1857, 1861). *History of Civilization in England* Third Edition, 2 Vols London: Parker, Son & Bourn

Bulhões, O G *et al.* (Jan–Mar 1977) '16 Articles', *Revista Brasileira de Economia* 31(1), pp 5–270

Bullock, Charles J (1939). *Vanderblue memorial collection of Smithiana* Cambridge, Mass: Harvard University Press

Cairncross, Alexander (144, 1976). 'The Market and the State', in Smith, Adam, pp 113–34

Campbell, Thomas D (1971). *Adam Smith's science of morals* London: Allen and Unwin

Coase, Ronald H (Oct 1976). 'Adam Smith's View of Man', *J Law Econ* 19(3), pp 529–47

—— (July 1977). '*The Wealth of Nations*', *Econ Inquiry* 15(3), pp 309–25

Coats, A W (138, 1975). 'Adam Smith and the Mercantile System', in Skinner and Wilson (eds), pp 218–36

Cole, Arthur H (Feb 1958). 'Puzzles of the *Wealth of Nations*', *Can J Econ* 24(1), pp 1–8

Dankert, Clyde E (1974). *Adam Smith: Man of letters and economist* Hicksville N Y: Exposition Press

Danner, Peter L (Dec 1976). 'Sympathy and Exchangeable Value: Keys to Adam Smith's Social Philosophy', *Rev Soc Econ* 34(3), pp 317–31

Di Nardi, Giuseppe (Dec 1976). 'Una riflessione sul pensiero smithiano', *Bancaria* 32(12), pp 1224–9

Eckstein, Günter (1967). *Adam Smiths Finanzwissenschaft. Eine Analyse in neuer Sicht* Nürnberg: Offsetdruck

Eltis, W A (138, 1975). 'Adam Smith's Theory of Economic Growth', in Skinner and Wilson (eds), pp 426–54

Foley, Vernard (1976). *The social physics of Adam Smith* West Lafayette Ind: Purdue University Press

Franklin, Burt and Cordasco, Francesco (1950). *Adam Smith, a bibliographical checklist: An international record of critical writings and scholarship relating to Smith and Smithian theory, 1876–1950* New York: Burt Franklin

Franklin, Raymond S (Dec 1976). 'Smithian Economics and Its Pernicious Legacy', *Rev Soc Econ* 34(3), pp 379–89

Friedman, Milton (1977). *From Galbraith to economic freedom* London: Institute of Economic Affairs

—— 'Adam Smith's Relevance for 1976', unpublished paper

Gäfgen, Gérard (1974). 'On the Methodology and Political Economy of Galbraithian Economics', *Kyklos* 27(4), pp 705–30

Giersch, Herbert (144, 1976). 'Mercantilism and Free Trade Today: Comment', in [Smith, Adam], pp 185–95

Gill, Emily R (Dec 1976). 'Justice in Adam Smith: The Right and the Good', *Rev Soc Econ* 34(3), pp 275–94

Gray, Alexander [Sir] (June 1976). 'Adam Smith', *Scot J Polit Econ* 23(3), pp 153–69

Grotius, Hugo (1625). *De iure belli ac pacis* Paris

Gürlichová, Stanislava (1976). 'Poznámky k systémovému přístupu v buržoazní ekonmické teorii v souvislosti s dílem A. Smithe' ['Notes on the Systems Approach in the Bourgeois Economic Theory in Connection with Adam Smith's Work'], *Politická Ekonomie* 24(3), pp 223–32

—— (1976). 'Adam Smith a dnešek' ['Adam Smith and the Present'], *Politická Ekonomie* 24(7), pp 655–8

Harberger, Arnold C (Sept 1971). 'Three Basic Postulates for Applied Welfare Economics: An Interpretive Essay', *J Econ Lit* 9(3), pp 785–97

Harrington, Michael (1976). *The Twilight of Capitalism* New York: Simon and Schuster

Hasbach, Wilhelm (1891). *Untersuchungen über Adam Smith und die Entwicklung der Politischen Ökonomie* Leipzig: Duncker and Humblot

Hayek, Friedrich A (1948). *Individualism and economic order* Chicago: University of Chicago Press

Heilbroner, Robert L (138, 1975). 'The Paradox of Progress: Decline and Decay in the *Wealth of Nations*', in Skinner and Wilson (eds), pp 524–39

—— (Summer 1976). 'The Adam Smith Nobody Knows', *J Portfolio Manage* 2(4), pp 65–6

Heretik, Štefan (1976). 'Dvesto rokov ekonomickej vedy: K výročiu Smithovho Boha tstvo národov' ['Two Hundred Years of the Economic Science: To the Bicentennial of Smith's *Wealth of Nations*'] *Ekonomický Čhasopis* 24(10), pp 921–37

Herland, Michel (1977). 'A propos de la définition du travail productif: Une incursion chez les grands anciens', *Revue Économique* 28(1), pp 109–33

Heuss, Ernst (1965). *Allgemeine Markttheorie* Tübingen: Mohr

Hicks, J R (1969). *A theory of economic history* London: Oxford University Press

Hochman, Harold M and Rodgers, James D (1969). 'Pareto Optimal Redistribution', *Amer Econ Rev* 59(4), pp 542–57

Hollander, Samuel (1973, 1976). *The economics of Adam Smith* Toronto and Buffalo: University of Toronto Press

—— (1976). 'The Historical Dimension of the Wealth of Nations', *Transactions of the Royal Society of Canada Series* IV Vol XIV, pp 277–92

—— (Feb 1977). 'Smith and Ricardo: Aspect of the Nineteenth-Century Legacy', *Amer Econ Rev* 67(1), pp 37–41

Howell, Wilbur S (138, 1975). 'Adam Smith's Lectures on Rhetoric: An Historical Assessment', in Skinner and Wilson (eds), pp 11–43

Hunter, L C (144, 1976). 'The Labour Market: Comment', in [Smith, Adam], pp 260–5

Hutchison, Terence, W (Sept 1976). 'The Bicentenary of Adam Smith', *Econ J* 86(343), pp 481–92

—— (Oct 1976). 'Adam Smith and the *Wealth of Nations*', *J Law Econ* 19(3), pp 507–28

Jaffé, William (Feb 1977). 'A Centenarian on a Bicentenarian: Leon Walras's *Eléments* on Adam Smith's *Wealth of Nations*', *Can J Econ* 10(1), pp 19–33

—— (ed) (1965) *Correspondence of Leon Walras and related papers* 3 Vols Amsterdam: North-Holland

Jensen, Hans E (Dec 1976). 'Sources and Contours of Adam Smith's Conceptualized Reality in the *Wealth of Nations*', *Rev Soc Econ* 34(3), pp 259–74

Jevons, William Stanley (1965). *The principles of economics and other papers* New York: Kelley

Jöhr, Walter A (1975). *Galbraith und die Marktwirtschaft* Tübingen: Mohr

Johnson, Harry G (1976). 'The Relevance of *The Wealth of Nations* to Contemporary Economic Policy', *Scot J Polit Econ* 23(2), pp 171–6

Kaldor, Nicholas (1972). 'The Irrelevance of Equilibrium Economics', *Econ J* 82(328), pp 1237–55

Keynes, John Maynard (1971–3). *The collected writings of John Maynard Keynes.* Edited by the Royal Economic Society, New York: St Martin's Press

Kurz, Heinz D (Oct 1976). 'Adam Smiths Komponententheorie der relativen Preise und ihre Kritik' ['Adam Smith's Component Parts Theory of Relative Prices and its Critics'], *Z ges Staatswiss* 132(4), pp 691–709

Lasarte, Javiar (1976). *Economía y hacienda al final del antiguo régimen Dos estudios* Madrid: Instituto de Estudios Fiscales

Leduc, Gaston (Sept–Oct 1976). 'Adam Smith et la pensée française', *Rev d'Econ Polit* 86(5), pp 795–803

Lindgren, J Ralph (1973). *The social philosophy of Adam Smith* The Hague: Martinus Nijhoff

—— 'Adam Smith's Solution to the Paradox of Value', unpublished paper

List, Frierich (1841, 1959) *Das Nationale System der politischen Ökonomie* Volume 1. Edited by A Sommer Tübingen: J G Cotta

Lowe, Adolph (138, 1975). 'Adam Smith's System of Equilibrium Growth', in Skinner and Wilson (eds), pp 415–25

Lutfalla, Michel (Sept–Oct 1976). 'Sur une réédition abrégée de la Richesse des nations', *Rev d'Econ Polit* 86(5), pp 804–5

Lynn, Arthur D Jr (1976). 'Adam Smith's Fiscal Ideas: An Eclectic Revisited', *Nat Tax J* 29(4), pp 369–78

Macfie, Alec L (1967). *The Individual in society: Papers on Adam Smith* London: Allen and Unwin

MacMillan, James A (Nov 1976). 'A Critique of Benefit-Cost Analysis Guide', *Can J Agr Econ* 24(3), pp 50–4

Mann, Fritz K (Oct 1976). 'Adam Smith—The Heir and the Ancestor', *Z ges Staatswiss* 132(4), pp 683–90

Medick, Hans (1973). *Naturzustand und Naturgeschichte der bürgerlichen Gesellschaft* Göttingen: Vandenhoeck and Ruprecht

Meek, Ronald L (1967). *Economics and ideology and other essays: Studies in the development of economic thought* London: Chapman and Hall

—— (Winter 1976). 'New Light on Adam Smith's Glasgow Lectures on Jurisprudence', *Hist Polit Econ* 8(4), pp 439–77

—— (Dec 1973). and Skinner, Andrew S 'The Development of Adam Smith's Ideas on the Division of Labour', *Econ J* 83(332), pp1094–1116

Mihalik, István and Endre, Szigeti (1976). 'Egy klasszikus mü jubileumára. Kétszáz éves A Smith': '*A nemzetek gazdagsága*' simü müve' ['On the 200th Anniversary of the *Wealth of Nations*'], *Közgazdasági Szemle* 23(5), pp 596–606

Mill, John Stuart (1848). *Principles of political economy* London: Parker and Co, New York: Kelley, 1965

Mini, Piero V (1974). *Philosophy and economics: The origins and development of economic theory* Gainesville: University of Florida Press

Montesquieu, Baron de (1748). *De l'ésprit des lois* Genf

Morrow, Glen R (1923). *The ethical and economic theories of Adam Smith* Ithaca, New York: Cornell University Library

Moss, Laurence S (Winter 1976). 'The Economics of Adam Smith: Professor Hollander's Reappraisal', *Hist Polit Econ* 8(4), pp 564–74

Mossner, Ernest C (1969). *Adam Smith: The biographical approach* Glasgow: University of Glasgow

Müller-Armack, Alfred (1977). 'Die zentrale frage aller Forschüng: Die Einheit von Geistes-und Naturwissenschaften', *Ordo Jahrbuch für Ordnung von Wirtschaft and Gesellschaft*, 28, pp 13–23

Münch, Kläus N (1976). *Kollektive Güter und Gebühren* Göttingen: Vandenhoeck and Ruprecht

Musgrave, Richard A (Nov 1974). 'Symposium: Rawls's *A Theory of Justice:* Maximin, Uncertainty, and the Leisure Trade-off', *Quart J Econ* 88(4), pp 625–32

—— (144, 1976). 'Adam Smith on Public Finance and Distribution', in [Smith, Adam] pp 296–319

Myers, M L (Sept 1976). 'Adam Smith's Concept of Equilibrium', *J Econ Issues* 10(3), pp 560–75

Napoleoni, Claudio (1975). *Smith, Ricardo, Marx* New York: Wiley, Halsted Press

Newton, Isaac [Sir] [Newtono, Isaaco] (1714). *Philosophiae Naturalis Principia Mathematica*, Amsterdam: Editio Ultima

—— (1872, 1963). *Mathematische Prinzipien der Naturlehre.* Edited by J Ph Wolfers, Darmstadt: Wissenschaftliche Buchgessellschaft

O'Brien, Denis P (Winter 1976). 'Customs Unions: Trade Creation and Trade Diversion in Historical Perspective', *Hist Polit Econ* 8(4), pp 540–63

——(1976). 'The Longevity of Adam Smith's Vision: Paradigms, Research Programmes and Falsifiability in the History of Economic Thought', *Scot J Polit Econ* 23(2), pp 133–51

—— (144, 1976). 'Smith's Contribution in Historical Perspective: Comment', in [Smith, Adam], pp 63–7

Peacock, Alan T (138, 1975). 'The Treatment of the Principles of Public Finance in *The Wealth of Nations*', in Skinner and Wilson (eds), pp 553–67

Petrella, Frank (Spring, 1970). 'Individual, Group, or Government? Smith, Mill and Sidgwick', *Hist Polit Econ* 2(1), pp 152–76

Phelps Brown, E H (144, 1976). 'The Labour Market', in [Smith, Adam], pp 243–91

Popper, Karl R (1963, 1965). *Conjectures and refutations: The growth of scientific knowledge.* Second edition. London: Routledge and Kegan Paul

Pufendorf, Samuel A (1979). *De Iure Noturae et Gentium* Frankfurt/Lepizig

Rae, John (1895, 1965) *Life of Adam Smith* New York and London: Kelley

Rawls, John (1972). *A theory of justice* Oxford: Oxford University Press

Recktenwald, Horst Claus (1951). 'Zur Lehre von den Marktformen', *Weltw Archiv* 67(2), pp 298–326

—— (1973). *Political economy: A historical perspective.* Translation of 1971 German edition London: Collier Macmillan

—— (1975). '*Adam Smith heute und morgen*', *Kyklos* 28(1), pp 5–22

—— (1976). *Adam Smith: Sein Leben und sein Werk* Munich: Beck Verlag

—— (ed) (1976). *Secular trends of the public sector* Paris: Edition Cujais

Reisman, David A (1976). *Adam Smith's sociological economics* London: Croom Helm; New York: Barnes and Noble Books

Ricardo, David (1951–73). *The works and correspondence of David Ricardo* 11 vols. Edited by Piero Sraffa, Cambridge: Royal Economic Society

Richardson, G B (138, 1975). 'Adam Smith on Competition and Increasing Returns', in Skinner and Wilson (eds), pp 350–60

Rimlinger, Gaston V (Dec 1976). 'Smith and the Merits of the Poor', *Rev Soc Econ* 34(3), pp 333–44

Robbins, Lionel [Lord] (1976). *Political Economy, past and present: A review of leading theories of economic policy* London: Macmillan Press

Robertson, H M (Dec 1976). 'Euge! Bell! Dear Mr Smith: The Wealth of Nations, 1776–1976', *South Afr J Econ* 44(4), pp 378–411

Rohrlich, George F (Dec 1976). 'The Role of Self-Interest in the Social Economy of Life, Liberty and the Pursuit of Happiness, *Anno* 1976 and Beyond', *Rev Soc Econ* 34(3), pp 373–8

Roll, Eric [Sir] (Jan 1976). '*The Wealth of Nations, 1776–1976*', *Lloyds Bank Rev* (119), pp 12–22

Rosenberg, Nathan (August 1976). 'Another Advantage of the Division of Labor', *J Polit Econ* Part I, 84(4), pp 861–8

Ross, Ian S *Life of Adam Smith*. The Glasgow Edition of the Works and Correspondence of Adam Smith, associated volume. Oxford: Clarendon Press, forthcoming.

Roubal, Kvétoslav (1976). 'Adam Smith a vyvoj produktivní práce v procescu védeckotechnické revoluce v kapitalismu a socialismu' ['Adam Smith and the Development of Productive Labour in the Process of the Scientific and Technological Revolution under Capitalism and Socialism'], *Politická Ekonomie* 24(1), pp 1–8

Rowley, C K (144, 1976). 'Competition: The Product Markets Comment', in [Smith, Adam], pp 232–7

Samuels, Warren J (Oct 1973). 'Adam Smith and the Economy as a System of Power', *Rev Soc Econ* 31(2), pp 123–37

——(Summer 1976). 'The Political Economy of Adam Smith', *Nebr J Econ Bus* 15(3), pp 3–24

Samuelson, Paul A (March 1962). 'Economists and the History of Ideas', *Amer Econ Rev* 52(1), pp 1–18

——(Feb 1977). 'A Modern Theorist's Vindication of Adam Smith', *Amer Econ Rev* 67(1) pp 42–9

Schumpeter, Joseph A (1954). *History of economic analysis*. Edited from manuscript by Elizabeth B Schumpeter New York: Oxford University Press

Scott, William R (1937, 1965). *Adam Smith as student and professor* Glasgow: Jackson, New York: Kelley

(1976). *Scottish Journal of Political Economy* 'Wealth of Nations Bicentenary: A Symposium' 23(2)

Skinner, Andrew S (Nov 1972). 'Adam Smith: Philosophy and Science', *Scot J Polit Econ* 29(3), pp 307–19

——(1974). *Adam Smith and the role of the state* Glasgow: University of Glasgow Press

——(1974). 'Adam Smith: Science and the Role of the Imagination', in *Hume and the enlightenment: Essays presented to Ernest Campbell Mossner*. Edited by William B Todd, Edinburgh University Press; Austin: University of Texas, Humanities Research Center, pp 164–88

——(June 1976). 'Adam Smith: The Development of a System', *Scot J Polit Econ* 23(2), pp 111–32

—— (1976). 'Adam Smith and the American Economic Community: An Essay in Applied Economics', *J Hist Ideas* 37, pp 59–78

—— and Wilson, Thomas (eds) (1975). *Essays on Adam Smith* Oxford: Clarendon Press

Smith, Adam *An Inquiry into the nature and causes of the wealth of Nations*. Edited by Edwin Cannan, London: Methuen (1904)

—— *Theorie der ethischen Gefuhle* 2 Vols. Edited by Walther Eckstein, Leipzig: Felix Meiner (1926)

[Smith, Adam] *Adam Smith, 1776–1926: Lectures to commemorate the sesquicentennial of the publication of 'The Wealth of Nations'* by John M Clark *et al.* Chicago: University of Chicago Press (1928)

—— *The wealth of nations*. Books I–III. Edited by A S Skinner Harmondsworth, England: Penguin Books (1970, 1973, 1977)

—— *Der Wholstand der Nationen*. Translated by Horst Claus Recktenwald (with an introduction to all works, a biography and new bibliography, and with 23 pictures and graphics on growth) Munich: Beck Verlag (1974)

[Smith, Adam] *The market and the state: Essays in honour of Adam Smith*. Edited by Thomas Wilson, and Andrew S Skinner Oxford: Clarendon Press (1976)

—— *An Inquiry into the Nature and Causes of the Wealth of Nations*. The Glasgow Edition of the Works and Correspondence of Adam Smith. Vol II (2 Vol). Edited by R H Campbell, A S Skinner and W B Todd, Oxford: Clarendon Press (1976)

—— *The theory of moral sentiments*. The Glasgow Edition of the Works and Correspondence of Adam Smith. Vol I Edited by D D Raphael and A L Macfie Oxford: Clarendon Press (1976)

—— Correspondence of Adam Smith. The Glasgow Edition of the Works and Correspondence of Adam Smith. Vol VI Edited by E C Mossner and I S Ross Oxford: Clarendon Press (1977)

—— *Essays on philosophical subjects*. The Glasgow Edition of the Works and Correspondence of Adam Smith. Vol III Edited by D D Raphael and A S Skinner. Contributions from J C Bryce, I S Ross and W P D Wightman Oxford: Clarendon Press, forth

—— *Lectures on rhetoric and Belles Lettres* The Glasgow Edition of the Works and Correspondence of Adam Smith. Vol IV Edited by J C Bryce, Oxford: Clarendon Press forth

—— *Lectures on jurisprudence*. The Glasgow Edition of the works and Correspondence of Adam Smith Vol V. Edited by R L Meek, D D Raphael and P G Stein Oxford: Clarendon Press forth

Spengler, Joseph J (April 1959). 'Adam Smith's Theory of Economic Growth', *South Econ J* Pt I, 25, pp 397–415 and July 1959, Pt II 26, pp 1–12

—— (June 1976). 'Adam Smith on Population Growth and Economic Development', *Population Develop Rev* 2(2), pp 167–80

—— (Feb 1977). 'Adam Smith on Human Capital', *Amer Econ Rev* 67(1), pp 32–6

Spiegel, H W (Winter 1976). 'Adam Smith's Heavenly City', *Hist Polit Econ* 8(4), pp 478–93

Stewart, Dugald (1858). *The works of Dugald Stewart*. Volume 7, *Account of the life and writings of Adam Smith*. Edited by Sir William B Hamilton, Edinburgh: Constable

Stigler, George J (138, 1975). 'Smith's Travels on the Ship of State', in Skinner and Wilson (eds), pp 237–46

—— (Dec 1976). 'The Successes and Failures of Professor Smith', *J Polit Econ* 84(6), pp 1199–213

Sylos-Labini, P (144, 1976). 'Competition: The Product Markets', in [Smith, Adam], pp 200–32

Taylor, Overton H (1960). *A History of economic thought: Social ideals and economic theories from Quesnay to Keynes* New York: McGraw-Hill

Thal, Peter (ed) (1976). *Adam Smith gestern und heute. 200 Jahre 'Reichtum der Nationen'* (10 integrated contributions of a collective.) Glashütten Tannus: Detlev Auvermann

Thompson, Herbert F (May 1965). 'Adam Smith's Philosophy of Science', *Quart J Econ* **79**, pp 212–33

Thweatt, William O (1957). 'A Diagrammatic Presentation of Adam Smith's Growth Model', *Social Research* 24(2), pp 227–30

Tuchtfeldt, Egon (1976). 'Über die Staatsfunktionen bei Adam Smith', *Ordo Jahrbuch für die Ordnung von Wirtschaft und Gesellschaft* 27, pp 29–45

Viner, Jacob (141, 1928). 'Adam Smith and Laissez Faire', in [Smith, Adam], pp 116–55

—— (107, 1965). 'Guide to John Rae's Life of Adam Smith', in Rae, pp 1–36

—— (1928, 1968). 'Adam Smith', *Intern Encycl of Soc Sci,* pp 322–8

Waters, William R (Dec 1976). 'Social Economics of Adam Smith: Introduction', *Rev Soc Econ* 34(3), pp 239–43

Werner, Horst (1976). 'Adam Smith zur Reform der Weltwirtschaftsordnung', *Ordo Jahrbuch für Ordnung von Wirtschaft und Gesellschaft* 27, pp 46–80

West, E G (March 1969). 'The Political Economy of Alienation: Karl Marx and Adam Smith', *Oxford Econ Pap* 21(1), pp 1–23

—— (138, 1975). 'Adam Smith and Alienation', in Skinner and Wilson (eds), pp 540–52

—— (Winter 1976). 'Adam Smith's Economics of Politics', *Hist Polit Econ* 8(4), pp 515–39

—— (Feb 1977). 'Adam Smith's Public Economics: Re-evaluation', *Canadian J Econ* 10(1), pp 1–18

Wilson, Thomas (144, 1976). 'Sympathy and Self-Interest', in [Smith, Adam], pp 73–99

Winch, Donald (144, 1976). 'Smith's Contribution in Historical Perspective: Comment', in [Smith, Adam], pp 67–72

Worland, Stephen T (Dec 1976). 'Mechanistic Analogy and Smith on Exchange', *Rev Soc Econ* 34(3), pp 245–58

NOTES

1 See Section III—(1) Methods of Inquiry below.

2 I estimate the number of those publications as about 350 in 1976. Unfortunately a bibliographic documentation centre for the vast and growing international literature on Smith does not yet exist. Both the *Vanderblue Memorial Collection of Smithiana* [23, Charles J Bullock, 1939] and Burt Franklin and Francesco Cordasco, *Adam Smith, A Bibliographical Checklist. An International Record of Critical Writings and Scholarship Relating to Smith and Smithian Theory 1876–1950* (with 446 titles) [35, 1950] are reliable sources (evidently with gaps), but obsolete.

Scholars interested in the Smith-literature 1950–78 have to rely on library records and bibliographic annexes in books and articles.

3   For further evidence and arguments and in order to save space, I am forced to quote more than I would prefer from my own contributions.

4   In a brief, yet very remarkable comment on Black's analysis, Denis P O'Brien indicates five ways in which historical perspective on Smith (and in general) changed; his article is of significance for other than historians of economics [101, 1976, pp 63–7].

5   Jacob Viner's often cited comment that 'an economist must have peculiar theories indeed who cannot quote from the *Wealth of Nations* to support his special purposes' [164, 1928, p 126] is, *mutatis mutandis,* valid for the whole work.

6   See footnote 29 below.

7   Metaphysical systems are for Smith mere fancies. Smith, the actual man, neither overrates selfishness, stupidity, and prejudice nor underrates fellow-feeling, prudence, and openness in *all* ranks.

8   In a letter to William Strahan, his publisher, written two years before his death, Smith confesses: 'I am a slow, a very slow workman, I do and undo everything I write at least half a dozen times before I can be tolerably pleased with it' (Facsimile in William R Scott [131, 1937, pp 374–6]). Even in his polemics, he writes with discipline and elegance. However compared, for instance, to Marx the polemics are insignificant.

Quite surely Smith's somewhat loose style (similar to that of Hugo Grotius, John Locke, and Baron de Montesquieu), repetitive and not too technical, full of a quiet humour, has rendered his works more accessible to the majority of readers. Despite this easy access, however, it is amazing how rarely and how uncarefully Smith's writings have been read. John K Galbraith has pertinently described this rather curious appearance at the Kirkcaldy symposium, 'With *Das Kapital* and the Bible, *Wealth of Nations* enjoys the distinction of being one of three books to which people may refer at will without feeling they should have read it.'

As a teacher Smith was, according to James Boswell the renowned biographer who attended his Glasgow lectures, beautiful, clear, accurate, perspicuous, really admirable, with none of 'that formal stiffness and pedantry too often found in Professors', quite the opposite of François Quesnay, whom Schumpeter thought was 'pedantic and doctrinaire to a degree and must have been an awful bore'. (For evidence, see Recktenwald [112, 1976].)

9   Yet not like a sententious German schoolmaster, Black [15, 1976, p 57] points to Cannan's somewhat curious way of criticising classical economics, his well known 'Tom Tulliver' approach (Viner). It seems to be only one or two Tullivers (who are 'very fond of birds, that is of throwing stones at them') in this generation.

10   See also Ronald H Coase [26, 1976, pp 537–40] and John Rae on Smith's opening prayers on natural religion [107, (1895) 1965, p 60].

11   See J Viner's 'Guide to John Rae's *Life of Adam Smith*' [165, 1965] and Recktenwald [112, 1976, pp 1–26].

12   Schumpeter [130, 1954, p 182]; also Recktenwald [112, 1976, pp 33–9].

13   Rae [107, 1965] and Recktenwald [112, 1976, pp 1–26].

14   See William Jaffé's magnificent *Correspondence of Léon Walras and Related Papers* (3 vols) [63, 1965]. Unlike Walras, Smith kept letter-writing to a minimum. Walras preserved every scrap of inscripted paper for posterity and his reputation. Somewhat frustratedly he confessed: 'The only immortality left for us to hope for is that of our own work. We must labour and enjoy the success of our labour by anticipation. This is the secret of morality and the secret of happiness' [63, 1965].

15 Unfortunately, the search for one of Foulis's busts, sold by bookshops in Glasgow has been unsuccessful so far.

16 For Smith, Newton's system was '. . . the greatest discovery that was ever made by man . . .' (*Astronomy* [148, forth]).

17 The interrrelated functions or effects making up the working of the 'imaginary machine'.

18 Issac Newton, *Auctoris Praefatio ad Lectorem* and *Libro Tertio* [97, 1714].

19 Smith's term 'experimental method' seems, therefore, to be false, at least misleading, if applied to economics. As to this central problem of research, see Alfred Müller-Armack [91a, 1977, pp 13–23].

20 Obviously an intuitive statement, not to be understood *prima facie*.

21 [65, 1965, pp 200–1]. See also Black [15, 1976, p 54] to whom I owe this quotation.

22 He had 'no great faith in political arithmetick' [145, *Wealth*, 1976, p 534].

23 By the way, Smith's favourite pursuits as a student were mathematics and natural philosophy at the university according to Dugald Stewart [155, 1858, Vol 7, p 7].

24 *Theory* [146, 1976, p 83]. As an example I point to the euphoria of some modern planners and programmers in the market and public sectors or to some prophecies in the Club of Rome report.

25 See W R Allen [2, 1977, pp 48–88].

26 See also Spengler [152, 1976; 153, 1977] and Anspach [6, 1976].

27 For further evidence see Wilhelm Hasbach [47, 1891, pp 201–2] and W Eckstein [140, *Wealth,* 1926]. As to conjectural history, see J R Hicks, *A Theory of Economic History* 53a, 1969.

28 Arthur H Cole [29, 1958], often quoted, has collected such 'puzzles' in the *Wealth*. He contrasts some cynical and harsh judgements to biographical statements on Smith's calm and steady character. In my judgement, Cole seems to overstate some false speculations and misses the fact that these historical illustrations do not weaken the conclusion. Thus, Smith was forced to use travellers' tales, in a few cases, a somewhat dubious source. Yet generally he used them as trade statistics critically and with some reserve (see *Wealth*, Introduction, [145, 1976, p 51]).

29 Smith derives the concept of moral obligation not from a metaphysical source but from mutually shared aversion and preferences, the 'respect for what are, or for what should be, or for what, upon a certain condition, would be, the sentiments of other people . . .' [146, 1976, p 263].

30 For a stimulating discussion of Smith's, Rawls' and modern theories of justice, see Richard A Musgrave [93, 1974] and E G West [171, 1976, pp 523–4].

31 To argue as Gunnar Myrdal does that Smith overlooks the conflict is quite surely a misinterpretation (so he holds: 'A sunny optimism radiates Smith's writing. He had no keen sense for social disharmonies, . . . he was blind to social conflict) (see Recktenwald [112, 1976, p 74]). I point merely to (a) the conflict between man's relentless pursuit of wealth and his love of ease and inactivity [145, *Wealth*, 1976, p 760] and (b) his institutional mechanism to protect society from 'the passionate confidence of interested falsehood' [145, 1976, p 496].

    Yet Smith does not *overrate* the conflict as Marx does, who makes it the central point in his dialectic theory. And Smith does not propose to settle the conflict by inhuman means.

32 For further evidence, see Hasbach [47, 1891], Campbell and Skinner (Introduction to *Wealth*) [145, 1976], Skinner [135, 1974], Ronald L Meek [83, 1976], Recktenwald [112, 1976], Lindgren [73, 1973].

33 Indeed the *Wealth*, partly overloaded by historical facts and long 'digressions', is a composite mixture, the outcome of a largely revised plan. Therefore, this was and

is one important source of misinterpretations even for the patient reader. And the author himself is responsible for such difficulties.

34   Thus, at times he may appear as a paradoxical writer. Of course, this is not a full explanation, e.g. for his somewhat curious labour theories of value, though his quantity of labour approach apparently is valid, but only at the first stage of economic development (and not in industrialised societies, of course, as Marxists, even today, hold).

35   See various examples, old and new ones in Black [15, 1976], Wilson [173, 1976], O'Brien [99, 1976; 100, 1976], and Recktenwald [112, 1976]. A catalogue of prejudices and distortions, which are still alive in modern textbooks, can be found in Friedrich List, *Das nationale System der politischen Ökonomie*, edited by A Sommer [74a, 1959]. On the other side, List acknowledged Smith's great performances, especially his *analytic* method.

36   Besides the German historians quoted above, Glen R Morrow [89, 1923], the earlier Viner [166, 1928], H J Bittermann [14, 1940], A L Macfie [78, 1967], H C Recktenwald [112, 1976], T D Campbell [25, 1971], R Anspach [5, 1972], and others reject the thesis of a radical conflict between Smith's *Theory* and *Wealth*.

37   Samuelson [129, 1977, p 43] points to other pseudo-problems that have monopolised the Smith-Ricardo literature.

38   Buckle's view '[Smith] makes man naturally selfish . . .' [21, 1861, p 353] seems obviously nonsense, but greatly influenced German economists in the nineteenth century. Schmoller's and the German Historical School's aversion to Smith and the English Classical School stems fundamentally from two considerations: 'materialism' (an egoistic theory of human nature) and method of deduction and equilibrium (see Recktenwald [112, 1976 pp 277–86]).

39   Perhaps such studies will contribute to avoid in the future what Donald N Winch rightly deplores, that 'the history of Smith's scholarship and the history of economists' views on Smith have frequently lived entirely separate lives' [174, 1976, p 71].

40   He warns us against wasting time in formulating an '*optimum optimorum*' or a 'fully ordered social system' (e.g. Boulding Grants Economy) before he states, 'To leave the Paretian territory does not mean that we are licensed to indulge in every kind of Utopian silliness whatever the camouflage of pedantic terminology' [173, 1976, p 92]. See also Harold M Hochman and James D Rodgers, 'Pareto Optimal Redistribution,' [54, 1969, p 59 pp 542–5]. For an opposite view to Wilson, see Musgrave who considers redistribution by government [94, 1976].

41   Similar to Hollander's mode in his profound study [55, 1973], but less formal.

42   Most interpreters of Smith's antimercantilist position, an analysis of impediments to the functioning of the markets, considered largely the restrictive regulations, which led to a serious misallocation of scarce resources.

43   'The Irrelevance of Equilibrium Economics' [68, 1972, p 1237 *passim*]. See also P Sylos-Labini's article [158, 1976, pp 200–32] and C K Rowley's comment [125, 1976, p 235].

44   For Smith *rivalry* characterises the bargaining on a competitive market, that is . . . a species of warfare of which the operations are continually changing, and which can scarce ever be conducted successfully, without such unremitting exertion of vigilance and attention . . .' [145, *Wealth*, 1976], a task for which a government department seems entirely unsuited.

45   For further evidence see my article 'Zur Lehre von den Marktformen' [109, 1951, pp 298–326] and Ernst Heuss, *Allgemeine Markettheorie* [53, 1965].

46   Coase [26, 1976, p 529]; Wilson [173, 1976, pp 88–92].

47 In addition, this is a central topic of the German Eucken school, a productive co-operation of economists and jurists whose contributions are commonly unknown in the Anglo-Saxon world. And it was a strong element in Erhard's economic policy.

48 See page 61.

49 For John Millar the principle of 'expediency' or efficiency and not of 'propriety' was the foundation of Smith's political economy. See the opposite views of Lindgren [73, 1973] and Hans Medick [81, 1973]; see also West [171, 1976] and Anspach [6, 1976, pp 494–514].

50 See page 73.

51 Smith writes that the performance of the sovereign's duty requires '. . . very different degrees of expence in the different periods of society' [145, 1976, p 709].

52 The most important source of inefficiency in the public sector, in my view, is this water-tight separation running up to 80 per cent of the revenues and expenditures in government budgets. To point to a similar problem: Our sacrifice theories, the basis of the argument for progressive taxation, sharply sever utility from spending income from the disutility of earning income. In geometry, the marginal utility curves compare only *one-half* of two persons' normal feelings or actions, completely ignoring the disutility functions; or to use Mark Blaug's metaphor, we play tennis, in this case as well, with the net down. Another puzzle or somewhat schizophrenic behaviour of some modern writers seems to be the attempts to reveal the demand or preference curve of public goods or the value of benefits in cost-benefit analysis by referring to the data of the market, the absolute failures of which they have so thoroughly proved (see A C Harberger, 'Three Postulates of Applied Welfare Economics: An Interpretive Essay' [45, 1971, pp 785–97]).

53 As is well known, Smith often proposes a 'mixed' reward. To this day we lack a sound theory and policy for fees and rewards in the public sector. See e.g. Blaug [138, Skinner and Wilson, 1975, p 569] and K N Münch, *Kollektive Güter und Gebühren* [92, 1976].

54 In a letter to William Cullen (*Correspondence* [147, 1977, no 173]) he writes on the Scottish universities: 'They are perhaps, upon the whole, as unexceptionable as any public institutions of that kind, which all contain in their *very nature the seeds and causes of negligency and corruption*, have ever been, or are ever likely to be' (italics added).

55 Recently Herbert Giersch has refuted some false arguments used in the North-South dialogue in applying Smith's fundamental principle of exchange and trade in a paper (forth).

56 As to the idealistic appeal of collectivism, Johnson [67, 1976, p 176] and my criticism [112, 1976, pp 50–62] of Schumpeter's argument.

57 As to the dialectic, see Karl Popper, *Conjectures and Refutations* [105, 1963, pp 312–35]. Meek holds Marx was an heir of Smith's sociology [82, 1967, pp 34–50]. See also A H Brown [18a, 1975, pp 253–9], Cairncross [24, 1976], and Wilson [173, 1976].

58 See Giersch [39a, 1976 pp 185–95] and Recktenwald [112, 1976, pp 277–86].

59 Smith himself forcefully claimed, as we know, in a lost letter of 1755, to have discovered before 1748 'the obvious and simple system of natural liberty', meant as an analytic principle and a set of political prescriptions, and he made it, we should add, objectively for the first time the pivot of an economic and social system. Other writers point to further truly original principles: his concepts of sympathy and the impartial spectator or his contribution to the theory of rhetoric and language ([58, Howell, 1975, pp 11–43], E Coseriu, 'Adam Smith und die Anfange der Sprachtypologie', quoted in Recktenwald [112, 1976, p 196]).

60   Schumpeter's interpretation of Smith's system of political economy is obviously as mistaken as Walras's. For evidence see p 69.

61   To round off Schumpeter's *laudatio*: He much admires Smith's *Essays* as 'crystallized fragments' of a great project, especially his favourite, the 'pearl', the *History of Astronomy* [130, 1954, p 182] and he rightly holds that the *Wealth* is the most successful not only of all books of economics but . . . of all scientific books that have appeared to this day' possibly excepting Darwin's *Origin of Species* [130, Schumpeter, p 181].

62   Smith read, observed, and listened engagedly and judicially, his criticism being, in general, extremely creative.

63   Be it more modernly interpreted as a Kuhnian paradigm or as a Lakatosian Research Programme with a hard and a weak core. See Blaug's most suggestive contribution [16, 1975] and O'Brien [100, 1976].

64   See e.g. Milton Friedman's refutation of Galbraith's nightmarish economic theory of our industrial system [37, 1977] and Walter A Jöhr's somewhat milder criticism [66, 1975] (and his argument with Gérard Gafgen's methodological position [39, 1974]). For further evidence, see my empirical test of Adolph Wagner's Law [113, 1978].

65   P A Samuelson, 'Economists and the History of Ideas' [128, 1962, p 7].

66   To avoid a false interpretation, I should note that our notions of micro- and macro-analysis, of course, do not correspond to this dichotomy.

67   I owe this citation to Karl R Popper's classic work [105, 1963].

68   More in Recktenwald [81, 1976, pp 74, 115].

CHAPTER SEVEN

Adam Smith and Economic Liberalism

Andrew S Skinner

Hume Occasional Paper No. 9
(The David Hume Institute 1988)

I

Adam Smith was born in 1723 and died in 1790. His life spanned events of great importance in Great Britain; the Rebellion of 1745 which was designed to restore the House of Stuart; the humiliation of France in 1763, which gave Britain a degree of influence which was only matched by that enjoyed by Holland in the seventeenth century; the beginning of the French Revolution.

These events are all very distant and yet Smith's teaching in certain areas commands and has commanded, support from a wide range of thinkers attracted by his eloquent claim that the sovereign should discharge himself from a duty:

> in the attempting to perform which he must always be exposed to innumerable delusions, and for the proper performance of which no human wisdom or knowledge could ever be sufficient; the duty of superintending the industry of private people, and of directing it towards the employments most suitable to the interest of the society (*WN*, IV, ix, 51).[1]

The celebration to mark the fiftieth anniversary of the book showed wide and continuing acceptance of this doctrine.

In 1876, at a dinner held by the Political Economy Club to mark the centenary of the *Wealth of Nations* one speaker identified free trade as the most important consequence of the work done by 'this simple Glasgow professor'. It was also predicted that 'there will be what may be called a large negative development of Political Economy tending to produce an important beneficial effect; and that is, such a development of Political Economy as will reduce the functions of government within a smaller and smaller compass'. It is hardly surprising that a contemporary leader in *The Times* could claim that 'the time is not yet distant when the supremacy of Adam Smith's teaching shall surpass his largest hopes'.[2]

Nor is Professor Stigler's famous claim, uttered a hundred years later on the occasion of the 1976 conference, lightly to be dismissed: 'Adam Smith is alive and well and living in Chicago'. Smith is, after all, a modern authority, in the eyes of the Chicago School and many others, including Mrs Thatcher.

It is not the intention of this paper directly to dispute Professor Stigler's claim, but rather to suggest that Smith's position is subtler and more informative than it sometimes appears. Especially is this the case when we see Smith's economic analysis in the context of his treatment of ethics and jurisprudence. When Smith was a professor in Glasgow he lectured on ethics, jurisprudence and economics in that order and we also know that he intended to publish a third book (on government) which would have completed a comprehensive system of the moral sciences; a grand design which was still possible to contemplate and largely to execute in his time.[3]

The main parts of Smith's great system represented by the *Theory of Moral Sentiments* (1759), the *Lectures on Jurisprudence*, and the *Wealth of Nations* (1776) are important of themselves, and also interrelated. The *Moral Sentiments*, based on the ethical part of the lecture course delivered in Glasgow, is primarily concerned with the way in which moral judgement is formed and in part designed to explain the emergence of those barriers which control our passions. The argument gives prominence to the emergence of general rules of conduct, including the rules of law, but also confirms that accepted standards of behaviour are related to environment so that they may vary in different societies at the same point in time and in the same society at different points in time. The lectures on jurisprudence, on the other hand, help to explain the emergence of government and its changing structure *through* time in terms of an analysis which features the use of four distinct socio-economic stages; the stages of hunting, pasture, agriculture and commerce. This dimension in Smith's thought has attracted the admiring attention of Marxist scholars.[4]

In the context of the *Wealth of Nations*, the main thrust of the argument is designed to explain the origin of the feudal form of government and the emergence of the stage of commerce. While the same points are made in the *Lectures*, the constitutional dimension is there more marked in the sense that Smith was concerned to explain a gradual shift in the balance of power which, at least in the peculiar circumstances of England, had led to the House of Commons assuming a position of some dominance.

The ethics and Smith's historical treatment of constitutional law were also closely linked with the analysis of political economy which was to follow.

The lectures on public jurisprudence help to specify the nature of the system of positive law which will be consistent with the attainment of the stage of commerce and throw some light on the form of government which might be expected. The same analysis helps to explain the structure of the modern economy and the emergence of a situation where all goods and services command a price. Here 'Every man . . . lives by exchanging, or becomes in some measure a merchant' (*WN*, I, iv, 1). If Smith gave prominence to the role of self-interest in this context and in this area of activity, auditors of the lectures on ethics, and readers of the *Moral Sentiments* would be aware that the drive to better our condition had a social reference; that 'it is chiefly from this regard to the sentiments of mankind, that we pursue riches and avoid poverty' (*TMS*, I, iii, 2, 1). Later in the book the position was further clarified when Smith stated that we tend to approve the *means*, as well as the *ends*, of ambition. 'Hence . . . that eminent esteem with which all men naturally regard a steady perseverance in the practice of frugality, industry, and application'; and esteem which is alone capable of sustaining such conduct, since in the normal course of events the 'pleasure which we are to enjoy ten years hence interests us to little in comparison with that which we enjoy today' (*TMS, IV*, 2, 8).

It is significant to note that the most complete discussion of the complex social psychology of the 'economic Man' is to be found in the *Moral Sentiments*—and especially in Part VI which was added in the last year of Smith's life.[5]

As far as the purely economic analysis is concerned, the familiar tale need not detain us; it is sufficient to be reminded that in the *Wealth of Nations* the theory of price and allocation was developed in terms of a model which made due allowance for distinct factors of production land, labour, capital and for the appropriate forms of return (rent, wages, profit). This point, now so obvious, struck Smith as novel and permitted him to develop an analysis of the allocative mechanism which ran in terms of interrelated adjustments in both factor and commodity markets. The resulting version of general interdependence also allowed Smith to move from the discussion of 'micro' to that of 'macro' economic issues, and to develop a model of the 'circular flow' which relies heavily on the distinction, already established by the Physiocrats, between fixed and circulating capital.[6]

But these terms, which were applied to the activities of individual under-takers, were transformed in their meaning by their application to society at large. Working in terms of period analysis, Smith in effect represented the working of the economic process as a series of activities and transactions which linked the main socio-economic groups (proprietors, capitalists, and wage-labour). In Smith's terms, current purchases in effect withdrew consumption and investment goods from the circulating capital of society; goods which were in turn replaced by virtue of productive activity in the same time period.

Looked at from one point of view, the analysis taken as a whole provides one of the most dramatic examples of the doctrine of 'unintended social outcomes', or the working of the 'Invisible Hand'. The individual undertaker (entrepreneur), seeking the most efficient allocation of resources contributes to overall economic efficiency; the merchant's reaction to price signals helps to ensure that the allocation of resources accurately reflects the structure of consumer preferences; the drive to better our condition contributes to economic growth. Looked at from another perspective, the work can be seen to have resulted in a great conceptual system linking together logically separate, yet interrelated, problems such as price, allocation, distribution, macro-statics and macro-dynamics.[7]

The argument is also buttressed by a series of judgements as to *probable* patterns of behaviour and *actual* trends of events. It was Smith's firm opinion, for example, that in a situation where there was tolerable security, 'The sole use of money is to circulate consumable goods. By means of it, provisions, materials, and finished work, are bought and sold, and distributed to their proper consumers' (*WN,* II, iii, 23). In the same way he contended that the savings generated during any (annual) period would always be matched by investment (*WN,* II, iii, 18); a key assumption of the classical system which was to follow. In the case of Great Britain, Smith also pointed out that real wages had progressively increased during the eighteenth century, and that high wages were to be approved of as a contribution to productivity (*WN,* I, vii, 44). The tone is buoyant with regard to economic growth, and is duly reflected in the policy stance which Smith was to adopt.

II

Smith's prescriptions, with regard to economic policy, followed directly on the analysis just considered. He called on governments to minimise their 'impertinent' obstructions to the pursuits of individuals. In particular he recommended that the statutes of apprenticeship, and the privileges of corporations should be repealed on the ground that they adversely affect the working of the allocative mechanism. In the same chapter Smith pointed to the barriers to the deployment of labour generated by the Poor Laws and the Laws of Settlement (*cf. WN,* I, x, c; IV, ii, 42).

He also objected to positions of privilege, such as monopoly powers, which he regarded as creatures of the civil law. The institution was again represented as impolitic and unjust: unjust in that a position of monopoly is a position of unfair advantage, and impolitic in that the prices of the goods so controlled are 'upon every occasion the highest which can be got' (*WN,* I, vii, 27).

In this context we may usefully distinguish Smith's objection to monopoly in general from his criticism of one manifestation of it; namely, the mercantile system, described as the 'modern system' of policy, best understood 'in our own country and in our own times' (*WN,* IV, 2). In Smith's view the most dramatic example of this policy was to be found in the regulations which controlled the relationship between Britain and America, and which were designed in effect to create a single economic community based upon complementary activities and markets. But again he noted that such a policy was liable to 'that general objection which may be made to all the different expedients of the mercantile system; the objection of forcing some part of the industry of the country into a channel less advantageous than that in which it would run of its own accord' (*WN,* IV, v, a, 24).[8]

But if this is the general position with which Smith is usually associated it should be noted that he was prepared to justify a wide range of policies, all of which have been carefully catalogued by Jacob Viner in his justifiably famous article on 'Adam Smith and Laisser Faire' (1928). For example Smith was prepared to justify the use of stamps on plate and linen as the most effectual guarantee of quality (*WN,* I, x, c, 13), the compulsory regulation of mortgages (*WN,* I, ix, 16) and government control of the coinage. In addition he defended the granting of temporary monopolies to mercantile groups on particular occasions, to the inventors of new machines, and, not surprisingly, to the authors of new books (*WN*, V, i.e. 30).

Four broad areas of intervention are of particular interest, in the sense that they involve wider issues of general principal. First, Smith advised governments that where they were faced with taxes imposed by their competitors in trade retaliation could be in order especially if such an action had the effect of ensuring the 'repeal of the high duties or prohibitions complained of'. Secondly, Smith advocated the use of taxation, not simply as a means of raising revenue, but as a means of controlling certain activities, and of compensating for what would now be known as defective telescopic faculty, i.e. a failure to perceive our long-run interest. In the name of the public interest, Smith supported taxes on the retail sale of liquor in order to discourage the multiplication of alehouses (*WN*, V, ii, g, 4) and differential rates on ale and spirits in order to reduce the sale of the latter (*WN*, V, ii, k, 50). To take another example, he advocated taxes on those proprietors who demanded rents in kind rather than cash, and on those leases which prescribe a certain form of cultivation. In the same vein, we find Smith arguing that the practice of selling a future revenue for the sake of ready money should be discouraged on the ground that it reduced the working capital of the tenant and at the same time transferred a capital sum to those who would use it for the purposes of consumption (*WN*, V, ii, c, 12).

The examples are few, but the basic principles are extremely important and capable of wide application. Smith is here suggesting that the state is justified in intervening to offset the consequences of ignorance and lack of knowledge or fore-thought on the part of individuals or groups of individuals.

Smith was also well aware, to take a third point, that the modern version of the 'circular flow' depended on paper money and on credit; in effect a system of 'dual circulation' involving a complex of transactions linking producers and merchants, dealers and consumers (*WN*, II, ii, 88); transactions that would involve cash (at a level of the household) and credit (at the level of the firm). It is in this context that Smith advocated control over the rate of interest, set in such a way as to ensure that 'sober people are universally preferred, as borrowers, to prodigals and projectors' (*WN*, II, iv, 15).[9] He was also willing to regulate the small note issue in the interests of a stable banking system. To those who objected to this proposal, he replied that the interests of the community required it, and concluded that 'the obligation of building party walls, in order to prevent the communication of fire, is a violation of natural liberty, exactly of the same kind with the regulations of the banking trade which are here proposed' (*WN*, II, ii, 94).

Although Smith's monetary analysis is not regarded as amongst the strongest of his contributions, it should be remembered that the witness of the collapse of major Banks in the 1770s was acutely aware of the problems generated by a sophisticated credit structure. It was in this context that Smith articulated a very general principle, namely, that 'those exertions of the natural liberty of a few individuals, which might endanger the security of the whole society, are, and ought to be, restrained by the laws of all governments; of the most free, as well as of the most despotical' (*WN*, II, ii, 94). One wonders what he might have made of the recent stock market crash.

While the state must provide for the important services of justice and defence, emphasis should be given, finally, to Smith's contention that a major responsibility of government must be the provision of certain public works and institutions for facilitating the commerce of the society which were 'of such a nature, that the profit could never repay the expence to any individual or small number of individuals, and which it, therefore cannot be expected that any individual or small number of individuals should erect or maintain' (*WN*, V, i, c, 1). In short he was concerned to point out that the state would have to organise services or public works which the profit motive alone could not guarantee.

The examples of public works which Smith provided include such items as roads, bridges, canals and harbours—all thoroughly in keeping with the conditions of the time and with Smith's emphasis on the importance of transport as a contribution to the effective operation of the market and to the process of economic growth. But although the list is short by modern standards, the discussion of what may be called the 'principles of provision' is of interest for the emphasis given to situations where market forces *alone* will not generate services or facilities which are necessary to the economic well-being of the whole.

So far we have treated the linkages between the parts of Smith's course in a particular way; that is by looking forward from the ethics and the jurisprudence to the economic analysis, and thus to the policy prescriptions which have just been considered. But there is also a sense in which it is useful to look back to the ethics and the jurisprudence from the vantage point supplied by the *Wealth of Nations*.

III

With regard to the ethics, the most important aspect is surely to be found in Smith's concern with the social and psychological costs of economic growth.[10]

Two major issues arise:

It will be recalled that for Smith moral judgement depends on our capacity for acts of imaginative sympathy and that such acts can only take place within the context of some social group (*TMS*, III, i, 3). However, Smith also observed that the mechanism of the impartial spectator might well break down in the context of the modern economy, due in part to the size of some manufacturing units and of the cities which housed them.

Smith observed that in the actual circumstances of modern society, the poor man could find himself in a situation where the 'mirror of society' (*TMS*, III, i, 3) was inoperative. As Smith noted, the 'man of rank and fortune is by his station the distinguished member of a great society, who attend to every part of his conduct, and who thereby oblige him to attend to every part of it himself'. But, Smith went on, the 'man of low condition', while 'his conduct may be attended to' so long as he is a member of a country village, 'as soon as he comes into a great city, he is sunk in obscurity and darkness. His conduct is observed and attended to by nobody, and he is therefore very likely to neglect it himself, and to abandon himself to every sort of low profligacy and vice' (*WN*, V, i, g, 12); a problem unlikely to be offset by membership of the family, since the prevailing mode of earning subsistence makes it easy for its members to 'separate and disperse, as interest or inclination may direct' (*TMS*, VI, ii, 1, 17, 13).

In the modern context, Smith suggests that the individual thus placed would naturally seek some kind of compensation, often finding it not merely in religion but in religious sects: that is, in small social groups within which the individual can acquire 'a degree of consideration which he never had before' (*WN*, V, i, g, 12). Smith noted that the morals of such sects were often disagreeably 'rigorous and unsocial',[11] and recommended two policies to offset this.

The first is learning, on the ground that science is 'the great antidote to the poison of enthusiasm and superstition'. It is interesting to observe that what Smith had in mind was an informed 'middling' rank of men whose influence would support the poor. In this context, Smith suggested that government should act 'by instituting some sort of probation, even in the higher and more difficult sciences, to be undergone by every person before he was permitted to exercise any liberal profession, or before he could be received as a candidate for any honourable office of trust or profit' (*WN*, V, i, g, 14).

The second remedy was through the encouragement given to those who might expose or dissipate the folly of sectarian bitterness by encouraging an interest in painting, music, dancing, drama—and satire (*WN,* V, i, g, 15).[12]

If the problem of solitude and isolation consequent on the growth of cities explain Smith's first group of points, a related trend in the shape of the division of labour helps to account for the second. In discussing this important source of economic benefit (which is emphasised to an extraordinary degree in the *Wealth of Nations*) Smith noticed that it could involve costs. Or, as Smith put it in one of the most famous passages from the *Wealth of Nations*:

> In the progress of the division of labour, the employment of the far greater part of those who live by labour, that is, of the great body of people, comes to be confined to a few very simple operations; frequently to one or two. But the understandings of the greater part of men are necessarily formed by their ordinary employments. The man whose whole life is spent in performing a few simple operations, of which the effects too are, perhaps, always the same, or very nearly the same, has no occasion to exert his understanding, or to exercise his invention in finding out expedients for removing difficulties which never occur. He naturally loses, therefore, the habit of such exertion, and generally becomes as stupid and ignorant as it is possible for a human creature to become (*WN,* v, i, f, 50).

It is the fact that the 'labouring poor, that is the great body of the people' must necessarily fall into the state outlined that makes it necessary for government to intervene.

Smith's justification for intervention is, as before, market failure, in that the labouring poor, unlike those of rank and fortune, lack the leisure, means, or (by virtue of their occupations) the inclination to provide education for their children (*WN*, V, i, f, 53). In view of the nature of the problem, Smith's programme seems rather limited, but he did argue that the poor could be taught 'the most essential parts of education . . . to read, write, and account' together with the 'elementary parts of geometry and mechanics' (*WN*, V, i, f, 54, 55).

It is interesting to observe in this context that Smith was prepared to go so far as to infringe the natural liberty of the subject, at least where the latter is narrowly defined, in recommending that the 'public can impose upon almost the whole body of the people the necessity of acquiring those most essential parts of education, by obliging every man to undergo an examination or probation in them before he can obtain the freedom in any corporation or be allowed to set up any trade either in a village or town corporate (*WN*, V, i, f, 57).

Distinct from the above, although connected with it, is Smith's concern with the decline of martial spirit which is the consequence of the nature of the fourth, or commercial stage.

In the *Wealth of Nations* Smith seems to have had in mind the provision of some kind of military education which he supported as a contribution to the well-being of the individual.

He concluded that 'Even though the martial spirit of the people were of no use towards the defence of the society, yet to prevent that sort of mental mutilation, deformity and wretchedness, which cowardice necessarily involves in it, from spreading themselves through the great body of the people, would still deserve the most serious attention of government' (*WN*, V, i, f, 60). Smith went on to liken the control of cowardice to the prevention of 'a leprosy or any other loathsome and offensive disease'—moving Jacob Viner to add public health to Smith's already lengthy list of governmental functions.[13]

IV

Smith not only identified the various services which the state was expected to provide; he also gave a great deal of attention to the forms of organisation which would be needed to ensure efficient delivery.

In the discussion of defence, for example, he noted that the 'wisdom of the state' (*WN*, V, i, a, 14) would have to be deployed given the expense of modern warfare and the structure of the modern economy. Of the options open to Governments, he preferred a standing army to a militia because the former would be more specialised and therefore more efficient (*WN*, V, i, a, 14). Recognising the political dangers which were involved in this solution, he was careful to add that it would be acceptable only:

> where the sovereign is himself the general, and the principal nobility and gentry of the country the chief officers of the army; where the military force is placed under the command of those who have the greatest interest in the support of the civil authority, because they have themselves the greatest share of that authority (*WN*, V, i, a, 41).

Smith argued that since the (great) expense involved was laid out 'for the general benefit of the whole society', it ought to be defrayed 'by the general contribution of the whole society, all the different members contributing, as nearly as possible, in proportion to their respective abilities' (*WN*, V, i, i, 1).

In the case of justice, Smith contended that the sovereign has the duty 'of protecting, as far as possible, every member of the society from the injustice or oppression of every other member of it' (*WN*, V, i, b, 1). Here he contended that effective provision of so central a service depended crucially on a clear separation of the judicial from the executive power (*WN*, V, i, b, 23).

As Alan Peacock has pointed out, Smith's efficiency criteria are distinguished from this basic issue of organisation, the argument being, in effect, that the services provided by attorneys, clerks, or judges should be paid for in such a way as to encourage productivity.[14] Smith also ascribed the 'present admirable constitution of the courts of justice in England' to the use of a system of court fees which had served to encourage competition between the courts of king's bench, chancery, and exchequer (*WN*, V, i, b, 20, 21). A further interesting and typical feature of the discussion is found in Smith's argument that although justice is a service to the whole community, none the less, the costs of handling specific *causes* should be borne by those who give occasion to, or benefit from, them. He therefore concluded that the 'expence of the administration of justice . . . may very properly be defrayed by the particular contribution of one or other, or both of those two different sets of persons, according as different occasions may require, that is, by fees of court' (*WN*, V, i, i, 2), rather than by a charge on general funds.

Smith's treatment of justice is of interest because it reveals many of the basic principles which underlie his discussion of public finance. In general Smith believed that the state should ensure that services are provided indirectly (rather than by means of provision organised and controlled from the centre); that such services should be self-financing wherever possible, and especially that those services should be 'so structured as to engage the motives and interests of those concerned'.[15]

In the case of elementary education he argued that the British Government should ensure provision by setting up institutions similar to the Scottish Parish Schools:

> where children may be taught for a reward so moderate, that a common labourer may afford it; the master being partly, but not wholly paid by the publick; because if he was wholly, or even principally paid by it, he would soon learn to neglect his business (*WN*, V, i, f, 55).

The 'incentive' argument is also eloquently developed in Smith's treatment of universities where he argued that degrees can be likened to the statutes of apprenticeship (*Corr*, 177) and protested against the idea of universities having a monopoly of higher education (*Corr*, 174). In particular Smith objected to a situation where professors enjoyed a stable and high income irrespective of competence or industry (*WN*, V, i, f, 7). In the same context he argued in favour of free movement of students between teachers and institutions (*WN*, V, i, f, 12,

13) as a means of inducing teachers to provide appropriate services. Smith concluded:

> The expence of the institutions for education and religious instruction is . . . beneficial to the whole society, and may, therefore, without injustice, be defrayed by the general contribution of the whole society. This expence, however, might perhaps with equal propriety, and even with some advantage, be defrayed altogether by those who receive the immediate benefit of such education and instruction, or by the voluntary contribution of those who think they have occasion for either the one or the other (*WN*, V, i, i, 5).

The theme was continued in the discussion of 'public works' where Smith suggested that the main problems to be addressed were those of equity and efficiency.

With regard to *equity*, Smith argued that public works such as highways, bridges, and canals should be paid for by those who use them and in proportion to the wear and tear occasioned. At the same time, he argued that the consumer who pays the charges generally gains more from the cheapness of carriage than he loses in the charges incurred:

> The person who finally pays this tax, therefore, gains by the application, more than he loses by the payment of it. His payment is exactly in proportion to his gain. It is in reality no more than a part of that gain which he is obliged to give up in order to get the rest. It seems impossible to imagine a more equitable method of raising a tax (*WN*, V, i, d, 4).

In addition, he suggested that tolls should be higher in the case of luxury goods so that by this means 'the indolence and vanity of the rich is made to contribute in a very easy manner to the relief of the poor, by rendering cheaper the transportation of heavy goods . . .' (*WN*, V, i, d, 5).

Smith also defended the principle of direct payment on the ground of *efficiency*. Only by this means, he argued, would it be possible to ensure that services are provided where there is a recognisable need; only in this way would it be possible to avoid building roads through a desert for the sake of some private interest; or a great bridge 'thrown over a river at a place where nobody passes, or merely to embellish the view from the windows of a neighbouring palace; things which sometimes happen, in countries where works of this kind are carried on by any other revenue than that which they themselves are capable of affording' (*WN*, V, i, d, 6). In the same vein he argued against government 'taking the management of the turnpikes into its own hand', and settling the charges, on the ground that the tolls levied would come to reflect the needs of the state rather than of the roads; that such charges would be highly regressive, and that 'it would be still more difficult, than it is at present, to compel the proper application of any part of the turnpike tolls' (*WN*, V, i, d, 14).

Smith also argued that while governments must be responsible for establishing major public works, care should be taken to ensure that the services were administered by such bodies or under such conditions as made it in the interest of individuals to do so effectively. Smith tirelessly emphasised the point, already noticed in the discussion of justice, namely, that in every trade and profession 'the exertion of the greater part of those who exercise it, is always in proportion to the necessity they are under of making that exertion' (*WN*, V, i, f, 4). On this ground he approved of the expedient used in France, whereby a construction engineer was made a present of tolls on a canal for which he had been responsible—thus ensuring that it was in his interest to keep the canal in good repair.

Smith used a number of such devices: advocating for example that the administration of roads would have to be handled in a different way from canals because of course they are passable even when full of holes. Here he suggested that the 'wisdom of parliament' would have to be applied to the appointment of proper persons, with 'proper courts of inspection' for 'controlling their conduct, and for reducing the tolls to what is barely sufficient for executing the work to be done by them' (*WN*, V, i, d, 9).

Smith also recognised that such services could not always be paid for by those who used them, arguing that in such cases 'local or provincial expences of which the benefit is local or provincial' ought, so far as possible, to be no burden on general taxation, it being 'unjust that the whole of society should contribute towards an expence of which the benefit is confined to a part of the society' (*WN*, V, i, i, 3). But here again it is argued (in the interests of efficiency) that such services 'are always better maintained by a local and provincial administration, than by the general revenue of the state, of which the executive power must always have the management' (*WN*, V, i, d, 18).

It is also worth noting that even where recourse has to be made to general taxation, Smith argued that such taxes should be imposed in accordance with the generally accepted canons of taxation;[16] that so far as possible such taxes should avoid interference with the allocative mechanism, and that they ought not to constitute disincentives to the individual effort on which the working of the system has been seen to depend (for example, taxes on profits).

V

The historical dimension of Smith's work also affects the treatment of public policy, noting as he did that in every society subject to a process of transition, 'Laws frequently continue in force long after the circumstances, which first gave occasion to them, and which could alone render them reasonable, are no more' (*WN*, III, ii, 4). In such cases Smith suggested that arrangements which were once appropriate but are no longer so should be removed, citing as examples the laws of succession and entail which were represented by Smith as the remnants of a past, feudal society. While Smith's treatment of justice and defence provide remarkable examples of his capacity to deploy historical materials, perhaps the most interesting aspect of the discussion from the standpoint of the emphasis on Smith and public policy, arises from the broadly constitutional dimension of his historical treatment of jurisprudence, to which we drew attention at the outset.

It will be recalled that for Smith the fourth economic stage could be seen to be associated with a particular form of social and political structure which influence the outline of government and the context within which it must function. It may be noted in this connection that Smith associated the fourth economic stage with the advent of freedom in the 'present sense of the term'; that is, with the elimination of the relation of direct dependence which had been characteristic of the feudal agrarian period. Politically, the significant and associated development appeared to be the diffusion of power consequent on the emergence of new forms of wealth such as trade and manufacture which, at least in the peculiar circumstances of England, had been reflected in the increased significance of the House of Commons as compared to the House of Lords.[17]

In elaborating on this theme, Smith suggested that 'free governments' of the kind established in England and confirmed by the Revolution Settlement in the late seventeenth century inevitably operate within a particularly sensitive political and economic environment.

Smith drew attention to the fact that modern government of the British type was a complex instrument. Smith seems to have felt, for example, that the management of Parliament through the distribution of offices was 'a necessary feature of the British mixed government' (*Cf. WN*, IV, vii, c, 69);[18] a point which is in turn linked to the fact that the pursuit of office was itself a 'dazzling object of ambition': a competitive game with as its object the attainment of 'the great prizes which sometimes come from the wheel of the great state lottery of British politics' (*WN*, IV, vii, c, 75).

Smith added, in a passage which reflects the psychological assumptions of the *Theory of Moral Sentiments* (I, iii, 2, 'Of the Origin of Ambition'), that:

> Men desire to have some share in the management of publick affairs chiefly on account of the importance which it gives them. Upon the power which the greater part of the leading men, the natural aristocracy of every country, have of preserving or defending their respective importance, depends the stability and duration of every system of free government (*WN*, IV, vii, c, 74).

This point leads on to another which was emphasised by Smith, namely that the same economic forces which had served to elevate the House of Commons to a superior degree of influence had also served to make it an important focal point for sectional interests—a development which could seriously affect the legislation which was passed and thus affect that extensive view of the common good which ought ideally to direct the activities of Parliament, in fulfilling the functions of government outlined above.

It is recognised in the *Wealth of Nations* that the landed, moneyed, manufacturing, and mercantile groups all constitute special interests which could impinge on the working of government. Smith referred frequently to their 'clamorous importunity', and in speaking of the growth of monopolies pointed out that government policy 'has so much increased the number of some particular tribes of them, that, like an overgrown standing army, they have become formidable to the government, and upon many occasions intimidate the legislature' (*WN*, IV, ii, 43). In this connection it was suggested that the nature of the colonial relationship with America had been the product of the 'sneaking arts of underlying tradesmen'. He concluded that: 'Of the greater part of the regulations concerning the colony trade, the merchants who carry it on, it must be observed, have been the principal; advisers. We must not wonder, if, in the greater part of them, their interest has been more considered than either that of the colonies or that of the mother country' (*WN*, IV, vii, b, 49). Indeed Smith went further in suggesting that the legislative power possessed by employers generally could seriously disadvantage other classes in society. As he put it: 'Whenever the legislature attempts to regulate the differences between masters and their workmen, its counsellors are always the masters. When the regulation, therefore, is in favour of the workmen, it is always just and equitable; but it is sometimes otherwise when in favour of the masters' (*WN*, I, x, c, 61; *cf.* I, viii, 12, 13). Smith thus insisted that any legislative proposals emanating from this class:

> ought always to be listened to with great precaution, and ought never to be adopted till after having been long and carefully examined, not only with the most scrupulous, but with the most suspicious attention. It comes from an order of men, whose interest is never exactly the same with that of the publick, who have generally an interest to deceive and even to oppress the publick, and who accordingly have, upon many occasions, both deceived and oppressed it (*WN*, I, xi, p 10).

But at the same time, Smith noted that governments on the English model were likely to be particularly sensitive to public opinion—and as frequently constrained by it. Smith made much of the point and in a variety of ways. He noted, for example, that even if the British Government of the 1770s had thought it possible voluntarily to withdraw from the current conflict with America it could not pursue this eminently rational course. As he remarked in a *Memorandum* addressed to Alexander Wedderburn, Solicitor-General in Lord North's administration at the time of Saratoga; 'tho this termination of the war might be really advantageous, it would not, in the eyes of Europe appear honourable to Great Britain; and when her empire was so much curtailed, her power and dignity would be supposed to be proportionally diminished. What is of still greater importance, it could scarce fail to discredit the Government in the eyes of our own people . . . (it) . . . would have everything to fear from their rage and indignation at the public disgrace and calamity, for such they would suppose it to be, of thus dismembering the empire' (*Corr*, 383).

Smith gave a great deal of attention to the general problems presented by the confirmed habits and prejudices of a people and to the need to adjust legislation accordingly. For example, he likened the fear of engrossing and forestalling in discussing the corn trade, 'to the popular terrors and suspicions of witchcraft' (IV, v, b, 26), and described the law dealing with the exportation of wheat as one which 'though not the best in itself, is the best which the interests, prejudices, and temper of the Times would admit of' (IV, v, b, 63). The reference to Solon in the context of the previous discussion finds an echo in the *Moral Sentiments* (VI, ii, 2, 16) where it is stated that when the legislator: 'cannot conquer the rooted prejudices of the people by reason and persuasion, he will not attempt to subdue them by force . . . He will accommodate, as well as he can, his public arrangements to the confirmed habits and prejudices of the people; and will remedy as well as he can, the inconveniences which may flow from the want of those regulations which the people are averse to submit to. When he cannot establish the right, he will not disdain to ameliorate the wrong; but like Solon, when he cannot establish the best system of laws, he will endeavour to establish the best that the people can bear.'[19]

In short, we have to add government failure[20] to the problem of market failure, where the former may be related to the problem of structure as well as to public opinion—ironically, one of the most important pillars of freedom.

VI

While the modern reader has to make a considerable effort to understand Smith's intentions, students of his course in Glasgow and perhaps contemporary readers of his work, would quite readily perceive that the different parts were important of themselves and also that they display a certain pattern of inter-dependence. As we have seen, the ethical argument indicates the manner in which general rules of conduct emerge, and postulates the need for a system of force-backed law, appropriately administered if social order is to be possible. The treatment of jurisprudence showed the manner in which government emerged and developed through time, and threw some light on the actual content of rules of behaviour which are likely to prevail in the four different socio-economic states.

It would also be evident to Smith's students that the treatment of economics was based upon psychological judgements (such as the desire for status) which are only explained in the ethics, and that this branch of Smith's argument takes as given the particular socio-economic structure which is appropriate to the fourth economic stage, that of commerce.

The modern reader too will find much instruction in Smith's work, especially if the separate parts are seen, as Smith intended they should be, as making the parts a greater whole; an achievement which invites us to consider that economics, ethics, and jurisprudence should be seen as the essential components of what is now known as a system of social science.

This is not, of course, to minimise the importance of what many regard as Smith's major achievement.

The *Wealth of Nations* did, after all, provide the basis of classical economics in the form of a coherent, all-embracing account of 'general interconnexions'.[21] As Jacob Viner has pointed out, the source of Smith's originality lies in his 'detailed and elaborate application to the wilderness of economic phenomena of the unifying concept of a co-ordinated and mutually interdependent system of cause and effect relationships which philosophers and theologians had already applied to the world in general'.[22]

It was this aspect of the *Wealth of Nations* which led Smith's biographer, Dugald Stewart, to comment on its beautiful progression of ideas, and to draw a parallel between it and the mathematical and physical sciences (Stewart, IV, 22). In the words of another contemporary (and trenchant critic), Smith's completed work would be regarded as an 'Institute of the Principia of those laws of motion, by which the operations of the community are directed and regulated and by which they should be examined'.[23] The analogy with Newton is particularly apt, especially in view of Smith's admiring assessment in the concluding sections of the *Astronomy*, and in the *Lectures on Rhetoric* (*LRBL*, ii, 133–4).

The 'laws of motion' of the economy to which Thomas Pownall referred exposed the point that the exchange economy functioned effectively as a consequence of the activities of individuals who were unconscious of the end which these activities served to promote, namely benefit to society at large. Smith's general policy prescriptions follow:

In the words of a later commentator, Lord Robbins, Smith bequeathed to his successors in the classical school an opposition to conscious paternalism; a belief that 'central authority was incompetent to decide on a proper distribution of resources'. But above all Smith developed an important argument to the effect that economic freedom 'rested on a two fold basis: belief in the desirability of freedom of choice for the consumer and belief in the effectiveness, in meeting this choice, of freedom on the part of producers'.[24] Smith added a dynamic dimension to this theme in a passage which reminds us that his interests were not narrowly academic. As Smith made clear in his discussion of the Corn Laws:

> That security which the laws in Great Britain give to every man that he shall enjoy the fruits of his own labour, is alone sufficient to make any country flourish, notwithstanding these and twenty other absurd regulations of commerce; and this security was perfected by the revolution, much about the same time that the bounty was established. The natural effort of every man to better his condition, when suffered to exert itself with freedom and security, is so powerful a principle, that it is alone, and without any assistance, not only capable of carrying on the society to wealth and prosperity, but of surmounting a hundred impertinent obstructions with which the folly of human laws too often encumbers its operations (*WN*, IV, v, b, 43).

This is Smith's true position; a position which helps to explain continuing interest in his work. Yet it is also important for the modern reader to recall that the agenda for action by governments was partly determined by Smith's choice of the problems to be addressed. He was not, for example, concerned (as Steuart had been) to analyse or to consider the socio-economic problems which are likely to be involved in the transition from a primitive version of the exchange economy to the relatively elaborate capital using system which actually attracted his attention. Nor was Smith concerned with the problem of regional imbalance or underdeveloped economies generally. Moreover, Smith's views on economic adjustments were relatively long run which alllowed him to discount certain areas of concern. As J A Schumpeter once remarked of the German economist, von Justi, 'he was much more concerned than A Smith with the practical problems of government action in the short run vicissitudes of his time and country . . . His laisser-faire policy was laisser faire plus watchfulness, his private enterprise economy a machine that was logically automatic but exposed to breakdowns and hitches which his government was to stand ready to mend . . . his vision of economic policy might look like laisser faire with the nonsense left out'.[25]

This was not Smith's position. Yet even given this, the list of government functions is, as we have seen, quite impressive serving to remind the modern reader of two important points.

First, that Smith's list of recommended policies was longer than some popular assessments suggest. Smith emphatically did not think in terms of 'anarchy plus the constable', to use Carlyle's phrase. As Jacob Viner has observed:

> Adam Smith was not a doctrinaire advocate of laisser-faire. He saw a wide and elastic range of activity for government, and he was prepared to extend it even further if government, by improving its standard of competence, honesty, and public spirit, showed itself entitled to wider responsibilities.[26]

Another commentator, A L Macfie, once humorously remarked, on reviewing Viner's list of specific policies garnered from the *Wealth of Nations*, that 'they add up to suggest a formidable state autocracy; a socialist spread of controls that would make some modern socialist's eyes pop'.[27]

As Robbins has noted, in making a different but related point:

> The English Classical Economists never conceived the system of economic freedom as arising *in vacuo* or functioning in a system of law and order so simple and minimal as to be capable of being written down on a limited tablet of stone (or a revolutionary handbill) and restricted to the functions of the night-watchman. Nothing less than the whole complex of the Benthamite codes—Civil, Penal and Constitutional—was an adequate framework for their system.[28]

Second, it is important to recall the need to distinguish between the principles which Smith used in justifying intervention (which may be of universal validity) and the specific agenda which he offered (and which may reflect his understanding of the situation which he actually confronted at the time of writing).

The principles which justify intervention are, after all, wide-ranging in their implications. On Smith's argument, the state should regulate activity to compensate for the imperfect knowledge of the individuals; it is the state which must continuously scrutinise the relevance of particular laws and institutions; the state which has a duty to regulate and control the activities of individuals which might otherwise prove damaging to the interest of society at large, and it is the state which must make adequate provision for public works and services (including education) in cases where the profit motive is likely to prove inadequate. Such basic principles are open to wide application notably in the circumstances of a modern society. It is this point which helps to explain Eric Roll's judgement that Smith and Keynes 'would find much common ground in respect of the broad principles that should guide the management of the economy'.[29]

Smith would surely have had sympathy with Keynes' reading of a different situation, which led him to defend an enlargement of government activity 'both as the only practicable means of avoiding the destruction of economic forms in their entirety and as the condition of the successful functioning of individual initiative'.[30]

We are reminded of E R Seligman's warning to readers of the 1910 edition of the *Wealth of Nations*, namely that they must avoid 'absolutism' and respect the point that recent 'investigation has emphasised the changing conditions of time and place and has emphasised the principles of relativity'.[31] It is not appropriate uncritically to translate Smith's policy prescriptions from the eighteenth to the twentieth century—moreover this would be quite inconsistent with Smith's own teaching. Smith's work was marked by relativity of perspective—dominant features of the treatment of scientific knowledge in the essay on *Astronomy* and the analysis of rules of behaviour in the ethics.

The interpretation of Smith's intentions and the process of forming a judgement as to his relevance today are not easy tasks. Yet there are some areas of immediate interest which are less ambiguous but which have not attracted quite as much attention as they deserve.

First, there is the issue of market failure. There can be no doubt that if Sir James Steuart and Adam Smith adopted different perspectives on the economic process, they agreed on at least one proposition, namely that governments must intervene in this event simply because there is no alternative agency. The problem which remains to perplex us, is exactly that which exercised our eighteenth-century predecessors and over which they differed: it is the problem of how and with what degree of confidence we can identify just where and when markets have failed. To intervene too readily may involve some distortion of market forces; to delay too long may generate unacceptable social and economic costs.

Second, we should note the attention which Smith gave to the general problem of government failure. As we have seen, he offered a sophisticated analysis of the structure of modern government and the pressures to which it is subject, treating all of this as an integral part of the discussion of economic policy and of public finance. Smith would certainly have been surprised to find Professor Tullock referring to a *newly* established 'economics of politics' in a book published two hundred years after his own.[32]

Finally, more attention could be given to Smith's concern that the state should ensure the provision of important services but at the same time arrange that they are so organised as to ensure efficient delivery. This is the aspect of the book which should appeal to Mrs Thatcher—and also perhaps to Mr Gorbachev. Smith would not have been surprised at such an unlikely association, believing as he did that the principles of human nature were constant over time and place, irrespective of differing political philosophies.

REFERENCES

References to Wood (1983) give date of article on first publication, followed by volume and page number. References to Smith's works employ the usages of Glasgow edition, that is,

WN	The *Wealth of Nations*;
TMS	*Theory of Moral Sentiment*;
Astronomy	'The History of Astronomy', from *Essays on Philosophical Subjects* (EPS);
Stewart	Dugald Stewart, 'Account of the Life and Writings of Adam Smith';
LJ (A)	*Lectures on Jurisprudence*, Report dated 1762–3;
LF (B)	*Lectures on Jurisprudence,* Report dated 1766;
LRBL	*Lectures on Rhetoric and Belles Letters*;
Corr	*Correspondence of Adam Smith*;
EAS	*Essays on Adam Smith,* ed A S Skinner and T Wilson (1975)

In the Glasgow edition, *WN* was edited by R H Campbell, A S Skinner and W B Todd (1976);

TMS, by D D Raphael and A L Macfie (1976);

Corr, by E C Mossner and I S Ross (1977);

EPS, by W P D Wightman (1980);

LJ (A) by R L Meek, D D Raphael, and P G Stein (1978), and *LRBL*, by J C Bryce (1983). Oxford University Press.

References to *Corr* give page number.

References to *LJ* and *LRBL* give volume and page number from the *MS*.

All other references provide section, chapter, and paragraph number in order to facilitate the use of different editions.

For example:

Stewart, I, 12 Dugald Stewart 'Account', Section I, para 12.

TMS, I, i, 5, 5 *TMS*, Part I, section i, chapter 5, para 5.

WN, V, i, f, 26 *WN*, Book V, chapter i, section 6, para 26.

NOTES

1   This claim is one of those leading principles which Smith dated from the lectures which were delivered in Edinburgh (1748–51). See Stewart (IV, 35).
2   This paragraph is based on Black (1976), 50–1.
3   *Cf.* the advertisement to the sixth edition of *TMS*.
4   *Cf.* Roy Pasçal (1938) and R L Meek (1967). The economic dimension is also emphasised by David Reisman (1976).
5   See for example, T Wilson (1976).
6   *Cf.* Skinner (1979), chapter 5.
7   See for example, Richardson (1975) and Lowe (1975).
8   *Cf.* Skinner (1979), chapter 8.

9 This argument gave rise to Jeremy Bentham's letter XIII in the Defence of Usury (1787). The materials are included in *Corr*, Appendix C.
10 *Cf*. Joseph Cropsey (1975) and Robert Heilbroner (1975). The theme of 'alienation' has been developed by E G West (1975); Robert Lamb (1973) and D N Winch (1978), chapter 5. On the treatment of education, see M Blaug (1975).
11 Smith suggested that the state should encourage a number of religious sects in the interest of stability (i.e. a kind of competitive equilibrium) at *WN*, V, i, g, 16.
12 To this extent, Smith regarded types of labour, previously defined as unproductive (*WN*, II, iii) to be indirectly productive of benefit.
13 Viner (1928), Wood, i, 162.
14 A T Peacock (1975), *EAS*, 553–67.
15 Rosenberg (1960), 68; *cf*. Ricketts (1978).
16 See *WN*, V, ii, b.
17 See Forbes (1975) and Winch (1978) for analyses of Smith's politics.
18 Forbes, *Op. cit*. 183.
19 *Cf*. Haakonssen (1981), 97, 164.
20 Sir James Steuart also gave a great deal of attention to the constraints imposed on the sovereign by economic laws. See Skinner (1966), lxxxi. A O Hirschman (1977) contrasts the positions adopted by Steuart and Smith in this respect. The problem of government failure has been highlighted by E G West (1976).
21 Lionel Robbins (1953), 172.
22 Viner (1928), Wood, i, 143.
23 Thomas Pownall (1776), in *Corr* 354.
24 Robbins, *Op. cit*. 12.
25 Schumpeter (1954), 172.
26 Viner, Wood, i, 164.
27 Macfie (1967), Wood, i, 348.
28 Robbins, *Op. cit*. 188.
29 Roll (1976), Wood, ii, 154.
30 J M Keynes (1936), 380.
31 E R A Seligman (1910), xv.
32 Gordon Tulloch (1976), 2.

AUTHORITIES

Black, R D C (1976). 'Smith's Contribution in Historical Perspective', in T Wilson and A Skinner (eds) *The Market and the State: Essays in Honour of Adam Smith*, 42–63
Blaug, M 'The Economics of Education in English Classical Political Economy', *EAS*, 568–99
Cropsey, J 'Adam Smith and Political Philosophy', *EAS*, 132–53
Forbes, D 'Sceptical Whiggism, Commerce and Liberty', *EAS*, 179–201
Haakonssen, K (1981). *The Science of a Legislator: the Natural Jurisprudence of David Hume and Adam Smith*
Heilbroner, R L 'The Paradox of Progress: Decline and Decay in the *Wealth of Nations*', *EAS*, 524–39
Hirschman, A O (1977). *The Passions and the Interests*
Keynes, J M (1936). *The General Theory of Employment, Interest and Money*
Lamb, R (1973). 'Adam Smith's Concept of Alienation', *Oxford Economic Papers*, 25

Louve, A 'Adam Smith's System of Equilibrium Growth', *EAS*, 415–25

Macfie, A L (1967). 'The Moral Justification of Free Enterprise. A Lay Sermon on an Adam Smith Text' (first published in *Scottish Journal of Political Economy*, vol 14); Wood, vol 1 (1983), 342–50

Meek, R L (1967). *Economics and Ideology and Other Essays: Studies in the Development of Economic Thought*

Pascal, R (1938). 'Property and Society: The Scottish Contribution of the Eighteenth Century', *Modern Quarterly*, 1

Peacock, A T 'The Treatment of the Principles of Public Finance in the *Wealth of Nations*', *EAS*, 553–67

Pownall, Thomas, (1776). *A Letter from Governor Pownall to Adam Smith Corr*, appendix A

Reisman, D (1976). *Adam Smith's Sociological Economies*

Richardson, G B 'Adam Smith on Competition and Increasing Returns', *EAS*, 350–60

Ricketts, M (1978). 'Adam Smith on Politics and Economics' in *The Economics of Politics*, *IEA* Readings, 18

Robbins, L (1953). *The Theory of Economic Policy in English Classical Political Economy*

Roll, E (1976). 'The *Wealth of Nations* 1776–1976', first published in *Lloyds Bank Review*, 119: Wood, vol 2, 146–55

Rosenberg, N (1960). 'Some Institutional Aspects of the *Wealth of Nations*' first published in *Journal of Political Economy*, vol 18; Wood, vol 2, 105–20

Schumpeter, J A (1954). *History of Economic Analysis*

Seligman, E R A (ed) (1910). *Wealth of Nations*

Skinner, A S (ed) (1966). *Sir James Steuart: Principles of Political Economy*

Skinner, A S (1979). *A System of Social Science: Papers Relating to Adam Smith*

Tulloch, G (1976). *The Vote Motive*.

Viner, J (1927). 'Adam Smith and Laisser-Faire', first published in *Journal of Political Economy*, vol 35; Wood, vol 1 (1983), 143–67

West, E G 'Adam Smith and Alienation. Wealth Increases, Men Decay?', *EAS*, 540–52

West, E G (1976). 'Adam Smith's Economics of Politics', first published in *History of Political Economy*, vol 8; Wood, vol 1, 581–600

Wilson, T (1976). 'Sympathy and Self-Interest' in the *Market and the State* 73–99

Winch, D (1978). *Adam Smith's Politics. An Essay in Historiographic Revision*

Wood, J C (1983). *Adam Smith, Critical Assessments*, 4 vols

The Longevity of Adam Smith's Vision: Paradigms, Research Programmes and Falsifiability in the History of Economic Thought

D P O'Brien

Scot. Jnl. of Pol. Econ. June 1976

The historical importance of Adam Smith as an economist is without any real parallel in the entire development of economics. When Keynes died *The Times* wrote that 'To find an economist of comparable influence one would have to go back to Adam Smith.' (*The Times*, 1946). But Keynes has only been dead for thirty years so that, although his influence has been enormously wide throughout a greatly enlarged body of professional economists, it will take historians of the distant future to decide whether he ever attained a sway comparable to that achieved by the *Wealth of Nations*. Smith's legacy remains the standard of comparison.

Smith's huge achievement was to provide the foundation for the whole of Classical economics. Of course he did not build up the body of thought which we now know as Classical economics single handed; Ricardo's contribution cannot be disregarded and indeed one major study of Classical economics is actually entitled *Ricardian Economics* (Blaug, 1958). But, in the last resort, Classical economics *is* conceivable without Ricardo, whose influence progressively waned from 1830 if not before; while it is quite inconceivable without Adam Smith and the *Wealth of Nations*. This article will aim to trace the way in which Classical economics developed out of the *Wealth of Nations* and how its importance survived well beyond what we think of as the Marginal Revolution. Having traced the pattern, an attempt will be made to see which of the philosophies of the history of science drawn respectively from the works of Popper, Kuhn, and Lakatos will help us to understand the progress of Smith's influence during the development of Economics.

THE SMITHIAN BASIS OF CLASSICAL ECONOMICS

It seems indisputable that the basic vision of the economic system, as a *system*, was supplied for the whole of Classical economics (and beyond) by Adam

Smith. The concept was of an economic system with knowledge and decision-taking as an individual responsibility within a framework of law, justice, and security of property provided by government. Partly because of this framework the effects of individual decisions coalesced into a systematic whole affecting society. Within the framework, individuals pursued their self-interest—but it was self-interest shot through with social values.[1] It is important to appreciate this. Any interpretation of the view of self-interest propounded in the *Wealth of Nations* which does not take account of the 'sympathy' theory propounded in the *Theory of Moral Sentiments* (Smith, 1759, Part I, Section III, Ch III) will be seriously misleading. This pursuit of self-interest within the framework of law, and of social values which permeated both the law and the self-interest, produced a resource allocation which was conducive to economic growth, as capital owners sought to take advantage of *new* profit opportunities, products and techniques. It produced an allocation of resources which, though it may not have been optimal—Smith did not possess the concept of optimality in our sense which may or may not have been his loss—was relatively *superior* to anything that government allocation of resources could produce instead.

Since it was relatively better (and thus the best that an *imperfect* world could manage) it implied a harmony between social and self-interest—as defined above.

It is true, as we shall see, that this optimistic view did come into question for a time when Ricardo's influence was at its zenith. For Ricardo believed that there was a real disharmony involved in the system of economic relationships, in that the interests of the landlords conflicted with those of the rest of the community. But this view found relatively little support and certainly not long-lasting support. The majority of the Classical economists, while conceding, as indeed Smith had done in specific instances, that there was always the possibility of areas of disharmony, preferred to take the view that the landlords had mistaken their real interests. Ricardo's attempts to show that, for instance, it was against the interests of the landlords to introduce improvements, were regarded as unsuccessful by his fellows. In general Smith's vision predominated.

It was not, of course only a general vision which Adam Smith gave to Classical economics. In a number of specific areas the analysis provided in his great book was either taken over entirely or used as the basis for more developed treatments by later writers.

Most fundamental of all, Smith's vision of growth was taken over whole and entire by Classical economics. It is true that Ricardo gave it a peculiar twist through his particular version of the stagnation thesis. But the idea of growth as the interaction of capital accumulation, division of labour, technical change, and population increase, was the fundamental one which Classical economics retained. Spanners could be thrown into these works by, for instance, the premature depression of the rate of profit via the Corn Laws: but the interactions in those works were accepted by all. So, with the exception of Ricardo's tax chapters (and their reproduction by James Mill), was the Smithian treatment of the *finance* of government. McCulloch's *Treatise,* the great public finance work of Classical economics (McCulloch, 1845), is wholly Smithian. Only J S Mill really tried to advance the analysis by introducing Utilitarianism into the discussion of tax incidence.

To have provided the whole of the basic vision of Classical economics, *and* the growth theory for a set of economic ideas which were *fundamentally* concerned with growth, would have been an enormous achievement on its own. But Adam Smith would not have expected all that he wrote to be taken over whole and entire. He believed in the evolution of systems of knowledge, not in the arrival at a final and immovable truth.[2] So it was appropriate that elements in his system provided the basis for later Classical developments. On the subjects of population and of wages Smith laid the foundations for all the later Classical treatments. His book contained a loose version of Malthus' population mechanism: Malthus made it rigid but in the hands of his successors—this is particularly true of the work of McCulloch and of Senior but it is also applicable to that of J S Mill—it became a loose fluid relationship very similar in its essence to that envisaged by Smith. The embryo wage-fund in the *Wealth of Nations* (part of Smith's growth model, like his population mechanism) was rigidified—especially by McCulloch, Ricardo, and Senior— and then partially relaxed again. The analysis of *relative* wages in the *Wealth of Nations* was retained intact throughout virtually all the Classical treat-ments—the only development being the introduction, by J S Mill and Cairnes, of non-competing groups. The Smithian treatment of rent—both price-determined and price-determining, without any indication of how these two concepts might be reconciled—provided the basis for the Classical rent theory developed by Malthus, West and Ricardo—though, through neglect of transfer earnings, their analysis was, in important respects, while clearer, less satisfactory than that from which it sprang.

The Smithian view of profit as interest plus a risk premium provided the basis for the later, more detailed, treatments of the components of the profit reward by Tooke and McCulloch: and his view of the savings mechanism (with his vagueness as to whether the rate of time preference was zero, positive, or negative) led to the later developments, by Rea and J S Mill, while the ambiguities in the *Wealth of Nations* about the *origin* of the interest agio made necessary the development of the theory of abstinence by Senior and J S Mill.

Smith's value theory was enormously influential. His adoption of a cost of production theory of value gave a stamp to virtually the whole of Classical value theory. Even the Ricardian version, which differed from Smith's in important respects (since it recognised labour as the only major input and, being designed as a part of the Corn Law model, was concerned, via the Invariable Measure, with the measurement of progress towards the stationary state) was still a constant cost, supply-determined-price model. Moreover, the succesors of Ricardo gradually turned his value theory back into a Smithian one so that when we reach J S Mill we find a Smithian value theory (except for the elimination of rent as a price-determined surplus) back in office. Even the subjective value theorists, at least Say and those influenced by him, took Smith's preservation of the Pufendorf-Hutcheson position in his treatment of market value as the starting point.[3]

In other areas, not surprisingly, developments went far beyond what the *Wealth of Nations* had to offer. Classical international trade theory, it is true, started from the Smithian concept of absolute advantage. The source of supply for a commodity which entered into international trade was, in this view, simply that place where the absolute input requirements were lowest. But Torrens and Ricardo were faced with the problem of showing that a country could still gain from trade if it was superior to other countries in all respects. Their solution to this, in the form of the theory of comparative costs, was a major advance on what Smith had to offer, particularly as Torrens (and later J S Mill) developed a theory to explain the division of the gains arising from trade on the basis of comparative advantage, through the theory of reciprocal demand. This was pure theory at its very best: and Ricardo must undoubtedly be given the credit for many of these achievements. For it was he who provided the impetus to pure theorising in this area. Yet even here, for those who were not pure theorists, the Smithian vision of trade on the basis of absolute advantage, and the concept of the interaction of trade and growth (as stressed by Smith rather than by Ricardo whose analysis was essentially static) were probably more important. In particular, there was the so called vent-for-surplus doctrine which saw countries engaging in international trade so as to rid themselves of surplus commodities in which they had an absolute advantage and which they were producing in ever increasing amounts as economic growth took place. Such surpluses could then be exchanged for commodities which were not produced under favourable domestic conditions. In nineteenth-century Britain, with its fast growing manufacturing sector which was in advance of any other country in the world for so long, this must have seemed an intuitively reasonable approach.

Another Smithian concept which must have had an intuitive appeal was the one that trade, by introducing new products, stimulated effort, enterprise, and further trade. Indeed this was a point which Malthus—under Smith's influence—made to Ricardo in discussing the gains from trade (Viner, 1937, pp 528–9). These gains could not, then, be assessed solely in terms of the increased productivity of resources in obtaining, indirectly through trade rather than directly through domestic production, a *given* range of commodities.

In the field of monetary theory Classical economics also went far beyond what Smith had to offer. The basic concept of the nature and role of money, supplied by Smith (and, *inter alia,* Joseph Harris) did of course stay with Classical economics. The 'great wheel of circulation and distribution' (Smith, 1776, I, 279), the peculiar qualities of the precious metals, the economising effects of paper money, and the use of banking likened to 'wagon ways through the air' which left the roads free for pasture (Smith, 1776, I, 304)—all these stayed with Classical economics. But Classical monetary theory, as one of the really great achievements of the Classical economists, went far beyond this. Starting from Hume's exposition of the price-specie-flow mechanism (of which Smith knew, of course) (Smith, 1763, p 197) it went on to the self-regulating distribution of the precious metals, inflation, the theory of an inconvertible paper currency under a free exchange rate, the theory of a convertible currency under a fractional reserve system, and the credit multiplication of bank deposits—Torrens and Pennington being, of course, the authors who achieved this last. Adam Smith had the perhaps dubious distinction in the two great monetary controversies, the Bullion debate and the Currency and Banking debate, of being the author of the Real Bills Doctrine (later re-named the Doctrine of Reflux) which was quite clearly on the losing side of these debates.

But all this is hardly surprising. Not only did Adam Smith never conceive of a science (including, for this purpose, economics) as having reached, or being likely to reach, the end of its development; but the great steps forward in monetary and international trade theory were stimulated by pressing practical economic problems resulting from a degree of growth and development in the British economy which Smith did not live to see. This may also explain why his view of the complementarity of labour and machinery and his neglect of the problem of aggregate demand failures—Say's Law is of course embryonically in the *Wealth of Nations*—both came under some pressure, especially in the second and third decades of the nineteenth century. Yet eventually Smith's view prevailed on both these matters: despite Barton and Ricardo, the majority of the Classical economists, while conceding that the installation of machinery could harm labour in the short run (and thus being prepared to advocate cushioning measures to mitigate this short-run harm) were firmly of the opinion that in the *long run* there was no such conflict. Similarly, on the question of aggregate demand, Lauderdale and Malthus found very few supporters for their fears that capital-stock adjustment problems would lead to demand failures in a growing economy.

On matters of policy and the *role* (as distinct from the finance, touched on earlier) of government, new problems, emerging in the century after the *Wealth of Nations*, brought forth new insights and recommendations from the Classical economists. Yet Smith's influence proved extremely durable, not only in giving the Classical economists the pragmatic approach to intervention which characterised their recommendations—intervention was, at bottom, only a way of producing the correct framework so that individual and social interests coincided as far as possible, and Smith himself had been prepared to recommend intervention in a number of areas—but also on some specific matters. In particular the Smithian view that colonies were a wasteful construction for the benefit of merchants:

> To found a great empire for the sole purpose of raising up a people of customers, ... is ... a project altogether unfit for a nation of shopkeepers; but extremely fit for a nation whose government is influenced by shopkeepers. Such statesmen, and such statesmen only, are capable of fancying that they will find some advantage in employing the blood and treasure of their fellow-citizens, to found and maintain such an empire. (Smith, 1776, II, 114)

was for long highly influential with the Classical economists, although, as Professor Donald Winch has shown (Winch, 1965), it was ultimately largely superseded by the new wave of 'scientific colonisation'—McCulloch being the only major figure amongst the Classical economists to remain faithful to Smith's original view.

The Smithian Vision Beyond 1870

In discussing the longevity of Adam Smith's vision we have, of course, to focus in the first instance on Classical economics. But to provide a complete picture of the durability of the view of the economic world set forth in the *Wealth of Nations* we have to go well beyond the era of Classical economics. Where there is no obvious date at which to draw a line (and Smith's influence is still clearly with us in a number of areas) it is I think worth showing how a basically Classical approach (and hence a basically Smithian one) continued to be characteristic of main-stream economics works well after 1870 and the beginning of the era that we now think of as the Marginal Revolution.

When we look at a work published as late as the second edition of Nicholson's *Elements* (Nicholson, 1909), we find that there are fifty-five separate sub-headings in the index under 'Adam Smith' and thirty-eight under 'J S Mill' while Marshall rates twenty-nine page references but no sub-headings at all. When we look at the details of the text we find *traces* of the Marginal Revolution: but little more. The distinction between total and marginal utility (Nicholson, 1909, pp 23–8) is recognisably post 1870: and this has some influence (though actually remarkably little) on the treatment of value later in the book. But the treatment of wages for instance is largely confined to a review of the wage-fund and a vague productivity theory. The latter is not marginal productivity; and Smith may be said to have had both a wage-fund and a vague productivity theory.

Sidgwick's discussion in his *Principles* (Sidgwick, 1887) is also Classical, and remarkably unmarked by the Marginal Revolution, despite the acknowledgements in his preface to such diverse authorities as Jevons, Cairnes, Marshall, Hearn and F A Walker. Criticism from Edgeworth and Wicksteed is also acknowledged in the second edition. Yet, despite the statement that Sidgwick believed himself to 'owe most to Jevons' *Theory of Political Economy,* the leading ideas of which have been continually in my thoughts' (Sidgwick, 1887 p v.) we find the treatment of value and those of wages, and of interest and capital, apparently innocent of Jevonian influence. The work as a whole is marked by a broad common sense very reminiscent of Adam Smith.

Another example is the famous work by C F Bastable, *Public Finance* (Bastable, 1892). This is, in design and spirit, an updated version of McCulloch's classic *Treatise* (McCulloch, 1845) although the treatment is considerably broadened in content by including the expenditure as well as the revenue side of government.

Of course, it is true that, during the period after 1870, the leaders of the profession both in England and abroad, men like Jevons, Marshall, Wicksteed, Edgeworth, Walras and Menger and their followers, were forging ahead in developing the system of economics which we now associate with that era in the history of economic thought. But if we consider the works which were offered by other men, men in influential academic positions and sometimes (as in the case of Sidgwick) men with a considerable intellectual reputation, we find the hand of Adam Smith still lying heavy upon the pages.

The Waxing and Waning of the Smithian Star

The enormous longevity of Adam Smith's influence, and the quite fundamental nature of his contribution to Classical economics, can then hardly be disputed. But it would be misleading to give the impression that Smith's influence was constant throughout the era of Classical economics. It was not. It was not only the post 1870 era which saw a decline in Smith's influence.

From the publication of the *Wealth of Nations* in 1776 through to the economic events of the Napoleonic Wars, Smith's great book was clearly the dominant work on economics. But then there arose a new star. Monetary events and the era of inconvertibility raised problems which were not covered in the *Wealth of Nations*; and increasing corn prices, coupled with agricultural protection, raised questions about the future courses of both economic growth and of income distribution. On the first score, the great Bullion debate succeeded in developing monetary theory to a pitch far higher than that achieved by Adam Smith; while on the second, Ricardo's system, in the form of his corn model, provided an analysis of the corn question (including, under this head, growth prospects and the macro-economic distribution of income) which economists, or at least the leaders amongst them, found highly persuasive. Part of this new wave proved long lasting. The monetary theory not only lasted but was refined and developed further as the century progressed. But then there was nothing in it which was inconsistent with the basic Smithian analytical approach. The corn model, however, suffered a severe decline— there is first hand testimony to this in a report of the proceedings of the Political Economy Club (Political Economy Club, 1921, pp 223–4)—a decline so severe indeed that by 1846 even the attack on the Corn Laws themselves probably owed as much to Smith as to Ricardo. In particular, McCulloch's analysis of the likely course of corn prices in the absence of protection was made on the basis of an absolute advantage model; and McCulloch was highly influential. Nevertheless, a bastard form of the Ricardian corn model lingered on in the publications of the Anti-Corn-Law League and other of the cruder supporters of free trade, who endeavoured to persuade the working population that repeal was in their interests, as it would lead to cheap bread, while persuading the manufacturers that repeal was in their interests as it would lead to cheap labour. But as far as the leaders amongst the Classical economists were concerned the Smithian system—still bearing Ricardian scars, especially in the work of J S Mill, but recognisably Smithian for all that—remained in the ascendant for the remainder of the Classical era. From 1870 onwards there developed, of course, the phenomenon known as the Marginal Revolution. But this was a slow progress although, unlike the Ricardian ascent, it was not due to be reversed. However, because it was slow, the Smithian view of the world continued to be the stock in trade of economists long after shining new tools had been refined and developed. For the most part these tools remained long unused in dealing with any real economic problem.[4]

Smith's influence then fluctuated, and was of varying pervasiveness during (and beyond) the era of Classical economics. But there is a large (and growing) body of literature in the history and philosophy of science which purports to provide an explanatory framework for the rise, ascendancy, and fall of bodies of ideas. It is then interesting to see how these perform as explanations of the vicissitudes of Smith's influence.

THEORIES OF THE HISTORY OF SCIENCE

(i) *The Popperian Falsificationism*

Popperianism as a theory of what scientists actually do (as distinct from what they *ought* to do, which is surely its main purpose) can be dismissed fairly quickly; not necessarily because of any intrinsic lack of merit on its home ground of the natural sciences, but because several critical features of its schema are missing in the history of economics.

The Popperian schema sees scientific progress as taking place through the formulation of hypotheses which are then subject to testing. Falsifiability is the hallmark of true science. A hypothesis will survive so long as it is not falsified by testing or—outside the domain of the naïve or dogmatic falsificationists, of whom Popper is not one—until such falsification is accepted as conclusive by the general body of scientists. It is fairly obvious why this approach need not detain us very long in the context of the present discussion. For Smith's ideas were not subjected to a testing programme of falsification; indeed, unlike Ricardo, Smith offered very few unambiguous predictions which would invite attempts at falsification. Nor, of course, was there any serious use of statistical apparatus to test Smith's ideas. We cannot, then, explain the longevity of the Smithian vision by reference to a long period of successful testing followed by ultimate failure (while a number of writers—Nicholson, Sidgwick and Bastable—persisted in judging that the tests were inconclusive). This would be a pretentious caricature of the history of our subject during the nineteenth century. The Popperian apparatus simply does not help us here. It should hardly be necessary to say that there were none of the 'crucial experiments' which Popper sees as occurring in the history of natural science.

(ii) *The Kuhnian Revolutions*

The ideas put forward in Kuhn's charming and deeply impressive *Structure of Scientific Revolutions* (Kuhn, 1962) are now well known to economists. We have had the concept of a paradigm introduced, and this concept—that view of what science (or sometimes a branch of it) is about and what and how it does its work, which is accepted by the 'scientific community'—governs all 'normal scientific' activity *including the actual process of testing*. 'Normal science' is a puzzle-solving activity; failure to solve the puzzles suggested by a particular paradigm reflects on the scientist not the paradigm, except at a time of crisis when a paradigm is under attack. The process of paradigm replacement, when a new paradigm comes to be accepted by the scientific community, is a 'Scientific Revolution'.

This is all a much more relativist way of looking at science than that offered by Popper—though it should be said that Kuhn has attempted to deny the charge of relativism.[5] Crucial to this aspect of the argument is the idea that paradigms are incommensurable (so that we cannot speak of *progress*) and that testing (because it involves accepted instruments and techniques developed under the reign of any particular paradigm) is very much paradigm-dominated. Falsification then becomes a paradigm-limited operation.

Described baldly in this way Kuhn's system sounds very much less persuasive than it seems when presented by its author buttressed with numerous examples from the history of several branches of natural science. Yet in many ways it is, *for economists*, a much more illuminating way of looking at their subject than that supplied by Popper. This is for two reasons. Firstly although the concept of paradigm has come under considerable attack from philosophers—one of Kuhn's supporters handed a great weapon to his opponents by painstakingly passing a period spent in hospital recording twenty-one different uses of the term by Kuhn in his book (Masterman, 1970)—it is actually a very helpful one. It can be seen to be useful when we consider a paradigm as a pair of spectacles through which we see the world. This is the interpretation suggested by Kuhn's discussion of the concept in connection with Gestalt psychology (Kuhn, 1962, pp 111ff.) Secondly, it is helpful because one of the important things which a paradigm does is to limit our view of what is the proper area of scientific concern. The changes of focus which occurred with the (eventual) triumph of the Marginal Revolution (and then, later on, with the Keynesian Revolution) have often been noticed by economists; and here the Kuhnian approach is illuminating. But does all this help us to understand the vicissitudes of Adam Smith's ideas?

It is perfectly possible to regard the *Wealth of Nations* as providing a paradigm—that of self-interest pursuit and decentralised decision-taking in a growth context viewed as producing a relatively best state of affairs and relatively efficient allocation of resources. So far, so good. But, if we are to take Kuhn's apparatus seriously within the context of the history of economic thought, we need to address ourselves to two vital sets of questions.

Firstly, did Ricardo's system provide an alternative paradigm—a different way of looking at the world from that provided by the Smithian paradigm? Now it certainly fulfilled one of Kuhn's paradigm functions—that of insulating scientists from important problems; and we can see this exhibited very clearly in Ricardo's discussion of tax matters in which he managed to avoid altogether dealing with the burning tax question of his day, the income tax. But, if Ricardo's system really did offer an alternative paradigm, were the economic events of the Napoleonic wars truly the occasion for a 'crisis' which led to its replacing the Smithian paradigm? This seems doubtful, although a case could certainly be made for it. But supposing that we do accept all this, there seems to be no provision within Kuhn's apparatus for the old paradigm to come back and replace the new one. Yet, as we have seen, this is effectively what happened in the course of the development of Classical economics with the return of Smith's influence to predominance. However, if Ricardo was *not* really offering an alternative paradigm, we are forced to conclude, as we might in any case conclude if we were not satisfied by the evidence for the existence of a 'crisis' and of 'anomalies', that Kuhn's apparatus, in its interesting form (as distinct from its watered-down form)[6] has nothing of interest to say about the vital developments in economics between 1815 and 1825, the period of Ricardian ascendancy.

Moreover, it would be hard to sustain the view that the Ricardian and Smithian paradigms were 'incommensurable'. This perhaps requires some amplification. In support of his view Kuhn argues that, for instance, the Einsteinian and Newtonian paradigms are incommensurable (Kuhn, 1962, pp 100–2) because terms come to mean different things—Space, Time, and Mass mean, he asserts, different things in terms of the two different paradigms. But can we say that wages, subsistence, capital, or population, have different meanings in the works of Smith and Ricardo? Only value acquired a different meaning. Yet perhaps it should be conceded that there was *an element* of incommensurability; for when McCulloch attempted to introduce Ricardian corn model elements into the Smithian growth model they failed to graft (O'Brien, 1970, Ch 12).

The first set of questions about the applicability of Kuhn's apparatus to the history of Smith's economics cannot then be answered entirely in favour of the application of the apparatus. The second set of questions that we have to ask ourselves about the use of Kuhn's theory of the history of science in explaining the history of Smith's bequest, relates to the whole collection of 'normal science' 'puzzle solving' and 'anomalies' that are so important to Kuhn in his view of natural science. It does seem that these questions can be answered even less satisfactorily. What is in question, it should be emphasised, is not their applicability in a natural science context: it is the use of these concepts in a discussion of classical economics. For it does seem clear that very little 'puzzle solving' was engaged in by the Classical economists, and that this concept of activity does not transplant from natural to social science any more easily than Popper's 'testing' or 'falsification'. Moreover it is extremely hard, even today, to envisage a situation in economics when a research failure would reflect on the researcher.

It does seem clear that Classical economics was not really a mature science in the Kuhnian sense—even though it probably did have a scientific community (O'Brien, 1975, pp 11–16).

But what about the post 1870 developments? Here it seems to me that Kuhn's approach does help a little. For the Smithian spectacles *were* gradually replaced. Although, as we have seen, they continued in use past the turn of the century, the economists' switch from the growth context to static optimisation is well enough documented; and with this came a change in the range of the subject. Population, for instance, which Smith had given a central role in his vision of the growth process, faded out from the economic literature. Even Marshall's attempt to include some discussion of it in his *Principles* seems in retrospect only a Marshallian act of filial piety. Moreover there was, at least in the British Isles, some sense if not of 'crisis' at least of *decay* in the subject of economics before the publication of Jevons' *Theory*. (Jevons, 1871.) Another of Kuhn's characteristics of paradigm change is present during this era: that the solutions had all been at least partially anticipated (by Senior, W F Lloyd, and Longfield). In addition there really does seem to have been a major communication problem between the old and new schools during this era, as Cairnes' total incomprehension of Jevons' work makes very clear (Cairnes, 1888, p iv). Moreover, the Continental dimension to the Marginal Revolution, which has made Kuhn seem less applicable to events after 1870 in the view of some writers, on the grounds that there was no crisis in European economics, is of no importance, because we are talking about the *British* scientific community in this context.

So Kuhn's apparatus is not valueless: and, by getting rid of Popper's concept of a crucial experiment,[7] Kuhn does offer a philosophy of the history of science which has distinctly more applicability to economics than has Popper's. Nevertheless Kuhn's apparatus seems to throw little light on some of the most interesting developments, especially those in the early years of the nineteenth century, and boldly transplanting it from the natural sciences seems, to put it mildly, a little premature.

(iii) *Lakatosian Research Programmes*

The late Imre Lakatos offered another view of the history of science which has also attracted attention from economists.[8] Here we have the vital concept of *Research Programmes*, which comprise whole sets of related theories in place of Popper's theories or Kuhn's paradigms. Research programmes are always appraised in competition with each other (so that one may replace another without a 'crisis') and are of two forms—*progressive* and *degenerating*. Into which box a particular programme fits is a matter of judgement for the community of scientists at any particular point in time; and this judgement will dictate which programme attracts adherence from scientists.

A programme consists of a hardcore, a negative heuristic, a positive heuristic, and a belt of auxiliary hypotheses. The hardcore is the basic, unchallengeable (and unprovable) set of assumptions, metaphysical in nature, which are at the centre of the research programme. The negative heuristic protects the hardcore from disproof by suggesting how auxiliary hypotheses may be changed to protect the hardcore from potentially damaging experimental results. The positive heuristic indicates a plan of procedure for testing and improving the explanatory power of the research programme; and from following this positive heuristic we develop a number of subsidiary theories.

A research programme is progressive if it predicts novel facts, and if some of these are confirmed by experimental work. (Note the return to verification in contrast to the Popperian falsification—though Lakatos makes little of this.) A programme is degenerating if it fails to predict novel facts, if the facts it does predict are not confirmed, and if further novel facts have to be accommodated into the theory by *ad hoc* stratagems.

In all this the concept of a 'novel fact' is rather critical and it has passed through several stages of development in Lakatos' work. The version of this concept proposed by Zahar did however seem to meet with Lakatos' approval.[9] Zahar offers the following concept: 'A fact will be considered novel with respect to a given hypothesis if it did not belong to the problem-situation which governed the construction of the hypothesis'. (Zahar, 1973, p 103.) Facts which were known, then, before the construction of an hypothesis, which were not involved in its formulation, *but which are explained by it*, then come into the category of novel facts.

Lakatos explicitly thought of his apparatus as applicable to social science and indeed he was instrumental in the convening of a conference at Nafplion in order to test its usefulness in explaining the history of economics. Moreover, he gives social science examples in his discussions (although he was highly— and explicitly—skeptical about the scientific pretentions of psychology and sociology[10]). Marxism, for instance, is viewed by Lakatos as the classic case of a degenerating scientific research programme on the grounds that it has failed to predict any new facts since 1917, the facts it has predicted have not been confirmed, and it has had to adopt a series of *ad hoc* stratagems to accommodate uncomfortable new facts as they have appeared.

What happens when we apply the Lakatosian vision to Smith's grand progress? There does seem little dout that, interpreted generously, it provides vastly more illumination than the Popperian or Kuhnian approaches. Let us initially adopt a generous stance. Then, in terms of this apparatus we can interpret the initial success of the research programme of the *Wealth of Nations*, the challenge from the Ricardian research programme, which was at first apparently successful, the continuation over a fairly lengthy period of the Malthusian research programme, and the final phase of the Smithian research programme as a degenerating one in the hands of Nicholson *et al.*

The Smithian hardcore contained the concept of self-interest pursuit on the basis of individual knowledge, this being superior to governmental knowledge, leading to a relative optimum in a context of growth, through the operation of the division of labour and technical advance combined with capital accumulation. The positive heuristic indicated that free trade should be adopted and that regulations interfering with the liberty to pursue economic activity should be removed. Subsequent observation of what happened to the economy under this sort of regime, as well as the study of economic history to see how other regimes had fared, was also indicated. Economic growth resulted from the progressive adoption of the Smithian prescriptions; and trade increased welfare. However, the programme was a little vague in its predictions about the effects on growth and income distribution of restrictions on the imports of basic foodstuffs: and with a rising price of corn the Ricardian research programme, sharing much of the same hardcore but with changes in that hardcore on the score of the harmony of individual and social interests, then came into competition with the Smithian one. Class conflict was not part of the Smithian hardcore so there does seem to have been a hardcore change which is necessary for a change in approach to qualify as a new research programme rather than simply as a *'problem shift'*. Class conflict was certainly not a 'novel fact' in the latest (Zahar's) sense because it was intimately involved in the formation of the theory; and this degree of involvement suggests that a hardcore change had taken place.

The associated positive heuristic then indicated that the Corn Laws should be repealed and that the consequent avoidance of the stationary state should then be observed. It also predicted (though again this was not truly 'novel' in Zahar's sense because it was intimately bound up with the theory's construction) that stagnation would ensue if the Corn Laws were not repealed. When this prediction failed the research programme moved into its degenerating phase and *ad hoc* stratagems were employed, notably by J S Mill in whose *Principles* (Mill, 1848) the Ricardian predictions became 'tendencies' which might or might not be observed depending upon the strength of (non-observable) countervailing tendencies.

During roughly the same period as the ascendancy of the Ricardian research programme the Malthusian one, derived very directly from Adam Smith, was also in operation, though it had of course a very narrow base of acceptance. The hardcore contained a number of the same elements as Smith's but it also contained (and gave very special weight to) a number of elements which were either not present in Smith's hardcore or which were unimportant there. These included fundamental propositions about sexual proclivities, and possible agricultural progress, as well as propositions about property distribution. The positive heuristic indicated that population and birth, marriage and death rates should be studied both at home and in other countries, and that measures (such as denial of poor relief) should be taken to deal with growth of population. Malthus also attacked the problem of corn prices and rising rents. But his population predictions were not confirmed; and his rent theory, tacked on as an auxiliary hypothesis to a hardcore very similar to Smith's, in contrast with Ricardo whose rent theory was an integral part of the entire system, meant that his research programme failed to attract support and the judgement that it was progressive. This argument seems plausible when one compares Malthus' two essays on the corn question (Malthus, 1814, 1815), and also the publications by McCulloch which were in part based on them (McCulloch, 1816a, 1816b) with Ricardo's *Essay on Profits* (Ricardo, 1815)—and indeed one can see clearly how McCulloch, as an emergent member of the community of economists at that time, switched his allegiance from the Malthusian to the Ricardian research programme,[11] in turn abandoning that for a return to the Smithian one. Yet we have, in pursuing this line of argument, to be honest, and to concede that Malthus offered important predictions about deflation and the burden of the National Debt which were, to a considerable extent, borne out by events: and this success did not save his programme.

Once the Smithian research programme was re-established as the ascendent one it developed new life; and the concept of the savings function and the nature of the profit reward were developed from Smith's rather than Ricardo's hints by Senior, Rea, and J S Mill. Finally, in the era of the Marginal Revolution, more and more economists, especially the younger ones, came to see the Smithian research programme as a degenerating one. It no longer predicted novel facts, and as some countries moved away from free trade in the last part of the nineteenth century it was necessary to adopt *ad hoc* stratagems to explain why this did not harm them. Similarly, it was necessary to adopt *ad hoc* devices to explain a degree of concerted action in the form of cartels (replacing competition) in Germany which went far beyond what was considered part of the Smithian research programme. (Clapham, 1923, pp 309–22.)

Yet it all fits *too* well; and there are some disquieting questions left. For one thing, there are basic ambiguities about what constitutes the hardcore and what constitutes the auxiliary hypotheses, so that Professor Mark Blaug is able to argue, in a brilliant paper, that the same hardcore was common to the Smithian, Ricardian, and Marginalist developments and that each of these simply involved a progressive problem shift within a given research programme. (Blaug, 1974, pp 19–20). In contrast, it was argued above that there were separate research programmes involved for the earlier part of the period; and for the later part it seems equally permissable to argue that there was a hardcore change because the maximising individual of the Smithian hardcore, one who is always in search of *new* opportunities, is replaced by the individual who accepts a permanently fixed range of opportunities. But obviously Professor Blaug's interpretation is entirely defensible. There is then considerable ambiguity in the Lakatosian concepts; and one is left wondering whether Lakatos' system's ability to internalise so much of intellectual history (which was Lakatos' criterion for a good theory of the history of science) is due to such ambiguities. As Professor Blaug himself remarks, in noting his disagreement with S Latsis: 'two Lakatosians need not agree on how to apply MSRP [the Methodology of Scientific Research Programmes] to a particular case in question.' (Blaug, 1974, p 23n).

There are other disquieting features too. The Marginal Revolution did not really involve the prediction of any novel facts at all—it was hardly a novel idea that demand curves sloped downwards. The interaction of demand and supply to determine price was to be found in several Classical research programmes—Malthus' in particular. Indeed the whole idea of 'novel facts' becomes a little strained when applied to economics; the predictions of the 'research programmes' were, with the exception of Ricardo, a good deal too vague and unspecific.

When we look at what happened to the Smithian research programme in the Marginal Revolution another ambiguity of the Lakatosian approach manifests itself. We can see what is involved if we consider the following Venn diagrams.

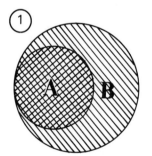 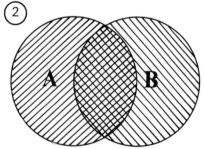

Diagram 1 is Popperian. Scientific advance proceeds by accretion. The area of scientific knowledge is continually increasing through the trial (of hypotheses) and error discovery (through falsification) process. Thus it is true that for Popper $A \subset B$, where set B is the set of scientific knowledge after some progress in the trial and error process and set A is the set of scientific knowledge before the progress has taken place. For instance, in Popper's view, Newton's results become a special case of Einstein's more general ones. Diagram 2 is Kuhnian. We have only those elements in A ∩ B which are common between paradigms. The elements in A∩B are the anomalies which the new paradigm—referring to the range of scientific questions in set B— is able to solve but which the old paradigm—referring to the set of scientific questions in set A—was unable to solve. Now the difficulty with Lakatos is to know which of the Venn diagrams applies to him. One of his critics[12] has claimed that for a research programme to be progressive, not a single old anomaly need be explained. If this is so, the change of focus of economics which occurred with the decline of the Smithian research programme in the last part of the nineteenth century, is within Lakatos' system; and, additionally, the fact that the failure of the Smithian programme to explain economic developments in Germany was not remedied by the arrival of Marginalism which had the same regard for competition, need not bother us. But Lakatos himself seems to be unclear on this matter; and this is disturbing because we have a real ambiguity on an important aspect of the whole schema.

There are other difficulties which suggest themselves. The standards of judgement used by economists in appraising a research programme can only be defined *ex post*; and hence a Progressive scientific research programme can only be distinguished from a Degenerating one *ex post*. One man's degenerating programme is another man's progressive programme as the continued existence of Marxist economics should remind us. There is indeed a danger that the system can be used to explain everything and that the circumstances are not conceivable in which it could be proved wrong. This is precisely the (valid) objection made by both Popper and Lakatos to Freudianism and Marxism.[13] This danger is all the more real because of the lack of a time dimension in Lakatos and because of Lakatos' insistence that we should use a history of science which internalises most of what has occurred—the more successful this is, the more difficult it becomes to envisage a set of facts it would not fit.

There is also a very real difficulty in applying Lakatos' apparatus when we take into account monetary and trade theory in discussing Classical economics. For a great chunk of the Ricardian research programme, in the form of the theory of comparative costs, survived and prospered even when the rest of the programme had foundered; and in an age when the British prided themselves on their superiority over the rest of the world in just about every matter,[14] the prediction of the theory of comparative costs that, in such a situation of superiority, trade would still be beneficial, was not irrelevant. Similarly, the monetary theory which was taken over by Ricardo prospered after the demise of his programme. However, this last is less serious because the theory did not originate with Ricardo but with Hume and the Bullionists like Thornton, and it was perfectly compatible with the *Wealth of Nations*.

A little nit-picking is probably in order then. But Lakatos' apparatus does seem to help us to understand what happened to Smith's economic programme, and, the difficulty over novel facts after 1870 notwithstanding, to provide some insight into both its rise, its temporary eclipse, its resurgence, and its decline.

Conclusion

Adam Smith, as we saw at the beginning of the discussion is, with Keynes, one of the two most influential economists the world has ever known. To explain the longevity of his influence, and the power of his system to make a come-back when temporarily eclipsed, is not easy. But of all the philosophies of the history of science which deserve to be taken seriously [15] that of Lakatos seems the most successful in explaining the history of Smith's unparalleled achievement.

NOTES

1   *Cf.* Samuels (1966) and Hirsch (1975).
2   *Cf.* Thomson (1965), p 233. See also Smith's own remarkable venture into the history of science (Smith, 1795) especially the deeply impressive essay on the 'History of Astronomy' (*ibid.* pp 3–93).
3   See Smith (1776), I, 57–65 and Bowley (1972), pp 12–13.
4   In the late 1950s a lecturer in the University of London, committed to giving a course of lectures on applied economics, was told by his professor that whatever applied economics was, it was *not* the application of economic theory. Similarly, the late Professor Ely Devons asked in *Essays* published in 1961 'Applied Economics—The Application of What?' (Devons, 1961). It would be going too far to claim that this was entirely representative; and N Jha's book (Jha, 1973) gives plenty of instances of attempts to apply the Marshallian tools. But if we leave the specialist pages of the *Economic Journal*, on which Jha's study is based, and look at the much wider field of industrial economics, we find an enormous gap between theory and 'applied economics' as late as the 1950s.
5   The relativism of Kuhn's early work is most marked in his (1962) chapter IX. See also Kuhn in Lakatos and Musgrave (1970, pp 11–12). For a distinct retreat on this matter see, however, *ibid.* p 264.
6   For a discussion of the retreat made by Kuhn from the position advanced in the first edition of his book see Musgrave (1971).
7   Lakatos has also rejected the Popperian concept of a crucial experiment (Lakatos and Musgrave, 1970, pp 120, 154–9).
8   See in particular the outstanding discussion by M Blaug (1974). I am, like a number of others, deeply indebted to this paper for introducing Lakatos' work in the context of economics.
9   According to Zahar (1973, pp 101–3), Lakatos had a concept of 'novel fact' in his 1968 (pp 381–7) which was so narrow that it would have given Einstein no credit for explaining Mercury's perihelion because it had been recorded long before General Relativity was proposed. Then in his 1970 (p 155–7) Lakatos, in deference to the opinion of physicists, modified his opinion by saying that in the light of a new theory some known facts could become novel ones. But this was so wide as to be fatal to his programme.
10   For Lakatos' outspoken attitude see his 1971 (pp 102, 119) and the reference in his 1970 (p 176) to 'proliferating intellectual garbage' and to 'intellectual pollution which may destroy our cultural environment'.
11   This assertion is made poker-faced, so to speak, in the text, in order to make as good a case for Lakatos as possible before moving on to examine the defects in that case. However, it has to be said that McCulloch was a very eclectic writer and that even

in his (1816a) which shows a friendly—indeed deferential attitude towards Malthus which is in marked contrast to his later attitude (O'Brien, 1970, p 35 and *n*, and contrast p 6 of McCulloch's 1816a where Malthus is referred to as 'the great political economist'), McCulloch's solution to the problem of fixed payments in deflation, raised by Malthus, was a reduction in interest payments on the National Debt, while Malthus' solution was agricultural protection. Moreover, although McCulloch's attitude remained friendly in his 1816b (*ibid.* pp 133, 198–201) he drew there on a very wide range of authors indeed. But having said that, there is no doubt that the Ricardian 'research programme' had not, at that stage, secured McCulloch's adherence. There are very few references to Ricardo and only one to the vital *Essay on Profits* (Ricardo, 1815).

12   This and other points are to be found in the critically penetrating essay by Koertge (Koertge, 1971). The specific criticism referred to in the text is Koertge p 162.
13   Popper (1963), pp 34–5; Lakatos (1970), p 92.
14   For a striking illustration of this see J S Mill (1848), p 105*n*.
15   It seems to me impossible to read Popper's treatment of dialectic (Popper, 1963, p 312–35) and still take seriously the various half-baked 'dialectical explanations' of the history of economics which have appeared.

REFERENCES

Bastable, C F (1892). *Public Finance* London: Macmillan
Blaug, M (1958). *Ricardian Economics* New Haven and London: Yale University Press
—— (1974). Kuhn versus Lakatos or Paradigms versus Research Programmes in the History of Economics
Bowley, M E A (1972). The Predecessors of Jevons—the Revolution that wasn't *Manchester School*, 40, pp 9–29
Cairnes, J E (1888). *The Character and Logical Method of Political Economy* 2nd edition repr New York: A M Kelly, 1965
Clapham, Sir J (1923). *The Economic Development of France and Germany* 2nd edition. Cambridge: Cambridge University Press
Devons, E (1961). 'Applied Economics—The Application of What?', in *Essays in Economics* London: Allen & Unwin
Hirsch, F (1975). 'The Bagehot Problem', *Warwick Economic Research Papers*, No 65
Jevons, W S (1871). *The Theory of Political Economy* (ed) R D C Black, London: Penguin, 1970
Jha, N (1973). *The Age of Marshall: Aspects of British Economic Thought* 2nd edition. London: Frank Cass
Koertge, N (1971). Inter-Theoretic Criticism and the Growth of Science, pp 160–73, in R C Buck and R S Cohen (eds), *Boston Studies in the Philosophy of Science*, Vol III, 1971. Dordrecht: Reidel
Kuhn, T S (1962). *The Structure of Scientific Revolutions* 2nd ed enlarged. Chicago: University of Chicago Press, 1970
Lakatos, I (1968). 'Changes in the Problem of Inductive Logic', in *The Problem of Inductive Logic* pp 315–417. Amsterdam: North-Holland Publishing Co
—— (1971). 'History of Science and Its Rational Reconstruction', in R C Buck and R S

Cohen (eds), *Boston Studies in the Philosophy of Science* Vol VIII, 1971. Dordrecht: Reidel

——, & Musgrave, A (1970). *Criticism and the Growth of Knowledge* London: Cambridge University Press

McCulloch, J R (1816a). *An Essay on a Reduction of the Interest of the National Debt, proving that this is the only possible Means of Relieving the Distress of the Commercial and Agricultural Interests* London: J Mawman

—— (1816b). *An Essay on the Question of Reducing the Interest of the National Debt; in which the Justice and Expediency of that Measure are fully Established* Edinburgh: D Brown

—— (1845). *A Treatise on the Principles and Practical Influence of Taxation and the Finding System* (ed) D P O'Brien. Edinburgh: Scottish Academic Press, 1975

Malthus, T R (1814). *Observations on the Effects of the Corn Laws, and of a Rise and Fall in the Price of Corn on the Agricultural and General Wealth of the Country* London: J Murray

—— (1815). *The Grounds of an Opinion on the Policy of Restricting the Importation of Foreign Corn* London: J Murray

Masterman, M (1970). The Nature of a Paradigm, pp 59–89, in *Lakatos & Musgrave* (1970)

Mill, J S (1848). *Principles of Political Economy with Some of their Applications to Social Philosophy* (ed) W J Ashley, London: Longmans, Green & Co, 1929

Musgrave, A E (1971). 'Kuhn's Second Thoughts', *British Journal for the Philosophy of Science* **22,** pp 287–97

Nicholson, J S (1909). *Elements of Political Economy* London: A & C Black

O'Brien, D P (1970). *J R McCulloch. A Study in Classical Economics* London: Allen & Unwin

—— (1975). *The Classical Economists* Oxford: Clarendon Press

Political Economy Club (1921). *Proceedings* Vol VI Centenary Volume. London: Macmillan

Popper, K R (1963). *Conjectures and Refutations. The Growth of Scientific Knowledge* London: Routledge and Kegan Paul

Ricardo, D (1815). *An Essay on the Influence of a Low Price of Corn on the Profits of Stock.* London: John Murray. Reprinted in *The Works and Correspondence of David Ricardo* (ed) P Sraffa. Cambridge: Cambridge University Press, 1951, Vol IV, pp 9–41

Samuels, W (1966). *The Classical Theory of Economic Policy* Cleveland Ohio: World Publishing Co

Sidgwick, H (1887). *The Principles of Political Economy* London: Macmillan

Smith, A (1759). *The Theory of Moral Sentiments; or, an Essay Towards an Analysis of the Principles by which Men Naturally Judge Concerning the Conduct and Character, First of their Neighbours, and Afterwards of Themselves.* New (ed) London 1853 repr New York: A M Kelley, 1966

—— (1763). *Lectures on Justice, Police, Revenue and Arms* (ed) E Cannan, Oxford: Clarendon Press, 1896

—— (1766). *An Inquiry into the Nature and Causes of the Wealth of Nations* (ed) E Cannan, 2 volumes. London: Methuen, 1904. Reprinted London 1950

—— (1795). *Essays on Philosophical Subjects* London: T Cadell

Thomson, H F (1965). 'Adam Smith's Philosophy of Science', *Quarterly Journal of Economics,* 79, pp 212–33

Times (1946). Lord Keynes obituary, 22 April 1946, reprinted in S E Harris (ed). *The New Economics. Keynes' Influence on Theory and Public Policy* London: Dennis Dobson, 1948

Viner, J (1937). *Studies in the Theory of International Trade* London: Allen & Unwin, reprinted 1964

Winch, D (1965). *Classical Political Economy and Colonies* London: G Bell

Zahar, E (1973). 'Why did Einstein's Programme Supersede Lorentz's?', *British Journal for the Philosophy of Science* 24, 1, pp 95–123; 2, pp 223–62

CHAPTER NINE

Sir James Steuart: Economic Theory and Policy

Andrew S Skinner

*Philosophy and Science in the
Scottish Enlightenment*
ed Peter Jones (John Donald, 1989)

SYSTEM

One of the most important features of Sir James Steuart's career was his extensive knowledge of the Continent. The Foreign Tour (1735–40) and exile as a result of his association with the Jacobites (1745–63) meant that by the end of the Seven Years' War Sir James had spent almost half of his life in Europe. In this time he mastered four languages (French, German, Spanish and Italian); facts which may help to explain Joseph Schumpeter's judgement that 'there is something un-English (which is not merely Scottish) about his views and his mode of presentation' (1954, p 176n).

In the course of his travels Steuart visited a remarkable number of places which included Antwerp, Avignon, Brussels, Cadiz, Frankfurt, Leyden, Liège, Madrid, Paris, Rome, Rotterdam, Tübingen, Utrecht, Venice and Verona. He seems, moreover, consistently to have pursued experiences which were out of the common way. For example, when he settled at Angoulême not long after his exile began, he took advantage of his situation to visit Lyons and the surrounding country. During his residence in Tübingen, he undertook a tour of the schools in the Duchy of Württemberg. Earlier he had spent no less than fifteen months in Spain where he was much struck by the irrigation schemes in Valencia, Mercia, and Granada; the mosque in Cordoba, and the consequences of the famine in Andalousia in the Spring of 1737.[1] In fact very little seems to have been lost and it is remarkable how often specific impressions found their way into the main body of the *Principles*. In his major book Steuart noted the economic consequences of the Seven Years' War in Germany, the state of agriculture in Picardy, the arrangement of the kitchen gardens round Padua, and the problem of depopulation in the cities of the Austrian Netherlands[2]—not as isolated examples, but as a part of the broader fabric of the argument as a whole.

The critical point to note is that a broad fabric of argument *is* present, reflecting Steuart's attempt to produce a single great conceptual system, linking the most interesting branches of modern policy, such as *'population, agriculture, trade, industry, money, coin, interest, circulation, banks, exchange, public credit* and *taxes'* (p 7). As Paul Chamley has pointed out, Steuart's attempt to produce a systematic treatise shows that he sought to include economics in the body of organised science, and that as such it conforms to the design of the *Encyclopédie* as described by D'Alembert (1965, p 50).

Steuart's desire to produce a *scientific* system whose parts are linked by common principles shows a certain similarity, as to *motive,* with that later articulated by Adam Smith—and the parallel extends to the former's attempt to *organise* his discourse by 'contriving a chain of ideas, which may be directed towards every part of the plan, and which, at the same time, may be made to arise methodically from one another' (p 28). The intention is therefore clear. It was rather the execution of the plan which presented Steuart with his initial difficulties; difficulties which were compounded by the sheer mass of material which was available to him and by the lack of a single clear model on which to base his account.[3]

Indeed Steuart himself, in the Preface to the *Principles,* explicitly drew attention to the difficulties under which he laboured precisely because he thought they would be of interest to the reader at the time of writing (pp 5–6):

> I have attempted to draw information from every one with whom I have been acquainted: this however I found to be very difficult until I had attained to some previous knowledge of my subject. Such difficulties confirmed to me the justness of Lord Bacon's remark, that he who can draw information by forming proper questions, must be already possessed of half the science (pp 5–6).

In approaching the problems involved, Steuart chose to adopt the broadly historical perspective associated with his friend David Hume whose essays he had read closely. Steuart too had taken a hint from what the late revolutions in the politics of Europe had pointed out to be the regular progress of mankind, from great simplicity to complicated refinement (p 28).[4]

The approach was to find expression in a number of areas which include sociology, politics and economics. The outcome was distinctive, not least as a result of Steuart's sensitivity to the issue of scientific method (Skinner, 1966), p lx). He was also acutely aware of the diversity of conditions in the countries which he had visited, and of the problems of economic development.

HISTORICAL ANALYSIS

Steuart made use of a theory of stages, now recognised as a piece of apparatus which was central to the historical work notably of the Scottish School.[5] He cites, for example, the Tartars and Indians as relatively primitive socio-economic types of organisation (p 56) while concentrating primarily on the third and fourth stages—the stages of agriculture and commerce. In the former case, Steuart observed that those who lacked the means of subsistence could acquire it only through becoming dependent on those who owned it; in the latter, he noted that the situation was radically different in that all goods and services command a price. He concluded, in passages of quite striking clarity:

> I deduce the origin of the great subordination under the feudal government, from the necessary dependence of the lower classes for their subsistence. They consumed the produce of the land, as the price of their subordination, not as the reward of their industry in making it produce (p 208).

He continued: 'I deduce modern liberty from the independence of the same classes, by the introduction of industry, and circulation of an adequate equivalent for every service' (p 209).

Steuart was also aware of the political aspect of these changes, and its effect upon the state:

> From feudal and military, it is become free and commercial. I oppose freedom in government to the feudal system, to mark only that there is not found now that chain of subordination among the subjects, which made the essential part of the feudal form.

He continued:

> I oppose commercial to military; because the military governments now are made to subsist from the consequences and effects of commerce only; that is, from the revenue of the state, proceeding from taxes. Formerly, everything was brought about by numbers; now numbers of men cannot be kept together without money (p 24).

Steuart noted that the gradual emergence of the stage of commerce had generated new sources of wealth which had affected the position of Princes:

> The pre-rogative of Princes, in former times, was measured by the power they could constitutionally exercise over the *persons* of their subjects; that of modern princes, by the power they have over the *purse* (p 290). [6]

Perhaps with the fate of his former Jacobite associates in mind, Steuart also observed that 'an opulent, bold, and spirited people, having the fund of the Prince's wealth in their own hands, have it also in their power, when it becomes strongly their inclination, to shake off his authority' (p 216).

The change in the distribution of power which was reflected in the changing balance between proprietor and merchant led Steuart to the conclusion that 'industry must give wealth and wealth *will* give power' (p 213). As an earnest of this position, he drew attention (in his Notes on Hume's *History*) to the reduced position of the Crown at the end of the reign of Elizabeth: a revolution which appears 'quite natural when we set before us the causes which occasioned it. Wealth must give power; and industry, in a country of luxury, will throw it into the hands of the commons' (p 213n). [7]

There is a further side to the analysis in that Steuart was concerned not only to contrast and compare the feudal and exchange economies, but also to consider the process of transition between them. In doing so, he started from a position where property was mainly in land, where the relationship between landlord and vassal or tenant was primarily based on service and where rents were chiefly paid in kind. To these institutions he added small towns, mainly located around the great seats, and composed of the few tradesmen and manufacturers who were necessary. Cities were represented as ecclesiastical centres which, significantly, had gradually 'formed themselves by degrees into small republics' (p 60).

More rapid change came with trade, especially to the Americas and the East Indies, providing a stimulus to manufacturing and commerce on the model of the Hanstowns. While there is something of a parallel with Smith (*Wealth of Nations*, Book III), it is equally important to note that Steuart's analysis provides a link between economy, community, and state.

THE THEORY OF POPULATION

The analysis of the emergence of the exchange economy is not untypical of the period and intrinsically interesting even if Steuart did consider that it was more properly the province of the science of politics than of political economy strictly defined. But he also argued that the subjects reviewed above were not 'altogether foreign to this' science, i.e. to economics (p 208), illustrating the truth of the remark by deploying the 'stadial' thesis in a purely economic context. The technique finds illustration in a number of fields, and generally involves the use of the stages of society treated as *models* which gradually increase in complexity. As Steuart put it, in constructing any body of theoretical knowlege:

> Every branch of it must, in setting out, be treated with simplicity, and all combinations not absolutely necessary, must be banished from the theory. When this theory again comes to be applied to examples, combinations will crowd in, and every one of these must be attended to (p 227).

The first analytical problem to which Steuart addressed himself was that of population where his stated purpose was 'not to inquire what numbers of people were found upon the earth at a certain time, but to examine the natural and rational causes of multiplication' (p 31). In so doing he stated that the 'fundamental principle' is 'generation; the next is food' (*Ibid.*), from which it follows that where men live by gathering the spontaneous fruits of the soil (the North American Indian model), population levels must be determined by their extent:

> From what has been said, we may conclude, that the numbers of mankind must depend upon the quality of food produced by the earth for their nourishment; from which, as a corollary may be drawn.
>
> That mankind have been, as to numbers, and must ever be, in proportion to the food produced; and that the food produced will be in compound proportion to the fertility of the climate, and the industry of the inhabitants (pp 36–7).

Where some effort is applied to the cultivation of the soil (the agrarian stage), Steuart recognised that the output of food and therefore the level of population would grow. But here again he drew a distinction between cultivation for subsistence, which was typical of the feudal stage, and the application of industry to the soil as found in the modern situation where goods and services command a price, and where the potential for economic growth (and therefore population) is greatly enhanced.[8]

Perhaps two major points arising from this argument deserve further notice.

To begin with, attention should be drawn to the emphasis which Steuart gives to the interdependent state of the sectors in his model of the exchange economy, recognising as he did that '*Agriculture among a free people will augment population, in proportion only as the necessitous are put in a situation to purchase subsistence with their labour*' (p 40). Secondly, Steuart gave a good deal of attention to the point that the whole process depended on 'reciprocal' wants and that there are cases where the limited extent of the latter will constrain economic development and population growth:

> Experience everywhere shows the possible existence of such a case, since no country in Europe is cultivated to the utmost: and that there are many still where cultivation, and consequently multiplication, is at a stop. These nations I consider as being in a *moral incapacity* of multiplying: the incapacity would be *physical*, if there was any actual impossibility of their procuring an augmentation of food by any means whatsoever (p 42).

Although we cannot review the theory in any detail here, it can be said that in Book I we confront a single major theme, the theory of population; a theory which while owing a great deal to David Hume (and possibly to Cantillon) nonetheless represents one of Steuart's most distinguished contributions and one of the best examples of his capacity for the systematic deployment of different levels of abstraction. But equally characteristic of his mode of argument is the fact that the theory is built up in such a way as to permit him to provide an account of the modern or exchange economy (the last of the 'models' used above), thus gradually widening the scope of the inquiry while still preserving a coherent 'chain of ideas'.

THE EXCHANGE ECONOMY

In dealing with the *nature* of the exchange economy, it is significant that Steuart made little use of the division of labour in the Smithian sense of the term (although he does cite the example of the pin at page 158). On the other hand, he gave great emphasis to the *social* division of labour in using the basic sectoral division to be found in Cantillon, Hume, Mirabeau, and Quesnai's *Encyclopedie* articles:

> we find the people distributed into two classes. The first is that of the farmers who produce the subsistence, and who are necessarily employed in this branch of business; the other I shall call *free hands*; because their occupation being to procure

themselves subsistence out of the superfluity of the farmers, and by a labour adapted to the wants of the society, may vary according to these wants, and these again according to the spirit of the times (p 43).

In both cases productive activity involves what Steuart defines as *industry*, namely, '*the application to ingenious labour in a free man, in order to procure, by means of trade, an equivalent, fit for supplying every want*'. *Trade*, on the other hand, is defined as '*an operation by which the wealth, or work, either of individuals, or of societies, may, by a set of men called merchants, be exchanged, for an equivalent, proper for supplying every want, without any interruption to industry, or any check upon consumption*' (p 146). The whole pattern is carried on through the use of *money*, also defined, with characteristic care as '*any commodity, which purely in itself is of no material use to man . . . but which acquires such an estimation from his opinion of it, as to become the universal measure of what is called value, and an adequate equivalent for anything alienable*' (p 44).

For Steuart the modern system was clearly an exchange economy characterised by a high degree of dependence between forms of activity and the individuals who carried them on, so that the idea or ideal of a free society emerges as involving '*a general tacit contract, from which reciprocal and proportional services result universally between all those who compose it*' (p 88). Later Steuart was to state an hypothesis of obvious relevance to the situation under review in remarking that 'the principle of self-interest will serve as a general key to this inquiry; and it may, in one sense, be considered as the ruling principle of my subject, and may therefore be traced throughout the whole. This is the main spring . . .' (p 142).

But the main underlying theme remains that of the interdependence of economic phenomena; a theme which brought Steuart quite logically to the treatment of price and allocation.

As far as the supply price of commodities is concerned, Steuart noted two elements: 'to wit, the real value of the commodity, and the profit upon alienation'. Real value was defined in such a way as to include three elements:

> The first thing to be known of any manufacture when it comes to be sold, is how much of it a person can perform in a day, a week, a month, according to the nature of the work.
> The second thing to be known, is the value of the workman's subsistence and necessary expence, both for supplying his personal wants, and providing the instruments belonging to his profession, which must be taken upon an average as above . . .
> The third and last thing to be known, is the value of the materials, that is the first matter employed by the workman. . . . These three articles being known, the price of the manufacture is determined. It cannot be lower than the amount of all three, that is, than the real value; whatever it is higher, is the manufacturer's profit (pp 160–1.

He went on to note that in a position of *equilibrium*, prices are found in the adequate proportion of the real expence of making the goods, with a small addition for profit to the manufacturer and merchant (p 189)

As far as the *process* of price determination was concerned, Steuart contended that the outcome of the 'contract' would be determined by competition between and among buyers and sellers:

> *Double competition* is, when, in a certain degree, it takes place on both sides of the contract at once, or vibrates alternately from one to the other. This is what restrains prices to the adequate value of the merchandize (p 172).

Thus, for example, if there is a relative shortage of some commodity, there may be competition between buyers in order to procure limited supplies, causing prices to rise. In the event of an excess supply, for example of a perishable commodity such as fish, there will be competition between sellers to rid themselves of excess stocks, thus causing prices to fall below their equilibrium values. Both cases present examples of what Steuart called 'simple competition' prevailing in effect in one side of the 'contract' only.

Two points follow from this argument: first, that a 'balance' between demand and supply does not of itself indicate a position of equilibrium; and, second, that the process of bargaining will normally affect both parties to the exchange.

Steuart was thus able to offer a definition of *equilibrium* but also a statement of a *stability* condition in noting that:

> In proportion therefore as the rising of prices can stop demand, or the sinking of prices can increase it, in the same proportion will competition either the rise or the fall from being carried beyond a certain length (p 177).

Finally, it should be noted that Steuart was aware, in general terms, of the allocative functions of the market. As he put it:

> Trade produces many excellent advantages; it marks out to the manufacturers when their branch is under or overstocked with hands. If it be understocked, they will find more demand than they can answer; if it be overstocked, the sale will be slow (p 158).

Arguments such as these are obviously broadly 'static' in character but in fact are to be found in a setting which illustrates that preoccupation with long-run dynamics which characterised the argument of the first Book, thus presenting the reader with yet another change of focus.

Economic Trends

Adam Smith would have had little difficulty in appreciating the broadly optimistic assessment which Steuart offered with regard to economic growth. It is readily apparent that Steuart saw no reason to doubt the potential for economic development in the context of the *exchange* economy. Here, and for the first time in an *institutional* sense:

> Wealth becomes *equably distributed*; . . . by *equably distributed* I do not mean, that every individual comes to have an *equal* share, but an equal chance, I may say a certainty, of becoming rich in proportion to his industry (*Works*, 1805, ii, 156).

Steuart also argued that the potential for economic growth was almost without limit or certain boundary in the current 'situation of every country in Europe'—and especially France, 'at present in her infancy as to improvement, although the advances she has made within a century excite the admiration of the world' (p 137). An equally dramatic confirmation of the general theme is to be found in the chapter on machines, which he considered to be 'of the greatest utility' in 'augmenting the produce or assisting the labour and ingenuity of man' (p 125)[9]

Again in the manner of Smith (and indeed Adam Ferguson), it was Steuart's contention that the modern economy had opened up new forms of demand and new incentives to industry. In a passage reminiscent of Smith's *Moral Sentiments* (which he may have read), Steuart drew attention to man's love of ingenuity and to the fact that the satisfaction of one level of perceived wants tends to open up others by virtue of a kind of 'demonstration' effect (p 157).[10]

The general point at issue is best caught by Steuart's earlier (but recurring) contrast between the feudal and modern systems:

> *Men were then forced to labour because they were slaves to others; men are now forced to labour because they are slaves to their own wants* (p 51).

But Steuart was to offer a further application of the thesis just considered which was to have a significant effect on his policy recommendations.

It will be recalled that Steuart's definition of equilibrium required that the balance between supply and demand be such that 'prices are found in the adequate proportion of the real expence of making the goods, with a small addition for profit to the manufacturer or merchant'. It was Steuart's view that this definition, originally applied to particular commodities, must also apply to *all* goods, thus suggesting, as in the case of Smith's *Lectures,* an intuitive grasp of the general interdependence of economic phenomena. Indeed this perspective seems to dominate Steuart's treatment of the long run, where he argues in effect that the balance of work and demand, *taking the economy as a whole*, is likely to change over time with consequent effects on the components of real value and on the relationship between real value and price (as described above).

Some causes of change were easily explained. Steuart recognised that taxes, for example, could affect the prices of commodities. He also drew attention to a tendency for the prices of primary products (subsistence and materials) to rise over time, especially as the result of 'the increase of population, which may imply a more expensive improvement of the soil' (p 198). But the most significant problem, for Steuart, was located on the demand side.

It was in this connection that he drew attention to two problems of particular importance. First, he suggested that the long-run trend would be for the balance of demand to preponderate (i.e. over supply), thus suggesting a tendency for prices to rise over time and to generate higher levels of profit. In this connection he suggested that higher profits 'subsisting for a long time . . . insensibly become *consolidated* or, as it were, transformed into the intrinsic value of goods' in such a way as to become 'in a manner necessary' to their existence (p 193). Secondly, and related to the above, Steuart distinguished between *physical* and *political* necessities, where the former is defined almost in biological terms as *'ample subsistence where no degree of superfluity is implied'* (p 269). He added:

> The nature of man furnished him with some desires relative to his wants, which do not proceed from his animal oeconomy, but which are entirely similar to them in their effects. These proceed from the affections of his mind, are formed by habit and education, and when once *regularly established*, create another kind of necessary which, for the sake of distinction, I shall call *political* (p 270).

Steuart went on from this point to suggest that the political necessary was 'determined by birth, education or habit' and 'rank' in society, clearly recognising that it is 'determined by general opinion only, and therefore can never be justly ascertained' (p 271). But he was clear in respect of one point; namely, that there will be a tendency for the accepted definition of political necessary to rise over time, with consequent effects on the supply prices of commodities. The importance of this argument was to emerge in the next stage of the exposition: the treatment of international trade.

In the second book Steuart dropped the assumption of the closed economy and proceeded to examine the issue of international trade. Characteristically, he traced the interrelationship between developed and undeveloped nations in terms of the distinction between active and passive trade, which had already been established by Malachy Postlethwayt.[11] Here the purpose was to examine the positive impact of foreign demand on a backward economy in terms of an argument which would not have disgraced one of Adam Smith's most notable disciples, the French economist, J B Say,[12] who in effect elaborated on an argument which is implicit in Smith's Book III.

Equally striking is the fact that Steuart treated different *states* as competitive firms:

> The trading nations of Europe represent a fleet of ships, every one striving who shall get first to a certain port. The statesman of each is the master. The same wind blows upon all; and this wind is the principle of self-interest, which engages every consumer to seek the cheapest and the best market. No trade wind can be more general, or more constant than this (p 203).

Steuart's treatment of international trade takes as its basic premiss the proposition that economic conditions and performance will differ even in the context of relatively developed nations whose trade he described as 'active'.

He was clearly aware of variations caused by 'natural advantages' such as access to materials, transport and the nature of the climate (p 238), as befits a close student and admirer of 'the great Montesquieu' (p 121). To these he added the form of government in arguing that 'trade and industry have been found to flourish best under the republican form, and under those which have come nearest to it' (p 211).[13] But equally important for Steuart were the spirit of a people and 'the greater degree of force' with which 'a taste for refinement and luxury in the rich, an ambition to become so, and an application to labour and ingenuity in the lower classes of men' manifested themselves in different societies at any one point in time and over time.

He also believed that there are likely to be variations in the extent to which the definition of 'political necessary' changes through time and the rate and extent to which the 'balance' of demand tends to preponderate in different countries. Steuart was acutely conscious of the sheer variety of economic conditions and indeed noted early in the book that:

> If one considers the variety which is found in different countries, in the distribution of property, subordination of classes, genius of people, proceeding from the variety of forms of government, laws, climate, and manners, one may include, that the political oeconomy of each must necessarily be different (p 17).

The number of possible 'combinations' opened up by the proposition that growth rates and other characteristics will vary is virtually endless. In recognition of this point Steuart employed three broad classifications, all of which may derive from Mirabeau's *Friend of Man* (1756): the stages of infant, foreign, and inland trade. [14]

ECONOMIC POLICY

The duties of the statesman in the economic sphere are clear: having defined the essence of the exchange economy as involving a 'general tacit contract', Steuart went on to note that 'Whenever . . . anyone is found, upon whom nobody depends, and who depends on everyone, as is the case with him who is willing to work for his bread, but who can find no employment, there is a breach of contract and an abuse' (p 88). In Steuart's view, the true purpose of the science of political economy.

> is to secure a certain fund of subsistence for all the inhabitants, to obviate every circumstance which may render it precarious, to provide every thing necessary for supplying the wants of the society, and to employ the inhabitants (supposing them to be freemen) in such a manner as naturally to create reciprocal relations and dependencies between them (p 17).

As in the case of Smith, the justification for intervention is market failure although Steuart's position with respect to the functions of the state in fact arises directly from the areas of analysis and policy with which he was primarily concerned. [15]

Looking back over the arguments which we have reviewed, it is appropriate firstly to recall Steuart's interest in *pre*-modern societies and in the *emergence* of the exchange economy. Steuart's concern with society in a process of transition is reflected in his attempt to formulate policies designed to deal with the problems generated by *historical* developments; developments which had caused cities to expand, and feudal retainers to be dismissed. It is in this context that the statesman is invited to consider the employment of redundant nobles and of the 'multitudes of poor' together with the all-important issue of the

means of communication (such as good roads). Steuart suggested that the
historical and contemporary record would also provide an invaluable guide to
the problems which would confront a statesman who adopted a self-conscious
policy of economic *and therefore* of social development. It was Steuart's
contention that in many cases the transition from a state of 'trifling industry'
and subsistence farming (which could be described as the primitive version of
the stage of commerce) could not occur without the interposition of the
sovereign (p 108). In a striking passage, which reminds the reader of his
remarkable range of experience, Steuart observed that:

> Pipers, blue bonnets, and oat meal, are known in Swabia, Auvergne, Limousin, and
> Catalonia, as well as in Lochaber: numbers of idle, poor, useless hands, multitudes
> of children, whom I have found to be fed, nobody, knows how, doing almost
> nothing at the age of fourteen . . . If you ask why they are not employed, their
> parents will tell you because commerce is not in the country: they talk of commerce
> as if it was a man, who comes to reside in some countries in order to feed the
> inhabitants. The truth is it is not the fault of these poor people, but of those whose
> business it is to find out employment for them (*ibid.*).

Steuart's general interest in regional issues is a marked feature of the
Principles and was to find further expression in his *Considerations of the
Interest of the County of Lanark in Scotland*, which was first published in 1769
under the name of Robert Frame. This short work was explicitly designed to
illustrate general principles by reference to a particular case; namely that of a
backward county in which Steuart resided and which supplied corn to the
neighbouring city of Glasgow. Steuart was concerned to demonstrate the
impact of the city's demand for agricultural products on an undeveloped
region (*Works,* v, p 321). He also drew attention to the fact that economic
development had enhanced local demand, and thus temporarily reduced the
supply of food available for sale outwith the region.

From the point of view of the city, the fact that local supply was fitful had
lent support to the proposed Forth and Clyde Canal which was intended to link
the two coasts and further to improve the market for grain. Steuart clearly
welcomed this development, while warning his contemporaries that its *short-
run* effect would be to *ruin* local agriculture *unless* steps were taken to further
the cause of agricultural improvement and of the local infrastructure.[16] In
particular he contended that the infant industry argument which merchants
had applied to the textiles of Paisley should be extended to agriculture (*Works,*
v, p 308). He also advocated high and stable prices for agricultural products,
while calling for a granary scheme which would in effect secure supplies and
stabilise incomes at a level which was consistent with improvement.[17]

Steuart also gave a great deal of attention to policy with respect to
international trade, in emphasising the need for protection in particular cases.

For example, Infant Trade represents that situation 'known in all ages, and
in all countries, in a less or a greater degree' and which is antecedent to
supplying the wants of others. Here the ruling principle

> is to encourage the manufacturing of every branch of natural productions, by
> extending the home-consumption of them; by excluding all competition with

strangers; by permitting the rise of profits, so far as to promote dexterity and emulation to invention and improvement; by relieving the industrous of their work, as often as demand for it falls short; and, untill it can be exported to advantage, it may be exported with loss, at the expense of the public (p 263).

At the same time Steuart suggested that the statesman must control profit levels so that when the real value of commodities indicates that they are competitive in the international context, trade may begin. In the same vein he argued that while protection is essential if industry is to be established (p 262), 'the scaffolding must be taken away when the fabric is completed' (*Works, ii,* 235).

In the case, of *foreign trade*, taken as representing the attainment of a competitive stage, the policies recommended are simply designed to retain the capability: here the ruling principles are 'to banish luxury; to encourage frugality; to fix the lowest standard of prices possible; and to watch, with the greatest attention, over the vibrations of the balance between work and demand. While this is preserved, no internal vice can affect the prosperity of it' (p 263).

Inland Trade, on the other hand, represents a situation where a developed nation has lost its competitive edge. Here the basic preoccupation must be the maintenance of the level of employment. He also recognised the importance of the balance of payments in advocating a restrictive monetary policy, and concluded:

> I will not therefore say, that in every case which can be supposed,   certain restrictions upon the exportation of bullion or coin are contrary to good policy. This proposition I confine to the flourishing nations of our own time (p 581).

In the state of inland trade, the basic problem was to keep domestic price levels as low as possible with a view to taking advantage of the difficulties of others. With the possible exception of Holland, it was Steuart's contention that because all nations would suffer the same long-run trends, but at different rates, it followed that:

> as industry and idleness, luxury and frugality, are constantly changing their balance throughout the nations of Europe, able merchants make it their business to inform themselves of these fluctuations, and able statesmen profit of the discovery for the re-establishment of their own commerce (p 296).[18]

Finally, it may be noted that although Steuart presents the three stages as being representative of various states of an economy, he also made the point that industries or regions within any *given* economy might manifest characteristics of all of them at any particular point in time:

> I shall only add, that we are not to suppose the commerce of any nation confined to any one of the three species. I have considered them separately, according to custom, in order to point out their different principles. It is the business of statesmen to compound them according to circumstances (p 265).

GOVERNMENT AND CONSTRAINT

In view of the emphasis which Steuart placed on the statesman it is important to bear in mind that he was not speaking of 'ministers of state, and even such as are eminent for their knowledge in state affairs' (p 16n), nor yet of a particular type of government. As he put it, within the context of the *Principles* the *statesman* is taken to be a 'general term to signify the legislature and supreme power, according to the form of government' (p 16). Steuart spoke

> of governments only which are conducted systematically, constitutionally, and by general laws; and when I mention princes, I mean their councils. The principles I am enquiring into, regard the cool administration of their government; it belongs to another branch of politics, to contrive bulwarks against their passions, vices and weaknesses, as men (p 217).

In a political sense the statesman is an essentially abstract concept, which reminds us once more that Steuart differentiated more clearly than most between economics, politics and ethics:

> Did I propose a plan of execution, this supposition, I confess, would be absurd; but as I mean nothing further than the investigation of principles, it is no more so, than to suppose a point, a straight line, or an infinite, in treating of geometry (16, m, 3).

Yet the discussion is not wholly abstract.

Steuart gave a great deal of emphasis to the constraints confronting the statesmen, in drawing attention, much as Smith had done, to the importance of the 'spirit' of a people as 'formed upon a set of received opinions relative to three objects: morals, government, and manners' (p 22)—opinions of such significance 'that many examples may be found, of a people's rejecting the most beneficial institutions, and even the greatest favours, merely because some circumstances had shocked their established customs' (p 27). Linked to the above, but separate from it, was Steuart's concern with the subject's imperfect knowledge of the purposes of particular policies—indeed he pointed out in the Preface that although the work may 'seem addressed to a statesman, the real object of the inquiry is to influence the spirit of those whom he governs'. He went on to note that 'A people taught to expect from a statesman the execution of plans, big with impossibility and contradiction, will remain discontented under the government of the best of kings' (pp 12–13).

To such constraints must be added those of a broadly constitutional kind in that the major instruments of modern policy (for example public debt and taxes) have to be sensitively applied if they are not to be counterproductive. Steuart also noted that the advent of the modern economy had led to a shift in the balance of political power as noted above (*Cf.* Winch, 1978).

But perhaps the most important element in what A O Hirschman (1977) has recently called Steuart's 'deterrence model' of government is the emphasis given to the role of purely economic laws. For Steuart, the statesman 'is neither master to establish what oeconomy he pleases, nor, in the exercise of his sublime authority, to overturn at will the established laws of it, let him be the most despotic monarch upon earth' (p 16). Later he wrote:

When once a state begins to subsist by the consequences of industry, there is less danger to be apprehended from the power of the sovereign. The mechanism of his administration becomes more complex, and . . . he finds himself so bound up by the laws of his political oeconomy, that every transgression of them runs him into new difficulties (p 217).

This point did not go unnoticed.

When the *Principles* was reviewed in 1767, it was in the main criticised for the role ascribed to the statesman. The point was repeated in the reviews of Steuart's *Works* (1805) when the *Monthly* complained that the author had committed a 'capital and injurious mistake' when insisting on the 'statesman's constant superintendence over trade'.[19] Yet the same reviewer perceptively remarked that:

a reader of the present day will most prize, in these volumes, their illustration of the influence of political economy on civil government; which places in the strongest light the mischiefs of arbitrary rule, and which exhibit it as not less prejudicial to its depositaries than to their subjects. This very momentous question, is no where, to our knowledge, so satisfactory treated.

The reviewer of the Playfair edition of the *Wealth of Nations* in the same journal, noted that:

Wide as have been the excursions of Dr Smith into politics and statistics, he never discussed the influence of the true principles of political economy over civil government. This fine subject, however, has been treated by Sir James Steuart with considerable success.[20]

CONCLUSION: STEUART AND SMITH

The lives of Steuart and Smith, like their careers, scarcely touched. Steuart was called to the bar in 1735 two years before Smith became a student in Glasgow. Having embarked on the Foreign Tour in the same year, Sir James returned to Scotland at the very time that Adam Smith went to Oxford as the Snell Exhibitioner (1740). By the time Smith left Oxford in 1746, Steuart was already in exile, and when in 1764 the Professor left for France as tutor to Buccleuch, Steuart had just returned to Scotland. At this time he was busily engaged in completing a work which was published within a year of Smith's return from France. In their later years, the two men lived on opposite sides of the country: Smith as a government official based in Edinburgh, and Steuart as a country gentleman living in Lanarkshire, having abandoned all hopes of further official recognition.[21]

Smith's position with regard to the *Principles* has not emerged with any clarity.[22] While it is known that he owned a copy of the book, he made no mention of it even in respect of areas where Steuart had provided relevant information—notably with regard to the Bank of Amsterdam where Smith claimed in the advertisement to the fourth edition of the *Wealth of Nations* that 'no printed account had ever appeared to me satisfactory, or even intelligible'. Steuart's interesting account of Law's Bank suffered the same fate, as did his careful analysis of the Scottish Banks (Book IV, Part 2).[23]

On the other hand, it is reported that Smith had 'been heard to observe that he understood Sir James's system better from his conversation than from his volumes' (Rae, 1895, p 63). It is also known that Smith wrote to William Pulteney on 4 September 1772, to the effect that:

> I have the same opinion of Sir James Stewart's book that you have. Without once mentioning it, I flatter myself, that every false principle in it, will meet with a clear and distinct confutation in mine (*Correspondence*, Letter 132).

Yet such a statement does not preclude recognition of the fact that there were principles in the book which were not incorrect. Reading the work in 1767, the author of the essay on 'Astronomy' could hardly fail to appreciate Steuart's scientific purpose; his concern with the emergence of the 'present establishments in Europe', the successful deployment of the 'theory of stages' which Smith himself had used in his *Lectures,* or the interest shown by a *trained lawyer* in the relationship between the mode of subsistence and the patterns of authority and subordination. There is a similar emphasis on the importance of 'natural wants' as a stimulus to economic activity, and the same broadly sociological dimension to a discussion which features so strongly in Smith's ethics.

In terms of economic analysis Smith would have confronted a sophisticated theory of population, an advanced theory of the determination of prices, and the same clear grasp of the interdependence of economic phenomena that marked his own early work in the *Lectures on Jurisprudence*. Other and more general parallels are to be observed in Steuart's awareness of the enormous potential for economic growth and in his appreciation of the contributions made by international trade to the process (p 119).

If this is hardly surprising in view of the influence exerted by David Hume[24] on both his friends, it might also be claimed that the *Principles* outstrips the economic sections of the *Lectures* in terms of technical sophistication.

But the *Wealth of Nations* differs from the *Principles* analytically; especially in respect of Smith's clear distinction between factors of production (land, labour, capital), and categories of return (rent, wages, profit), and in Smith's use of a macro-economic model of the circular flow which was informed throughout by physiocratic teaching. It can plausibly be argued that Smith's visit to Paris in 1766 transformed the analytical structure envisaged in the *Lectures* quite fundamentally: a transformation effected by Smith's knowledge of economic models of which Steuart was unaware in the late 1750s, when Books I and II were completed.[25]

There is a further contrast. In the case of Smith there is a clear presumption against interference by government—although that is not to be taken to mean that Smith saw a limited role for the state.[26] But in Steuart's work, 'the science of domestic policy' is consistently directed to the 'statesman'. His government is 'continually in action'. As he noted: 'In treating every question of political oeconomy I constantly suppose a statesman at the head of government, systematically conducting every part of it' (p 122).

Economists have long been troubled by a contrast which makes it all too easy to conclude that Smith was in some sense 'enlightened' whereas Steuart was not. Without wishing further to comment on the issue by way of direct comparison, it may be helpful to recall the distinction between the principle which justifies intervention (such as market failure) and the specific agenda which is presented. The point is of course that while the basic principle may claim wide validity, the agenda actually presented will depend on the author's perception of the problems to be addressed.

In Steuart's case there may be a genuine difference, as compared to Smith, in respect of the confidence with which he believed governments could identify just when and where markets have failed (*Cf.* Skinner, 1986). But there are other, perhaps more fundamental, differences in approach which are easier to assess.

The *Wealth of Nations* succeeded in supplying a great conceptual system whose component parts had a perceived relevance in an industrial age which Smith did not see, and which continued to meet the needs of the modern science of economics long after his death.[27] Steuart, in contrast, sought immediate relevance in an institutional sense, and thus gives the reader some inkling of the problems of economic and social policy actually to be confronted at the time of writing.[28] It is perhaps in this respect that Steuart has been somewhat neglected by economists—and by students of the Scottish Enlightenment. A number of areas commend themselves to our attention.

To begin with, it should be emphasised that while Smith and others gathered information about remote peoples, Steuart exploited a unique if unwanted opportunity with respect to contemporary Europe. In the course of his travels he visited, as we have seen, a number of places which would be remarkable even by modern standards and which is astonishing given the problems of communication at the time. It is scarcely surprising that Dugald Stewart, the most perceptive of commentators on Adam Smith, should have recommended his students to begin their study of political economy with the *Wealth of Nations* and then proceed to the *Principles* as a work which contained 'a great mass of accurate details' gleaned by 'personal observation during a long residence on the Continent' (1857, ix, 458). Dugald Stewart may also have intended his students to appreciate a very different perspective, in that Sir James's stance was European rather than English in orientation.

Secondly, we should note Steuart's interest in the variety of economic conditions which were likely to face competing nations, and the fact that this position, once adopted, made it difficult for him to formulate a simple or straightforward policy position. For Steuart everything was seen to depend on the circumstances prevailing:

> Were industry and frugality found to prevail equally in every part of these great political bodies, or were luxury and superfluous consumption, everywhere carried to the same height, trade might, without any hurt, be thrown entirely open. It would then cease to be an object of a statesman's care and concern (p 296).

But there is a certain realism in Steuart's general conclusion:

> Nothing, I imagine, but an universal monarchy, governed by the same laws, and administered according to one plan, well concerted, can be compatible with an universally open trade. While there are different states, there must be separate interests; and when no one statesman is found at the head of these interests, there can be no such thing as a common good; and where there is no common good, every interest must be considered separately (p 365). [29]

Thirdly, attention should be drawn to Steuart's interest in 'that spirit of liberty, which reigns more and more every day, throughout all the polite and flourishing nations of Europe' (p 18). He was acutely aware of a current 'revolution in the affairs of Europe': '*Trade* and *Industry* are in vogue: and their establishment is occasioning a wonderful fermentation with the remaining fierceness of the feudal constitution' (p 215).

In fact, Steuart, notably in Book I of the *Principles,* directly addressed a problem, which is implicit in the analysis of the third book of the *Wealth of Nations,* but which was not *explicitly* considered by Smith: namely, the *economics* of the process which finally resulted in the emergence of the fourth stage of commerce in its *advanced* form. *Steuart's* model is that of 'primitive accumulation' in *contrast* to Smith where 'the process of primitive accumulation has now been completed' (Kobayashi, 1967, p 19). [30] The same point has been made by Michael Perelman in noting that Steuart *directly* addressed the problems of a *primitive* version of the stage of commerce (1983, p 454) in a way which led Marx to appreciate his sensitivity to historical differences in modes of production (*op. cit.* p 468). [31]

It is a striking fact that although Smith uses primitive and advanced versions of the stages of pasture and agriculture (*Wealth of Nations,* Book III), he does *not* consider the primitive case of the stage of commerce.

It should be noted that although Steuart was to introduce a great number of changes to his text between 1767 and 1780 (the year of his death), he did *not* introduce materials which reflect a reading of the *Wealth of Nations,* or of physiocratic writing. The reason is not analytical deficiency; rather Steuart believed the model of primitive accumulation to have intrinsic merit and *continuing relevance*: as indeed it does to this day where the economic and social conditions which he *actually* confronted are duplicated.

The model, and the use made of it, constitutes a uniquely valuable contribution to our understanding of the 'stadial' thesis. This was, in fact, matched by Steuart's analysis, primarily in Book II, of the 'rich country, poor country' relationship recently noticed by Istvan Hont (1983). As Dr Hont has reminded us, this major debate began with the publication of Hume's *Political Discourses* and ended in one version (for variation in economic performance is still a major problem), with Lauderdale's *Inquiry into the Nature and Origin of Public Wealth* (*op. cit.* Ch 11). [32]

It may be also suggested that more attention should be given to Steuart's appreciation of the wider, historical, significance of his own preoccupation with policy. The whole object of the exercise, as we have seen, was to obviate the effects of *relatively* short-run problems; of what Steuart called 'sudden revolutions'. At the same time, the purpose of policy is, for example, to protect employment levels and to encourage or induce economic growth and the social changes associated with it. Even in the more purely political sphere Steuart observed the effects of intervention: 'in our days, we have seen those who have best comprehended the true principles of the new plan of politics, arbitrarily limiting the power of the higher classes, and thereby applying their authority towards the extension of public liberty' (p 216).

The point is made with greater clarity in the course of a critique of the 'principles' of M de Montesquieu, who deduced the origin of many laws, customs, and even religions, from the influence of climate':

> This great man reasoned from fact and from experience, and from the power and tendency of natural causes, to produce certain effects, when they are not checked by other circumstances; but in my method of treating this subject, I do not suppose that these causes are ever to be allowed to produce their natural and immediate effects, when such effects would be followed by a political inconvenience: but I constantly suppose a statesman at the head of government, who makes every circumstance concur in promoting the execution of the plan he has laid down (p 238).

Policy itself was recognised to be an instrument of *change*, thus suggesting that while the emergence of the 'present establishments' in Europe could be adequately explained in terms of the eighteenth-century vision of a 'science' of history, the future course of events could be affected by contemporary interpretation of its meaning and direction. This is a point of some importance, and not least for our understanding of Smith's own work in the field.

Finally, it should not be forgotten that Steuart can be regarded as an *economist* who had an acute grasp of the methodology to be applied and who did much to differentiate this particular branch of the social sciences from others. In recent years it has been fashionable to refer to 'available languages'—for example, of natural jurisprudence or of civic humanism. Steuart uses the language of economics in a way which is recognisably modern but which also reminds us of those links which exist between the *Principles* and an older, seventeenth-century tradition dating back at least to the works of Sir William Petty (see Roncaglia, 1986).

Surely there is enough here to suggest that Steuart was also a worthy contributor to an 'Augustan Age' (p 6), and that assessment of his contribution can only effectively be made once the *commentator* has freed himself from Smith's long shadow?

Yet the task, important though it may be, will not be easy. Even the urbane Donald Winch has recently remarked of Steuart's *Principles* that 'the difficulties in making this part of Smith's context are well-known. To put it bluntly, one has to take on board a Jacobite traitor tainted with Continental notions, and an author whose work was largely ignored by his Scottish contemporaries' (1983, p 268).[33]

'A traitor tainted with Continental notions . . .' The point echoes comments made in the reviews of 1767 which accused Steuart of *imbibing prejudices abroad, 'by no means consistent with the present state of England, and the genius of Englishmen'* (p 4). Steuart replied that his work, 'will not, in general, correspond to the meridian of nation opinions anywhere' (*Ibid.*). He went on: 'Can it be supposed, that during an absence of near twenty years, I should in my studies have all the while been modelling my speculation upon the standard of English notions?' 'If from this work I have any merit at all, it is by divesting myself of English notions, so far as to be able to expose in a fair light, the sentiments and policy of foreign nations, relatively to their own situation' (pp 4–5). Could Smith, so pre-eminently a citizen of the world, have disagreed with so praiseworthy a *sentiment*?

NOTES

This essay partially 'conflates' the arguments of Skinner (1981) and (1985). I am indebted to the editors of the journals concerned for permission to reproduce a number of passages. This article was first published in *Philosophy and Science in the Scottish Enlightenment* (ed) Peter Jones (Edinburgh, 1989) and is reprinted with the permission of the publishers, John Donald. The present version differs from the origin in respect of the ordering of the section on economic policy.

References to Steuart's *Principles* (1767) are given in parenthesis and are to the Skinner edition (1966). Biographical details are drawn from the latter work together with P Chamley (1963, 1965). There is an interesting chapter on Steuart in a forthcoming study by J E King (Lancaster)

1   Steuart wrote two interesting letters from Spain, dated 5 and 17 March 1737, addressed to Thomas Calderwood, his brother-in-law, and Charles Mackie. Laing *MS*, Edinburgh University. The former is reprinted in Chamley (1965), pp 127–9.
2   Steuart's treatment of land-use theory was the subject of the presidential address to the Regional Science Association of the USA in 1980, by Martin J Beckman (1981); *Cf.* W J Stull (1986).
3   Steuart was familiar with the works of Sir William Petty, Hume's *Essays* (in French translation) and with Mirabeau's *Friend of Man* (1756). The edition used was that published prior to Mirabeau's meeting with Quesnai, but would have made him familiar with the substance of Cantillon's teaching. For a list of authorities cited by Steuart, see Skinner (1966), p 739.
4   He added: 'I am far from being of the opinion that this is the only road to happiness, security and ease: though from the general taste of the times I live in, it be the system I am principally employed to examine' (p 214). It is in this light that we are to read the following chapter (Book II, Ch 14 on Lycurgus Plan, entitled, 'Security, Ease, and Happiness, No Inseparable Concomitants of Trade and Industry'.
5   See R L Meek (1976). Steuart's analysis of the relationship between the mode of subsistence and the patterns of authority and dependence are mainly located in Book II, Ch 12—where, like Smith, he appears as a critic of the contract theory of government.
6   Steuart continued: 'I know of no Christian monarchy (except, perhaps, Russia) where either the consent of states, or the approbation and concurrence of some political body within the state, has not been requisite to make the imposition of taxes constitutional' (p 290).
7   Steuart's manuscript writings are detailed in Skinner (1966), pp 741–3.
8   *Cf.* Hume, 'Of the Populousness of Ancient Nations', in Rotwein (1955), where a similar argument is advanced. M A Akhar has drawn attention to the presence of a model in Steuart's work (1978, 1979).

9   See especially, Book I Ch 19.

10 Steuart went on: 'Let any man make an experiment of this nature upon himself, by entering into the first shop. He will nowhere so quickly discover his wants as there. Everything he sees appears either necessary, or at least highly convenient; and he begins to wonder (especially if he be rich) how he could have been so long without that which the ingenuity of the workman alone had invented, in order that from the novelty it might excite his desire; for when it is bought, he will never once think of it, perhaps, nor ever apply it to the use for which it first appeared so necessary' (p 157). *Cf.* Smith, *Theory of Moral Sentiments*, Part IV, Ch 1, 'Of the Effect of utility upon the Sentiment of Approbation'. See also Loasby (1986), p 17.

11 The point is made by Johnson (1937) p 225.

12 *Cf.* J B Say (1821), Book I, Ch 15. For further comment on the regional dimension in Say's formulation of 'his' famous 'law', see Skinner (1967).

13 The argument is elaborated in Book II, Ch 13.

14 See Chamley, *op. cit.* pp 77–82.

15 Steuart's emphasis was not on planning *ad hoc*, but on the 'corporate state'. See the paper with this title given by Walter Eltis for the British Association, in R D C Black (1986).

16 Steuart's thesis was that with the development of local roads and of agriculture, the proposed Canal would improve the operation of the market and further stimulate agriculture in Lanark. He addressed the problem of good roads in pamphlets published in 1766 and 1770. *Cf.* the arguments of his son, General Sir James Steuart (1805).

17 See Steuart's *Memorial on the Corn Laws*, dated 10 October 1777, reprinted in Chamley, *op. cit.* pp 140–2 and Skinner (1966), pp 737–8; see also Skinner, *op. cit.* pp iii–iv, for an analysis of the debate for and against free trade in corn.

    See also Steuart's *Dissertation on the Policy of Grain* (1759), *Works*, vol 5. Eltis has argued that Steuart's position anticipated that of the modern EEC (*op. cit.* p 44).

18 Steuart's use of the thesis of 'growth and decay' is to be interpreted in the light of this statement; *op. cit.* p 195, *Cf.* p 196n.

19 The main commentaries appeared in the *Monthly* and *Critical* Reviews for 1767. Assessments of the *Works* were published in the *Annual* (1805) and *Monthly Review* (1806). James Mill contributed a critical piece to the *Literary Journal* (1806).

20 *Monthly Review,* Vol 50 (1806), pp 115 and 123.

21 In 1772, Steuart was invited by the East India Company to advise on currency problems in Bengal. The Report was published as the *Principles of Money Applied to the State of the Coin in Bengal* (*Works,* Vol 5). See especially S R Sen (1957), Ch 10. Smith's name may also have been mentioned to the Company, see Rae (1895), pp 253–4. On Steuart's monetary analysis, see esp D Vickers, *Studies in the Theory of Money, 1690–1776* (1960).

22 *Cf.* Chamley, *op. cit.* pp 67–9.

23 There is also an interesting (and hitherto largely un-noticed) treatment of unproductive labour in Book II, Ch 26.

24 Hume may have assisted Steuart when the latter was preparing for publication. See Skinner (1966), p xiv. In a letter dated Coltness, 10 November 1767, Steuart refers to the 'many proofs you have given me of your friendship' (Burton, 1849, p 174). Hume's patience was somewhat strained in the course of a jocular debate about Mary Queen of Scots; see Skinner (1966), p 742.

25 Steuart left France just before the outbreak of war with England and finished the first two books of the *Principles* in Germany, during the course of 1759. Chamley, *op. cit.* pp 130–7; 138–9. For the present writer's views as to Smith's debt to

Physiocracy, see Skinner (1979), Ch 5. A comprehensive analysis of physiocratic work, which includes both commentary and translations, is to be found in Meek (1962).

26   See Skinner (1986).

27   See especially Caton (1985) and *Cf.* Kindleberger (1976).

28   A rather similar contrast is drawn by A L Macfie when comparing Smith's position with that adopted by his pupil John Millar, where the latter is shown to have been interested in *reform*, while the 'truest final image of Adam Smith seems to me to be the system weaver, his mind ever moving on to further logical consequences' (1961), p 203. See also Raschid (1982) and (1986) for an extremely interesting assessment of the reception accorded to the two works at the time of writing, and *Cf.* Anderson and Tollison (1984).

29   Steuart added: 'But as this scheme of laying trade quite open, is not a thing likely to happen, we may save ourselves the trouble of enquiring more particularly into what might be its consequences' (p 36).

30   Kobayashi has also suggested that Steuart's emphasis on primitive accumulation may explain the popularity of the work in contemporary Ireland and Germany. See also Chamley, *op. cit.* pp 88–9.

31   The relationship between Steuart and Hegel has also been noted, especially by Paul Chamley (1963) and (1965).

32   Steuart's analysis of the relationship between relatively developed and undeveloped economies is a feature of his critique of Hume's doctrine of the 'specie flow' (Book II, Ch 28, 29). Later in the book the argument is extended to include a clear distinction between the balance of trade and the balance of payments (pp 489, 494). Steuart also argued that the flow of specie from a relatively undeveloped country (for example Scotland) could be irreversible (p 500), arguing that banks should borrow abroad to fund current deficits while continuing to support domestic credit in the interests of development (pp 505–20). See also Walter Eltis, *op. cit.*

33   There is an interesting letter written by Elizabeth Mure of Caldwell and addressed to Steuart's sister, Mrs Calderwood which touches on her brother's politics (Chamley, 1965, pp 115–17). Elizabeth Mure wrote:

> Were we by the fireside alone, no doubt I could give you more information than most people now alive, but those incidents are improper for a publication.
>   Our friend's notion of government would ill suit the rage for freedom (I may call it) that now reigns in this country, and is fast running on to licentiousness. His ambition was to have an active share in a government that he approved of, and was a Jacobite on some whig principles, but not the whole of them . . . had that revolution taken place which he wished, he would have been the first man in the state.

Elizabeth Mure's affectionate remembrance was dated 20 December 1787—a little more than *seven* years after Steuart's death.

REFERENCES

Akhar, M A (1978). 'Steuart on Growth', *Scottish Journal of Political Economy* Vol 25
—— (1979). 'An Analytical Outline of Sir James Steuart's Macro-economic Model', *Oxford Economic papers* Vol 31
Anderson, G M and R D Tollison (1984). 'Sir James Steuart as the Apotheosis of Mercantilism and his Relation to Adam Smith', *Southern Economic Journal* Vol 51
Beckmann, J (1981). 'Land-use theory then and now: a tribute to Sir James Steuart', in *Papers Regional Science Association* Vol 48
Black, R D C (ed) (1986). *Ideas in Economics* London
Burton, J H (1849). *Letters of Eminent Persons Addressed to David Hume* Edinburgh
Caton, H (1985). 'The Pre-Industrial Economics of Adam Smith', *Journal of Economic History* Vol 45
Chamley, P (1963). *Economie Politique et Philosophie chez Steuart et Hegel* Paris
—— (1965). *Documents Relatifs à Sir James Steuart* Paris
Eltis, W (1986). 'Sir James Steuart's Corporate State' in R D C Black (ed)
Hirschman, A O (1977). *The Passions and the Interests, Political Arguments for Capitalism before its Triumph* Princeton
Hont, I (1983). 'The Rich Country—Poor Country debate in Scottish Classical Political Economy', in Hont and Ignatieff (ed) *Wealth and Virtue: The Shaping of Political Economy in the Scottish Enlightenment* Cambridge
Johnson, E A G (1937, 1960). *Predecessors of Adam Smith* New York
Kindleberger, C (1976). 'The Historical Background: Adam Smith and the Industrial Revolution', in T Wilson and A S Skinner (eds), *The Market and the State: Essays in Honour of Adam Smith* Oxford
Kobayashi, N (1967). *Sir James Steuart, Adam Smith and Friedrich List* Tokyo
Loasby, B (1986). 'Marshall's Economics of Progress', in *Journal of Economic Studies* Vol 13
Macfie, A L (1961). 'John Millar', *Scottish Journal of Political Economy* Vol 8
Meek, R L (1962). *The Economics of Physiocracy* London
—— (1967). 'The Rehabilitation of Sir James Steuart', in *Economics and Ideology and Other Essays: Studies in the Development of Economic Thought* London
Perelman, M (1983). 'Classical Political Economy and Primitive Accumulation', *History of Political Economy* Vol 15
Rae, John (1895). *Life of Adam Smith* London
Raschid, S (1980). 'The Policy of Laisser Faire during Scarcities', *Economic Journal* 90
—— (1982). 'Adam Smith's Rise to Fame: A Re-examination', *The Eighteenth Century, Theory and Interpretation* Vol 23
—— (1986). 'Smith, Steuart and Mercantilism', *Southern Economic Journal* Vol 52
Roncaglia, A (1985). *Sir William Petty: The Origins of Political Economy* New York
Rotwein, E (1955). *David Hume: Writings on Economics* Edinburgh
Say, J B (1821). *A Treatise on Political Economy* transl C R Prinsep, London
Schumpeter, J A (1954). *History of Economic Analysis* London
Sen, S R (1957). *The Economics of Sir James Steuart* London
Skinner, A S (1966). *Sir James Steuart: Principles of Political Oeconomy* (ed) Edinburgh and Chicago
—— (1967). 'Say's Law: Origins and Content', *Economica* Vol 34

—— (1979). *A System of Social Science: Papers Relating to Adam Smith* Oxford

—— (1981). 'Sir James Steuart: Author of a System', *Scottish Journal of Political Economy* Vol 28

—— (1985). 'Sir James Steuart: A Perspective on Economic Policy and Development', *Quaderni di storia dell' economia politica* Vol 3

—— (1986). 'Adam Smith, Then and Now' in Black

Smith, Adam (1959). *The Theory of Moral Sentiments* (ed) A L Macfie and D D Raphael, Oxford, 1976

—— (1776). *An Inquiry into the Nature and Causes of the Wealth of Nations* (ed) R D Campbell, A S Skinner and W B Todd, Oxford, 1976

Steuart, Sir James (1759). *A Dissertation on the Policy of Grain, with a view to a Plan for preventing scarcity or exorbitant prices, in the Common Markets of England* (Works, Vol 5)

—— (1766). *Observations on the Advantages arising to the Public from Good Roads, particularly of the Utility of a short and easy Communication between the Firths of forth and Clyde; with Remarks on the Present Roads Leading to Glasgow* Glasgow

—— (1767). *Principles of Political Oeconomy: being an Essay on the Science of Domestic Policy in Free Nations* (ed) A S Skinner, Edinburgh and Chicago, 1966

—— (1769). *Considerations on the Interest of the County of Lanark in Scotland; which (in several respects) may be applied to that of Great Britain,* Works Vol 5

—— (1770). *Sketch of a Plan for Executing a Set of Roads over the County of Lanark* Glasgow

—— (1805). *Works, Political, Metaphyisical, and Chronological* 6 Vols, London

Steuart, General Sir James (1805). *Remarks on the proposed Bill for the Improvement of the Roads in the County of Lanark, by Statute Labour* Glasgow

Stewart, D (1854–60). *Works* (ed) Sir William Hamilton, 10 Vols Edinburgh

Stull, W J (1986). 'The Urban Economics of Adam Smith', *Journal of Urban Economics* Vol 20

Tribe, K P (1984). 'Cameralism and the Science of Government', *Journal of Modern History* Vol 56

Vickers, D (1960). *Studies in the Theory of Money 1690–1776*

Winch, D (1978). *Adam Smith's Politics: An Essay in Historiographic Revision* Cambridge

Winch, D (1983). 'Adam Smith's enduring particular result', in Hont and Ignatieff

CHAPTER TEN

Sir James Steuart's Corporate State

Walter Eltis

Ideas in Economics,
ed R D C Black (Macmillan, 1986)

It is well known that Smith and Hume have had great influence on conservative economic policy in the twentieth century. Hume argued that the balance of payments was self-correcting so that governments could ignore the international implications of their policies, and that money was neutral in the long run so that monetary expansion offered no long-term benefits. Smith showed that the demand for labour depended on the capital stock and its effectiveness which would be maximised if capital was always allowed to earn the highest possible return. This required that the allocation of capital be in no way interfered with by government regulation and control, and that all investment decisions be taken by those who actually stood to benefit. It followed that workers' living standards would be maximised if capitalists were left entirely free to invest in whatever they regarded as the most profitable ways, while the role of government was restricted to the creation of an environment where capitalist property rights were guaranteed. Government investments would reduce living standards because they would yield less than private investments since those who took the decisions would have no inducement to get them right. All interference with trade would make workers poorer because the effectiveness of the capital stock would be reduced. Government consumption would be still more damaging because it would actually reduce the capital stock and not merely its effectiveness. The connection between these propositions and twentieth-century conservative economic policy is patent.

Eighteenth-century economics left a wholly different legacy which is less well known. An eighteenth-century Scottish aristocrat, Sir James Steuart, went into exile in 1745 (as a prospective Minister if the Stuarts had triumphed)[1] where he absorbed a good deal of the interventionism which prevailed in Europe, and published a 1,200 page treatise, *An Inquiry into the Principles of Political Oeconomy,* in 1767 after his return from the continent.[2] This offered his countrymen heavy taxation, an unlimited public debt, monetary expansion to reduce interest rates to 2 per cent, import controls, export subsidies, government-managed corporations, and the Agricultural Policy which the EEC went on to adopt 200 years later. Still more astonishingly he described as, 'the most perfect plan of political oeconomy . . . anywhere to be met with' (218), one where there was no private property, no imports, no foreign travel, and no private consumption beyond the barest necessities. The potential effectiveness of such a society where the entire non-agricultural population was available for war was such that if any European nation adopted it, 'every other nation' would be obliged 'to adopt, as far as possible, a similar conduct, from a principle of self-preservation'. (227)

In the period of Keynesian ascendancy, Steuart's economics was preferred to Smith's by admirers of his cheap money and full employment policies,[3] and a distinguished Indian planner welcomed his collectivism and justification for unlimited intervention,[4] but soviet economists have yet to follow up the admiration for Steuart which Marx repeatedly expressed.[5]

An Inquiry into the Principles of Political Oeconomy was referred to by Smith in 1772 in a well-known letter to William Pulteney: 'Without once mentioning it [Steuart's book], I flatter myself, that every false principle in it, will meet with a clear and distinct confutation in mine'.[6] Smith succeeded so well that Steuart remarked shortly before his death that a book of equal length about his dog would have excited as much interest as the treatise on political economy which occupied eighteen years of his life.[7]

As with most economists who merit attention, Steuart's conclusions, including his twentieth-century policy proposals, follow straightforwardly from his premises. The present restatement will start with an account of Steuart's assumptions and how these led him to conclude that a nation would suffer a variety of economic maladjustments leading to inevitable economic decline, in the absence of very detailed interventions by an enlightened *statesman*. The actual policies Steuart put forward to enable a nation to develop fully its physical and human resources and so prevent the economic decline which would otherwise be inevitable, will be the subject of the second part of the paper. Finally something will be said about Smith's reasons for regarding these policies as utterly misconceived. It will become evident that the sharply different policy implications of these two major eighteenth-century economic treatises have echoes, and indeed, considerably more than echoes, in the economic debates of the 1980s.

Sir James Steuart's Assumptions and how they led him to conclude that only an Enlightened Statesman could prevent Severe Economic Maladjustment and Decline

Steuart divided the people of a country into two classes, 'The first is that of the farmers who produce the subsistence, and who are necessarily employed in this branch of business; the other I shall call *free hands*; because their occupation being to procure themselves subsistence out of the superfluity of the farmers, and by a labour adapted to the wants of the society, may vary according to these wants, and these again according to the spirit of the times'. (43)

Steuart anticipated Malthus in linking population closely to the growth of agricultural output. The non-agricultural population which depends on the surplus that farmers produce for the consumption of 'free-hands' will rely on powers of coercion in a society where slavery prevails, but most of Steuart's book is concerned with market economies, and here the amount that farmers produce in excess of their own needs will depend on the range of manufactured goods which can be offered in exchange for their surplus food, and since these will be more extensively available in a monetised than a barter economy, agricultural productivity and therefore the size of the agricultural surplus will also vary with the degree of monetisation:

> When once this imaginary wealth (money) becomes well introduced into a country, luxury will very naturally follow; and when money becomes the object of our wants, mankind become industrious, in turning their labour towards every object which may engage the rich to part with it; and thus the inhabitants of any country may increase in numbers, until the ground refuses farther nourishment. (45)

Steuart was convinced like Malthus that the level of agricultural productivity and output would vary sharply with the effective demand of other classes for food. If the demand for food falls for any reason:

> The laziest part of the farmers, disgusted with a labour which produces a plenty superfluous to themselves, which they cannot dispose of for any equivalent, will give over working, and return to their ancient simplicity. The more laborious will not furnish the food to the necessitous for nothing . . . Thus by the diminution of labour, a part of the country, proportional to the quantity of food which the farmers formerly found superfluous, will again become uncultivated.
>
> Here then will be found a country, the population of which must stop for want of food; and which, by the supposition, is abundantly able to produce more. Experience every where shews the possible existence of such a case, since no country in Europe is cultivated to the utmost: and that there are many still, where cultivation, and consequently multiplication, is at a stop. (41–2)

Agriculture and industry therefore have to grow together. Industrial growth provides the incentives for farmers to produce the surpluses which industry's free hands require for their subsistence,[8] 'agriculture, when encouraged for the sake of multiplying inhabitants, must keep pace with the progress of industry; or else an outlet must be provided for all superfluity'. (41)

The free hands whom the agricultural surplus supports (who amounted to approximately half the population in the Britain of 1767 according to Steuart (54–5)) may produce manufactures for home consumption or for export, provide personal services for the wealthy, or be employed by the state in the armed forces, or else to produce public works or services, The 'wants of society' and the 'spirit of the times' will determine which of these predominate.

Steuart believed a historical sequence which is often found is that the development of agriculture is first associated with a reciprocal growth in manufacturing. As industry develops, costs are low initially because surplus labour can be drawn cheaply from the land ('The desertion of the hands employed in a trifling agriculture' (183)) while industrialists have not yet become accustomed to high personal incomes which will in due course be 'consolidated' into manufacturing prices. Industry will then be internationally competitive, and there will be a fruitful period in which the free hands are predominantly employed in industry to produce luxuries for home consumption and for export. This will produce a comfortable period in which there is parallel growth in industry and agriculture, but industrial expansion contains the seeds of subsequent decline.

First, the relative price of food will rise and raise wages in a Ricardian manner:[9]

> Now the augmentation of food is relative to the soil, and as long as this can be brought to produce, at an expence proportioned to the value of the returns, agriculture without any doubt, will go forward in every country of industry. But as soon as the progress of agriculture demands an additional expence, which the natural return, at the stated prices of subsistence, will not defray, agriculture comes to a stop, and so would numbers, did not the consequences of industry push them forward, in spite of small difficulties. The industrious then, I say, continue to multiply, and the consequence is, that food becomes scarce, and that the inhabitants enter into competition for it.
>
> This is no contingent consequenc.·, it is an infallible one; because food is an article of the first necessity, and here the provision is supposed to fall short of demand. This raises the profits of those who have food ready to sell; and as the balance upon this article must remain overturned for some time . . . these profits will be consolidated with the price, and give encouragement to a more expensive improvement of the soil . . .
>
> This augmentation on the value of subsistence must necessarily raise the price of all work . . . (197)

The consequent rise in wages and the prices of manufactures will weaken industrial competitiveness, reduce exports of manufactures and increase imports.

At the same time as industry advances, any high profits and wages which are earned over any considerable period will tend to be consolidated into the income levels that producers come to expect, and a subsequent weakening of demand will not reduce their incomes to the former level. Moreover, as industry advances, all kinds of barriers to competition will develop, and manufacturers will acquire peculiar privileges which enable them to sustain prices at high levels. According to Steuart, monopoly and monopsony are widespread, and departures from perfect competition will be greater, the more mature a country's industry, so in time any successful country will become increasingly vulnerable to international competition.

Finally export markets will inevitably weaken and competition from imports increase as foreign industry develops as it must.

> when the inhabitants themselves foolishly enter into competition with strangers for their own commodities; and when a statesman looks coolly on, with his arms across, or takes it into his head, that it is not his business to interpose, the prices of the dexterous workman will rise above the amount of the mismanagement, loss, and reasonable profits, of the new beginners; and when this comes to be the case, trade will decay where it flourished most, and take root in a new soil. (205)

As soon as foreign manufacturers begin to outcompete domestic producers, a country will find it increasingly difficult to employ its free hands in industry.

> Trade having subsisted long in the nation we are now to keep in our eye, I shall suppose that, through length of time, her neighbours have learned to supply one article of their own and other people's wants cheaper than she can do. What is to be done? Nobody will buy from her, when they can be supplied from another quarter at a less price. I say, what is to be done? For if there be no check put upon trade, and if the statesmen do not interpose with the greatest care, it is certain, that merchants will import the produce, and even the manufactures of rival nations; the inhabitants will buy them preferably to their own; the wealth of the nation will be exported; and her industrious manufacturers will be brought to starve. (284)

The lost jobs due to increasing import penetration present considerable problems for a society in Steuart's analysis because the economy's 'free hands', approximately half the labour force, will necessarily have to find work outside agriculture, but he does not believe that there is a satisfactory mechanism to clear the labour market at an acceptable wage. He believes that attention should be continually focused on the relationship between *demand* and *work* in an economy:

> when we say that the balance between work and demand is to be sustained in equilibrio, as far as possible, we mean that the quantity supplied should be in proportion to the quantity *demanded*, that is, *wanted*. While the balance stands justly poised, prices are found in the adequate proportion of the real expence of making the goods, with a small addition for profit to the manufacturer and merchant. (189)

If demand falls while work (or potential supply) remains unchanged, 'reasonable profits will be diminished', and perhaps workmen will be obliged to sell 'below prime cost' with the result that 'workmen fall into distress, and that industry suffers a discouragement'. If on the contrary demand exceeds work, 'the manufacturers are enriched for a little time, by a rise of profits', 'but as soon as these profits become *consolidated* with the intrinsic value, they will cease to have the advantage of profits, and, becoming in a manner necessary to the existence of the goods, will cease to be considered as advantageous'. The continual tendency for import penetration to rise will reduce demand in relation to work with the result that manufacturers will be 'forced to starve' (192–4).

A further result of increased imports is that any consequent balance of payments deficit will lead to a continual drain of the precious metals, and therefore a loss of part of the money supply:

> if. . . a nation . . . be found to consume not only the whole work of the inhabitants, but part of that of other countries, it must have a balance of trade against it, equivalent to the amount of foreign consumption; and this must be paid for in specie, or in an annual interest, to the diminution of the former capital. Let this trade continue long enough, they will not only come at the end of their metals, but they may render themselves virtually tributary to other nations, by paying to them annually a part of the income of their lands, as the interest due upon the accumulated balances of many years' unfavourable trade. (359)

Steuart rejects Hume's argument that a loss of specie will produce self-correcting adjustments in relative prices.

A loss of specie will continue indefinitely in a country which is spending more than its national income so that it not only suffers adverse trade but also a continual need to sell real assets to foreigners and to borrow internationally:

> [Mr Hume] is led from his principles to believe, that there is no such thing as a wrong balance of trade against a nation, but on the contrary thinks that the nature of money resembles that of a fluid, which tends every where to a level . . . [N]othing is so easy, or more common than a right or a wrong balance of trade; and I observe, that what we mean by a balance, is not the bringing the fluid to a level, but either the accumulating or raising it in some countries, by the means of national industry and frugality, which is a right balance; or the depressing it in others, by national luxury and dissipation which is a wrong one. Thus the general doctrine of the *level* can only take place, on the supposition that all countries are equally frugal and industrious . . . (1767, i, 515–16)

Steuart also objects to Hume's assumption that prices will rise smoothly in countries which gain specie and fall in those which lose gold and silver, because an increased supply of the precious metals may stagnate in countries with surpluses, where, because of all the imperfections in competition, 'prices remain regulated as before, by the complicated operations of demand and competition'. (363)[10] If a gold inflow does not raise prices:

> What then will become of the additional quantity of coin, or papermoney? . . . if upon the increase of riches it be found that the state of demand remains without any variation, then *the additional coin* will probably be locked up, or converted into plate; because they who have it, not being inspired with a desire of increasing their consumption, and far less with the generous sentiment of giving their money away, their riches will remain without producing more effect than if they had remained in the mine . . . Let the specie of a country, therefore, be augmented or diminished, in ever so great a proportion, commodities will still rise and fall according to the principles of demand and competition . . . Let the quantity of coin be ever so much increased, it is the desire of spending it alone which will raise prices. (344–5)

A drain of money in countries with deficits is liable to produce irreversible adverse effects if there is an accompanying decline in the degree of monetisation, which is so important to the creation of incentives to produce. If a country with a trade deficit is also borrowing internationally, or selling assets to foreigners, because its aggregate expenditure exceeds its domestic production, which can all too easily occur in a country with declining real incomes, then, as in the case of Ireland (where the improvidence of heirs is supposedly shifting property rights to England):

> so soon as . . . demand . . . comes to fail, for want of money, or industry, in Ireland, to purchase it, what remains on hand will be sent over to England in kind; or, by the way of trade, be made to circulate with other nations (in beef, butter, tallow, &c.) who will give silver and gold for it, to the proprietors of the Irish lands. By such a diminution of demand in the country, for the fruits of the earth, the depopulation of Ireland is implied; because they who consumed them formerly, consume them no more; that is to say, they are dead, or have left the country. (371)

Thus adverse specie flows as a result of lack of demand for domestic produce, may lead to demonetisation and depopulation.

Steuart was deeply concerned that a country which threw its frontiers open to international competition, could easily arrive at a situation where its manufactures were overpriced, with the result that it had a chronic tendency to raise its imports and to export less. At the same time the monopolistic and restrictive practices which emerged while its industry was internationally viable would prevent prices from falling to a competitive level, for in so many states, 'domestic luxury, taxes, and the high price of living, have put out of a capacity to support a competition with strangers' (1767, i, 505). If foreigners are nevertheless permitted to sell manufactures freely to an increasingly fickle population which often prefers foreign goods merely because they are foreign, domestic industry will provide employment for diminishing numbers of 'free hands'. There will then be an inevitable excess of 'work' or potential output over 'demand' resulting in inevitable unemployment and starvation for industrial workers. The failure of domestic manufacturing will moreover reduce demand for surplus food from the farmers, for there will be insufficient demand from 'free hands' to buy up the agricultural surplus. The continuing loss of the domestic money supply which accompanies these adverse trends will compound the decline in both industry and agriculture, which, Steuart believed, had often occurred in the past as once prosperous states fell:

> If . . . there be found too many hands for the demand, work will fall too low for workmen to be able to live; or, if there be too few, work will rise, and manufactures will not be exported.
>
> For want of this just balance, no trading state has ever been of long duration, after arriving at a certain height of prosperity. We perceive in history the rise, progress, grandeur, and decline of Sydon, Tyre, Carthage, Alexandria, and Venice, not to come nearer home. (195)

But this decline in great manufacturing nations is avoidable because:

> When a nation, which has long dealt and enriched herself by a reciprocal commerce in manufactures with other nations, finds the balance of trade turn against her, it is her interest to put a total stop to it, and to remain as she is, rather than to persist habitually in a practice, which, by a change of circumstances, must have effects very opposite to those advantages which it produced formerly. Such a stop may be brought about by the means of duties and prohibitions, which a statesman can lay on importations, so soon as he perceives that they begin to preponderate with respect to the *exportations* of his own country. (1767, i, 504)

The further stages of historical development of a nation therefore depend on the decisions of statesmen, and the second part of this paper will be concerned with Steuart's detailed theory of state intervention.

Sir James Steuart's Theory of Economic Policy

Steuart was very optimistic about the motivation of statesmen and their desire to further economic welfare. Like Smith, he believed that self-interest is the ruling principle which governs humanity, and 'From this principle, men are engaged to act in a thousand different ways, and every action draws after it certain necessary consequences'; but self-interest will not similarly influence the conduct of a statesman,[11] 'Self-interest, when considered with regard to him, is public spirit; and it can only be called self-interest, when it is applied to those who are to be governed by it.' (142) Steuart's statesman desires nothing less than to plan the functioning of the whole economy in order to advance the good of all:

> When the statesman knows the extent and quality of the territory of his country, so as to be able to estimate what numbers it may feed; he may lay down his plan of political oeconomy, and chalk out a distribution of inhabitants, as if the number were already compleat. It will depend upon his judgement alone, and upon the combination of circumstances, foreign and domestic, to distribute, and to employ the classes, at every period during this execution, in the best manner . . . (384)

Steuart's statesman requires vast knowledge in order to plan the economy successfully:

> There is no governing a state in perfection, and consequently no executing the plan for a right distribution of the inhabitants, without exactly knowing their situation as to numbers, their employment, the gains upon every species of industry, the numbers produced from each class. (70)
>   The more perfect and more extended any statesman's knowledge is of the circumstances and situation of every individual in the state he governs, the more he has it in his power to do them good or harm. I always suppose his inclinations to be virtuous and benevolent. (333)

Steuart's statesman becomes indispensable as soon as a country's industry begins to become less competitive in relation to foreign producers, because that is the point from which employment, output and population will continually fall if the statesman 'looks coolly on, with his arms across, or takes it into his head, that it is not his business to interpose'. What should the statesman then do to preserve industry at its peak? His desire above all is to sustain the nation's capital at this maximum level.

> The first object of the care of a statesman, who governs a nation, which is upon the point of losing her foreign trade, without any prospect or probability of recovering it, is to preserve the wealth she has already acquired. No motive ought to engage him to sacrifice this wealth, the safety alone of the whole society excepted, when suddenly threatened by foreign enemies. The gratification of particular people's habitual desires, although the wealth they possess may enable them, without the smallest hurt to their private fortunes, to consume the productions of other nations; the motive of preventing hoards; that of promoting a brisk circulation within the country; the advantages to be made by merchants, who may enrich themselves by carrying on a trade disadvantageous to the nation; to say all in one word, even the supporting of the same number of inhabitants, ought not to engage his consent to the diminution of national wealth. (293)

Since it is a loss of trade competitiveness that is threatening the wealth of the nation, the statesman's immediate desire will be to restrict imports and encourage exports so as to attempt to overcome the increasing competitive advantages of other nations. The statesman will need to have extremely detailed knowledge if he is to restrict imports to the best effect:

> He must first examine minutely every use to which the merchandize imported is put: if a part is re-exported with profit, this profit must be deducted from the balance of loss incurred by the consumption of the remainder. If it be consumed upon the account of other branches of industry, which are thereby advanced, the balance of loss may still be more than compensated. If it be a means of supporting a correspondence with a neighbouring nation, otherwise advantageous, the loss resulting from it may be submitted to, in a certain degree. But if upon examining the whole chain of consequences, he find the nation's wealth not at all increased, nor her trade encouraged, in proportion to the damage at first incurred by the importation; I believe he may decide such a branch of trade to be hurtful; and therefore that it ought to be cut off, in the most prudent manner . . . (293)

The declining competitiveness of exports can be counteracted in a variety of ways. Most directly, exports can be subsidised. '[P]ublic money must be made to operate upon the price of *the surplus* of industry only so as to make it exportable, even in cases where the national prices upon home consumption have got up beyond the proper standard'. (235) An example of a proposal to subsidise exports is:

> Let me suppose a nation which is accustomed to export to the value of a million of sterling of fish every year, to be undersold in this article by another which has found a fishery on its own coasts, so abundant as to enable it to undersell the first by 20 *per cent*. In this case, let the statesman buy up all the fish of his subjects, and undersell his competitors at every foreign market, at the loss to himself of perhaps £250,000. What is the consequence? That the million he paid for the fish remains at home, and that £750,000 comes in from abroad for the prices of them. How is the £250,000 to be made up? By a general imposition upon all the inhabitants. This returns into the public coffers, and all stands as it was. If this expedient be not followed, what will be the consequence? That those employed in the fishery will starve; that the fish taken will either remain upon hand, or be sold by the proprietors at a great loss; they will be undone, and the nation for the future will lose the acquisition of £750,000 a year. (256-7)

If the decline in exports is the result of an inevitable Ricardian rise in food and raw material prices as the country develops, then the statesman may use public money to counteract the adverse effects on competitiveness of these fundamental developments:

> When the progress of industry has augmented numbers, and made subsistence scarce, he must estimate to what height it is expedient that the price of subsistence should rise. If he finds, that, in order to encourage the breaking up of new lands, the price of it must rise too high and stand high too long, to preserve the intrinsic value of goods at the same standard as formerly; then he must assist agriculture with his purse, in order that exportation may not be discouraged. This will have the effect of increasing subsistence, according to the true proportion of the augmentation required, without raising the price of it too high. (200)

If it is a consolidation of previous inflated incomes that has made export prices unduly high, new export producers can be set up in green field sites uncontaminated with consolidation:

> All methods . . . should be fallen upon to supply manufacturers with new hands; and lest the contagion of example should get the better of all precautions, the seat of manufacturers might be changed; especially when they are found in great and populous cities, where living is dear: in this case, others should be erected in the provinces where living is cheap. The state must encourage these new undertakings; numbers of children must be taken in, in order to be bred early to industry and frugality . . . (251)

Steuart also supports a state role in the day-to-day management of industrial companies:

> in the infancy of such undertakings . . . the want of experience frequently occasions considerable losses; and while this continues to be the case, no complaints are heard against such associations. Few pretend to rival their undertaking, and it becomes at first more commonly the object of raillery than of jealously. During this period, the statesman should lay the foundation of his authority; he ought to spare no pains nor encouragement to support the undertaking; he ought to inquire into the capacity of those at the head of it; order their projects to be laid before him; and when he finds them reasonable, and well planned, he ought to take unforeseen losses upon himself: he is working for the public, not for the company; and the more care and expence he is at in setting the undertaking on foot, the more he has a right to direct the prosecution of it towards the general good. This kind of assistance given, entitles him to the inspection of their books; and from this, more than any thing, he will come to an exact knowledge of every circumstance relating to their trade. (391)

It will already be evident that Steuart's interventionism is not confined to industry, because fisheries are also receiving support, and the statesman's purse has been opened to agricultural improvement. In 1759, before his return from exile, he wrote a paper which was only published in 1805 in which he proposed 'a Policy of Grain' in 'the Common Markets of England'. In this he proposed that the government should be prepared to buy up all the grain that farmers were prepared to produce at 'the minimum price expedient for the farmers', sell all that could be sold at 'the maximum price expedient for the wage-earners', and store any excess in state granaries. This proposal for the Common Markets of England in grain which he wrote for his countrymen from Tübingen has, of course, become the extremely controversial policy of grain of the European Common Market.

The detailed interventions in industry and agriculture which have been set out, were avoidable while industrial and agricultural growth were compatible with international competitiveness, but they become increasingly necessary as soon as foreign industry threatens to undermine the employment of the country's 'free hands'. Actual intervention in industry would of course be unnecessary if there was blanket protection against all imports. But a consequence of this would be that domestic monopoly incomes would grow and the home production of an extensive range of luxury consumer goods for the landlords and the recipients of consolidated monopoly incomes would occupy the free hands who formerly produced for international markets. But a shift into luxury production where domestic producers have no need to fear foreign competition has several disadvantages:

> The consequences of *excessive luxury, moral and physical,* as well as the dissipation of private fortunes, may render both the statesman, and those whom he employs, negligent in their duty, unfit to discharge it, rapacious and corrupt. (267)

The growth of domestic luxury production will tend to encourage the formation of large private fortunes. The need to compete internationally acted as a constraint in the former period, but there is now no limit to the extent to which prices can be raised. This will lead to great personal inequalities; and the growth of private fortunes which will tend to dominate money markets also threatens the power and prestige of the state. Here there are remedies:

> The statesman looks about with amazement; he, who was wont to consider himself the first man in the society in every respect, perceives himself eclipsed by the lustre of private wealth, which avoids his grasp when he attempts to seize it. This makes his government more complex and more difficult to be carried on; he must now avail himself of art and address as well as of power and authority. By the help of cajoling and intrigues, he gets a little into debt; this lays a foundation for public credit, which, growing by degrees, and in its progress assuming many new forms, becomes from the most tender beginnings, a most formidable monster, striking terror into those who cherished it in its infancy. Upon this, as upon a triumphant war-horse, the statesman gets a-stride, he then appears formidable anew; his head turns giddy; he is cloaked with the dust he has raised; and at the moment he is ready to fall, he finds, to his utter astonishment and surprise, a strong monied interest, of his own creating, which, instead of swallowing him up as he apprehended, flies to his support. Through this he gets the better of all opposition . . . (181-2)

Steuart saw great potential advantages from the establishment of state controlled banks and issues of government bonds to create paper assets, and he believed that these would simultaneously raise the money supply and reduce interest rates. He argued that John Law's Mississippi scheme could have been successful in France with only a few minor modifications in the manner in which it was set up and administered; and that this would have established a long-term rate of interest of 2 per cent in France (557-63).

As well as asserting his authority via the market for public debt, a statesman also has the power to tax, which offers to governments the most powerful means to influence the economy and society:

> By taxes a statesman is enriched, and by means of his wealth, he is enabled to keep his subjects in awe, and to preserve his dignity and consideration.
>
> By the distribution of taxes, and manner of levying them, the power is thrown into such hands as the spirit of the constitution requires it should be found in. (304)
>
> [T]he intention of taxes as I understand them, is to advance only the public good, by throwing a part of the wealth of the rich into the hands of the industrious poor . . . (334)

In addition to furthering income redistribution and social improvement, large sums of public money are needed to finance Steuart's policies to sustain the competitiveness of industry, so tax revenues will become increasingly necessary as foreign industry advances:

> [T]axes become necessary; in order, with the amount of them, to correct the bad effects of luxury, by giving larger premiums to support exportation. And in proportion as a statesman's endeavours to support by these means the trade of his country becomes ineffectual, from the growing taste of dissipation in his subjects, the utility of an opulent exchequer will be more and more discovered; as he will be thereby enabled both to support his own authority against the influence of a great load of riches thrown into domestic circulation, and to defend his luxurious and wealthy subjects from the effects of the jealousy of those nations which enriched them. (336–7)
>
> Another use of taxes, after the extinction of foreign trade, is to assist circulation, by performing, as it were, the function of the heart of a child, when at its birth that of the mother can be of no farther use to it. The public treasure, by receiving from the amount of taxes, a continual flux of money, may throw it out into the most proper channels, and thereby keep that industry alive, which formerly flourished, and depended upon the prosperity of foreign commerce only.
>
> In proportion, therefore, as a statesman perceives the rivers of wealth . . . which were in brisk circulation with all the world, begin to flow abroad more slowly, and to form stagnations, which break out into domestic circulation, he ought to set a plan of taxation on foot, as a fund for premiums to indemnify exportation for the loss it must sustain from the rise of prices, occasioned by luxury; and also for securing the state itself, against the influence of domestic riches, as well as for recompensing those who are employed in its service. (337–8)

The need for high taxation in order to finance Steuart's industrial policies is underlined by the need to pay high salaries to administer them. As the role of government increases, it needs to attract a proportion of those with high ability to execute the vast array of tasks which Steuart has in mind, and top people (which meant aristocrats to Steuart who had lived more in France than in Smith's Edinburgh and Glasgow) need to be well paid:

> Is it not very natural, that he who is employed by the state should receive an equivalent proportioned to the value of his services? Is it to be supposed, that a person born in a high rank, who, from this circumstance alone, acquires an advantage in most nations, hardly to be made up by an acquired abilities, will dedicate his time and his attendance for the remuneration which might satisfy an inferior? The talents of great men deserve reward as much as those of the lowest among the industrious; and the state is with reason made to pay for every service she receives. (337)

Steuart also needed high taxation in order to finance his full employment policies, and these have attracted much favourable twentieth-century attention:[12]

> The nation's wealth must be kept entire, and made to circulate, so as to provide subsistence and employment for every body. (1767, i, 506)

The more money becomes necessary for carrying on consumption, the more it is easy to levy taxes; the use of which is to advance the public good, by drawing from the rich, a fund sufficient to employ both the *deserving,* and the *poor*, in the service of the state . . . (1767, i, 512–13)

If there is insufficient demand for labour:

When home-demand does not fill up the void, of which we have spoken, a vicious competition takes place among those that work for a physical-necessary; the price of their labour falls below the general standard of subsistence . . .

A statesman therefore, at the head of a luxurious people, must endeavour to keep his balance [between 'work' and 'demand'] even; and if a subversion is necessary, it is far better it should happen by the preponderancy of the scale of demand. Here is my reason for preferring this alternative.

All subversions are bad, and are attended with bad consequences. If the scale of work preponderates, the industrious will starve, their subsistence will be exported; the nation gains by the balance, but appears in a manner to sell her inhabitants. If the scale of demand preponderates, luxury must increase, but the poor are fed at the expence of the rich, and the national stock of wealth stands as it was. (1767, i, 506–7)

The poor should be employed above all on public works to carry through major investments in the social infrastructure:

If a thousand pounds are bestowed upon making a fire-work, a number of people are thereby employed, and gain a temporary livelihood. If the same sum is bestowed for making a canal for watering the fields of a province, a like number of people may reap the same benefit, and hitherto accounts stand even; but the firework played off, what remains, but the smoke and stink of the powder? Whereas the consequence of the canal is a perpetual fertility to a formerly barren soil. (1767, i, 519)

I say that whoever can transform the most consumable commodities of a country into the most durable and most beneficial works, makes a high improvement. If therefore meat and drink, which are of all things the most consumable, can be turned into harbours, high roads, canals, and public buildings, is not the improvement inexpressible? This is the power of every statesman to accomplish, who has subsistence at his disposal; and beyond the power of all those who have it not. (383)

As policies which require public expenditure are pushed further, rates of taxation and borrowing will have a continual tendency to increase, and Steuart believed that taxation should rise continually as competitiveness declines and the government has to create a demand for labour to fill the gap left by declining foreign sales. He was convinced that higher taxation would have a clear tendency to raise effective demand, since the state definitely spends what might only be partly spent if left in private hands:

[T]axes promote industry; not in consequence of their being raised upon individuals, but in consequence of their being expended by the state; that is, by increasing demand and circulation . . .

> Every application of public money implies a want in the state; and every want supplied, implies an encouragement given to industry. In proportion, therefore, as taxes draw money into circulation, which otherwise would not have entered into it at that time, they encourage industry; not by taking the money from individuals, but by throwing it into the hands of the state, which spends it; and which thereby throws it directly into the hands of the industrious, or of the luxurious who employ them.
>
> It is no objection to this representation of the matter, that the persons from whom the money is taken, would have spent it as well as the state. The answer is, that it might be so, or not; whereas when the state gets it, it will be spent undoubtedly. (725–6)

If the demand-side effects of higher taxation are favourable as Steuart and present-day Keynesians insist for precisely these reasons, what of the supply-side effects which are now so often believed to be unfavourable? Steuart differed from almost all his successors in that he believed that higher taxation would actually have *favourable effects upon supply*.

> When in any country the work of manufacturers, who live luxuriously, and who can afford to be idle some days of the week, finds a ready market; this circumstance alone proves beyond all dispute, that subsistence in that country is not too dear, at least in proportion to the market prices of goods at home; and if taxes on consumption have, in fact raised the prices of necessaries, beyond the former standard, this rise, cannot, in fact, discourage industry: it may discourage idleness; and idleness will not be totally rooted out, until people be forced, in one way or other, to give up both superfluity and days of recreation. (691)
>
> When the hands employed are not diligent, the best expedient is to raise the price of their subsistence, by taxing it. By this you never will raise their wages, until the market can afford to give a better price for their work. (695)

Since higher taxation will thus have favourable effects upon both *demand* and *supply*,[13] there really are no problems in raising it whenever this is necessary for the financing of social, or industrial, or full employment policies. Steuart's attitude to private incomes has twentieth-century echoes:

> [M]y original plan, . . . was to keep constantly in view those virtuous statesmen who think of nothing but the good of their subjects. Taxes and impositions in their hands, are the wealth of the father of the family; who therewith feeds, clothes, provides for, and defends every one within his house. (703)
>
> If the money raised be more beneficially employed by the state, than it would have been by those who have contributed it, then I say the public has gained, in consequence of the burden laid upon individuals; consequently the statesman has done his duty, both in imposing the taxes, and in rightly expending them. (709)

With economic activity increasingly concentrated in public hands where normal market incentives do not apply, there are clear risks of abuse which Steuart recognised, and he recommended penalties for economic sabotage which have been widely applied in the twentieth century; though not quite his insistence that the appropriate method of execution for the abuse of public money was drawing and quartering (the eighteenth-century penalty for high treason) and not mere hanging (the penalty for highway robbery):

> [I]f there be a crime called high treason, which is punished with greater severity than highway robbery, and assassination, I should be apt (were I a statesman) to put at the head of this bloody list, every attempt to defeat the application of public money, for the purposes here mentioned . . . If severe punishment can . . . put a stop to frauds, I believe it will be thought very well applied. (257)

Steuart was of course far ahead of his time in his eulogies of high taxation, and in the emphasis he placed on the public sector. He recognised this, but because he was confident that his argument was logically correct, he believed a time would surely come when his propositions would also be politically acceptable:

> In treating of taxes, I frequently look no farther than my pen, when I raise my head and look about, I find the politics of my closet very different from those of the century in which I live. I agree that the difference is striking; but still reason is reason, and there is no impossibility in the supposition of its becoming practice. (1767, i, 514)

Steuart's attitude to public debt is equally modern, but here it is Latin America that has gone furthest in the directions he advocated. He reasoned that there is no limit to the heights that domestically held public debt can reach. He first posed the question:

> If the interest paid upon the national debt of England, for example, be found constantly to increase upon every new war, the consequence will be, that more money must be raised on the subject for the payment of it. The question then comes to be. First, How far may debts extend? Secondly, How far may taxes be carried? And Thirdly, What will be the consequence, supposing the one and the other carried to the greatest height possible? (645)

Steuart's answer is that, 'debts may be increased to the full proportion of all that can be raised for the payment of the interest', and the land-tax, for instance:

> may be carried to the full value of all the real estate of England. The notion of actually imposing 20 shillings in the pound upon the real value of all the land-rents of England, appears to us perfectly ridiculous. I admit it to be so; and could I have discovered any argument by which I could have limited the rising of the land-tax to any precise number of shillings under twenty, I should have stated this as the maximum rather than the other. (646)

But the upper limit to government debt is not even the level where the interest upon it equals the revenue of a 100 per cent land-tax plus all the other taxes which can be levied. '[T]he state will then be in possession of all that can be raised on the land, on the consumption, industry and trade of the country; in short, of all that can be called income, which it will administer for the public creditors.' (646) In effect, the property rights of all former property owners will then have been transferred to the state, since their wealth no longer yields a net of tax income, but there will then be a new set of property owners, the holders of public debt, or gilt-edged stock. The government can go on to finance still further borrowing by taxing their income at 100 per cent, and so an, *ad infinitum*:

> If no check be put to the augmentation of public debts, if they be allowed constantly to accumulate, and if the spirit of a nation can patiently submit to the natural consequences of such a plan, it must end in this, that all property, that is income, will be swallowed up by taxes; and these will be transferred to the creditors, the state retaining the administration of the revenue.
>
> The state, in that case, will always consider those who enjoy the national income as the body of proprietors. This income will continue the same, and the real proprietors will pay the taxes imposed; which may be mortgaged again to a new set of men, who will retain the denomination of creditors; until by swallowing up the former, they slip into their places, and become the body of proprietors in their turn, and thus perpetuate the circle. (1767, ii, 633-4)

Such reasoning appeared strange to Steuart's contemporaries, but the analytical device he is using which is extremely familiar today is the limiting case. He says, 'Do not be put off from raising taxes when this appears correct in the short term, for there is no theory which says that a land-tax, for instance, cannot be raised to 100 per cent; and Britain (levying just four shillings in the pound) is far short of that. Do not be put off from borrowing for fear of the size of the public debt, because immeasurably greater debt is conceivable'. Finally, to explain his praise for a wholly collectivist and egalitarian society which has been remarked on,[14] do not fear to restrict freedom of choice in consumption by restricting imports and taxing the better off heavily in order to reduce their luxury consumption, because a society which pushed such trends immeasurably further would still be agreeable to live in, and militarily formidable to boot. In each of these examples, Steuart is careful to point out that they are chimerical. Thus, the scheme of taxing property owners at 100 per cent in order to finance massive government borrowing, and then going on to tax the holders of giltedged shares in order to provide the interest to finance still more borrowing is 'destitute of all probability; because of the infinite variety of circumstances which may frustrate such a scheme'. (647) As for the egalitarian collectivist society where none consume imports or luxuries, this has been, 'introduced purposely to serve as an illustration of general principles, and as a relaxation to the mind, like a farce between the acts of a serious opera'. (227) Steuart's solid and substantial argument is the detailed case he consistently develops for the establishment of what is nowadays called 'a corporate state', where the interests of both capitalists and workers as producers are paramount. His fundamental approach to economy and society is summarised in the passage below:

> Cities and corporations may be considered as nations, where luxury and taxes have rendered living so expensive, that goods cannot be furnished but at a high rate. If labour, therefore, of all kinds, were permitted to be brought from the provinces, or from the country, to supply the demand of the capital and smaller corporations, what would become of tradesmen and manufacturers who have their residence

there? If these, on the other hand, were to remove beyond the liberties of such corporations, what would become of the public revenue, collected in these little states, as I call them?

By the establishment of corporations, a statesman is enabled to raise high impositions upon all sorts of consumption; and notwithstanding these have the necessary consequence of increasing the price of labour, yet by other regulations . . . the bad consequences thereby resulting to foreign trade may be avoided, and every article of exportation be prevented from rising above the proper standard for making it vendible, in spite of all foreign competition . . .

Cities having obtained the privilege of incorporation, began, in consequence of the powers vested in their magistrates, to levy taxes: and finding the inconveniences resulting from external competition (foreign trade), they erected the different classes of their industrious into confraternities, or corporations of a lower denomination, with power to prevent the importation of work from their fellow tradesmen not of the society . . . Nobody ever advanced, that the industry carried on in *towns*, where living is dear, ought to suffer a competition with that of the *country*, where living is cheap . . . (286–7)

Steuart himself underlines the importance of this example of a social contract between rulers who tax, and unionised citizens whose livelihood they then protect from competition, when he summarises this chapter:

I shew how [incorporated cities] may be considered as so many states, which domestic luxury , taxes, and the high price of living, have put out of a capacity to support a competition with strangers (that is with the open country) which here represents the rest of the world. I show the reasonableness of such exclusive privileges, in favour of those who share the burthens peculiar to the community, in so far only as regards the supply of their own consumption; and I point out, by what methods any discouragements to industry may be prevented, as often as that industry has for its object the supplying the wants of those who are not included in the corporation.

From the long and constant practice of raising *taxes* within incorporated cities, I conclude, that *taxes* are a very natural consequence of luxury, and of the loss of foreign trade; and as Princes have taken the hint from the cities, to extend them universally, it is no wonder to see foreign trade put an end to, in consequence of such injudicious extensions. (1767, i, 504–5)

Steuart thus perceived a parallel between a country which is no longer competitive in trade and therefore incapable of providing employment for its 'free hands', and a mature city state, and he proposed that the remedies for the problems of the mature nation were precisely those that successful city states had discovered in their efforts to sustain an adequate standard of living for all within their corporations. The full range of Steuart's policy proposals is explicable in this context,[15] and also the extensive support for very similar policies in the twentieth century by those who see the problems of their countries in similar terms.

It is thus central to the analysis of the Cambridge Economic Policy Group that British industry ceased to be internationally competitive in the 1970s, for reasons which echo several of Steuart's and the consequent damage to employment to which they attach the same overriding importance can only be averted by import controls and positive job-creating industrial policies which resemble those that Steuart specifically outlined. At the same time, like Steuart, they foresee little damage from higher taxation, heavier government borrowing and a narrower range of availability of 'luxury' consumer goods.[16] Similar analyses have naturally emerged elsewhere.

Smith considered this analysis entirely mistaken in 1776. This paper will conclude with a summary of why he objected so strongly to Steuart's interventionist policies. The reasons for his opposition to Steuart's corporatist approach naturally have much in common with the arguments used today by those who oppose moves towards a corporate state in the Britain of the 1980s.

WHY ADAM SMITH BELIEVED THAT SIR JAMES STEUART'S POLITICAL OECONOMY WAS MISTAKEN

There are several obvious reasons why Smith believed strongly that Steuart's analysis was misconceived. First and most fundamentally, his view of the knowledge, skill and motivation of statesmen was entirely different. The contrast between Steuart's omniscient and benevolently intentioned statesmen, and those to be found in the *Wealth of Nations* below[17] could hardly be greater:

> The statesman, who should attempt to direct private people in what manner they ought to employ their capitals, would not only load himself with a most unnecessary attention, but assume an authority which could safely be trusted, not only to no single person, but to no council or senate whatever, and which would nowhere be so dangerous as in the hands of a man who had folly and presumption enough to fancy himself fit to exercise it. (456)

> What is the species of domestick industry which his capital can employ, and of which the produce is likely to be of the greatest value, every individual, it is evident, can, in his local situation, judge much better than any statesman or lawgiver can do for him. (456)

As well as lacking the knowledge of entrepreneurs, Smith also believed that statesmen were by nature extravagant, and prone to maladministration:

> The uniform, constant, and uninterrupted effort of every man to better his condition, the principle from which publick and national, as well as private opulence is originally derived, is frequently powerful enough to maintain the natural progress of things towards improvement, in spite both of the extravagance of government, and of the greatest errors of administration. (343)

The eighteenth-century readers of Smith and Steuart who actually determined which would be taken seriously, recognised Smith's statesmen, but not Steuart's Utopian supermen (who re-emerged only in the detailed blueprints for 'the economics of control' which followed 'the Keynesian revolution')[18] There is one point where some of the statesmen whom Steuart must actually have encountered surface, when he writes,

> In my inquiries. I have constantly in my eye, how man *may* be governed, and never how *he* is governed. How a righteous and intelligent statesman may restrain the

liberty of individuals, in order to promote the common good; never how an ignorant and unrighteous statesman may destroy public liberty, for the sake of individuals. (708)

It is precisely because Smith described how man *is* governed, while Steuart merely sought to show how he *may be* governed that his analysis carried extra conviction to his contemporaries. And today there is an equal difference between those who believe governments have sufficient information to execute complex interventionist policies in order to maximise social welfare functions over immense (and sometimes infinite) time horizons, and those who believe that in practice politicians will often be concerned with little more than the parochial interests of their own party over a period little longer than the memory of an electorate. These 'realists' are as unready as Smith to expect benefits from government control over the minutiae of economic life.

An equally far-reaching objection to Steuart stemmed from Smith's belief that economies were sufficiently self-correcting in the short term to avoid many of the ills that Steuart predicted. In particular, in the *Wealth of Nations* the demand for labour always depends on the capital stock, and this will be used most effectively if it is allowed to earn as much profit as possible for those who own it. The prosperity of workers which Smith and Steuart both desired depended on continual growth in the stock of capital, and Smith analysed the conditions which can be expected to contribute to accumulation with great care. It has been widely pointed out that potential supply in Steuart's economy, 'work' as he calls it, is merely the available labour force.[19] Smith's perception that 'stock' influences the demand for labour is lacking. Even if many of Steuart's full employment policies actually raised demand in the short term, they would undoubtedly reduce the rate of capital accumulation afterwards, and therefore reduce the demand for labour in the medium term. Smith did not refer to the possibility of unused capital even in the short term, but even if the short run is conceded to Steuart, the lack of a concept of 'stock' means that he fails to provide an analysis of the progression of the demand for labour, and of how the growth of government expenditure may inhibit this, and of how private saving will generally increase it. Today there is equal disagreement between those like Steuart who focus on the correction of immediate demand deficiencies at whatever cost, and those like Smith who believe that the trend demand for labour must react favourably if the appropriate conditions for long-term private sector capital accumulation can be established.

Finally, because he believed that private capitalists would always be able to find profitable openings for the physical capital at their disposal, Smith had no need for the paraphernalia of the corporate state:

> The general industry of the society never can exceed what the capital of the society can employ. As the number of workmen that can be kept in employment by any particular person must bear a certain proportion to his capital, so the number of those that can be continually employed by all the members of a great society, must bear a certain proportion to the whole capital of that society, and never can exceed that proportion. No regulation of commerce can increase the quantity of industry in any society beyond what its capital can maintain. It can only divert a part of it into a direction into which it might not otherwise have gone . . . (453)

If foreign competitors provided some goods more cheaply than home producers, Smith's industrialists can be expected to switch their capital to the production of alternative products. An eighteenth-century capital stock consisted largely of food and raw materials which could be used to produce a variety of final products. If one of these became uncompetitive, production could switch to others at a trivial cost in comparison with the twentieth-century penalty for having to switch capital out of textiles, a car, or an aircraft industry, because these are losing out to foreigners. Smith believed that competition would always steer the capital stock into the directions which would maximise returns. Steuart believed that the extent of domestic competition was extremely limited, and that the superior knowledge of the statesman would generally enable him to out-think the market, and that the powers of government to limit competition would in any case ensure that whatever the statesman produced was sold. Smith believed that such departures from the competitive process would misdirect investment, and reduce the aggregate returns a nation derived from its physical capital. Today there are equally those who wish to set up a corporate state behind tariff walls, and others who believe that maximum competition will ensure that the best use is made of a country's productive resources.

A vital difficulty which economies encounter today that never occurred to Smith is that a country's general price or cost level may be stuck above those of competitors. Smith readily accepted Hume's argument that gold losses by such a country would reduce its domestic costs and prices to a level where domestic markets cleared. Today's market economists are perfectly ready to echo Smith and Hume, but Steuart's rejection of Hume's argument because many domestic costs and prices are fixed independently of the money supply, and because a country can lose gold cumulatively like Ireland and never find equilibrium, also finds eloquent and persuasive support. It is difficult to believe that eighteenth-century economies had sufficient wage and price rigidities to defeat Hume's argument, but in the Britain of 1985 Steuart's belief that a country's wage or price structure can get so far out of line that its industries cannot remain sufficiently competitive to sustain full employment is accepted by many ranging from the Cambridge Economic Policy Group to the Chancellor of the Exchequer.

NOTES

1   The best accounts of Sir James Steuart's life are to be found in Skinner (1966) and Chamley (1965).
2   References and quotations, will, wherever possible, be to the Scottish Economic Society's 1966 edition, edited by Andrew Skinner, and page references will be to this edition, unless a passage is only to be found in the original edition in which case a page reference will be preceded by 1767. The publishers of the 1966 edition unfortunately insisted on the omission of approximately one-quarter of Steuart's text.
3   See, in particular, Sen (1957), Stettner (1945), and Vickers (1959) and (1970)

4   See Sen (1957), 'Steuart's historical and evolutionist approach, his views on the economic structure, his conception of labour as a social category, his theory of perpetual crisis facing the exchange economy, his analysis of inner contradictions as transforming one economic stage into another, his treatment of Spartan communism and general anti-individualist bias had undoubtedly a profound influence on Marx' (pp 187–8).

5   There are, for instance, thirteen references to Steuart in the first volume of *Capital*, 'Sir James Steuart, a writer altogether remarkable for his quick eye for the characteristic social distinctions between different modes of production' (p 314); and 'Sir James Steuart is the economist who has handled this subject [population] best. How little his book, which appeared ten years before the *Wealth of Nations*, is known, even at the present time, may be judged from the fact that admirers of Malthus do not even known that the first edition of the latter's work on population contains, except in the purely declamatory part, very little but extracts from Steuart, and in a less degree, from Wallace and Townsend' (p 333).

6   See, Smith, *Correspondence*, p 164. Skinner (1981) in his magisterial article written to commemorate the bicentenary of Steuart's death, discounts the evident contempt for Steuart's economics that this letter conveys: 'it will be noted that remarks such as these are not overtly hostile or even hypercritical, and that Smith's reply to Pulteney cannot be fully assessed until the latter's opinion is known' (p 39).

7   See Skinner (1966), p lv, and Steuart (1767) vol 2 p 646

8   See Eagly (1961) for an account of the importance of incentives and aspirations in Steuart.

9   Hollander (1973) has drawn attention to the presence of agricultural diminishing returns in Steuart.

10 The relationship between Steuart's monetary theory and the quantity theory is discussed in detail in Skinner (1967), and Skinner also explains (1981) the importance for Steuart's interventionist approach to economic policy of his rejection of Hume's self-correcting specie flow propositions.

11 Skinner (1962) provides a valuable account of the relationship of Steuart's politics to his economics.

12 See especially, Vickers (1959) and (1970), Meek (1967), Schumpeter (1954), Hutchison (1978) and Stettner (1945).

13 It is not easy to reconcile Steuart's argument here that higher taxation may have *favourable* effects on the supply produced by, for instance, farmers, with the propositions referred to above (pp 45–6) that the availability of a greater variety of manufactures in exchange for food will often persuade them to produce more. Brian Loasby drew my attention to this contradiction, which may be a by-product of Steuart's evident desire to set out a strong case for high taxation.

14 Anderson and Tollison (1984) suggest that Steuart seriously desired the establishment of an egalitarian collectivist society of this kind, without referring to the context in which he outlines his account of this society. Their doubts about the uncritical praise for Steuart's interventionism in the secondary literature are similar to those in the present article

15 Skinner (1966) has suggested that Steuart 'appeared too often in the guise of a "political matron" (p lxxxii). This is certainly a plausible interpretation of his attitude to policy, but it is also possible that he was systematically setting out the case for the establishment of 'a corporate state' rather than outlining a series of piecemeal remedies for every difficulty.

16 See the successive issues of the *Cambridge Economic Policy Review*, which this group published from 1975 to 1981, after which they apparently lost hope of influencing policy in Britain, for the publication of the Review ceased.

17 Page references are to the Glasgow Edition of the *Wealth of Nations,* edited by
    R H Campbell and A S Skinner.
18 Sen (1957) has suggested that, 'It would not be any great exaggeration to say that
    A P Lerner's chapter on functional finance seems almost a paraphrase of Steuart'
    (p122).
19 See, for instance, Meek (1967) and Akhtar (1978 and 1979). In 1979 Akhtar wrote
    'The most serious flaw in his treatment is that it completely neglected the subject
    of capital accumulation, and the role of capital in the production process' (p 301).
    Perelman (1983) has shown that there are valuable accounts of primitive
    accumulation in Steuart.

REFERENCES

Akhtar, M A (1978). 'Steuart on Growth', *Scottish Journal of Political Economy* 25,
    pp 57–74
——— (1979). 'An Analytical Outline of Sir James Steuart's Macroeconomic Model',
    Oxford Economic Papers 31, pp 283–302
Anderson, G M and R B Tollison (1984). 'Sir James Steuart as the Apotheosis of
    Mercantilism and His Relation to Adam Smith', *Southern Economic Journal* 51, pp
    456–68
Cambridge Economic Policy Group (1975–81). *Cambridge Economic Policy Review*
    Farnborough: Gower
Chamley, P (1965). *Documents Relatifs à Sir James Steuart* Paris: Dalloz
Eagly, R V (1961). 'Sir James Steuart and the Aspiration Effect', *Economica* 28, pp
    53–81
Hollander, S (1973). *The Economics of Adam Smith* Toronto: Toronto University Press
Hume, D (1752). *Political Discourses,* Edinburgh
Hutchison, T W (1978). *On Revolutions and Progress in Economic Knowledge*
    Cambridge: Cambridge University Press
Lerner, A P (1944). *The Economics of Control* New York: Macmillan
Malthus, T R *An Essay on the Principle of Population as it Affects the Future
    Improvement of Society* London
Marx, K (1867) *Capital* Moscow: Progress Publishers for Lawrence & Wishart, 1974,
    reprint
Meek, R L (1967). *Economics and Ideology and Other Essays* London: Chapman and
    Hall
Perelman, M (1983). 'Classical Political Economy and Primitive Accumulation: The
    Case of Smith and Steuart', *History of Political Economy* 15, pp 451–94
Ricardo, D (1817). *On the Principles of Political Economy and Taxation* London
Schumpeter, J A (1954). *History of Economic Analysis* New York: Oxford University
    Press
Sen, S R *The Economics of Sir James Steuart* London: Bell
Skinner, A S (1962). 'Sir James Steuart: Economics and Politics', *Scottish Journal of
    Political Economy* 9, pp 275–90
——— (1966). 'Biographical Sketch', and 'Analytical Introduction', in the Scottish
    Economic Society's edition of Sir James Steuart, *Principles of Political Oeconomy*
    Edinburgh: Oliver & Boyd

—— (1967). 'Money and Prices: A Critique of the Quantity Theory', *Scottish Journal of Political Economy* 14, pp 275–90

—— (1981). 'Sir James Steuart: Author of a System', *Scottish Journal of Political Economy* 28, pp 20–42

Smith, A (1776). *An Inquiry into the Nature and Causes of the Wealth of Nations*. Republished as R H Campbell and A S Skinner (eds) *The Glasgow Edition of the Works and Correspondence of Adam Smith*, II Oxford: Oxford University Press, 1976

—— (1977). *The Correspondence of Adam Smith*, E C Mossner and I S Ross (eds) *The Glasgow Edition of the Works and Correspondence of Adam Smith*, VI Oxford: Oxford University Press

Stettner, W F (1945) 'Sir James Steuart on the Public Debt', *Quarterly Journal of Economics* 59, pp 451–76

Steuart, Sir James (1759). *A Dissertation on the Policy of Grain, with a view to a Plan for preventing scarcity or exorbitant prices in the Common Markets of England* in Sir James Steuart (ed) *Works, Political, Metaphysical and Chronological* (1805)

—— (1767). *An Inquiry into the Principles of Political Oeconomy: being an Essay on the Science of Domestic Policy in Free Nations* 2 vols London. Reprinted (abbreviated) for the Scottish Economic Society in 2 vols, A Skinner (ed) Edinburgh: Oliver & Boyd, 1966

—— (1805). (ed)*Works, Political, Metaphysical and Chronological*, 6 vols London

Vickers, D (1959). *Studies in the Theory of Money 1690–1776* Philadelphia: Chilton

—— (1970). 'The Works, Political, Philosophical and Metaphysical of Sir James Steuart: A Review Article', *Journal of Economic Literature* 7, pp 1190–5

CHAPTER ELEVEN

The Rehabilitation of Sir James Steuart[1]

R L Meek

Economics, Ideology and other Essays (Chapman & Hall, 1967)

I

The phenomenon of 'rehabilitation' is a peculiarly modern one, at any rate in the field of economic theory. In this field, indeed, one could almost say that prior to the 1930s there were no real 'rehabilitations' at all: the different schools which followed one another as the science developed usually contented themselves with demolishing their immediate predecessors, and made little attempt to claim affiliation with the earlier schools which these predecessors had in their day themselves supplanted. There were, of course, cases where writers unknown to, or misunderstood by, their contemporaries were rediscovered: Boisguillebert was in a sense 'rehabilitated' by the Physiocrats and von Thünen by the Marginalists; and Marx was diligent in tracking down anticipations of his theory of surplus value in the work of earlier writers. List, in a rather different sense, can be said to have 'rehabilitated' the Mercantilists—though in the sphere of economic policy rather than of theory. But cases where basic elements in the theoretical work of a once-famous author were discovered to have relevance and importance to a later era were very rare indeed.

During the last twenty-five years or so, however, there has been something of a swarm of rehabilitations—dating, perhaps, from Keynes' well-known essay on Malthus and the kind words which he subsequently spoke on behalf of the Mercantilists and that 'brave army of heretics' which included Mandeville, Gesell and Hobson.[2] The beginnings of general equilibrium theory have been found in the medieval Schoolmen, and of input-output analysis in Quesnay's *Tableau Economique*. Mrs Robinson sees her own work on the problems of overall growth of the economy as being in a sense 'a revival of the classical theory'.[3] And Dr Sen, in an interesting book[4] which is my point of departure in the present essay, suggests that Sir James Steuart should properly be regarded as a pioneer of our modern 'economics of control'.

What has caused this remarkable contemporary increase in the propensity

220

to rehabilitate? Partly, no doubt, a sense of insecurity. Theory rarely keeps pace with history: serious lags develop and accumulate, but they remain more or less unnoticed by the orthodox until some shattering event (the slump of 1929, Keynes's *General Theory*, Khrushchev's speech on Stalin) forces recognition of the fact that theory has got out of touch with reality. Then follows a period of profound intellectual questioning, in which the reign of complacency and dogmatism begins to come to an end, and people start asking themselves whether certain earlier ideas rejected by current orthodox theory may not have had something in them after all.

But the reappraisals of past systems of thought which occur during such periods of questioning tend to be *ex post* rather than *ex ante*. Parallels with the past are usually drawn after, rather than before, the orthodox theory begins to be decisively developed in new directions. Consider, for example, some of the main changes which have taken place in economic theory in our own times.

Take value theory. Most historians of economic thought would probably agree that the long period of development in this field prior to Adam Smith was marked by two basic features—first, a transition from the idea that the 'value' of a commodity was the price at which it *ought* to sell on the market to the idea that it was the price at which it *actually did* sell; and second, the working out of a fairly rudimentary supply-and-demand theory to explain how this market price was fixed. Then came the Classical economists, who, while accepting the notion that prices were fixed by supply and demand, sought for a more fundamental explanation of the *level* at which supply and demand fixed them in the normal case. Here their main emphasis was placed, of course, on the cost which lay behind supply. The Marginalists posed the general problem of value in similar terms, but placed their main emphasis on the utility which lay behind demand. But then a new tendency began to develop—towards a general equilibrium theory of price which in effect by-passed the whole problem of value as it was conceived by the Classical and Marginalist economics, and endeavoured to explain prices (to put it very crudely) in terms of the mutual interaction of supply and demand. Once this new approach had become respectable, it was only a question of time before the pre-Classical economists began to be rehabilitated as its progenitors. In Schumpeter's great reinterpretation of the history of economic analysis, for example, the salient feature of the whole period up to 1790 appears as the development of the elements of a 'full-fledged theory of demand and supply',[5] and the work of Adam Smith and Ricardo appears as a sort of 'detour[6] from the historical line of economists' endeavours.

Then again, take the theory of economic development. The problem of growth and development had been one of the leading preoccupations of the later Mercantilists, and had also constituted the basic subject-matter of Classical political economy. So much so, indeed, that the very concept of a distinction between static and dynamic analysis (which was later to be popularised by J S Mill) was quite alien to Smith and Ricardo. Gradually, however, interest in the problem of 'scarcity'—i.e. the question of how scarce means could most efficiently be allocated between competing ends—came to co-exist with, and eventually almost to replace, interest in the problem of development. Criteria of economic welfare were evolved with more or less exclusive reference to the degree of efficiency displayed in the allocation of a given set of scarce means, and the problem of the factors determining the rate of increase in these scarce means themselves was discussed only by Marxists and those (like Schumpeter) who had been stimulated to supply alternative answers to the questions which Marx had propounded. Then, with remarkable suddenness, the problem of economic development, in both mature capitalist economies and under-developed countries, was placed on the agenda once again. And following on this resurgence of interest in 'the nature and causes of the wealth of nations', the work of the Classical economists in the dynamic field has begun to be reconsidered. No doubt it will not be very long before a new reinterpretation of the history of economic thought appears in which the work of all the post Ricardian theorists who ignored the problem of development is claimed to be a 'detour' from the historical line of economists' endeavours.

Finally, take the so-called 'economics of control'. The economics of the pre-Classical schools usually rested on the assumption that an economy could not possibly work effectively if left to itself. A greater or lesser degree of intervention by the State was regarded as necessary if an economy was to grow and develop, and political economy was visualised as the art of guiding economic policy. This assumption gradually gave way to the revolutionary idea that under a régime of free capitalist competition private vices could be automatically transmuted into public benefits: allow each man to use his labour and his capital in the manner which seemed most profitable to him, and the net result could be the maximisation of society's economic welfare. The division was not in fact quite as clear-cut as this, of course: interventionists can quote Smith's *Wealth of Nations* and anti-interventionists Steuart's *Political Oeconomy* for their purposes. But the break with the older ideas was none the less a real one for that. The role of the State was in effect reduced from that of actually guiding economic affairs to that of providing a suitable legal and political framework within which economic affairs might safely be left to guide themselves. In our own times, however, bitter experience has led the great majority of economists to question a number of the basic assumptions of *laissez-faire,* and all but a few last-ditchers are now prepared to advocate certain important measures of State interference with the free market mechanism. As a result, some of the pre-Smithian economists are now being rehabilitated, and the history of economic thought is once again being reinterpreted. 'Two divergent paths', writes Dr Sen, 'were pointing outwards from the milieu of Mun and Petty and Locke. Steuart followed the one which was later to lead to economic individualism.'[7]

So, after a long period in which scarcely anyone was rehabilitated, we pass to a relatively short period of a quarter of a century or so in which scarcely anyone has *not* been rehabilitated. We are reminded of the Dodo, who, on being asked who had won the race, replied after a great deal of thought: '*Everybody* has won, and *all* must have prizes.' But do they really deserve them? Let us consider first the particular case of Sir James Steuart, and then, in the light of this, some of the more general problems which are involved.

II

Steuart was surely the unluckiest of men: seldom has one great work been so completely and so soon eclipsed by another as Steuart's *Inquiry into the Principles of Political Oeconomy* was by Smith's *Inquiry into the Nature and Causes of the Wealth of Nations*. Smith, it must be confessed, seems to have been rather patronising about Steuart. In a letter to Pulteney, written in 1772, he says: 'I have the same opinion of Sir James Steuart's book that you have. Without once mentioning it, I flatter myself that any fallacious principle in it will meet with a clear and distinct confutation in mine.'[8] This was hardly cricket. As Dr Sen correctly points out, however, Smith was not playing cricket but 'fighting a grim crusade the success of which depended on the effectiveness of his slogan'.[9] Smith was a better strategist and a better stylist than Steuart, which no doubt partly accounts for his victory. But he also had a better theory—or at any rate a theory which corresponded better with the *zeitgeist* of his time. Mercantilism, however enlightened—and Steuart's Mercantilism was very enlightened indeed—has had its day. An illuminating extract from Luigi Cossa's *Introduction to the Study of Political Economy* admirably sums up the verdict on Steuart delivered by subsequent generations:

> Could Adam Smith have a more preposterous precursor than this defender of the omnipotence of the State, whose one idea is to combine privileged corporations with unrestricted competition, and who will allow free banking if only all banks will issue unconvertible scrip? More than an ordinary allowance of pedantry must be thrown into the balance, before Adam Smith and the physiocrats can be so much as weighed in the same scales with a writer who, like Steuart, confuses money with capital, value with price, and wages with profits.[10]

Amid a chorus of abuse of this type, the still small voice of Marx, proclaiming Steuart as 'the first Briton who elaborated the general system of bourgeois economics',[11] and praising him for standing 'more firmly on historical ground' than most of his eighteenth-century contemporaries,[12] remained unheeded.

Nevertheless Cossa was not entirely wrong. There was indeed an important sense in which Steuart did 'confuse money with capital, value with price, and wages with profits'. The important thing to appreciate, however, is that these three 'confusions', in so far as they were in fact present, all sprang from one and the same source: Steuart's failure to take proper account of the emergence in agriculture and manufacture of a new social class—the class which used capital in the employment of wage labour, and as a result gained a profit bearing a more or less regular proportion to the amount of capital laid out. The 'two principal Classes of a People' which Steuart distinguishes are the 'farmers', who produce enough for their own subsistence plus a surplus, and the 'free hands', who in effect 'live upon the surplus of the farmers'.[13] The class of 'free hands' is divided into two sub-classes: 'The first, those to whom this surplus directly belongs [*i.e.* the landlords], or who, with a revenue in money already acquired, can purchase it. The second, those who purchase it with their daily labour or personal service.'[14] The essential point to be noted here is that the class of 'farmers' and the second sub-class of 'free hands' may clearly include both capitalists and wage-earners, but the distinction between these latter classes is not recognised by Steuart as being relevant to the economic problems under consideration. In particular, Steuart tends to regard 'profit' merely as a synonym for 'gain', or at best as a sort of superior wage which may accrue under certain circumstances to *any* 'farmer' or member of the second sub-class of 'free hands'. Broadly speaking, any net reward (over and above the cost of raw materials, tools of trade and personal subsistence) received by anyone engaged in production or trade is classified as 'profit', whether its recipient happens to be an employer, a wage-earner, or a worker on his own account.[15] We look in vain in Steuart for any definite formulation of the new concept of profit which Smith was to popularise—the concept of profit as an income accruing exclusively to employers of wage-labour and bearing a regular proportion to the amount of their capital. This is no doubt what Cossa was referring to when he spoke of Steuart's 'confusion of money with capital' and 'wages with profits'. Steuart was hardly alone in this 'confusion', of course: the model of the economy which he used was not essentially different from that of Cantillon, or Quesnay, or Hume, or indeed from that of the Smith of the *Glasgow Lectures*. But the gulf between Steuart's concept of profit and that of the *Wealth of Nations* is certainly a deep and important one.[16]

Steuart's concept of profit leads directly to that 'confusion of value with price' of which Cossa spoke. The prices of goods, says Steuart, are made up of two component parts—the 'real value' and the 'profit upon alienation'.[17] The real value (roughly the average physical cost of production) is known when the quantity of labour required to produce the commodity, 'the value of the workman's subsistence and necessary expence', and 'the value of the materials' are known. 'These three articles being known,' concludes Steuart, 'the price of manufacture is determined. It cannot be lower than the amount of all the three, that is, than the real value; whatever it is higher, is the manufacturer's profit. This will ever be in proportion to demand, and therefore will fluctuate according to circumstances.' Given his concept of profit, this was as far as Steuart could possibly have gone in showing 'how trade has the effect of rendering [prices] first and determined'. Given the Smithian concept of profit as a class income accruing solely to those who used capital in the employment of wage-labour, however, a further important analytical advance could be made. A high degree of competition, it could be said, did not eliminate profits, but merely reduced them to an average or 'natural' level. Profit on capital at this 'natural' rate could then be postulated as a constituent of the supply price of the commodity concerned, to which its market price would in the long period tend to conform. No longer was there a sort of floating element which 'fluctuated according to circumstances' in the prices of commodities: older theories of price like Steuart's began to appear not only as relatively indeterminate but also as involving a 'confusion of value with price'.[18]

Nevertheless, Steuart was not quite as far removed from the Classical position as he is usually made out to have been. He insists that although the 'profit upon alienation' may vary with the degree of competition, the 'real value' never can,[19] provided that we estimate its three constituent elements 'upon an average'.[20] In   several places, too, he recognises that under competition profits will be reduced to the 'proper standard',[21] to a 'reasonable' level,[22] and so on. 'While the balance [of supply and demand] stands justly poised,' he says in one place, 'prices are found in the adequate proportion of the real expence of making the goods, *with a small addition for profit to the manufacturer and merchant*'.[23] And in his interesting comments on what he calls the 'consolidation of profits' he seems to visualise a situation in which profits are incorporated into the supply prices of commodities—'transformed into the intrinsic value of the goods', as he puts it.[24] All in all, then, it seems wrong to regard Steuart purely as a 'supply and demand' theorist: he was clearly feeling his way forward from a mere supply and demand theory towards the Classical approach to the value problem. This view is reinforced by another feature of Steuart's work to which Dr Sen correctly draws attention—the fact that his theory of prices was intended as an integral part of a general theory of social dynamics,[25] just as were the value theories of Smith, Ricardo and Marx.

Steuart's 'one idea', said Cossa, was 'to combine privileged corporations with unrestricted competition'. This is of course a rather absurd exaggeration, but the remark does point to another significant feature of Steuart's work which most commentators prior to Dr Sen tended to neglect. By Steuart's time 'unrestricted competition' was coming more and more to dominate the economic scene, although it was still alloyed to a considerable extent with various elements of monopoly. Because of this, Steuart felt himself obliged to conduct his enquiry into 'Trade and Industry' on the basis of the assumption that 'the principle of self-interest' was the 'ruling principle' of his subject,[26] and to give a full analysis of the working of competition, both restricted and unrestricted. He was obliged to recognise, too, that when the 'scales' of supply and demand were evenly balanced there was no need for the statesman to interfere. Up to this point he is at one with the Classical economists. Where he differs from them is in his estimate of the capacity of the system to readjust itself after the balance has for some reason been disturbed. Even in the case of a short-run tendency for one of the 'scales' to preponderate, Steuart maintained, it was the duty of the statesman to interfere—not, indeed, by taking anything out of the heavy scale, but rather by 'gently . . . load[ing[the opposite scale'. For example, 'when the scale of demand is found to preponderate, he ought to give encouragement to the establishment of new undertakings, for augmenting the supply, and for preserving prices at their former standard'.[27] And in the case of long-run maladjustments it was even more incumbent upon the statesman to interfere, since long-run maladjustments were both more certain to occur and more serious in their effects than short-run maladjustments. Steuart's *Political Oeconomy* is in essence a book of advice to the statesman on the appropriate measures of intervention which he ought to adopt when the economy deviates—as in Steuart's view it must inevitably and constantly tend to do—from the ideal of free competition. Many of the measures which he recommends are formally similar to those which Keynesians have recommended for dealing with the business cycle, such as public works, fiscal measures, and changes in the rate of interest; and the comparison which Dr Sen makes between Steuart's *Political Oeconomy* and A P Lerner's *Economics of*

Control is perhaps not too far-fetched. But such comparisons should not be pushed too far. Whereas modern Western welfare economists usually take the view that deviations from the optimum exist in spite of the general tendency of the system to return to a balanced position, Steuart usually takes the view that deviations from the optimum exist because of the general tendency of the system to move away from a balanced position. To Steuart, in other words, the balance of supply and demand is more an *ideal* position than an 'equilibrium' position in the Classical and modern sense of the word.

There is another point which should be borne in mind before we claim Steuart as a pioneer of modern interventionist theory and say with Dr Sen that 'had not the brilliance of Adam Smith and the *laissez-faire* spirit of the nineteenth century combined to cast him into oblivion, it is quite possible that the school of thought which Malthus, List and Keynes took so long to build up might have been more rapidly developed'.[28] I think there is little doubt that if Steuart had in fact won out over Smith in the eighteenth century the result would have been most unfortunate for both economic practice and economic theory. In the field of practice, it can probably be said that at that time progress demanded an extension of economic freedom for the individual capitalist and a minimisation of measures of State control over economic life. In the field of theory, progress demanded improvements in the analysis of the actual working of a free exchange economy and further attempts to discover the basic laws underlying its operation and development. A victory for Steuart would surely have inhibited progress in both these fields. A century and a half later, when capitalism had passed from its competitive to its monopolistic stage and was beginning to show ominous signs of decrepitude, the times did indeed become ripe for a sort of 'revival' of certain pre-Smithian ideas, including those of Steuart. But the revival of these ideas did not mean that economics had simply gone round in a circle: the ideas were revived on a higher plane, precisely as a result of the crucial analytical work which the anti-interventionists had carried out in the intervening period.

A doctor examines an infant, and declares that it is suffering from a serious disease which requires a particular type of treatment. Other doctors examine the child, and find that it seems to be developing in a reasonably healthy way and that the treatment recommended by the first doctor would be likely to inhibit its development. They therefore neglect pathological considerations, and proceed to investigate the general principles of the child's bodily structure and the laws of its growth. Eventually, much later, when the child has grown into an old man, it begins to develop the very disease which the first doctor diagnosed, and it becomes clear that the germs of this disease had in fact been present in it from infancy. The remedies originally prescribed by the first doctor are therefore applied, but owing to the knowledge of bodily structure and growth which has been acquired in the meantime as a result of the work of other doctors, these remedies can now be greatly improved and applied much more effectively. Steuart can be called a pioneer of modern interventionist theory only in the sense that the first doctor can be called a pioneer of the modern methods of treatment.

One of the most interesting features of Steuart's work is what Dr Sen aptly describes as his 'historical, institutional and on the whole evolutionist approach'.[29] Steuart does not merely postulate the existence of a society divided into 'farmers' and 'free hands': he also shows in some detail how such a society came into being and developed. Broadly, he argues that population must always be in proportion to the produce of the earth. At first, man lives on the spontaneous fruits of the soil; then the pressure of population and the desire for improvement lead him to 'add his labour and industry to the natural activity of the soil'.[30] Gradually individuals are either compelled (by means of the institution of slavery) or induced (by means of the multiplication of human wants and the encouragement of exchange) to produce a surplus of food over and above their own subsistence, thus providing a material foundation for the growth of a class of 'free hands' who live on the surplus produce. It is only with the emergence of this new class that a 'free society' comes into being. The main motive forces in each stage of social development are conceived by Steuart as being basically economic in character,[31] and this emphasis on the primacy of economic factors is retained throughout the whole work—as, for example, in the following characteristic passage:

> The great alteration in the affairs of Europe within these three centuries, by the discovery of America and the Indies, the springing up of industry and learning, the introduction of trade and the luxurious arts, the establishment of public credit, and a general system of taxation, have entirely altered the plan of government every where.
> From feudal and military, it is become free and commercial.[32]

The same general attitude can be found in Steuart's discussions of the territorial division of labour and localisation of industry, the effect of the influx of precious metals from America, and 'the general principles of *subordination* and *dependence* among mankind'.[33] All these, Dr Sen says, 'indicate an attempt at an economic interpretation of history which is certainly unusual for the times when Steuart lived and wrote'.[34]

'Unusual', however, only up to a point. The most striking fact which emerges from a reading of Steuart is surely his close intellectual kinship in this respect with the members of the Scottish Historical School of the eighteenth century.[35] This kinship, curiously enough, is not recognised by Dr Sen, who in fact goes so far as to say of the members of the Scottish Historical School that 'every characteristic feature of their general outlook differed from that of Steuart'.[36] But it can hardly be denied that the *most* 'characteristic feature of their general outlook' was precisely a 'historical, institutional and on the whole evolutionist approach', coupled with a bias towards an 'economic interpretation of history'. Men like Hume, Smith, Kames, Robertson, Ferguson and Millar may have objected to Steuart's political views and thought little of his economics, but in the field of 'theoretical or conjectural history' which they were opening up they must surely have recognised him as something of a kindred spirit. In this respect at any rate Steuart was much more in tune with his times than Dr Sen appears to suspect.[37]

III

Dr Sen, then, makes out a good case for regarding Steuart as a thinker of considerable calibre whom subsequent generations have unjustly neglected, and whose basic ideas make rather more sense in the economic context of the twentieth century than they did in that of the eighteenth. If the 'rehabilitations' of the present day went no further than this, no objection could properly be made to them. Unfortunately, however, few of the modern rehabilitators have been able to resist the temptation of using their rehabilitation as the basis for a complete reinterpretation of the history of economic thought, and it seems to me that as a result we are in grave danger of losing all sense of perspective when we look at past theoretical systems.

The trouble is that reinterpretation is too easy a game to play. A new theory becomes fashionable—a new theory of value, say, or a new theory of employment. Now since the problems of value and employment have been looked at from so many different angles during the two or three centuries of the existence of economics as we know it today, the chances are that the new theory will turn out upon investigation to be not entirely new. A similar type of approach will be found to have been adopted (albeit in a very different context) by economists X, Y and Z at various periods in the development of economic thought. If we now abstract these theories of X, Y and Z from their historical context, we are ready to make our reinterpretation. We can, if we like, adopt what might be called the teleological approach, and visualise the new theory as 'the divine event to which the whole creation moves', judging the performances of individual economists 'according to whether they hastened or retarded its arrival'.[38] The emphasis here will be on continuity, so that the work of any of the opponents of X, Y and Z who managed to get the whip hand over them for any length of time will have to be described as a detour from the historical line of economists' endeavours. Or alternatively, if X, Y and Z all lived a sufficiently long time ago we can adopt what might be called the apocalyptic approach. X, Y and Z can be represented in the guise of ancient and rather primitive prophets, whose ideas were rejected and whose followers were driven underground for a long period, at the end of which the theory they had espoused suddenly burst forth upon an astonished world. The number of new patterns in the development of economic thought which can be disclosed by the use of these and other methods of reinterpretation is quite surprising.

I do not deny, of course, that the use of these methods may have some pedagogical value (as in the case of Keynes' redefinition of the term 'Classical'), or that it may throw fresh light on neglected fields of study (as in the case of Schumpeter's rehabilitation of the Schoolmen). Nor do I deny that each generation must to some extent rewrite the history of economic thought in the light of its own theoretical discoveries. But before reorientating the whole history of economic thought towards these discoveries, one must be certain that they *are* genuine and important discoveries and not mere changes of fashion, and when estimating the place of past theories in the general stream of thought one must be careful not to abstract them from the particular historical context in which they were put forward. The latter point is especially important. If we abstract the views of an economist like Steuart from the general economic and intellectual milieu in which they were formulated, and then compare them with some of the views which are fashionable today, we will certainly discover a number of interesting formal parallels. But if we attempt a complete reinterpretation of the history of economic thought on the basis of these parallels the result is not likely to be very useful.

The essential point is this: Economics, in the form in which it has come down to us, has always been primarily concerned with the analysis of the system of market exchange. But however much an individual economist may think that he is laying down laws of market exchange which will be valid at all times and places, his analysis will almost inevitably be relative (in some significant sense of that word) to the particular historical stage of development through which the market exchange system happens to be passing at the time he writes. The general approach which he makes to the phenomena of market exchange will largely depend upon his general attitude to the socio-economic environment of his own time. This attitude will determine (*inter alia*) the answers which he gives to two all-important questions: (i) From what angle can exchange phenomena most usefully be analysed? and, (ii) Does the free exchange system maximise economic welfare?

Take the first question. When production for the market was still a comparatively rare and localised institution, the analysis of exchange phenomena was naturally conducted from the angle of 'supply and demand'. Gradually, however, as feudalism disappeared and capitalism began to advance, production for the market came more and more to dominate the economic scene, and the concept of a society which was in effect bound together by this type of production began to emerge. The economic tie which linked men to one another as producers of different commodities for the market came to be viewed as the 'chief cement'[39] binding society together. People who looked at the society of their times in this new light began to take the view that exchange phenomena should properly be analysed not only from the angle of 'supply and demand', but also (and indeed primarily) from the angle of the relations which men entered into with one another in production. The development of the Classical labour theory of value was closely associated with the emergence of this new viewpoint, and the Classical economists carried on the same tradition in so far as they can be said to have analysed the distribution of income in terms of class relations. After Ricardo's death, however, when capitalism went over from an offensive position against the landlords to a defensive position against the newly-organised working class, this way of looking at society came to appear distinctly dangerous to the more conservative economists, who began in effect to suggest that exchange phenomena could not be analysed 'scientifically' unless abstraction were made of the relations of production. Inevitably this line of thought led (through very tortuous paths) to the resurrection of something like the old 'supply and demand' type of approach which had characterised the pre-capitalist period of development. The other type of approach was taken over from the Classical economists by Marx, whose general attitude to the socio-economic system of his time was of course radically different from that of the orthodox economists.

The views of economists on the second question have also been quite largely determined by their general attitude towards the particular stage of development through which the market exchange system happened to be passing at the time they wrote. The idea that a free exchange system will maximise economic welfare is of course a comparatively recent one: it could scarcely have been put forward prior to the eighteenth century, when this new system began rapidly to rise to a position of predominance. The first opponents of the idea were men like Steuart and Malthus, 'reactionaries' in the technical sense, who tended to look back in longing towards certain institutions of the past which the new system was rapidly destroying. Steuart was suspicious of the advance of unrestricted competition and Malthus of the advance of unrestricted accumulation, and both advocated various measures of government intervention to alleviate the difficulties which they believed the new developments would entail. Their opponents, Smith and Ricardo respectively, took an entirely different view of the new system and its prospects, and their ideas won out largely because they were more in line with the demands of economic progress at the time. Then came those who turned away from the new system in revulsion because of the 'dark satanic mills' spawned by the industrial revolution, or because of the cyclical tendencies which the system was coming increasingly to display, and who looked forward to a more rational system which would eventually replace it. Finally in our own times there has been a revolt against certain aspects of the system from within the ranks of the orthodox economists themselves—a revolt motivated not by a desire to return to some older system or to advance to a new one, but rather by a wish to make the existing system work. And inevitably this latter development has led to a revival of interest in the measures of control advocated by men like Steuart and Malthus, and in the theoretical analyses which lay behind their proposals.

Economics, then, has grown up hand in hand with the system of market exchange, particularly in its capitalist stage of development. Conflicts between schools of thought have arisen partly because the different phases of development of the system require different modes of analysis (a Physiocratic world is different from a Smithian world; a Marshallian world is different from a Keynesian world), and partly because in each phase of development group struggles have emerged in which economists, like everyone else, have taken sides. Similarities and continuities can be detected partly because it is at bottom one and the same system (in its different phases of development) which economists have been analysing, and partly because certain attitudes expressed for a particular reason in a particular phase of development are sometimes expressed again for a very different reason in a very different phase of development. The point I have been trying to make in this essay is simply that it is wrong to interpret the history of economic thought on the basis of similarities of the latter type. An *interpretation* of the history of economic thought, if it is to be worthy of the name, must surely start by relating the major theories which have been put forward to the different phases of development through which the system of market exchange has passed. We cannot postulate the existence of a 'path' leading from Mercantilism to socialism merely on the basis of certain formal similarities between Steuart's work and the 'economics of control'. If we do so, we will certainly escape the Scylla of relativism, but we will do so only to drown in the Charybdis of teleology.

NOTES

1   This essay is an amended version of an article originally published (under another title) in *Science and Society*, Fall 1958.

2   J M Keynes, *Essays in Biography* (London, 1933), pp 95 ff, and *General Theory* (London, 1936), pp 333 ff.

3   Joan Robinson, *The Accumulation of Capital* (London, 1956), p vi.

4   S R Sen, *The Economics of Sir James Steuart* (Cambridge, Mass, 1957).

5   J S Schumpeter, *History of Economic Analysis* (New York, 1954), p 98.

6   *Ibid.* p 474. This view is criticised in the essay on *Economics and Ideology* which appears below, pp 196 ff.

7   Sen, *op. cit.* p 185.

8   J Rae, *Life of Adam Smith* (London, 1895), pp 253–4.

9   Sen, *op. cit.* p 3.

10   Cossa, *op. cit.* (tr. Louis Dyer, London, 1893) pp 234–5.

11   Marx, *Critique of Political Economy* (Chicago, 1904), p 65.

12   *Ibid.* p 267.

13   Steuart, *Political Oeconomy* (1767 ed), Vol I, pp 50 and 48.

14   *Ibid.* p 48.

15   This comes out very clearly in *ibid.* pp 317 ff where Steuart discusses the circumstances which may 'extend profits beyond the physical-necessary'. This is one of the very few passages in which Steuart specifically mentions the distinction between employers and wage-earners.

16   Smith's concept of profit is discussed in the next essay in the present volume.

17   Quotations in this paragraph from *Political Oeconomy*, Vol I, pp 181–2.

18   See pp 202–3 below.

19   *Political Oeconomy*, Vol I, p 199.

20   *Ibid.* p 182. Here Steuart comes very close to the concept of socially-necessary labour.

21   *Ibid.* p 490.

22   *Ibid.* p 199.

23   *Ibid.* p 217 (my italics).

24   *Ibid.* p 221. It should be noted that Steuart deplores this 'consolidation of profits', and claims that it can only come about if a monopoly situation arises which the statesman fails to correct.

25   Sen, *op. cit.* pp 70 ff.

26   *Political Oeconomy*, Vol I, p 162.

27   *Ibid.* p 491.

28   Sen, *op. cit.* p 153.

29   *Ibid.* p 19. 'In this respect,' Dr Sen remarks (pp 18–19), 'he may be regarded as one of the earliest exponents of that school of thought which Saint-Simon and Sismondi in France and Richard Jones and Karl Marx in England were to develop in the next century. As such he may also be regarded as a pioneer writer on the theory of economic growth.'

30   Steuart, *Political Oeconomy*, Vol I, p 21.

31   *Cf.* Sen, *op. cit.* p 49.

32   Steuart, *Political Oeconomy,* Vol I, p 10.
33   *Ibid.* p 238.
34   Sen, *op. cit.* p 49.
35   For an account of the work of the Scottish Historical School, see the essay on *The Scottish Contribution to Marxist Sociology.*
36   Sen, *op. cit.* p 183.
37   Since the appearance of the article upon which this essay is based, Mr A S Skinner, of Glasgow University, has published a number of pieces on Steuart in which proper emphasis is laid on this point. See in particular his article 'Sir James Steuart: Economics and Politics'.
38   G B Richardson, in a review-article on Schumpeter's *History of Economic Analysis* in *Oxford Economic Papers,* June 1955, p 142.
39   The phrase is that of Joseph Harris, *An Essay Upon Money and Coins* (1757), p 15, footnote. Steuart had much the same idea when he spoke of 'the reciprocal wants which the statesman must create, in order to bind the society together' (*Political Oeconomy,* Vol I, p 28).

Chapter Twelve

Foreword to David Hume's Political Discourses

Sir Alan Peacock

Introduction

There is wide agreement amongst British philosophers that the Scotsman David Hume (1711–76) is the greatest of them all; and his international reputation as a philosopher likewise places him amongst the giants. In his own day, however, his domestic reputation was based on his work as an historian and it was only in France that his philosophical work seems to have had an immediate appeal. His memorial stuck on a crag overlooking the centre of Edinburgh has inscribed on it 'David Hume: Historian' and it comes perhaps as a surprise to find that in the Authors' Catalogue of the London School of Economics and Political Science, where his name is revered, he is still classified as an historian! His reputation as an historian was well deserved and it will soon be seen how important a part his knowledge of history played in his economics.

It must also seem paradoxical today that his *Treatise of Human Nature* (1739), which revolutionised philosophical thinking, in his own words, 'fell deadborn from the Press', whereas his *Political Discourses* (1752), was an instant success both at home and overseas. Yet the latter work is frequently neglected in recent surveys of his intellectual contribution and stature, possibly because the lead in such surveys is inevitably taken by philosophers without a training in economics. Furthermore, the general neglect by economists themselves of the intellectual history of their subject, afraid that 'scholarship' is less prestigious than 'original thinking', has contributed to a lack of interest in Hume who is frequently classified as a mere precursor of Adam Smith.

There are at least three reasons why the *Political Discourses* deserves to be brought to the attention of the modern reader. In the first place, anyone interested in the history of economic ideas, who wants to avoid, in Lionel Robbins' words, 'provincialism in time' cannot fail to be struck by the power of Hume's intellect. Likely as not, if the reader is unfamiliar with Hume, he will find his application of his own technique of thinking to economic problems of a useful approach to the more fundamental philosophical ideas concerning the analysis of human nature. In the second place, if the reader has a basic knowledge of modern economic analysis, he will find some intriguing pre-echoes of this analysis in Hume's theories of money, interest and international trade—to name only three related topics in the *Discourses*—and some timely reminders of the fallacies underlying the all-pervasive doctrine of national self-sufficiency which renewed its hold on politicians in major industrial countries about a century ago. Lastly, like his younger friend Adam Smith, Hume's writings can be enjoyed as English literature, and, indeed, the bulk of his works were written for an educated but general public and not solely, as so often today, for some inner circle of specialists—some 'peer group'. For example, he was so anxious that his *Treatise of Human Nature* should not be forgotten that he wrote a fascinating *Abstract* of it, published in 1740 anonymously and only identified as Hume's work as late as 1938 and then by none other than Keynes himself, together with the Italian economist Piero Sraffa. Keynes who wrote what might be regarded as one of the last great works of literature in Economics—his *General Theory*—clearly recognised how important this short volume is as an 'essay in persuasion'.

This foreword elaborates the points made in this last paragraph with the purpose of making it easier for the reader to appreciate that these essays on widely different subjects are bound together by Hume's general approach to analysing human action. However, before examining Hume's treatment of economic subjects, some account must be given of his life and character. This is not simply because our interest may be aroused by the prospect that great thinkers may have lead interesting lives—sometimes this is far from being the case. Rather it is because Hume himself placed so much emphasis on personal impressions and experience as the foundation of our knowledge of both the physical and social world about us that his own impressions and experience give us interesting clues to his methods of reasoning.

LIFE AND CHARACTER

David Hume, the son of the owner of a small estate near the south-east corner of Scotland, was born in Edinburgh on 26 April 1711, the date being midway between the Union of the Scottish and English Parliaments which ended the political independence of Scotland in 1707 and the start of the first Jacobite rebellion (1715) in Scotland aimed at restoring the House of Stewart. Both these contiguous events were to exert a considerable influence on Hume's life. The Union of the Parliaments required Scots with political and intellectual ambitions to make themselves understood in both written and spoken English. Hume was to become a master of the English language and to be a vigorous opponent of 'Scotticisms' in literary works. This accounts for the curious list of Scots words which were to be avoided by his countrymen in their writings printed at the end of the *Political Discourses*. Hume's family were opposed to the Jacobites, as was Hume himself, but his impartiality as an historian led him to take a more balanced view of the Catholic House of Stewart than was considered proper by the churchmen who supported the ruling House of Hanover who were of course Protestants.

Hume was brought up on the small family estate very close to the small town of Duns in Berwickshire. There is a peculiar irony in the fact that the most famous Scots philosopher in Europe before Hume was the medieval theologian John Duns Scotus (*c.*1265–*c.*1308) who was brought up in Duns and was noted throughout the medieval world for his subtle proofs of the existence of God, whereas Hume was to become branded, misleadingly, as the philosopher of atheism. This locational affinity of Hume and Duns Scotus, if Hume was conscious of it, would not have been regarded by him as other than a chance event, though it is surely not devoid of interest. If the air of the Scottish Borders was congenial to study and speculation it was soon clear to Hume and his family that David would have to make his own way in the world and he dutifully enrolled at Edinburgh University at the age of eleven (not uncommon in the eighteenth century) but never took his degree (also not uncommon then) and studied law but without qualifying as an advocate. By the age of eighteen he had already resolved to become a 'man of letters' but did not wish to be a burden on his family.

He was then on the brink of developing his famous theory of causation. He abandoned the law, and, after a brief and unsuccessful incursion into business in Bristol, settled in provincial France where he could live on his very modest income. The last two years of his three years in France were spent in the small town of La Flèche in Anjou where the greater part of his *Treatise of Human Nature* was written. It is again ironic that he was stimulated by friendly argument with the Jesuit Fathers who allowed him to use their foundation's extensive library. They may not have been entirely aware that their young genial Scots friend had embarked on an intellectual adventure designed to undermine the influence of their College's most famous alumnus—René Descartes, the author of the famous *Discourse on Method* (1637).

The relevance of the *Treatise* for his economic thinking will be explored below. In a biographical context what is interesting is how this work affected Hume's contemporary position as a thinker. Looking at his philosophic speculations through the eyes of his contemporaries, here was an unknown young man from an isolated part of Northern Europe, who had the temerity to argue that in making even the simplest prediction, such as the relation between the length of time an egg is in boiling water and its texture, we generalise from past experience and can never be certain that the future will replicate the past; who stood Descartes's philosophy on its head by claiming that the motive force of man's actions was his tastes and preferences—his 'passions'—and that man's reasoning ability did and ought to serve his passions; who claimed, therefore, that moral actions could not be derived from reason, and, who, worst of all, could find no grounds for supporting the Christian belief that it had a monopoly of religious truth. Such speculations could be ignored but, *pace* Hume, they were not, for his opponents could see that they were formidably presented, as were his subsequent essays on moral philosophy, politics and economics which were soon to follow in 1742. Then in 1744 came the vital test when Hume presented himself as a candidate for the Chair of Ethics and Pneumatical Philosophy which had fallen vacant at Edinburgh University. The town authorities were swayed by a theological faction, including the Principal of the University, who charged Hume with atheism.[1]

He was not appointed, and the same fate befell him six years later when the theologians at Glasgow vetoed his appointment to the vacant Chair of Logic. The only teaching appointment that Hume was ever to hold was that of tutor to the Marquess of Annandale who turned out to be mad, and that lasted but a year.

Hume's problems of finding employment consonant with his wish to pursue his literary and philosophical activities was partly solved in other ways. Life amongst a coterie of Scots intellectuals in Edinburgh did much to restore his spirits and as *Political Discourses* bears witness, he became a literary as well as a social success, despite the persecution by the Church which lasted all his life. His friends secured him the appointment of Librarian of the Faculty of Advocates in 1752, which gained him a useful small addition to his money income and a substantial addition to his real income in the form of access to the library's excellent book stock. The use of this library, which he was allowed to retain after his resignation from the post in 1757, was an essential prerequisite for the preparation of Hume's great *History of England.* Modest but tangible success as an author and refusal to waste his energies battling with his bigoted opponents had bought him time to become the man of letters which he desired to be.

The *History* may not be read much today, but it is a landmark in eighteenth-century historiography. Before Hume, history was mostly written as narrative and often as an encomium of the ruling royal house. In keeping with his philosophy, he examines human motivation and the causes of change in society and with unusual detachment. Voltaire was to describe the work as 'perhaps the best ever written in any language' and to applaud 'a mind superior to his materials; he speaks of weaknesses, blunders, cruelties as a physician speaks of epidemic diseases'. The flavour of Hume's historical method can be savoured in several of the essays in *Political Discourses,* notably 'Of the Populousness of Ancient Nations'.

No later influences in Hume's life bear on the production of *Political Discourses* for the Second and last revision of the work appeared later in the same year as the First. Hume's later life, however, has an interest of its own and some consideration of his character has a bearing on his economic analysis.

It may be said that while Hume saw Edinburgh as the base of his intellectual endeavours, he consciously sought to gain experience from travel and even employment abroad. He made extended visits to London to test reactions to his work and to bargain with publishers of his works and those of Scots colleagues. He had many admirers South of the Border and gained the respect of his intellectual antagonists but although Adam Smith, now a firm friend, and Hume contemplated settling in London, they were never entirely at ease in a city where Scots were still regarded as potential rebels and where literary success depended so much on soliciting favours from the great aristocratic families. Today, it is easier for Scots to acquire the protective colouration which enables them to pass for Englishmen and even to market their abilities as professional Scots who are 'rough diamonds whom London polishes well'. Justifiable doubts remain amongst Scots intellectuals about the patronising attitude of some of their English counterparts and the curious blend of 'metropolitan parochialism' which 'foreigners', other than themselves, often remark upon.

Hume bought a house in Edinburgh in 1762 with the clear intention of settling there for a life of quiet contemplation. That was not to be. Local opposition to his work was now accompanied by professional jealousy. The following year, when diplomatic ties were renewed between the French and British after the Seven Years' War, Hume received an unexpected invitation to join the staff of the British Ambassador, Lord Hertford, with the prospect of becoming Secretary to the Embassy in Paris. After some hesitation he accepted, perhaps aware that the appointment had been made with at least the connivance of his growing number of French admirers. He found himself a great celebrity and 'le bon David', as they called him, was a distinct success both socially and professionally. He was not to return to settle in Edinburgh until 1769 for he was promoted to Under-Secretary of State (Northern Division), a post which included conduct of diplomatic negotiations with the Court of Catherine the Great of Russia. Another ironic twist to his career emanates from his duties which included writing the Royal Speech delivered annually by the King's representative to the General Assembly of the Church of Scotland! The more moderate members of that Church had cause to be grateful for his personal influence, though one wonders how far they deserved it.

The final return to Edinburgh is marked by his serenity and detachment and by the somewhat tardy recognition by his colleagues of his pre-eminence. This period is remembered best by economists for his close ties with Adam Smith whose *Wealth of Nations* appeared as the philosopher was dying, and which delighted him greatly. In the face of death he wrote *My Own Life*, a tantalisingly short but astute analysis of his own character and development. His moral courage in dying is on a par with that of Socrates. He quietly put his affairs in order, disturbing the morbidly curious James Boswell by his lack of fear that his own philosophy postulated that 'it was an unreasonable fancy that we should exist for ever'.

When, on 29 August 1776, his coffin was being carried out of his home, one of the large crowd was heard to remark, 'Ah, he was an Atheist'. A companion added, 'No matter, he was an honest man'.

In *My Own Life* Hume sums up his own character as follows:

> I was . . . a man of mild dispositions, of command of temper, of an open, social and cheerful humour, capable of attachment but little susceptible of enmity, and of great moderation in all my passions. Even my love of literary fame, my ruling passion, never soured my temper, notwithstanding my frequent disappointments. My company was not unacceptable to the young and careless as well as to the studious and literary; and as I took a particular pleasure in the company of modest women, I had no reason to be displeased with the reception I met with from them . . . I cannot say that there is no vanity in making this funeral oration of myself, but I hope it is not a misplaced one; and this is a matter of fact which is easily cleared and ascertained.

When the facts are ascertained from contemporary accounts of friends, colleagues and even intellectual opponents, it is clear that David Hume knew himself very well, which is not typically the case with great men. Space does not permit the documentation of views of contemporaries but Adam Smith, his special friend, is only a shade more generous than others when he closed a famous account of Hume's last days with the words: 'I have always considered him . . . as approaching as nearly to the idea of a perfectly wise and virtuous man, as perhaps the nature of human frailty will permit.'

The Methodology of Political Discourses

Having noted that Hume himself was motivated by a desire for literary fame, the initial question raised by the *Political Discourses*, is how was such a work to accord with this desire? What was Hume's marketing strategy?

The *Treatise on Human Nature* appeared anonymously and, although in time it was a *succès d'estime,* it was hardly a literary success. His next major venture *Essays: Moral and Political* (1742) appear to be modelled on the famous essays published in the London literary journal *The Spectator* by Joseph Addison (1672–1719). Like Addison and later Samuel Johnson (1709–1784), Hume writes his own marketing copy. In his essay 'On Essay Writing', he decries the separation of the world of learning from the conversible world, that is the world of the literary salon. The learned scholars lose by 'being shut up in Colleges and Cells, and secluded from the World of good Company'. The conversationists suffer from confining their attention to trivial and ephemeral issues. So Hume is going to bridge the gap by dealing with serious issues but using a manner of exposition which will appeal to the intelligent if not intellectual members of society. Like Johnson, he recognised that an appeal to the ladies was an essential part of the marketing strategy. He wrote in the same Essay: 'I am of Opinion, that Women of Sense and Education are much better Judges of all polite Writing then Men of the same degree of Understanding'. As we know, his strategy paid off, and, by all accounts, he had a distinguished female following!

In 'Of Commerce', the first essay in *Political Discourses*, Hume makes the same marketing 'pitch', but, encouraged no doubt by the success of his earlier essays, the tone is less ingratiating and the author exudes confidence. Hume attacks the 'shallow thinkers' who 'will never allow anything to be just which is beyond their own weak conceptions'. This is particularly true in the case of economic questions where generalising from individual experience is a particular weakness, as we are all touched by commercial and financial matters. What is clearly needed is some guidance from an 'abstruse thinker' but one, of course, endowed with a good style and a clear mind. In order to disarm his critics in advance, Hume adds 'there will occur some principles which are uncommon, and which may seem too refined for such vulgar subjects (i.e. commerce etc). If false, let them be rejected: but no one ought to entertain a prejudice against them, merely because they are out of the common road.'

Hume's marketing problem is therefore similar to an economist today writing for 'the intelligent layman', in say, a monthly periodical. He would have to wear his learning lightly in offering views on interesting subjects. There were, however, two important differences compared with a modern exponent of ideas looking for a wide audience. He wrote to convince his intellectual peers as well as an educated public, and, further, his ideas were likely to meet resistance by their very novelty.

Consider how a modern writer might approach such a subject as what causes economic growth to differ between countries. He would probably begin by defining growth, normally in terms of real income per head, presenting data on the growth in real income per head in different economies for a given period of time. He would then build a model of economic growth in which the most important constituent would be the motivation of individuals to accumulate the resources in order to produce growth, notably the accumulation of physical capital, human capital and the quantity of labour input. He would be bound to consider how far the organisation of human institutions, notably the system of government and the system of production, might hinder or promote growth. He would then test his explanation of growth against the data, with reference perhaps to econometric investigations. This methodology would also underpin a popular exposition even though the audience would have to be spared the agony of following the intricacies of economic analysis found in the professional economics journals!

It is clear that Hume could not call upon an elaborate set of national and international statistics produced by governments and international agencies. Historically, such data became available as a by-product of the administrative process in government, and there might not even exist any incentive to make public the data itself. The first detailed statistical analysis of his own country, Scotland, did not take place until after his death and was a mammoth *private* undertaking by the Scottish landowner, Sir Archibald Sinclair, who used the parish Ministers of the Church as his rapporteurs. This is not to say that Hume was not interested in descriptive statistics. On the contrary, the longest essay in *Political Discourses*, 'Of the Populousness of Ancient Nations', is an exhaustive investigation of a wide variety of classical sources designed to disprove the thesis that the ancient nations were more populous than those of Hume's day. If, therefore, survival and growth of population were taken as an indicator of human well-being—a proposition supported, incidentally, by Adam Smith—then comparisons between some past golden age and a 'desolate' eighteenth century were false. The use of population growth as an indicator of economic welfare was to be a subject of much controversy in the nineteenth century during the famous Malthusian debate, and Hume anticipates Malthus by his appeal to the available data.

The much more striking part of Hume's methodology is the application of his views on human nature which were derived from his *Treatise*. Our actions are derived from our 'passions'—our tastes and sentiments as they are called in the *Abstract*—and our reasoning powers which are developed and sharpened by our knowledge of the world about us are employed in order to promote our happiness. In the preliminary essay in *Political Discourses* entitled 'Of Luxury' Hume argues that human happiness consists of three ingredients—'action, pleasure and indolence' which are present in all of us though not necessarily in the same proportions. Moreover, these 'passions' are present in men at all times and in all countries. Hume has already laid the foundations on which the modern economic theory of human action is based, though the terminology has changed. We speak today of an individual 'utility function' in which the 'arguments' or determining forces are goods, leisure and work satisfaction. Moreover, his description of the 'passions' does not entail that individuals' satisfaction is independent of that of others. If individuals seeking happiness come into conflict with one another, they cannot change their natures but their reasoning powers sharpen their appreciation of the need to find ways of co-operating in order to resolve conflicts between themselves, otherwise, in the famous words of Thomas Hobbes, life may become 'solitary, poor, nasty, brutish and short'. Hume's views on the origins of government were already developed before the *Political Discourses* and cannot be considered in detail here. Sufficient, I hope, has been said to indicate that his view of human action entails the institution of a system of justice and promotion of security as a pre-condition for human happiness which is to be anything more than transitory. It is also a view of government which is dramatically different from those who derived principles of justice and security from some moral order, divinely inspired. However, co-operation between individuals was not regarded by Hume as purely a matter of expediency. Individuals derive positive pleasure from helping their friends, from preserving their friends' good opinion of them, and so they have recourse, as the essay 'On Luxury' stresses, to continuous social intercourse once they have progressed beyond barbarism. As it would be put today in an economics treatise, individual 'utility functions' are interdependent, though much economic analysis neglects this rather important ingredient derived from the classical works of Hume and Smith.

There is no identifiable growth model in Hume's work, as there is in Adam Smith's *Wealth of Nations*, but his emphasis on an examination of human motivation accords well with present-day presentations of the analysis of growth to both professional and lay audiences. The impetus to growth comes from the human desire for action—what Hume in the *Treatise* called the insatiable craving for exercise and employment. Moreover, such action complements the desire for pleasure and continuous pleasure throughout man's life span stimulates the desire to accumulate capital and to improve knowledge. The *Political Discourses* places more emphasis on the self-sustaining nature of the growth process, once resources accumulate. As the standard of living rises above subsistence levels, pleasures become more refined, and this stimulates a diversity of interests which 'carries improvements into every art and science . . . men enjoy the privilege of rational creatures, to think as well as to act, to cultivate the pleasures of the mind as well as those of the body'. To Hume, using a crude indicator of growth such as real income per head masks the importance of the pleasures of growing diversity in human society. While Hume argues that it would be impossible for these benefits not to be widely diffused throughout all classes, he is conscious of the need to explain the international differences in the degree of diversity. Why do people in the tropics not attain the degree of 'art and civility' of nations in temperate climates? Presumably, argues Hume in 'Of Commerce', because the tropics encourage indolence. Clothes and houses are less necessary as protection against the elements and the benefits of climate being equally distributed promote more equality of real income. Fewer quarrels are likely to arise between individuals so that a settled system of government is less necessary.

The affinity between Hume's model of human nature and these models encountered in modern economic analysis means that his view would be strongly at variance with that of modern psychologists. Ernest Gellner, for instance, in his profound book *The Psychoanalytic Movement* (1986) pokes gentle fun at Hume who seems to view man as 'a gourmet crossed with an accountant, with a touch of compasionate sensibility thrown in. He conducted his life by studying his palate and seeking to arrange for its greatest satisfaction, and his imaginative sympathy for others inclined him to favour their satisfaction too, if to a lesser degree than his own' (p 16). It is not that modern psychology would object to Hume's fundamental thesis regarding the dominant role of the passions in human action. The trouble is that Hume's passions are gentle and the impulses that they produce in us are easily brought into harmony with the world around us as our powers of reasoning and observation develop. This view of human nature could hardly explain the facts of history which Hume himself so ably presents, unless its many tragic episodes were caused primarily by natural disasters beyond man's control, which is clearly not the case. Indeed, it could be argued that the treatment of Hume himself by his fellow human beings, examples of which have already been given above, hardly accords with his own depiction of human action! The *Political Discourses* suggests at various points that economic progress offers the firm prospect that men will be more disposed to live in peace and harmony with one another but the evidence points in another direction. The anxieties associated with fear of poverty may disappear in affluent societies, but other anxieties are then more starkly revealed. Hence the grip on our imaginations of the ideas of Nietzsche and Freud which emphasis the dark instinctual drives which propel human beings into conflict with one another, and with themselves.

Economists confronted with criticism of the model of rational calculation embedded in their notion of human action are apt to take refuge in the proposition that they are only concerned with how people act in allocating their scarce resources and not with why they may act in a certain way. Such propositions as 'the quantity demanded of a commodity is sensitive to its price' or 'people's incentive to work depends on what they expect to be paid' contain reasonable hypotheses which are testable. If they fit the facts, then they can be used to explode common economic fallacies and to warn governments of the problems encountered in trying to control individual economic behaviour. It is not necessary to probe the dark recesses of the mind in order to support positive economic reasoning. It is when economists begin to speculate on broader questions such as the consequences of material advance that they are apt to get out of their depth. Hume's own approach to economic growth offers a clear illustration of these observations. In the essay 'Of Interest' he repeats the proposition that there 'is no craving of the human mind more constant and insatiable than that for exercise and employment'. He shows how the desire to accumulate resources leads to economic advance and how economic advance becomes associated with 'low profits and low interest'. His empirical checks may seem by today's standards to be rather casual, but his economic reasoning is both powerful and cogent. Hume is after 'bigger fish' than the majority of economists today, and his own audience certainly expected to learn how he would catch them. He wishes to demonstrate, as already indicated, that the growth of trade and commerce resolves conflicts within society and between nations. The debate on such a matter cannot be settled within the confines of an economic analysis which assumes that men are rational creatures.

THE MAJOR ECONOMIC THEMES

The remarks on Hume's methodology have made it possible to introduce aspects of Hume's treatment of some of the broad issues in economics, as they are treated in *Political Discourses*. Hume's reputation as an economist today rests less on these broad issues, in which he is perhaps overshadowed, unjustifiably I believe, by Adam Smith, and more on his handling of such subjects as the role of money and interest in the economy, international trade policy and the financing of government by taxes and by public debt. At least these are the subjects which warrant him a place in those economic texts which are more than simply teaching manuals designed to minimise the agony of having to pass examinations.

Consider the kind of discussion of the significance of money found in the financial press today. There is a clear agreement that money as a medium of exchange is essential for both national and international trade for otherwise specialisation of production and gains from exchanging products becomes impossible or intolerably inefficient. Hume makes much of this point towards the end of his essay 'Of Money' but clearly identifies money as an acceptable medium with gold and silver coin (specie) and he is suspicious of paper credit unless clearly convertible into specie. There is also clear agreement that there is some connection between a change in the quantity of money and the change in the level of prices, but disagreement about the transmission mechanism, the precise quantitative relationship between changes in money and changes in prices and the time it takes for the change in money supply to produce a change in prices. These disagreements worry governments who want to use the money supply as an instrument to promote policy objectives such as the control of inflation. Hume is usually given a 'good press' in economic texts for his discussion of such matters. He examines the facts and finds that over long periods of time the supply of specie has risen at a slower rate than the rise in prices. There is therefore a positive relationship established between money and prices, but it is not a proportional one. Why is this so? Because, Hume explains, it takes time for any price adjustment to take place and, in the course of that time period, the increase in demand produced by an increase in money supply may be counterbalanced by alterations in the goods available to be bought. Indeed, the expectation that demand will increase, encourages more production, though eventually prices must begin to rise as labour and materials become scarcer.

Hume's policy conclusion is interesting: 'It is of no manner of consequence, with regard to the domestic happiness of a state, whether money be in a greater or lesser quantity. The good policy of the magistrate consists in keeping it, if possible, still encreasing; because, by that means, he keeps alive a spirit of industry in the nation, and encreases the stock of labour, in which consists all real power and riches.' This maxim has an obvious affinity with the common Central Bank maxim that increasing the supply of money is mainly justified by the need to accommodate a growth in potential Gross Domestic Product. However, it should be noted that Hume is describing what is desirable and is not certain that what is desirable is also possible. In his essay 'On Public Credit' he makes it abundantly clear that governments should not rely on the expansion of paper credit as the means for controlling the supply of money. Increasing the government deficit by the issue of public stocks will bring about a lack of confidence in the currency and cause inflation rather than engender an expansion in output. Government can only influence the money supply, that is gold and silver coin, by creating the conditions which enable its citizens to expand and develop its trade with those in possession of specie or who produce gold and silver . . . 'a government has great reason to preserve with care its people and its manufactures. Its money, it may safely trust to the course of human affairs' (see the essay 'Of the Balance of Trade').

Hume's discussion of money is the point of departure for two further excursions into important economic problems. The first of these is his theory of interest. It was commonly asserted by his contemporaries that one of the advantages of increasing the money supply was that it lowered interest rates. Typically, Hume begins by asking the question: how do we test this proposition? Presumably if the assertion were true, countries with relatively large money supplies would have relatively low interest rates. This is not found to be the case. Then he argues that the assertion is implausible in any case. Doubling the money supply, for example, only means that if you lend me so much labour and so many commodities, I have to repay you the equivalent money value in labour and commodities plus some interest which is a proportion of the equivalent money value. There is no reason to suppose that that proportion of equivalent value would alter simply because the value of labour or commodities had doubled in money terms. Further proof is offered by Hume in the form of historical evidence to back up his 'cross-section' study of countries; 'an effect always holds proportion with its cause. Prices have risen near four times since the discovery of the Indies; and it is probable gold and silver have multiplied much more: But interest has not fallen much above half. The rate of interest, therefore, is not derived from the quantity of precious metals' (See 'Of Interest').

Hume therefore uses his knowledge of history to refute a common hypothesis of the time, but turns back to the *Treatise* as the basis of his own explanation of the determination of interest rates. We have to look at the motives for supplying funds and for borrowing them. Concentrating on the fall in interest rates as countries develop, he explains this phenomenon in the following way. Countries develop because of the human desire for 'exercise and employment', as already stated. This is associated with a greater desire to provide for the future by saving. At the same time the 'opportunity cost' of saving diminishes because the growth of commerce produces growing competition amongst merchants which lowers the rate of profit. Accordingly, merchants accept more willingly a lower rate of return on lending. Thus 'an encrease in commerce by a necessary consequence, raises a great number of lenders, and by that means produces lowness of interest'. Space hardly allows extensive discussion of this interesting analysis, but it must be noted that Hume is considering only long-term, gradual changes in the economy. Consider his example of the 'miracle' where every citizen in Great Britain wakes up to find £5 in his pocket. According to Hume, all that would happen is that prices would double and the rate of borrowing and lending would not change. However, Hume has already argued that price adjustments take time, and, if this is so, the extra money could be saved rather than spent unless every person anticipates an immediate rise in the prices of all goods. The extra saving would lower interest rates, though in the longer run, these could rise again as individuals have to pay more for goods. Furthermore, Hume seems to envisage a society where borrowing is used solely in order to finance present consumption and not for the purchase of capital equipment. The level of interest rates simply reflects the degree of advancement of the economy. It does not influence its advancement. There is a good deal of controversy on this point, even today. If the money supply can be used to reduce interest rates, even temporarily, and this were to stimulate the demand for increasing and improving the capital stock, then a change in the interest rate in the short run might affect economic growth in the long run—so the argument goes.

It is a short step from this proposition to the policy recommendation that a government should use monetary policy in order to prevent interest rates from rising, even temporarily, so that capital investment is not discouraged. We can only speculate on how Hume would have replied to this argument. One supposes that even if he were to admit that governments could control the monetary supply, keeping down interest rates by monetary policy would suggest to Hume that the expected rise in prices would raise the costs of investment goods which would counteract any attractions to invest because interest rates had fallen. The debate continues until this day!

The second excursion derived from Hume's view of money is to be found in his analysis of international trade. Hume examines the famous mercantilist view that a country is rich or poor according to whether its stock of specie or precious metals is large or small. This view led naturally to the proposition that a country should aim at amassing gold and silver by maintaining a positive balance of trade with its neighbours, for example by discrimination against foreign imports which would have to be paid for in specie. Hume argues that this policy is both undesirable and impossible to operate in the long run. Suppose, says Hume, a situation where specie flows into Britain as a result of some measure which increases the balance of payments surplus. The increase in money raises prices so that neighbouring countries cannot afford to buy from us whereas their commodities become relatively cheaper. Money flows out. The outflow of money acts as a correcting mechanism for it results eventually in a fall in domestic wages and prices which restores domestic competitiveness. A kind of natural economic law is at work which preserves the money supply in trading countries in proportion to 'the art and industry of every nation' (See 'Of the Balance of Trade'). Of course, a country might attempt to cut itself off completely from other countries and run a siege economy but, Hume argues, this would reduce its standard of living. He illustrates this very graphically by the consequences of the barriers to trade between France and Britain: 'We lost the French market for our woollen manufactures, and transferred the commerce of wine to Spain and Portugal, where we buy worse liquor at a higher price.' Hume was to develop this argument much further in essays written after the *Political Discourses*. His international trade analysis is much admired today by international economists. They argue that if international gains from trade are to be fully realised, then countries who try to manipulate their money supply so that it fails to conform with their command over internationally accepted currency will find themselves facing major adjustment problems as their prices of internationally traded goods fall out of line with those of trading partners. Free trade in internationally traded goods, some of them argue, requires a return to the Humeian 'rules' of expansion and contraction of the increase in domestic money supply according to movements in each country's balance of payments. A continuing surplus in a major country matched by deficits in others, would require the surplus country to increase the percentage growth in its money supply, whereas the deficit countries would have to contract their percentages. The reasons why governments act otherwise are not mentioned by Hume, but his own analysis of human nature can easily be used to explore them. The process of adjustment to the 'natural'level of money in any country takes time and is painful to those who have to take cuts in their relative wages and prices in order to regain their international markets. Hume prefers to end on a note of idealism which anticipates that of the founders of the European Economic Community. In a later essay written in 1758 entitled 'Of the Jealousy of Trade', he closes with a statement on the consequences of autarkic trade policies:

> were our narrow and malignant politics to meet with success, we should reduce all our neighbouring nations to the same state of sloth and ignorance that prevails in Morrocco and the coast of Barbary. What would be the consequence? They could send us no commodities: They could take none from us: Our domestic commerce itself would languish for want of emulation, example and instruction: And we ourselves should fall into the same abject condition, to which we have reduced them. I shall therefore venture to acknowledge, that, not only as a man, but as a British subject, I pray for the flourishing commerce of Germany, Spain, Italy, and even France itself!

The present-day interest in Hume as an economist now extends to the analysis of the government as an economic entity. Although Hume includes in his *Political Discourses* his fascinating essay on 'Idea of a Perfect Common-wealth', the content of this essay concerns the process through which government power should be exercised. To understand Hume's recommendations, it is necessary to go back to his previous essays on the origin of government and the principles which he believes should control its operations. A full discussion of Hume's theory of government would fill volumes. It can only be said here that he traces the origin of government from the need to devise an instrument for resolving conflicts about the use of resources where this cannot be achieved by negotiation in the market. He offers as an example his now famous case of the draining of a meadow which may be generally conceived as mutually beneficial amongst a group of men.

> Two neighbours may agree to drain a meadow which they possess in common, because it is easy for them to know each other's mind; and each must perceive that the immediate consequence of his failing in his part is the abandoning of the whole project. But it is very difficult, and indeed impossible, that a thousand persons should agree in any such action; it being difficult for them to concert so complicated a design, and still more difficult for them to execute it; while each seeks a pretext to free himself of the trouble and expense, and would lay the burden on others. Political society easily remedies both these inconveniences.

> 'Of the Origin of Government': Book III , *Treatise of Human Nature*

Governments, therefore, reduce the transactions costs amongst citizens who perceive that compulsory exactions to finance on indivisible benefit are a lesser evil than the risk that, if there were no government, the benefit could not be realised. This still leaves unresolved three vital questions: who should decide which projects should be undertaken, how can one check on the efficiency of those who undertake and administer them and how should the burden of financing them be divided amongst the beneficiaries? The reader can trace for himself Hume's answers to these difficult questions in the *Political Discourses*, notably in 'Of Taxes' and 'Of Public Credit' in which he clearly indicates that governments have to be prevented from actions which remove the incentives to save and to invest and which oppress the poor.

POSTCRIPT: HUME AS AN INSPIRATIONAL FORCE

Reputations of great thinkers fluctuate according to the intellectual fashions and preoccupations of the day. What of David Hume in the 1980s?

The author recently had occasion to test Hume's current reputation in jurisprudence and economics. Returning after many years as David Hume did, to live in Edinburgh, the author has set up The David Hume Institute devoted to the study of policy questions requiring a professional knowledge of law and economics. It is a response to a challenge familiar to Adam Smith and David Hume for it requires the development and promulgation of ideas on policy, but at a long distance from the seat of government. The author made contact with a number of prominent economists and lawyers who had a particular interest in what is now termed 'legal economics', asking them if they would associate themselves with this risky enterprise. They all accepted the invitation and three of them wrote tributes to Hume as one of the major influences on their thinking. What is striking is that all three of them—Friedrich Hayek, George Stigler and James Buchanan—have been awarded the Nobel Prize in

Economics. No better evidence need be offered of the power and penetration of David Hume's work and further commendation of it to the reader seems superfluous.

NOTE

1   The views of the bigots might be summed up in a 'clerihew', a peculiarly British form of epigram consisting of two rhyming couplets containing lines of different lengths and concerning some famous figure:

> David Hume
> Made Prelates Fume.
> As a Francophilic Freethinker
> How could he be other than an Insufferable Stinker?

AIDE MEMOIRE OF HUME'S LIFE

1707	Union of the Parliaments of England and Scotland.
1711	David Hume born in Edinburgh, Scotland.
1715	First Jacobite Rebellion in Scotland.
1722	Hume enters University of Edinburgh.
1734–7	Hume's first residence in France.
1739	Publication in London of *Treatise on Human Nature*.
1741	Publication in Edinburgh of *Essays: Moral and Political*.
1745	Hume rejected for the Chair of Ethics and Pneumatical Philosophy at the University of Edinburgh.
1745–6	Second Jacobite Rebellion led by Charles Edward Stuart ('Bonnie Prince Charlie').
1746	Hume appointed Judge Advocate to the military forces under the command of General St Clair engaged in an expedition (which proved unsuccessful) to attack the French ports in Brittany.
1751	Hume returns to Edinburgh
1752	Political Discourses published in Edinburgh. Hume appointed Librarian to the Faculty of Advocates, Edinburgh, a post held until 1757.
1754	First volume of Hume's *History of England* published in London.
1756–62	Seven Years' War between Britain and France.
1764	Diplomatic relations between Britain and France restored. Hume accompanies new British Ambassador to Paris as Secretary.
1767	Hume returns to London to become Under-Secretary of State.
1769	Final return of Hume to Edinburgh.
1776	Publication of Adam Smith's *Wealth of Nations* in London. David Hume dies.

A BIBLIOGRAPHICAL GUIDE

LIFE AND TIMES

The standard biography of David Hume is still Ernest Campbell Mossner's *The Life of David Hume*, Nelson, Edinburgh, 1954. Mossner's work quotes extensively from Hume's letters and reproduces Hume's *My Own Life* in full (Appendix A). Essential reading on eighteenth-century intellectual life in Scotland is *A Hotbed of Genius: The Scottish Enlightenment, 1730–90* (edited by Daiches, Jones and Jones), Edinburgh University Press, 1986. This work contains an excellent essay on Hume by Peter Jones and some delightful illustrations. This contribution owes much to both Mossner and Jones for factual information.

HUME'S PHILOSOPHY

The intrepid reader may wish to consult *A Treatise of Human Nature* (edited by L A Selby Biggs), Oxford University Press, 1978. That edition also contains the *Abstract of Human Nature* (1740), which has been separately edited and introduced by John Maynard Keynes and Piero Sraffa, published first in 1938 by Cambridge University Press and now published by Archon Books, Connecticut, USA, 1965. The complete *Essays, Moral Political and Literary,* have been reproduced by Liberty Classics, Liberty Fund, Indianapolis, 1985.

Commentaries on Hume's philosophy include A J Ayer, *Hume,* Oxford 1980, and the essay by Peter Jones mentioned above. His position in the development of psychology is most interestingly presented in Ernest Gellner, *The Psychoanalytic Movement or the coming of Unreason,* Paladin Books, Granada Publishing Ltd, London 1985.

HUME'S ECONOMICS

The standard work on Hume's economics is still *David Hume: Writings on Economics,* edited and introduced by Eugene Rotwein, Nelson, Edinburgh 1955. It contains a useful long introduction by Professor Rotwein, most of the essays contained in *Political Discourses* and relevant extracts from Hume's correspondence concerning economic questions.

Most respectable histories of economic thought now acknowledge the importance of Hume's contribution. Perhaps the most interesting appraisal of his work is still that of Joseph Schumpeter in his monumental *History of Economic Analysis,* Oxford University Press, 1954.

CHAPTER THIRTEEN

Hayek, the Scottish School, and Contemporary Economics

John Gray

The Boundaries of Economics
eds G C Winston and R F Teichgraber
(CUP, 1988)

In his own account of his intellectual formation, F A Hayek has always acknowledged his indebtedness to the thinkers of the Scottish school and, above all, to Ferguson, Smith, and Hume. Indeed, in his contributions to the intellectual history of classical liberal political economy and social philosophy, Hayek has gone so far as to distinguish two divergent and opposed intellectual traditions—that of the French Enlightenment, which he sees as inspired ultimtely by a variation of Cartesian rationalism, and that of the Scottish Enlightenment, with its roots in a Christian and skeptical recognition of the limits of human understanding—and has identified himself explicitly with the Scottish tradition. That Hayek's thought converges with that of the leading Scottish political economists on many fundamental questions is not in serious doubt and can easily be demonstrated. At the same time, the thought of the Scottish school is only one of the influences that have shaped Hayek's complex intellectual makeup, and these other influences, especially that of his teachers in the Austrian school, are responsible for many of the points of sharp and real divergence between Hayek and the Scottish philosophers. It is by virtue of these other influences that we may say that Hayek's thought diverges from that of the Scottish philosophers as often as it converges with it—and, often enough, in ways Hayek has not himself perceived.

It is by virtue of his debts to the Austrian economists, also, that Hayek's thought has been neglected in the mainstream of economic theory. Hayek's intellectual relations with his Austrian forebears are so complex, and his own methodological and theoretical perspective so distinctive, that explicit acknowledgement of his chief insights is rare in the literatures of conventional economic theory. Yet many distinctively Hayekian themes—such as the role of tacit information in co-ordinating market processes, the subjectivity of economic phenomena, and the function of markets as discovery procedures for preferences—surface in the more centrally situated works of Shackle, Arrow, and other mainstream economists. In short, whereas Hayek's explicit presence has at least since the Second World War been on the margins of economics, his characteristic theoretical insights are found at many growth points in the literatures of economics since that time. One of my goals in this chapter is to account for this paradoxical circumstance.

In seeking to uncover the complicated connections between Hayek, the Scottish writers, and contemporary economics, I address two central themes: the conception found in Hayek and the Scottish writers of the uses of knowledge in society and of the role of morality in sustaining a market order. One conclusion of my investigation is that Hayek has sometimes ascribed a uniformity of view to the Scottish thinkers that historical inquiry does not support. Another conclusion, which may be of interest chiefly to Hayekian scholars but which may be of broader concern to political economists and social theorists, is that Hayek's own thought is beset by conflicts and tensions that finally disable it as a system. The conclusion I reach is that, notwithstanding its ultimate failure, Hayek's system of thought retains considerable contemporary interest, both for the many important insights it encompasses and for its achievement in keeping alive political economy as an intellectual tradition whose subject matter and concerns transcend many contemporary disciplines. Notwithstanding Hayek's comparative neglect, the continuing vitality of his theoretical work is indicated by the many occasions on which his chief insights surface, often stated in different terminologies and within other conceptual frameworks, in a variety of areas in contemporary economics.

Distinctive elements in Hayek's system of thought

Hayek's system of thought comprises two major elements. The first is expressed in what I have elsewhere[1] called his *epistemological turn* in social philosophy. By this is meant his insistence that, against the dominant tradition in social and political theory, social institutions be assessed and compared by reference to their capacity to conserve, generate, transmit, and make use of knowledge rather than by their conformity to some preferred principles of political morality. It is not, to be sure that Hayek sees the production of knowledge by social institutions as an ultimate or intrinsic good. Instead, he argues that human goals, whatever they may be, are best assured of achievement when the growth of knowledge is promoted and existing knowledge effectively utilised. It is of vital importance in any attempt to understand Hayek's thought to grasp that he believes the knowledge-producing function of social institutions to apply across the board—not only to the central institution of market pricing, but also to law, morality, religion, and language. For Hayek, all these important social institutions are best conceived as vehicles for the conservation, transmission, and generation of knowledge. They are (so to speak) carriers or embodiments of knowledge held in practical form—as skills, traditions and practices—and they are an indispensable condition of our developing and using knowledge in its theoretical forms.

For Hayek, the problem of knowledge—the problem of how we are to make best use of the knowledge we have as well as the problem of how we are to acquire new knowledge—is the central problem of social order. It is also the central problem of economic theory. As he has put it:

> The peculiar character of the problem of a rational economic order is determined precisely by the fact that the knowledge of the circumstances of which we must make use never exists in concentrated or integrated form but solely as the dispersed bits of incomplete and frequently contradictory knowledge which all the separate individuals possess. The economic problem of society is thus not merely a problem of how to allocate 'given' resources—'if given' is taken to mean given to a single mind which deliberately solves the problem set by these 'data.' It is rather a problem of how to secure the best use of resources known to any of the members of the society, for ends whose relative importance only these individuals know. Or, to put it briefly, it is a problem of the utilisation of knowledge which is not given to anyone in particular. (Hayek 1976a: 77–8)

For Hayek, then, the economic problem is not one of allocating scarce resources to competing ends, but one of coping with the most fundamental scarcity of all, human knowledge. Market institutions are then understood as rational devices for the division of knowledge in society, as institutions whereby knowledge scattered and dispersed across society becomes nevertheless available through the price mechanism to the society as a whole. The market process is not according to this view an allocative mechanism but rather an epistemological device, a discovery procedure in which knowledge that could not be collected by a single mind (or committee of minds) is yet rendered accessible and usable for human purposes.

This conception of market institutions as an epistemological device is, perhaps, Hayek's most fundamental and original contribution to economic thought. It has echoes, no doubt, in recent studies in the economics of information, in which information is itself viewed as a costly commodity and in which practices such as advertising are theorised as rational devices for lowering information costs in the economy. At the same time, Hayek's conception of market institutions as a discovery procedure remains very different from that which animates studies in the economics of information. It is not that market processes lower the costs of information to economic agents, but that they allow participants to make use of information that would not otherwise be available to them at all. Invoking his contributions to the famous calculation debate between the Austrian economists and the theorists of market socialism such as Lange and Lerner, Hayek maintains that market prices embody information about preferences and relative scarcities that is available in no other way. One crucial argument he advances in support of this claim is the Polanyian[2] argument that much of the knowledge transmitted by market prices is tacit and local knowledge untheorised (and perhaps untheorisable) by its possessors. This kind of knowledge—the knowledge that may be expressed in entrepreneurial insight, for example—may well be unknown to its possessor. Market prices then embody knowledge of which market participants themselves may be ignorant. Arguing that social institutions in general are adaptations to our inevitable ignorance of most of the facts of the social world, Hayek maintains that market institutions in particular enable us to make use of knowledge we do not know we have.

The epistemological turn in Hayek's thought leads him, as we have seen, to view social institutions as knowledge-bearing phenomena. The second element in Hayek's thought seeks to promote an evolutionary conception of the emergence and development of social institutions. Generalising Menger's account of the rise of money as an unintended consequence of human action, Hayek submits that social institutions are (in Ferguson's phrase) results of human action but not of human design; they are artifacts but not constructs, having evolved as adaptations to changing circumstances and needs. No-one could have planned the central social institutions—law, morality, language and the market—and no-one understands their detailed functions. In general, Hayek develops an *evolutionary-functionalist* conception of the development of the major social institutions, in which it is maintained that their emergence and subsequent history can be explained by their contribution to the survival chances of the social groups that subscribe to them.[3] This second element of Hayek's thought is not a simple claim but a complex thesis. In part it is the claim that social institutions are the unintended consequences of the actions of individuals; it is a methodological individualist thesis about the explanatory reconstruction of social institutions. As such it remains controversial but not clearly indefensible. Hayek's evolutionary-functionalist claims are far more clearly disputable. To begin with, human history is too riddled with sheer contingencies for any monocausal model of institutional development to be at all plausible, and for this reason, a Darwinian explanation of the rise and fall of institutions comes up against many strong counter examples. For example, Hayek's suggestion that there is a sort of natural selection of religions,[4] in which religions favouring private property and family life prevail over others by virtue of the enhanced survival chances they afford the offspring of their practitioners, neglects the role that the capture of state power has often played in accounting for the triumph of religions over their rivals. In fact, the evolutionary turn in Hayek's thought seems open to all the criticisms and objections that disable the evolutionary-functionalist sociologies of Herbert Spencer, W G Sumner, and (perhaps) Marx.[5]

The two fundamental elements that distinguish Hayek's thought having been sketched, a few remarks on their difficulties and mutual relations may be in order. In the first place, though Hayek connects it with his thesis of the knowledge-bearing role of social institutions, the thesis that there is a sort of natural selection of institutions and practices is evidently wholly independent of it. One may grant the epistemological functions of social institutions and admit the vital contribution these functions make to human well-being without in any way endorsing Hayek's cultural Darwinism. This is to say that, from the competition or rivalry among social institutions, practices, and systems, nothing guarantees the success or survival of the institutions that are best in terms of productivity, efficiency, capacity to sustain human populations, or contributions to the growth of knowledge. It is, after all, one of the larger implications of the calculation debate that attempts at socialist central planning only squander available knowledge by making it unusable. In other words, the attempted suppression of market pricing in Stalinist-style socialist economies results only in a depletion of the common stock of human knowledge—knowledge that had hitherto been preserved or stored in market prices. If socialist economic institutions come to prevail over market institutions, then according to Hayek's own account this will lead to a massive impoverishment not only of living standards but also of the human capital of knowledge in society. There is nothing about human cultural evolution or institutional development that assures us that the institutions that are best in epistemological terms will be those that prevail. For this reason, the two fundamental theses of the Hayekian system are not only independent of one another; they may even on occasion come into conflict with each other. But what does all this say about Hayek's relations with the Scottish school?

HAYEK AND THE SCOTTISH PHILOSOPHERS ON THE USE OF KNOWLEDGE IN SOCIETY

The point of closest convergence between Hayek and the Scottish writers lies in their anti-Cartesian skepticism of systematic or comprehensive social reform by the use of the human reason. As Adam Smith puts it in a famous passage:

> The man of system . . . seems to imagine that he can arrange the different members of a great society with as much ease as the hand arranges the different pieces upon the chessboard. He does not consider that the pieces upon the chessboard have no other principle of motion beside that which the hand impresses upon them; but that, in the great chessboard of human society, every single piece has a principle of motion of its own, altogether different from that which the legislature might choose to impress upon it. If those two principles coincide and act in the same direction, the game of human society will go on easily and harmoniously, and is very likely to be happy and successful. If they are opposite or different, the game will go on miserably, and human society must be at all times in the highest degree of disorder.

The skeptical perspective expressed in this passage, in which is asserted the incapacity of human intelligence to capture the vast complexity of social life, is one found in most of the Scottish thinkers, and it has many echoes in Hayek. Like the Scottish thinkers, Hayek constantly asserts a contrast between civilisation and barbarism—between societies with developed systems of law and institutions of property, extended networks of trade and commerce, and a considerable measure of social and geographical mobility, on the one hand, and societies of a more autarchic, traditional, and agrarian sort, on the other. According to Hayek, the point of demarcation between these two categories lies in the uses made of knowledge in society. As he puts it, 'It might be said that civilisation begins when the individual in the pursuit of his ends can make use of more knowlege than he has himself acquired and when he can transcend the boundaries of ignorance by profiting from knowledge he does not himself possess' (Hayek 1960: 22). Human constitutional ignorance is not, however, abolished in civilised society; it is acknowledged and thereby diminished by reliance on institutions such as market pricing and by subscription to knowledge-bearing cultural traditions. Hayek (1960, 24) further qualifies the kind of ignorance to which the institutions of a civilised society are a response when he observes that 'the knowledge which any individual mind consciously manipulates is only a small part of the knowledge which at any time contributes to the success of his action.' And again: 'Scientific knowledge does not exhaust even all the explicit and conscious knowledge of which society makes constant use' (p 25). In summary, Hayek remarks that 'concurrent with the growth of conscious knowledge there always takes place an equally important accumulation of tools in this wider sense, of tested and generally adopted ways of doing things' (p 27).

Despite their many obvious points of affinity and convergence, the Hayekian doctrine of human constitutional ignorance is not merely a reiteration of the skeptical Scottish insistence on the limitations of human understanding. It is hardly a theory of ignorance at all, but rather an account of the primordially practical character of our social knowledge. Hayek's argument is a version of the thesis of the primacy of practice in the constitution of social knowledge that has been advanced in other forms by such philosophers as Wittgenstein, Ryle, Oakeshott, and Heidegger. In Hayek's work, as in Oakeshott's, the thesis that much social knowledge is always buried or stored in social practices and is often insusceptible to conscious recovery or rational reconstruction is used as a battering ram against various schemes for comprehensive social planning and reform—schemes that Hayek lumps together under the pejorative label of 'constructivism.' In this respect, Hayek's criticism of constructivist rationalism has something in common with Pascal's critique of Cartesianism. Both insist that much knowledge cannot be formalised in any systematic way and affirm that the project of reconstructing knowledge on indubitable foundations can only end in an impoverishment of our knowledge, including our moral knowledge. (We know that Descartes himself retreated from the project of reconstructing moral knowledge and opted for a provisional and conventional morality.) In Pascal's case, but not straightforwardly in Hayek's, the upshot of the critique of constructivist rationalism— which means here only the doctrine that all knowledge worthy of the title can, and perhaps should, be given a statement in theoretical or formal terms—was a sort of skeptical traditionalism in social and economic matters. Because Hayek is concerned, as Pascal was not and could not have been, with the necessary conditions of a large industrial society, his inference from the impossibility of constructivist rationalisms is different. For Hayek, the positive normative implication of the thesis that our social knowledge has always a profoundly practical character lies in the demand that individuals have an assured space of independence within which they may act on their own goals and with the aid of the tacit knowledge each uniquely possesses. In political terms this becomes the demand for strong private property rights under the rule of law. The primacy of tacit knowledge then yields a knowledge-based defence of property rights. This is, in effect, the reverse side of Hayek's epistemological arguments against socialist calculation.

Whereas their normative and political implications are the same, there is little in the writings of the Scottish philosophers that parallels Hayek's use of the idea of tacit knowledge. In Hume there is, as a result of his complex skeptical argumentation, the insistence that in the end we rely on natural belief in all our dealings with the world, but there is little that could be construed as a recognition, however oblique, of the importance of social institutions as stores or bearers of practical knowledge. In this connection, Hume differs radically from Burke, who explicitly defends traditions as bearers of knowledge otherwise inaccessible to any one generation of people and in whose writings there is an informal but pervasive reliance on a conception of tacit or practical knowledge. Burke here deviates, however, not only from Hume but from all the other major Scottish writers.

Hayek's position on tacit knowledge may well be an entirely original feature of his thought, since it seems to predate Polanyi's writings on the subject (see Gray 1986, 14-15). At the same time, it may also be interpreted as a development of the subjectivist analysis of social phenomena that Hayek inherited from his Austrian teachers. Though at first it figured as a theory of value, Austrian subjectivism soon came to be extended to such important institutions as money and to be used against objectivist positions in the theory of expectations. In Hayek's work a subjectivist account of social life is explicitly advocated (see, in particular, Hayek 1952), which has significant implications for the character and method of political economy. Among the Scots, as Myrdal and many others have observed, objectivist conceptions of economic value survived that led to an endorsement of the 'communistic fiction' of the economy as a household. For this reason, political economy was for the Scottish thinkers incompletely emancipated from the idea of a science of wealth, or *plutology*, which had figured in much mercantilist thought. Hayek, by contrast, makes a sharp distinction between an *economy*, in which resources are known and ranked in a hierarchy of importance by reference to an agreed scale of values, and a *catallaxy*, which is the vast network of exchanges, taking place without a hierarchy of values or common knowledge of the available resources, that constitutes the real economic life of society. Economic theory has as its subject matter this network of exchanges, not the allocational decisions that occur in a firm or a household, and is better called catallactics than economics. Hayek's subjectivist value theory leads naturally, then, to a conception of the subject matter of economic thought that is radically different from that of the Scots (based as it was on an objectivist, labour-based value theory). This does not mean, however, as I shall later maintain, that the Scots writers do not converge with Hayek on a broad general conception of political economy. What we have established is only that Hayek's neo-Austrian subjectivism leads him to a conception of market institutions and indeed economic life that is very different from any conception of them to be found among the Scots. Is there any greater convergence in their views of morality?

MORALITY AND SOCIETY IN THE SCOTTISH WRITERS AND IN HAYEK

The upshot of a powerful current in recent historiography is that the Scottish Enlightenment was significant in effecting a radical secularisation of political morality. In its most profound statement, John Dunn's (1985, chs 1–3) interpretation of the relations of John Locke with the Scottish philosophers, it is argued that Locke's thought is embedded (and is, indeed, barely intelligible outside of) a context of Christian theism. Whatever epistemological problems Locke may have in accounting for our knowledge of the divine will, all the moral force of natural law and natural rights in his system derives from their source in the will of the Deity. By contrast, in the Scottish writers, according to Dunn, a dissolution of all such theistic schemes is effected, with the result that morality, particularly political morality, is given a wholly naturalistic form. It is one of Locke's least appreciated anticipations of future intellectual developments, Dunn (1985, 54) avers, that the naturalistic reconstruction of morality by the Scottish writers may in the end prove unstable or at least inadequate as a basis for political legitimacy.

That the Scottish writers inherited a Lockean vision of civil society while at the same time divesting it of its foundations in a certain kind of Christian piety, and attempted to rest its justification on a largely secular basis, are claims that are easily substantiated by a survey of the principal Scottish writings. At the same time, it is easy for an account of this sort to neglect important differences among the Scottish writers. Whereas the secular character of David Hume's reconstruction of political morality is unambiguous and incontestable, the case of Adam Smith is more equivocal. The coincidence of private with public interest—which in the later and wholly secular thought of Bentham, James Mill, and the other Philosophic Radicals, was a contingency grounded institutional artifice—has in Smith the status of a natural law whose guarantor is in the end a beneficent Providence. It seems for this reason an exaggeration to assimilate the uncompromising secularism of Hume into the deistic naturalism of Smith. An even starker contrast is that of Hume with Burke, whose debts to Smith are well known. In Burke, the Whig presumption of progress in history rests securely on an explicitly providentialist histori-ography that has no echo in Hume. The latter's thought is largely lacking in any notion of progress, history being represented in pagan and Machiavellian fashion as a cycle of civilisation and barbarism. Whereas the lack of historical dimension in Hume's political thought has been over stated by many writers and has now been amply criticised,[7] it remains the case that his account of political life has a static quality that leaves him closer to Hobbes and Spinoza than to some of the other major Scottish thinkers such as Ferguson.

These differences in the degree of secular commitment among the Scottish writers have important implications for their links with Hayek. One way of illuminating this complex structure of influences is to note that Hayek himself fails to mark the contrasts I have mentioned above between Hume on the one hand and Burke and Smith on the other. He assimilates Burke together with all the Scottish philosophers into a single tradition of 'English' liberal thought (Hayek 1960, 55–6)—an assimilation that neglects the differences in degree of

secular commitment and the diversity of conceptions of historical development among the thinkers so grouped together. In spirit and outlook, Hayek is
closest to Burke, though Burke's providentialism undergoes in Hayek's
thought a secularist metamorphosis into a form of cultural Darwinism. The
view common to both Hayek and Burke of traditions as carriers of knowledge
accumulated across the generations fits well with the epistemological turn in
Hayek's social theory. At the same time, it suggests a number of hard problems
for Hayek's defence of liberal civil society and the market order. One problem
has already been intimated—the fact that nothing in Hayek's thought
guarantees that civil societies will in the end prevail over tyrannous ones. Such
an outcome could be assured only, if at all, in a historical theodicy that, like
Burke's, had an explicit theistic context. (Even in Burke, providentialism faces
notorious difficulties, vividly ventilated in the closing sections of the
Reflections, about how the victory of the French ideologues is to be accounted
for in providentialist terms.) The expectation that liberal civilisation will
become universal is in Hayek's thought, as it was in the earlier evolutionary
sociology of Herbert Spencer, a form of moral optimism that is justified by
nothing in the evolutionary theory itself.

Hayek's Burkean conception of moral tradition confronts another problem
created by his wholly un-Scottish endorsement of the moral attitudes of
Mandeville. As is well known, most of the Scottish thinkers, and in particular
Smith and Hume, were strongly critical of Mandeville's moral radicalism, in
which the achievements of civil society are shown to be dependent on a
toleration of human attributes—greed, lust, envy—condemned by inherited
Christian moral traditions. None of the Scottish writers was prepared to accept
Mandeville's equation, part ironic, part speculative of private vice with public
virtue. In this respect, the Scottish writers were able to combine their moderate
political radicalism with a robust moral conservatism. For Smith as much as
for Hume, the stability of civil society depended on the flourishing within it of
the traditional virtues, and in particular of honesty, sobriety, deference to
superior rank, and so on. The attitude of the Scottish thinkers to the moral
inheritance of Christianity may well have been a complex and ambivalent one,
since, as a whole school of intellectuals following Pocock has shown (see, e.g.
Winch 1978), Scottish thought during this period was not uninfluenced by civic
humanism with its sympathies for pagan moral life. None of the Scottish
writers followed Mandeville, however, in his readiness to deploy a subversive
critique of inherited moral traditions in the service of a defence of civil society.
What is noteworthy in Hayek is that he is ready to do precisely this, finding in
Mandeville the germs of many of the central themes of Scottish social theory.
As he puts it:

> ... His (Mandeville's) main contention became simply that in the complex order
> of society the results of men's actions were very different from what they had
> intended, and that the individuals, in pursuing their own ends, whether selfish or
> altruistic, produced useful results for others which they did not anticipate or
> perhaps even know; and, finally, that the whole order of society, and even all that
> we call culture, was the result of individual strivings which had no end in view, but
> which were channelled to serve such ends by institutions, practices and rules which

had also never been invented but had grown up by the survival of what proved successful.

It was in the elaboration of this wider thesis that Mandeville for the first time developed all the classical paradigmata of the spontaneous growth of orderly social structures: of law and morals, of language, the market, and of money, and also the growth of technological knowledge. (Hayek 1978, 253)

The problem generated for Hayek by his identification of Mandeville as the precursor of the Scottish school lies precisely in the contradictory relations between Hayek's Burkean moral conservatism and Mandeville's moral radicalism. This problem emerges explicitly when, in a recent book, Hayek (1976b) notes the emergence in modern cultures of 'unviable moralities,' that is, moralities that condemn the institutions on which contemporary civil societies rest. Hayek is here demanding a revision of the moral inheritance of modern society—a moral inheritance replete with elements he stigmatises as tribal and atavistic.[8] In so doing, however, he relinquishes his Burkean moral traditionalism and adopts a critical rationalist stance in regard to customary morality of precisely the sort he has elsewhere condemned. Furthermore, in criticising elements of inherited and contemporary morality for their inconsistency with the conditions of stability of civil society, Hayek effectively abandons the evolutionary ethics he has expressed ever more insistently in his recent writings. In abandoning evolutionary ethics, however, Hayek reveals the absence in his thought of any plausible moral theory—an absence that dissolves the unity of his system and leaves it without a compelling normative defence for the market order.

Hayek's relations with the Scottish school on questions of morality and society are, then, no less complex than those on questions of epistemology and the use of knowledge in society. His view of morality is less like that of the Scottish writers than he supposes and least like that of the Scottish philosopher he most admires, David Hume. This is not to say that Hayek's overriding concern with the moral foundations of a civil society is any less urgent than that of the Scots thinkers. He shares with them, and particularly with Smith and Ferguson, an anxiety that the actual evolution of commercial societies may throw up moral outlooks that are incompatible with the stability of the societies that have produced them. But it would be idle to pretend that there is in Hayek, any more than there is in Smith or Ferguson, a compelling moral response to what have later been called the cultural contradictions of capitalism.[9]

HAYEK'S RELATIONS WITH CONTEMPORARY ECONOMIC THEORY

We have seen that Hayek's intellectual relations with the Scottish writers are complex, sometimes obscure, and not always as Hayek himself conceives them. Hayek's account of his affinities with, and debts to, the writers of the Scottish school, like his intellectual historiography as a whole, is idiosyncratic and partisan. It is not surprising, then, that the authentic and distinctive contributions Hayek has made to the intellectual history of economic thought have found little echo in the dominant voices in the recent history of ideas. The manifest neglect of Hayek's theoretical work by the larger profession of economists is harder to explain. Part of the explanation, no doubt, is to be found in the accidents of Hayek's intellectual biography. His influence in the profession was probably at its height during his theoretical controversy with Keynes. Unlike Keynes, however, Hayek never embodied his economic thought in a general theory whose implications for public policy were made intelligible and explicit. For this reason, though Hayek's economic theory is eminently systematic in conception and intent, its systematic character was far from obvious. Furthermore, its policy implications appeared to many to be irrelevant or absurd during the two or three decades after the Second World War, when it seemed that Keynesian macro-economic policies were being implemented, and implemented successfully. Part of the reason for the neglect of Hayek's work in mainstream postwar economics is the brute historical fact that for several decades he appeared to be on the losing side in intellectual terms. Finally, his intellectual efforts after the war were not, in fact, principally in economic theory in any easily recognisable form, but instead in social philosophy.

These incidents in Hayek's intellectual biography tell us something, but not much about his neglect in postwar economics. A much deeper explanation lies in the elusive quality of Hayek's thought itself. If, as I have maintained, his relations with the Scottish writers are complicated and unclear, his relations with his Austrian forebears are no less difficult to specify. In methodology, Hayek never subscribed either to the Kantian a priori, apodictic-deductive method of von Mises or to the Aristotleian essentialism of Menger. His methodological position appears in fact to have owed much to Mach and to have anticipated in important respects that of Popper (though there are no less important differences between Hayek's and Popper's accounts of scientific methodology).[10] In particular, it remains very unclear what status Hayek ascribed to 'economic laws'. His opposition to the German historical school in economic theory is well known, but at times Hayek comes close to the view adumbrated explicitly by his sometime pupil, G L S Shackle,[11] that economics has more in common with law and medicine than it does with physics or mathematics. At times, indeed, Hayek comes close to the view, stated in postmodernist idiom in this volume by Donald McCloskey (see Chapter 2), that the economic way of thinking is but one way of talking about the social world—one that seeks to find intelligibility in certain kinds of patterns or *gestalten* that recur in our social experience.[12]

It is in the elusive originality of Hayek's methodological and theoretical outlook, then, that a large part of the explanation for his neglect by mainstream economics is plausibly to be found. It is to be found, most fundamentally, however, in certain specific features of Hayek's theoretical perspective, which deviate radically from the ruling paradigm in much conventional economic thinking. In his contributions to philosophical anthropology, Hayek has always theorised human beings as rule-following animals rather than utility maximising creatures. His theoretical contributions have, for this reason among others, been resistant to formulation in the utilitarian terms of neoclassical economics. Hayek has never subscribed to the fiction of *Homo economicus* or its related fiction, the notion of a distinct mode of economic life. For Hayek, the market process is only social exchange in its most explicit and accessible form. At the same time, Hayek has always repudiated the imperialist claims of a paneconomism (such as Gary Becker's) that theorises all human activity on a model of rational choice—a model that, for Hayek, only consecrates the Hobbesian (and Cartesian) myth of *Homo calculans*. The sphere of economic life is not, then, restricted to the market process; but neither is it all pervasive.

Hayek's marginality in contemporary economics may be accounted for, in significant part, accordingly, by reference to the elusive originality of his theoretical perspective, which assorts badly with the ruling idioms of theoretical discourse in postwar economics. It may well be, indeed, that Hayek's own methodological and philosophical perspective on economic theory failed to gain adherents or to exercise a compelling interest, not only by virtue of its subtlety, but because of unresolved problems in its foundations— problems that persuaded the few who have studied his thought that the systemic unity of his work is at bottom thoroughly compromised. Among economists, the most fundamentally important of those who have found incoherences in Hayek's system is Shackle, who has argued powerfully that Hayek's insistence on the limitation of human knowledge, and, most particularly, on the subjective character of our beliefs about the future, introduces a disequilibrating factor in economic life that Hayek's account of the market process does not sufficiently acknowledge. At the level of theory and policy, this is to say that Hayek's account of the market process fails to respond adequately to the insights, only partially developed by Keynes, into the macro-instability of the market process under conditions in which subjective expectations produce large-scale crisis (see Shackle 1972, Ch 22). Stated in the most general terms, Shackle's critique of Hayek lies in the proposition that Hayekian conceptions of social knowledge and unknowledge, when taken to their natural limit, have implications that are not recognised by Hayek himself and are ultimately subversive of his system. It is in the likely incoherence of Hayek's system of ideas taken as a whole, then, as well as in the fact of its considerable subtlety and originality, that we find the most persuasive explanation of the weakness of his direct influence. It is in these facts, again, that we can find an explanation of the many oblique borrowings of Hayekian insights in recent economic literatures.

Concluding remarks: Hayek, the Scottish school, and contemporary economics

The outcome of the survey I have conducted of the affinities between Hayek and the thinkers of the Scottish school on questions to do with the use of knowledge in society and the role of morality in sustaining a civil order is that the points of divergence are at least as striking as the elements of clear affinity between them. The distinctive elements in Hayek's own intellectual formation to which I alluded at the start, and above all the inheritance of Austrian subjectivism, in any case render the result of my survey *prima facie* plausible. It seems that Hayek in his contributions to the history of ideas has found continuities where discontinuities are more easily demonstrable and, at least in respect of his view of social institutions as epistemic devices, may even have underrated his own originality. Whereas an account of this general sort is attempted by Burke of moral traditions, I can think of no-one before Hayek who has represented the central institutions of the market itself as epistemic devices.

Distinctive and original as his own contributions to it are, Hayek shares with the Scottish thinkers a commitment to a discipline—political economy—and he has in common with them a definite conception of its subject matter. Though the term 'political economy' is not itself commonly used by the Scottish writers, there is in all of them, and especially in the writings of Smith, Ferguson, and Hume, the conception that it is the market process, and the conditions and characteristics of commercial society, that are the central subject matter of political economy. Both Hayek and the Scottish thinkers could not but view as retrograde the fragmentation of intellectual life that has occurred in the twentieth century, in which the subject matter of political economy has come to be viewed from a variety of rationally incommensurable disciplinary viewpoints—those of jurisprudence, sociology, moral psychology, political science, and economics, for example. Equally, both could not help but regret the fragmentation of economics itself into a host of specialist subdisciplines whose mutual relations and shared presuppositions were neglected and untheorised.

For all their many points of divergence, then, Hayek and the Scottish thinkers are at one in their commitment to political economy as a distinct discipline. They have in common a suspicion of conventional categories of understanding—a suspicion based on the belief that such disciplinary categories render elusive to us a social world that, insofar as it can be understood at all, must be understood in its totality. This holistic perspective shared by Hayek and the Scottish thinkers has been little evident in contemporary economics, with the interesting and significant exception of those who still work in a Marxian tradition. It is, perhaps, in carrying on the intellectual tradition that informs the present-day discipline of political economy, and injecting into it the distinctive Austrian themes of subjectivism and concern with the epistemic role of market institutions, that Hayek has made his chief contribution to intellectual life. Even if his own system of thought founders, his insights both contribute to the project of theorising social life as a whole that the Scottish philosophers initiated, and intimate a holistic perspective on the conditions and character of the market process from which conventional economics may still have something of fundamental importance to learn.

REFERENCES

Cohen, G A (1978). *Marx's Theory of History: A Defence* New York: Oxford University Press

Dunn, John (1985). *Rethinking Modern Political Theory* Cambridge University Press

Forbes, Duncan (1975). *Hume's Philosophical Politics* Cambridge University Press

Gray, John (1982). Philosophy, science, and myth in Marxism. *In Marx and Marxisms: Royal Institute of Philosophy Lectures* series 14 (ed) G H R Parkinson, pp 71–96. Cambridge University Press

—— (1986). *Hayek on Liberty,* 2d ed Oxford: Basil Blackwell

Hayek, F A (1952). *The Counterrevolution of Science* Glencoe, Ill, Free Press

—— (1960). *The Constitution of Liberty* University of Chicago Press

—— (1976a). *Individualism and Economic Order* London: Routledge & Kegan Paul

——(1976b). *Law, Legislation and Liberty: Vol 20 The Mirage of Social Justice* London: Routledge & Kegan Paul

—— (1978). *New Studies in Philosophy, Politics, Economics and the History of Ideas* London: Routledge & Kegan Paul

Polanyi, Michael (1951). *The Logic of Liberty* University of Chicago Press

—— (1962). *Personal Knowledge* London: Routledge & Kegan Paul

Shackle, G L S (1972). *Epistemics and Economics: A Critique of Economic Doctrine* Cambridge University Press

Winch, Donald (1978). *Adam Smith's Politics: An Essay in Historiographic Revision* Cambridge University Press

NOTES

1 See Gray (1986, pp 134–40).
2 Michael Polanyi invokes the idea of tacit knowledge in the context of an argument against central economic planning in his *Logic of Liberty* (1951, pp 114–22). The notion of tacit knowledge is developed in Polanyi's major work, *Personal Knowledge* (1962).
3 Hayek's evolutionary functionalism in respect of social institutions is discussed and criticised in Gray (1986, pp 135–8).
4 Hayek's conception of the natural selection of religions is advanced in his as yet unpublished work, *The Fatal Conceit: The Intellectual Error of Socialism.*
5 That Marx's historical materialism is a form of functionalism with affinities to Darwinian evolutionary theory has been argued by G A Cohen (1978) in his *Marx's Theory of History: A Defence.* I have criticised Cohen's Marxian evolutionary functionalism in my 'Philosophy, Science and Myth in Marxism' (Gray 1982, pp 71–96).
6 Hayek (1978, p 269) quotes this passage from Smith in his *New Studies in Philosophy, Politics, Economics, and the History of Ideas.*
7 For example, by Forbes (1975).
8 See Hayek (1976b) for an elaboration of this claim.
9 I refer here, of course, to the writings of Daniel Bell.
10 I have discussed the similarities and differences between Popper's views on scientific methodology and those of Hayek (Gray 1986, pp 10–13, 110–15, 136–7).
11 See Shackle's (1972, pp 28–39) masterpiece, *Epistemics and Economics: A Critique of Economic Doctrines,* on self-subsistent or non-self-subsistent sciences.
12 For Hayek's notion of pattern explanation and prediction, see Gray (1986, pp 79–81).

CHAPTER FOURTEEN

Rae on Political Economy

R W James

John Rae, Political Economist,
Vol I (Univ of Toronto Press, 1965)

In 1834, when Rae was thirty-eight years old, his book on political economy was published in Boston. Not only was this a major event in Rae's life, but his work was ultimately to exert a considerable influence on the development of the theory of capital. While it is desirable to examine certain aspects of Rae's contribution to political economy, it is not the intention to summarise or interpret the whole of Rae's book.[1] The immediate availability of the text makes this unnecessary. Nor does it appear desirable at this point to undertake an analysis of Rae's place in the history of economic thought. To some extent he borrowed and assimilated ideas from other people, but to trace such influences would involve a long digression and a great deal of conjecture. Instead it is proposed to single out some particular aspects of his work and to offer some explanatory remarks. The aspects dealt with will be limited to: (1) Rae's critique of Adam Smith; (2) Rae's theory of capital; (3) Rae on invention; (4) Rae on tariff protection; (5) Rae on luxury.

RAE'S CRITIQUE OF ADAM SMITH

In order to understand Rae's economics, it is essential first of all to appreciate his fundamental assumption concerning the growth of the capital or the wealth of a community. His contention is that there is a fundamental distinction between the factors governing the wealth of individuals and the factors governing the wealth of nations. His introductory remarks contrast two diverse policies designed to increase the national wealth. First there is the policy founded on the view that the encouragement of commerce and manufactures leads to an increase in national wealth and naturally therefore to an increase in the wealth of the individuals composing the nation. 'This view of the matter leads directly to a system of unceasing regulation and restraint.'[2] Second, there is an alternative claim that increases in the wealth of individuals must necessarily lead to greater national wealth. Any restraint or hindrance which impairs the ability of individuals to become wealthy must therefore be avoided lest it in turn leads to a diminution of the national wealth. This, of course, was Adam Smith's heroic contribution to the political life of the Western world.

Rae argues that both these systems were based on the faulty assumption of the identity of individual and national wealth, but he singled out Adam Smith for attack. He explained:

> My main object, in this book, is to show that the notion of the exact identity of the causes giving rise to individual and national wealth, on which the reasonings and arguments of Adam Smith all along depend, is erroneous, that consequently the doctrines he has engrafted on it, cannot be thus maintained, and are inconsistent with facts admitted by himself.[3]

There was nothing essentially new in Rae's argument. The same general ideas had been argued by the Earl of Lauderdale in his *Public Wealth* in 1804 and by Jeremy Bentham in his letter to Adam Smith on projects in arts written in 1787. Rae quotes from both these authors and was probably familiar with their criticisms.

Rae emphasised that individuals could become rich by the acquisition of larger shares of existing wealth while nations were constrained to create new wealth before they could become richer. Hard work and parsimony might help a person to become wealthy but the wealth of the nation as a whole could only grow with the help of the 'inventive faculty.' The implications of this view for economic policy were immediately clear. It was a cardinal requirement of policy to foster invention and to facilitate the transference of inventions from one country to another. This view further justified the intervention of the state in helping new industries by protective duties, bounties and other financial encouragement. Moreover, Rae believed that it was desirable for the state to encourage and support financially industrial research which would lead to new inventions. Rae's essential criterion for assessing economic policy as well as social behaviour was the effect on the accumulation of capital.

Rae's attitude to government intervention was in sharp contrast to the views expressed by many of the followers of Adam Smith. He quotes as an example a comment by Dugald Stewart in his *Account of the Life and Writings of Dr. Smith*:

> Little else is requisite to carry a state to the highest degree of opulence from the lowest barbarism but peace, easy taxes, and a tolerable administration of justice; all the rest being brought about by the natural course of things. All governments which thwart this natural course, which force things into another channel, or which endeavour to arrest the progress of society at a particular point, are unnatural, and to support themselves are obliged to be oppressive and tyrannical.[4]

Rae conceived that governments had, in fact, a real obligation to undertake policies which would benefit the economic welfare of the community. He contended that there existed certain social or economic laws which could be determined by truly scientific analysis and that these could lead legislators to the adoption of wise and beneficial policies. Rae had a deeprooted belief in man's perfectibility and in the possibilities of improvements in the intelligence and morality of a society. In one place he says specifically:

> . . . the result of a successful inquiry into the nature of wealth, would terminate in affording the means of exposing the errors that legislators had committed from not attending to all the circumstances connected with the growth of that wealth, whose progress it had been their aim to advance, and would so teach them, not that they ought to remain inactive, but how they may act safely, and advantageously; and that thus, it would maintain the analogy running through the whole of man's connexion with the trains of events going on about him, the course of which he governs by ascertaining exactly what it is. That here, as elsewhere, his advance in knowledge would show him his power, not his impotence.[5]

In part Rae's criticisms of Adam Smith stemmed from a fundamental difference in philosophic method. Rae was strongly influenced by the views of Francis Bacon on scientific method and argues vigorously that Smith's philosophy was not in accordance with the true inductive method described by Bacon. Rae claims that Smith's philosophy was essentially explanatory or systematic, saying:

> To me it appears that this philosophy is that of explanation and system, and that his speculations are not to be considered as inductive investigations and expositions of the real principles guiding the successions of phenomena, but as successful efforts to arrange with regularity, according to common and pre-conceived notions, a multiplicity of known facts.[6]

Rae quotes from Adam Smith's *History of Astronomy* the comment, 'A philosophical system is an imaginary machine invented to connect together in the fancy those different movements and effects, which are already in reality performed,' and emphasises that it is directly opposed to the views in Bacon's *Novum Organum*.

Rae summarises his dissent in the following trenchant paragraphs:

> . . . in my opinion the disciples and followers of Adam Smith, in claiming for the speculations contained in the Wealth of Nations, and for the doctrines they have founded on them, the rank of an experimental science, the conclusions of which are entitled to the same credence with other experimental sciences, act injudiciously, and by insisting on pretensions which are unfounded, injure the cause of that philosopher and conceal his real merits. If we view his philosophical system of the Wealth of Nations, or indeed any of his philosophical systems, as he views every such system, 'as an imaginary machine invented to connect together in the fancy those different movements and effects which are already in reality performed,' nothing of the sort can be more beautiful. A clear, orderly and extensive view is given of a vast number of interesting and important facts, connected by a few familiar principles. A great body of knowledge is thus brought before the mind in a shape which it can readily grasp, and easily command. The object being not to discover, but to arrange and methodize all the subordinate principles of the system are artfully bent so as to embrace the phenomena, and care is taken that the

imagination be not shocked by a view of matters that shall seem irreconcilable to the aspect of affairs which the contemplation of the world of life itself presents. Nor is it to be disputed that a general system of the sort, besides the pleasure and the advantage derived from it, is likely to be nearer the truth than speculations of the same nature, confined to particular parts.

The case, however, is completely altered, when the loose and popular principles on which such a system proceeds, are adopted as demonstrative axioms, the discoveries of real science, and are carried out to their extreme consequences. Their original purpose is then altogether changed, and instead of serving to bring before the mind a collection of facts, they lead it farther and farther away from truth and reality, into the barren and wearisome regions of mere verbal abstractions.[7]

RAE'S THEORY OF CAPITAL

Rae saw with great clarity the interaction of capital accumulation and social conditions. His interest in this problem stemmed from his youthful and ambitious scheme to study the causes which have made man 'what he is in various countries or has been in various times.'[8] Even before he emigrated, Rae obviously had some tentative views on the role of wealth in society and he found in Canada many opportunities for observing different kinds of societies in several stages of development. He became familiar with the primitive societies of the Indians, with the rough life in the backwoods, and with the characteristics of urban society in the colonial cities of Montreal and York. Much of Rae's theory of capital was the product of his own observations, confirmed by his knowledge of the writings of travellers in other undeveloped countries. He shows considerable familiarity with social conditions among the Romans, the ancient Germans and particularly the Chinese. His principal purpose was to analyse the factors which determined the accumulation of capital. His analysis is notable for its generality, its subtlety, and above all for its essential correctness.

Rae's theory of capital accumulation will be summarised under three broad headings: (a) the nature of capital; (b) the supply of capital; (c) the demand for capital. It must be recognised in advance that any summary of Rae is liable to be inadequate and distorted. The lucid sweep of his ideas is lost as well as the excellent literary quality of his writings.

(a) The nature of capital
Rae's concept of capital was amorphous and all-embracing. He adopted the term 'instrument' to describe durable capital and all other physical transformations whose use resulted in the occurrence of future events. He explained his choice of terminology in the following words:

> ... all those changes which man makes, in the form or arrangements of the parts of material objects, for the purpose of supplying his future wants, and which derive their power of doing this from his knowledge of the course of events, and the changes which his labor, guided by his reason, is hence enabled to make in the issue of these events, may be termed instruments.[9]

He explains that the term instruments as commonly used refers to mechanical devices such as levers, wedges, and more complex machines but that, despite the inconvenience, he needs a much more general concept. He gives an agricultural illustration and points out that the field, the wheat, the flour and the bread are all instruments. In short, any means to an end is an instrument. What are ordinarily treated as consumption goods are obviously instruments. Rae specifically refers to instruments which can easily be moved from place to place and exchanged. This class of instruments he calls goods or commodities.

All instruments have three characteristics in common. These are:

> 1 They are all either *directly* formed by human labor, or *indirectly* through the aid of other instruments themselves formed by human labor . . .
> 2 All instruments bring to pass, or tend, or help, to bring to pass events supplying some of the wants of man, and are then exhausted . . .
> 3 Between the formation and exhaustion of instruments a space of time intervenes. This necessarily happens because all events take place in time. Sometimes that space extends to years, sometimes to months, occasionally to shorter periods, but it always exists.[10]

Rae introduces two other terminological points in connection with instruments. First, he defines the *capacity* of an instrument as its power to produce events supplying human wants or a quantitative equivalent of the events. Second, he uses the term *exhaustion* to refer to the process by which instruments are again transformed into materials or dissipated. Food and fuel are exhausted quickly while machinery is worn out or exhausted gradually.

He then considers the question of measuring the capacity of instruments. The idea that capacity can be usefully measured in physical terms is rejected. Instead he proposes to measure capacity in terms of units of labour cost. He reasons that an equivalence exists between the events emanating from an instrument and the labour necessary to produce the same events in the absence of the instrument. He assumes a highly simplified system in which real wages are constant and uniform in a given society but different in different societies. He disclaims any intention of investigating the principles which govern wage rates and their variations and emphasises that his rigorous assumptions are intended merely to simplify the exposition.

The cost of production of instruments is also measured solely in terms of labour. Rae notes that labour alone seldom can be used to form instruments and that the co-operation of other instruments is necessary. However, he suggests as a further measure of simplification that the contribution of these co-operating instruments can be measured by an equivalent amount of labour. All this amounts to adopting a standardised and abstract daily wage as a *numéraire*.

There are thus three basic concepts in Rae's theory of capital accumulation. The first is their original cost measured in terms of labour inputs; the second is their capacity expressed as the equivalent of labour costs; and the third is the length of time elapsing between their formation and their exhaustion. He proposes to develop a method of classifying instruments which will express all possible interrelations of these three magnitudes.

This is done by arranging all instruments in a series, each term of which represents the number of years it will take for the instrument to yield double its original cost of formation. The place of an instrument in the series determines what he calls its *order*. He represents the series by the capital letters of the alphabet followed by the small letters and gives the following example: 'Instruments in the order C, in three years issue in events equivalent to double the cost of formation; of the order D, in four years; of the order Z, in twenty-six years; of the order *a*, in twenty-seven years, &c.'[11] He goes on to say that instruments in the neighbourhood of the order A will be said to belong to 'the more quickly returning orders' while instruments around the order of Z or beyond will be classed as 'the more slowly returning orders.' His general rule is that the proximity of an instrument to the order A is inversely related to the cost of production and the period of exhaustion and directly to its capacity. Rae freely admits that an instrument may not yield double its cost of production in an integral number of years and states that the order may in fact be between two succeeding members of the series. He provides also for the case in which an instrument is exhausted before it has yielded double its original cost. Here he derives the order by assuming a prolongation of the period of exhaustion until the necessary increase in the yield has been attained. The converse case occurs when an instrument yields more than double its cost before it is exhausted. Under such circumstances, its order will be determined by the length of time it took for the returns to amount to double the cost.

Rae devotes some attention to the assumption that all instruments are formed at one point of time and exhausted at another. He admits that the process of formation and exhaustion usually extends over a period of time, but contends that some average point can be taken to represent either the time of formation or exhaustion.[12] Rae formulates quite clearly the notion of an average period of production and an average period of exhaustion, but he attaches no economic significance to them.

Rae's conception that all instruments can be assigned a certain order is merely another way of saying that all instruments can be ranked according to their rate of yield. Each of Rae's orders corresponds to some unique rate of yield and it is a simple matter to derive the relationship between orders and rates of yield from the formula $(1+r)^x = 2$, where x is the order of the instrument, expressed in years, and r the percentage rate of yield. For example, the order A corresponds to a rate of yield of 100 per cent per annum, the order B to a rate of yield of 41–2 per cent per annum and the order N to slightly more than 5 per cent per annum.[13] It is now more usual to speak of rates of return, but it should be borne in mind that Rae's formulation was quite precise, though the terminology is unfamiliar and a little awkward.

To summarise briefly, Rae's concept of capital was that it consisted of instruments, each of which could be assigned to a certain order and each of which became exhausted and reverted to materials or simply disappeared in a specified period of time. The durability of instruments, has a central place in his theory of capital accumulation, and his analysis of the supply and demand factors influencing durability is the core of Rae's contribution to economic theory. He first considers the supply factors.

(b) *The supply of capital*

Rae distinguishes conceptually between durability and efficiency, both of which affect the capacity of instruments, but he concludes that increased durability usually implies increased efficiency, except for certain types of wearing apparel and hand tools or utensils. He discusses the characteristics of dwellings for purposes of illustration, saying:

> A dwelling-house is an instrument, aiding to bring to an issue events of various classes. It more or less completely prevents rain, damp, and the extremes of cold and heat, from penetrating to the space included within its area. It preserves all other instruments contained within it, in comparative safety. It gives those who inhabit it the power of carrying on unmolested, various domestic occupations, and of enjoying, undisturbed by the gaze of strangers, any of the gratifications or amusements of life of which they may be able and desirous to partake. Events of these sorts, it may bring to pass, for a longer or shorter time, or to a greater or less extent, within the same time. In the former case, the durability is increased, in the latter, the efficiency; in both, the capacity is augmented.[14]

He goes on to compare dwellings built of wood, lath, mud, plaster, and paper which would be habitable only for a few months or years with dwellings that might last for two or three centuries 'by employing stone, iron and the most durable woods, and joining and compacting them together, with great nicety and accuracy.' Assuming no change in efficiency, an increase in durability amounts to an increase in capacity which means that, in the cases of dwellings in particular, durability and capacity can be extended indefinitely.

But, to give increased durability to an instrument requires the expenditure of additional labour. Rae then undertakes to examine the relation between the marginal return from an increase in durability and the associated marginal cost. His analysis is in terms of undiscounted marginal returns and marginal cost and he concludes that when these two magnitudes are equal, increased durability will shift the instrument to a more slowly returning order. He compares a dwelling built to last thirty years with a similar dwelling costing twice as much and lasting sixty years. If the thirty-year house is of the order O, the sixty-year house will be of an order lying between X and Y. As durability is increased, under conditions where the marginal cost and the undiscounted marginal returns are equal, the rate of yield declines. Rae concluded that the marginal cost of increased durability must decrease in a geometric ratio if the rate of yield of an instrument is to remain unchanged. His own words are:

> If, therefore, continual additions be made to the durability of an instrument, it cannot be preserved at an order of equally quick return, unless the several augmentations be communicated to it, by an expenditure diminishing in a geometrical ratio; that is, in a ratio becoming indefinitely less, as it is continued.[15]

Rae saw dimly the significance of the equality of discounted marginal returns and marginal cost, but unfortunately he immediately denied that the implied behaviour of cost was possible. He visualised the process of geometrically decreasing marginal cost continuing indefinitely and concluded that this was an absurdity. If he had not thought in terms of indefinite durability, he might have stated the marginal conditions governing durability correctly.

As it was, Rae stated clearly the reasons for the increasing cost of imparting durability to instruments. His reasoning was that men use the cheapest and most abundant materials first and then must turn to more expensive processes or rely on diminishing and more costly supplies. He says:

> ... as the stock of materials which any society possesses, is limited, its members, if we suppose them to acquire no additional knowledge of the powers of those materials, and yet to add continually to the amount of instruments they form out of them, must at length have recourse to such as are either operated on with greater difficulty, or bring about desired events more sparingly or tardily. The efficiency of the instruments produced must therefore be generated by greater cost; that is, they must pass to orders of slower return.[16]

To this statement of the principle of diminishing returns Rae added a comment on the influence of technological change. He explained that new processes were continually being developed and that the more durable an instrument the greater the chances would be that it would become obsolescent and unable to compete with more recently created and improved instruments.

He concluded that a fall in the rate of yield was inevitable when the durability of instruments was increased, provided that technical knowledge was unchanged and the kind of materials available the same. The influence of technical progress on the formation of instruments is, of course, profound. Rae notes that the ability of barbarous nations to increase their capital equipment is limited but in technically advanced societies there does not seem to be an assignable limit to the amount of new instruments that could be formed. He says:

> One would not find it very easy to say, how much might be added, to the durability and efficiency, of dwelling-houses alone. The amount of the capacity for the facilitation of future transport, which might be embodied in railroads, returning ultimately much more than the cost of their formation, is incalculable; as is also, the degree to which mining operations might be extended. Even supposing all these, and many other instruments, to have acquired a vastly increased extent, both as concerns durability and efficiency; instead of limiting their farther increase, it would seem likely, rather to open up a still wider space, for the exertion of future industry in the formation of others.[17]

But, Rae says, so long as the state of the arts is stationary, the process of capital accumulation carries instruments gradually to the more slowly returning orders, that is, the marginal rate of yield falls. There is a limit to the willingness of individuals and societies to construct instruments of the more slowly returning orders and this is the decisive factor which retards capital accumulation. Rae then turns his attention to the circumstances which influence societies to halt the process of capital accumulation once a limiting rate of return has been reached.

(c) The demand for capital

Rae's central argument was that the formation of an instrument implied the sacrifice of a present good for a future good. Instruments characteristically yield future returns greater than present sacrifices; otherwise they will not be formed. The construction of instruments will continue in a society until a certain order is attained or alternatively until a certain rate of return is achieved. A point is finally reached where the willingness to make continued present sacrifices ceases and then the formation of instruments stops. Rae refers to the propensity to sacrifice present goods for future goods as the *effective desire of accumulation.* His explanation of this phenomenon deserves quotation:

> Were life to endure for ever, were the capacity to enjoy in perfection all its goods, both mental and corporeal, to be prolonged with it, and were we guided solely by the dictates of reason, there could be no limit to the formation of means for future gratification, till our utmost wishes were supplied. A pleasure to be enjoyed, or a pain to be endured, fifty or a hundred years hence, would be considered deserving the same attention as if it were to befall us fifty or a hundred minutes hence, and the sacrifice of a smaller present good, for a greater future good, would be readily made, to whatever period that futurity might extend. But life, and the power to enjoy it, are the most uncertain of all things, and we are not guided altogether by reason. We know not the period when death may come upon us, but we know that it may come in a few days, and must come in a few years. Why then be providing goods that cannot be enjoyed until times, which, though not very remote, may never come to us, or until times still more remote, and which we are convinced we shall never see. If life, too, is of uncertain duration and the time that death comes between us and all our possessions unknown, the approaches of old age are at least certain, and are dulling, day by day, the relish of every pleasure.
>
> A mere reasonable regard to their own interest, would, therefore, place the present very far above the future, in the estimation of most men. But, it is besides to be remarked, that such pleasures as may now be enjoyed, generally awaken a passion strongly prompting to the partaking of them. The actual presence of the immediate object of desire in the mind, by exciting the attention, seems to rouse all the faculties, as it were, to fix their view on it, and leads them to a very lively conception of the enjoyments which it offers to their instant possession. The prospects of future good, which future years may hold out to us, seem at such a moment dull and dubious, and are apt to be slighted, for objects on which the daylight is falling strongly, and showing us in all their freshness just within our grasp. There is no man perhaps, to whom a good to be enjoyed to day, would not seem of very different importance, from one exactly similar to be enjoyed twelve years hence, even though the arrival of both were equally certain.[18]

Why then, Rae asks, do people save when the benefits of future goods are not only uncertain but probably inferior? His answer is that people are not guided solely by selfish interests but are influenced by what he calls the social and benevolent affections. Man's pleasures derive from his ties to 'his kindred, his friends, his country, or his race.' Even when he dies, his sacrifices will not be lost if they continue to benefit the living. Rae admits that these motives are sometimes feeble and that 'the world is full of deceit hollowness and unhappiness,' but the existence of social and benevolent affections is nevertheless a real and important influence.

This influence is supplemented by reasoning and reflective habits arising out of the intellectual powers. The joys of the moment are tempered by reflection on the future and its prospects. The more man is concerned with the welfare of others, the more desirable it seems to make provision for the future. Intellectual power and affection for others strengthen and confirm the desire for accumulation.

Rae mentions a third influence—security. A healthy climate, a safe occupation, and expectancy of long life all make it more probable that the fruits of sacrifice will be gathered. Frugality is strongly influenced by geography and occupations. Sailors and soldiers are prodigals and so are the inhabitants of the West Indies, New Orleans, and the East Indies. The general prevalence of law and order and peace and tranquility affect the habit of saving. On the other hand, 'war and pestilence have always waste and luxury among the other evils that follow in their train.'

Rae's own summary of the three circumstances governing the desire to accumulate are:

> 1. The prevalence throughout the society, of the social and benevolent affections, or, of that principle, which, under whatever name it may be known, leads us to derive happiness, from the good we communicate to others.
> 2. The extent of the intellectual powers, and the consequent prevalence of habits of reflection, and prudence, in the minds of the members of the society.
> 3. The stability of the condition of the affairs of the society, and the reign of law and order throughout it. [19]

Rae takes note of the contemporary and earlier view that self-interest is the principal motive for saving. He deals with this as a special case, saying:

> If we confine our attention to the present times, and to particular parts of the globe, this may be readily admitted. Now, and in those places, a prudent regard to self-interest would doubtless prompt many individuals to cooperate effectively in the increase of the general means of enjoyment. But there is nothing more apt to mislead us, when investigating the causes determining the motions of any great system, than to take our station at some particular point in it, and, examining the appearances there presented to us, to suppose that they must be precisely similar through the whole sphere of action. Because, in Great Britain, a regard to mere self interest, may now prompt to a course of action leading to making a large provision for the wants of others, we are, in reality , no more warranted to conclude that it will do so always, and in every place, than were the ancients warranted to conclude, because, in their particular communities, the pursuit of wealth commonly generated evil, that it must therefore do so always and in every place. [20]

Rae's discussion of these sociological influences on the accumulation of capital is a brilliant piece of analysis and is brightened considerably by his gift for descriptive anecdotes. He shows here the broad sweep of his mind and his understanding of human motivation. This is deservedly the best known aspect of Rae's work. It is not usually recognised that it is only a part of an integrated theory of the supply and demand factors influencing capital accumulation. Because of its generality, his capital theory applied equally to the North American Indians and the ancient Romans.

Rae had the advantage of being able to observe the economic characteristics of an underdeveloped country at first hand and his knowledge of Canadian conditions in the 1820s and early 1830s clearly influenced his views of capital formation. The construction of roads and other public works was of major economic and political significance to the backwoods communities of Upper Canada and the durability of such instruments an immediate and practical issue. Confirmation of this appears in the following statement in *Lord Durham's Report;*

> I know, indeed, of no difference in the machinery of government in the old and new world that strikes an European more forcibly than the apparently undue importance which the business of constructing public works appears to occupy in American legislation. In speaking of the character of a government, its merits appear to be estimated by the public works which it has carried into effect. If an individual is asked how his own legislature has acted, he will generally say what roads or bridges it has made, or neglected to make, in his own district; and if he is consulted about changes in a constitution, he seems to try their soundness by calculating whether his neighbourhood would get more or better roads and bridges under the existing, or the proposed system.[21]

Rae's analysis of the role of durability in capital formation and the influence of sociological factors on capital accumulation is applicable with very little modification to the problems of underdeveloped countries in the middle of the twentieth century.

RAE ON INVENTION

The sections of Rae's book dealing with invention are a remarkable contribution to the literature of economics. From a purely literary point of view his work in this area is marked by lucidity and grace which is at least equalled by the generality and relevance of his economic analysis. Basically his concern is with the influence of invention on capital accumulation, a theme which he introduced in his early discussion of the difference between the wealth of individuals and the wealth of a society.

After a long and penetrating historical discussion of invention, Rae summarises the relation of invention to capital in a few pages. In essence, he sees invention as a force which makes labour more effective and thus reduces production costs. This not only increases the return on specific instruments, but the benefits are diffused throughout society. The instruments of the society are carried to more productive orders and its absolute capital and stock are correspondingly increased.

Invention and improvement permit the use of 'inferior or more stubborn materials' in production, and this process will continue until the total instruments arrive at an order corresponding to the effective desire of accumulation. The introduction of improvements leads to increases in the rate of return on capital and this contrasts with high rates of return associated with a low effective desire of accumulation in certain countries. He suggests that profits will generally be high in countries which are becoming wealthier and cites as an example the high rates of profit in North America arising out of 'the unintermitting transfer to that continent of European arts, and from the generation of new arts in the country itself.'

Rae is at his most eloquent in his comments on the personal characteristics of inventors. He speaks of the difference between 'real inventers' and 'mere compilers and repeaters' and goes on:

> It may be observed, too, that as of bards, so of authors, they who are mere compilers and repeaters, may be more successful than they who are real inventers, they may better suit their productions to particular times, tastes, and exigencies, and, besides, they can always find an audience prepared, by previous training, to applaud.
>
> The tendency of these pursuits is to withdraw those occupied in them, from the daily business of society. They fill not the places open for them, and which they are expected to fill; even when necessity pushes them for a time into them, and compels them to mingle with the crowd, they are marked as not belonging to it. Abstract and scientific truth can only be discovered, by deep and absorbing meditation; imperfectly at first discerned, through the medium of its dull capacities, the intellect slowly, and cautiously, not without much of doubt, and many unsuccessful essays, succeeds in lifting the veil that hides it. The procedure is altogether unlike the prompt determination, and ready confidence, of the man of action, and generally unfits, to a greater or less degree, for performing well the part. He, again, who dwells in the world of possible moral beauty and perfection, moves awkwardly, rashly, and painfully, through this of every day life, he is ever mistaking his own way and jostling others in theirs. To the possessors of fortune, these habits only give eccentricity; they affect those of scanty fortune, or without fortune, with more serious ills. Unable to fight their way ably, cautiously, and perseveringly, through the bustle of life, poverty, dependence, and all their attendant evils, are most commonly their lot.
>
> 'Toil, envy, want, the patron, and the jail,'
>
> are calamities, from the actual endurance of some of which, or the dread of it, they are seldom free. These, however, they share with other men; there are some peculiarly their own.[22]

The inventive faculty and the social and benevolent affections in a society are likely to be associated.

> ... though, in the individual, manifestations of the inventive faculty imply a superiority in some of the intellectual powers, they rather imply, in the society a preponderance of the social and benevolent affections. It is this general acuteness of moral sensation, and lively sympathy consequently with the pleasures arising to the individual, from the success of exertions for purposes of general good, that can alone excite, and nourish, the enthusiasm of genius.[23]

The progress of invention and the principles governing the accumulation of wealth are thus related but there are opposing forces at work in periods of social disturbance:

> Whatever disturbs, or threatens to disturb, the established order of things, by exposing the property of the members of the society to danger, and diminishing the

certainty of its future possession, diminishes also the desire to accumulate it. Intestine commotions, persecutions, wars, internal oppression, or outward violence, either, therefore, altogether destroy, or, at least, very much impair the strength of the effective desire of accumulation. On the contrary, they excite the inventive faculty to activity. . . . Whatever, therefore, breaks the wonted order of events, and exposes the necessity, or the possibility, of connecting them by some other means, strongly stimulates invention. The slumbering faculties rouse themselves to meet the unexpected exigence, and the possibility of giving a new, and more perfect order to elements not yet fixed, animates to a boldness of enterprise, which were rashness, had they assumed their determined places. Hence, as has often been remarked, periods of great changes in kingdoms or governments, are the seasons when genius breaks forth in brightest lustre. The beneficial effects of what are termed revolutions, are, perhaps, chiefly to be traced, to their thus wakening the torpid powers; the troubling of the waters they bring about, undoes the palsy of the mind. [24]

Rae on Tariff Protection

It would be difficult to improve on Rae's own summary of the factors influencing the growth of capital. Capital is increased, in his words:

I. By whatever promotes the general intelligence and morality of the society; and that, consequently, the moral and intellectual education of the people makes an important element in its progress . . .

II. By whatever promotes invention;

1. By advancing the progress of science and art within the community;

2. By the transfer from other communities of the sciences and arts there generated:

III. By whatever prevents the dissipation in luxury, of any portion of the funds of the community. [25]

The way in which 'the legislator' can influence the growth of capital will depend on legislative influences on these factors, but Rae purposely limited his consideration of the influence of the legislator in two areas: (a) the transfer of foreign arts to his own country; (b) the diversion to useful purposes of funds which would otherwise be dissipated in luxury.

Early in his book Rae had already introduced the question of international transfers of technical knowledge in his critique of Adam Smith. In that place, Rae argued at some length that in certain instances advantages in production could be acquired by borrowing methods developed in other countries. If by legislative action useful arts could be transferred from a distant country in such a way as to provide commodities at least as cheaply as they could be imported, there appeared to be ample justification for such a policy. The treatment at this place is fairly discursive, but near the end of the book his arguments become more succinct.

Here he repeated his contention that there were situations in which it was proper for the legislator to encourage the transfer of technical knowledge or 'useful arts' from one country to another. He enumerates three advantages of such transfers: (a) saving of the cost of transporting commodities; (b) the stimulation of invention with its consequently beneficial effects on capital formation; (c) the avoidance of interruption in the supply of essential imports because of wars or other causes. He states his case carefully, warning:

> But, while the legislator is called on to act, he is also called on to act cautiously, and to regulate his proceedings by an attentive consideration of the progress of events. He is never justifiable in attempting to transfer arts yielding utilities from foreign countries to his own, unless he have sufficient reason to conclude that they will ultimately lessen the cost of the commodities they produce, or are of such a nature, that the risk of waste to the stock of the community, from a sudden interruption to their importation from abroad, is sufficiently great to warrant the probable expense, both of the transfer and of maintaining the manufacture at home. It is his business first to ascertain these points, and to regulate his proceedings accordingly.[26]

Rae refers to several historical instances of 'injudicious conduct of the legislator,' and goes on to emphasise two factors which should encourage the transfer of a foreign art, an abundance of raw materials and great strength of the accumulative principle.

As practical devices Rae mentions premiums, bounties, and duties, suggesting that premiums may be useful to test the practicability of a transfer. If the transfer appears feasible it then may become desirable to introduce bounties or duties.

> In this way real capital, and healthy enterprise are directed to the art, the difficulties attending its introduction overcome in the shortest possible space, and the commodities yielded by it are produced at less outlay, and afforded at a less price than that, at which they were before imported.[27]

It should be emphasised that Rae's comments are a thoughtful and sophisticated statement of what came to be known later as the 'infant industry' argument for protection. It is, in fact, difficult to discover anything in Rae's detailed argument that is objectionable. Any reasonable person, no matter how ardent his free-trade convictions, would be compelled to agree with the justice of Rae's contentions.

Certainly Rae clearly recognised the advantages of freedom of trade. In one place, he says:

> In regard to articles supplying real wants, the more easy and unconstrained the communication, the more extended the production, the freer the competition, the farther, as we have seen, are the stocks of instruments of the societies exchanging carried towards the more quickly returning orders. Every step in advance in the course is equivalent, subject only to the risk of the communication being interrupted, to a real improvement.[28]

What is really remarkable is that Rae in the postscript to his preface appeared to ally himself with some of the crude protectionist arguments current in the United States in the 1820s and 1830s. In a way belying the tenor of the material in the text, Rae said at the beginning of the book in the postscript to the preface:

The practical bearings of that system [protection] on the condition of things in this republic, have been discussed so often, and with so much ability, that probably few new arguments or facts concerning it can be brought forward by any one, least of all can they be expected from a foreigner. Although, therefore, I look on the effects of the policy pursued by the legislature of the United States, as affording the best practical illustration hitherto existing of the correctness of some of the principles I maintain, I have scarcely at all referred to them for that purpose, but have contented myself with showing how the benefits resulting from the operations of the legislature, in this and in other similar cases, are to be accounted for. I have thus omitted much matter that would have appeared, had the work been published in England, but which, it seemed to me, would be at least superfluous here.[29]

As will be seen, the mere position of Rae's carelessly phrased comments on the protectionist controversy were to convey an unfortunate and largely erroneous impression to some of his readers.

RAE ON LUXURY

Rae suggested that vanity was one of the mainsprings of human motivation and that it had a retarding effect on capital accumulation. The mere desire of superiority over others stimulates the desire for 'commodities of which the consumption is conspicuous' and leads in some instances to an extravagant passion 'to have what others cannot have.' The social and benevolent affections and intellectual powers, on the other hand, counter and keep within bounds the indulgence of mere vanity. Rae suggests on the basis of historical evidence that vanity and luxury are not usual in societies where the effective desire of accumulation is high. Conversely, in savage societies, there is a marked propensity to make great sacrifices 'to have the means of decking their persons or habitations with something rare and costly.'

The difficulty with luxuries, Rae pointed out, was that their production left the absolute capital of a society unchanged. For the superiority enjoyed by one person from the acquisition of luxuries would be balanced by a corresponding feeling of inferiority on the part of another. Nevertheless, vanity may have some beneficial by-products if it stimulates the spread of invention. He suggests that certain exotic luxuries have been found to have a 'substratum of utility,' and mentions as examples, soap, silk and cotton fabrics, and glass.

Rae explains that scarcity and high price are essential characteristics of luxury. His comment about the celebrated northern Duchess who is quoted as saying, 'What a pity that eggs were not a sixpence the piece,' is indicative of his view. He implies that the demand for luxuries is such that an increase in price may lead to an increase in consumption. Conversely, the demand for luxuries may fall with a decrease in price. On the basis of his findings Rae had some original and stimulating suggestions respecting the taxation of luxuries.

In essence, Rae's point is that taxes on pure luxuries might yield substantial revenues without imposing a burden on the consumer. His illustrations, which feature alcoholic liquors, are interesting:

> In Great Britain rum is, I believe, at least double the price of whisky, and brandy still higher, the consumption, therefore, of the dearer article instead of the cheaper, must arise nearly altogether from vanity. In Canada, again, the price at which Scotch whisky is sold, is double the price of rum, and considerably above the price of brandy. The excess of its price above these other liquors must, therefore, be considered a luxury.[30]

In an accompanying footnote he explains that the price of Scotch whisky is ten shillings per gallon and Canadian whisky from two to three shillings. He recognises that taxes or duties designed to fall on luxuries, must be introduced very gradually:

> Men have generally a high opinion of the reasonableness of their conduct, and the correctness of their taste. They are apt to fancy that there is a real and very great enjoyment in expenses, which, in truth, have scarce any thing to recommend them but the gratification they afford to vanity. In like manner, when any article rises suddenly and greatly in price, when in their power, they are prone to adopt some substitute and relinquish the use of it. . . . Hence, were a high duty at once imposed on any particular wine, or any particular sort of cotton fabric, it might have the effect of diminishing the consumption very greatly, or stopping it entirely. Whereas, were the tax at first very slight, and then slowly augmented, the reasoning powers not being startled, vanity, instead of flying off to some other objects, would be apt to apply itself to them as affording a convenient means of gratification.[31]

He concludes his argument with a sensible and clear statement:

> As the great mass of commodities are in part utilities, in part luxuries, so, in transferring the manufacture of any of them from one country to another, it very frequently happens that, in as far as the article in question has real utility, the domestic soon equals the foreign variety. It is chiefly in a laborious finish, for the most part the result of the demands of vanity, that the former falls behind the latter. In such instances the operation of transferring the art from one country to another, by means of a protective duty, takes either very little, or nothing, from the revenue of individuals, and makes, it may be, a considerable addition to that of the legislator. Its general effects on the funds of the community, are directly, and indirectly, to advance the absolute capital of the society by the introduction of a new art, and, during the process, to give a considerable revenue to the legislator for the attainment of public objects, without encroaching at all, or but in a very slight degree, on the returns made by the industry or stocks of individuals.[32]

It is tempting to suggest, on the basis of some of Rae's comments, that he anticipated a great deal of modern economics. He did offer some surprisingly acute observations, but it may be unfair to emphasise Rae's overdone role as a forerunner of others. His work can be judged on its own merits. One point should perhaps be emphasised. Rae wove into his work erudite and interesting discussions of such things as luxury and conspicuous consumption,[33] the division of labour, taxation, the cost of production, and above all invention. But there is an essential unity about his work because nearly all his ideas are directly related to his theory of capital accumulation. The effect on capital accumulation of various modes of social behaviour including the activities of legislative bodies is Rae's touchstone.

NOTES

1 Some aspects have already been dealt with elsewhere. See, for example, the admirable article by Craufurd D W Goodwin, 'John Rae: Undiscovered Exponent of Canadian Banks', *Canadian Banker*, LXVI, Winter 1959, 110–15.

2 *New Principles*, 7.

3 *Ibid.* 8.

4 *Ibid.* 358.

5 *Ibid.* 361–2.

6 *Ibid.* 331.

7 *Ibid.* 350–1.

8 *Ibid.* iv.

9 *Ibid.* 87.

10 *Ibid.* 91–3.

11 *Ibid.* 101.

12 Rae was influenced by the contemporary view that land had some special indestructible or inexhaustible quality which set it apart from other instruments. He stated that the act of clearing land or rendering it fit for cultivation transformed it into an instrument of indefinite life. The tilling and seeding of the land forms another instrument which is subject to exhaustion. The distinction is ingenious but specious. It is strange how he could have proposed this after living in Canada where he must have seen cleared land revert to the bush after a relatively short period of neglect.

13 Rae shows the equivalence between orders and annual rates of return in *New Principles*, 195.

14 *Ibid.* 110.

15 *Ibid.* 112. This conclusion is challenged in Gustaf Åkerman's *Realkapital und Kapitalzins* (Stockholm, 1923). Åkerman, borrowing explicitly from Rae, conceives of the labour costs of manufacturing durable capital as consisting of a series, the first term being the amount required to make the capital last one year, the next term being the amount required to extend the life of the capital for another year, and so on. Åkerman states a rule that the average of the terms in the series must be decreasing before it is profitable to extend the life of capital. Åkerman's claim that Rae is wrong (pp 22 and 118) seems to reflect some confusion between the average and marginal behaviour of the terms of the series. Rae's contention that the series must form a decreasing geometric progression is quite correct and at the same time a more stringent condition than Åkerman's. See also Knut Wicksell, *Lectures on Political Economy* (New York, 1934), I, 259–61.

16 *New Principles* 113.

17 *Ibid.* 116–17.

18 *Ibid.* 119–20.

19 *Ibid.* 124.

20 *Ibid.* 124–5

21 Lucas (ed) *Lord Durham's Report*, II, 90.

22 *New Principles*, 213–14.

23 *Ibid.* 222.

24 *Ibid.* 222–3.

25 *Ibid.* 362.

26 *Ibid.* 367.

27 *Ibid.* 368.

28 *Ibid.* 310.

29   *Ibid.* ix.
30   *Ibid.* 372–3.
31   *Ibid.* 374–5.
32   *Ibid.* 375–6.
33   Rae used the phrases 'consumption is not conspicuous' and 'consumption is conspicuous' on pages 297 and 310 respectively of the *New Principles*. In this connection it is interesting to note J J Spengler's statement that 'Veblen knew Rae's work but did not cite it'. 'John Rae on Economic Development: A Note', *Quarterly Journal of Economics*, Aug 1959, 394, n 6.

CHAPTER FIFTEEN

John Rae's Theory of Capital and Economic Growth

Anthony Brewer

John Rae[1] was born in Scotland in 1796. After studying medicine and science at Edinburgh and elsewhere, he emigrated to Canada in 1822, and lived there for twenty-six years, mostly working as a school teacher in Hamilton, Ontario. His only significant work on economics, the *Statement of Some New Principles on the Subject of Political Economy* (1834, cited below as *NP*)[2] was written in Canada, and published in Boston, where it was sponsored by local business interests who supported protectionist policies. Much of his later life was spent in Hawaii, but he moved to New York shortly before his death in 1872. He is mainly remembered now for his contribution to capital theory, which anticipated many of the ideas now associated with Böhm-Bawerk and other Austrian and neoclassical writers, or perhaps as a 'sociological' critic of Adam Smith. There has been relatively little discussion of his theoretical framework as a whole. I will argue that Rae had a coherent view of the determinants of output, employment and economic growth, adding up to a distinctive account of the nature and causes of the wealth of nations.

Rae's theory was deliberately constructed as a critique of Adam Smith's *Wealth of Nations*. Like Smith, Rae assumed that population is endogenous, and grows in line with growth in the demand for labour. Unlike Smith, he treated capital in the same way, arguing that capital would accumulate rapidly whenever there were profitable investment opportunities, driving the rate of return on investment down to a minimum acceptable level set by the time preference of the community, just as population growth drives wages down to a minimum subsistence level, in the standard classical theory. The stocks of capital and labour are therefore determined by demand, with the scale of economic activity governed by the availability of land and natural resources. Economic growth can only occur if 'invention' creates new investment opportunities. Where Smith treated accumulation as the primary, independent cause of growth, Rae argued that it was no more than a passive response to technical change.

He deduced a case for government intervention to encourage technical change, particularly by protecting infant industries (introducing methods of production that are new to a particular area counts as technical change). He also showed a very clear understanding of the public good character of technical advance, and of the resulting divergence between private and social benefits.

CAPITAL AND PRODUCTION

Human beings satisfy their wants by working on the materials provided by the natural environment. Material production consists of the creation of 'instruments':

> ... every thing that man, for the purpose of gaining an end, brings to exist, or alters in its form, its position or in the arrangement of its parts, is an instrument.
>
> (*NP*, p 89)

It thus includes capital goods, work in progress, consumer durables, and stocks of consumer goods up to the instant of consumption. Instruments have three characteristics. First, they are produced by labour (*NP*, p 91). Second, they 'bring to pass . . . events supplying some of the wants of man, and are then exhausted (*NP*, p 92). Third, there is an interval of time between their formation and exhaustion (*NP*, p 93), i.e. between the input of labour and the resulting satisfaction of wants.

Rae first worked through a simple case, in which an instrument is assumed to be created at one instant, by an input of labour alone, and to yield its return at a subsequent single instant (a 'point input, point output' model). The cost can be measured in terms of labour as a numeraire, and the output ('capacity', in Rae's terms) by 'the amount of labour to which they are esteemed equivalent, by the owner of the instrument' (*NP*, p 92). Note that this amounts to a subjective theory of 'value' (returns are compared in terms of the labour they are 'esteemed equivalent' to), and that labour, or rather the wage of labour, is serving simply as a numeraire; there is no trace of a labour embodied theory of value. In this simple case, any investment ('instrument') can be described by three numbers: its cost, its capacity, and the time which elapses between investment and return.[3]

Rae then arranged all instruments into an order, according to their internal rate of return. His procedure was a little clumsy. First he considered instruments which yield exactly twice their cost, ranking them according to the time they take to yield this return (*NP*, pp 100ff): 'order A' takes one year, 'order B' takes two, and so on. These 'orders' can be converted to equivalent annual percentage rates of return (*NP*, p 195). Instruments which yield more or less than double the initial costs are assimilated to the ranking by putting them alongside those with the same (compound) rate of return. Instruments which are formed over a period of time, or yield returns over a period of time, are dealt with (in effect) by finding the discount rate which equates their present value to zero (see the elaborate numerical example, *NP*, pp 104–5). Where instruments are used to produce instruments, costs of production can be calculated by including the value of the instruments used up as inputs, in terms of labour commanded (*NP*, p 91).

Rae concluded that the amount of instruments (the capital stock) formed by any society depend on four factors. They are: (1) 'the strength and quality of the materials owned by it', (2) the 'effective desire of accumulation' (to be discussed below; essentially, the minimum acceptable rate of return), (3) the wage rate, and (4) the progress of invention. In modern terms, the capital stock, and all the other relevant variables, are determined by the supply conditions of land, capital, and labour, plus the state of technology.

Rae's category of 'materials' is the same as the modern category of 'land', that is, all non-produced natural resources. With given technology, output is limited by the available materials.

> Every society possesses a certain amount of materials capable of being converted into instruments. The surface of its territory, the various minerals lying below the surface . . . even perhaps the light and heat of the sun, are all to be regarded as materials, which, through the agency of the labor of its inhabitants, may be converted into instruments. The extent of the power, which the inhabitants of any state may possess, to convert into instruments the materials of which they have the command . . . increases . . . as their knowledge . . . increases.
>
> (*NP*, p 99)

Invention 'animates industry', but the amount of materials worked up 'must depend entirely' on the available materials (*NP*, p 262).[4]

Labour supply can be dealt with quickly. Rae took over the classical (Malthusian) assumption that labour is in elastic supply at a given real wage (which might differ between different societies), and treated the wage as given, for simplicity. Workers may substitute one good for another; it is the level of nourishment, clothing, housing, and so on that is taken to be fixed (*NP*, pp 97–8). An increase (or decrease) in wages lowers (or raises) returns on investments correspondingly (since wages are a cost).[5]

With given materials, and a given wage, it is always possible to increase output (in Rae's terms, to increase the capacity of the instruments of the society), by investing more, but only at the expense of lowering the rate of return ('moving the instruments formed continually onward in the series A B . . .' *NP*, p 109). Rae presented a number of examples and arguments to back up this version of the law of diminishing returns. He argued, for example, that

> as the stock of materials which any society possesses, is limited, its members, if we suppose them to acquire no additional knowledge of the powers of those materials, and yet to add continually to the amount of instruments they form out of them, must at length have recourse to such as are either operated on with greater difficulty, or bring about desired events more sparingly or tardily.
>
> (*NP*, p 113)

Note how explicitly the falling rate of return is ascribed to the fixity of the stock of materials or, in modern terms, to diminishing returns to a fixed supply of land.

The major weakness of Rae's analysis is the lack of any clear distinction between average and marginal returns on investment. The calculation of returns seems to apply to each instrument separately; once the calculation is done, instruments can be placed in order of returns. This would be no problem if the only relevant choice over any instrument was whether to construct it or not, independent of any other instrument. The extract quoted above illustrates the procedure; first produce the high yielding instruments, then, if necessary, those of lower yield. However, other examples presented by Rae (in the same chapter and elsewhere) involve either/or choices; either build a house of wood, or of stone.[6] In this case, the relevant question is obviously: what is the extra return on the extra cost of building in stone? There are examples in the book where Rae seems to have thought in this way, but it is not clear that he fully appreciated the distinction.[7]

INTERTEMPORAL CHOICE

There is, according to Rae, 'no limit to the capacity for the supply of future wants' (*NP*, p 118), if people are willing to accept a low enough rate of return, that is, if they are willing to wait long enough. He argued, however, that

> The formation of every instrument . . . implies the sacrifice of some smaller present good, for the production of some greater future good. If, then, the production of that future greater good. be conceived to deserve the sacrifice of this present smaller good, the instrument will be formed, if not, it will not be formed.

> (*NP*, p 118)

The equilibrium stock of capital is determined by the willingness of individuals to wait. If life and health were to last for ever, and if people were rational, they would always give up a smaller good for a larger (*NP*, p119). Since there is no limit to the capital that can be invested and yield a positive return, this would presumably mean that there would be no equilibrium: capital and output would both tend to infinity. Rae did not bother with this question, since life is 'the most uncertain of things'(*NP*, p 119), and people are in fact, impatient, and unwilling to wait. Purely selfish considerations would lead to a low 'effective desire of accumulation' (a high rate of time preference), and a low capital stock; a high effective desire for accumulation is the result of altruistic concern for one's descendants and for posterity generally (*NP*, p 121ff). (Rae frequently introduced moralistic considerations; he clearly felt that individuals *ought* to be concerned about the future). To begin with, Rae assumed that all individuals in a given society had the same preferences between present and future; the effects of differences between individuals are discussed at a later stage.

With given wages, natural resources, and technology, the equilibrium capital stock is determined by the 'effective desire of accumulation', measured by the slowest yielding 'order' of instrument that individuals are prepared to invest in. Both labour and capital are in elastic supply: labour at a given wage, capital at a given rate of return.

In modern terms, one could represent his model with a utility function of the form

$$V = \int_0^\infty e^{-\mu t} U(c) dt$$

where V represents utility, t is time measured from the present, U(c) is a sub-utility function showing the contemporaneous 'good' derived from a consumption vector c at any date, and μ is the rate of time discount (measuring the 'effective desire of accumulation'). An instrument could be represented by its effect on utility at time t, ΔU_t, which would be negative during the construction period, and positive once the returns start coming on. It has a rate of return of λ if

$$O = \int_0^\infty e^{-\lambda t} \Delta U_t dt$$

An instrument is worth constructing if $\lambda \geq \mu$, so all instruments satisfying this condition are constructed. Rae did not write it like this, of course, but his verbal formulation amounts to the same thing. Recall in particular that the returns on investment are measured in terms of the amount of labour (numeraire) they are 'esteemed equivalent' to (i.e. in terms of subjective utility), and that time preference is measured in terms of 'good' (subjective utility).

As it is presented here, and in Rae's initial statement, the theory is only directly relevant to the case of an isolated individual; Rae treated it as a model of a complete society by postponing consideration of differences between individuals (*Cf. NP*, p 198). Within any given society, he argued, there is a considerable degree of uniformity in preferences, because of the force of habit and example (*NP*, p 123). The rate of time preference is influenced by a number of features of the society. Longer life spans, greater security, and a culture which stresses provision for one's descendants or concern for the future of society in general, all lower the rate of time discount.

Rae stressed social factors affecting time preference very heavily, and discussed them at some length. So, for example, in China, a gerontocratic society placed power in the hands of the old, who could not look forward to much life expectancy, and felt few obligations to their descendants, and hence did not invest, while the Roman empire declined because of the corruption of morals, reluctance to marry, and lack of concern for descendants. Some writers see this 'sociological' element as an important feature of Rae's work,[8] I am mainly concerned here with the structure of Rae's economic model, so it does not matter very much why preferences are what they are.

In a market system, production is for exchange, because of the gains from specialisation and division of labour. The analysis in terms of subjective utility carries over with minor amendments.

> As all instruments exist solely to satisfy wants, so any man will consent to receive an instrument in exchange, or expect to give it in exchange, only as it is a means of supplying wants. It is the business of every man to adopt the readiest and easiest means he can devise to supply all coming needs, and it is solely because the medium of barter presents the readiest means of effecting this end, that he adopts it.

(*NP*, p 166).

The 'absolute value' of an instrument is determined by discounting the future benfits it is expected to yield, using labour as numeraire, its 'relative value' by its market price (*NP*, p 172). In equilibrium, the two must agree, provided 'the effective desire of accumulation of a community has had opportunity to work up the materials possessed by it' (*NP*, pp 172–3), and the interest rate must be brought into line with the (common) rate of return on investments (*NP*, p 196). Note that this implies a consistently subjective theory of value; all products are 'instruments', and are valued by discounting expected benefits, even if the date of consumption of (say) an item of food is no more than seconds away.

When individuals differ in their 'effective desire of accumulation', those with a relatively low desire of accumulation (high rate of time discount) value quick returning assets (consumer goods) above, and slow returning assets below, their market prices, so they (gradually) sell capital assets to those whose rate of time discount is lower. Presumably, a class of improvident individuals who own no saleable assets emerges. The result is that 'all instruments capable of transfer, are . . . at nearly the same orders' (*NP*, p 199), i.e. rates of return are equalised. The improvident, however, own cheap consumer durables with short lives (i.e. quicker than optimal returns), because ownership of consumer goods cannot be transferred without ceasing to consume their services altogether (*NP*, pp 199–200; consumer credit and rental arrangements were not then well developed).

Given time, then, a common rate of return on investment emerges in a given society, which reflects the general rate of time preference among its members, and this determines the size and composition of the stock of instruments (i.e. the capital stock). Whether average or marginal returns are equalised remains far from clear, Rae may have anticipated many elements of Austrian or neoclassical economics, but not marginalism.

The Importance of 'Invention'

Rae's main purpose was to argue that economic growth is governed by the rate of technical change ('invention'). With given technology, output depends on the available land ('materials'), labour, and capital ('instruments'). Labour is in elastic supply in the long run, at a subsistence wage, and so is capital, at a rate of return corresponding to the 'effective desire of accumulation' in the society. In the absence of technical change, an economy tends to a stationary state governed by the available 'materials' (i.e. by land scarcity).[9] This is, of course, no more than the standard classical view; Rae cited Smith's 'admission' that a country may 'come to have as great a quantity of stock . . . as the nature and extent of the territory will admit'(*NP*, pp 23–4). The difference is that Rae treated convergence to this stationary date (for given technology) as relatively rapid, attributing any sustained growth to continuing technical change, while Smith (and other classical economists) treated capital accumulation as the primary, independent, cause of continuing growth.

Figure 1 illustrates this argument. The stock of materials is given. The horizontal axis represents the capital stock, K, in terms of some numeraire, such as the (given) wage, and the vertical axis the common rate of return on investment (which is inversely related to the 'order of instruments', in Rae's terminology). Since population and employment are endogenous, K is an index of output and population, as well as capital, at least for given technology. F_0 shows the relation between K and r for the initial state of technology, which is shifted to F_1 by technical change. F_0 and F_1 are drawn so that there is no limit to the capital stock which will yield a positive return, as Rae insisted.

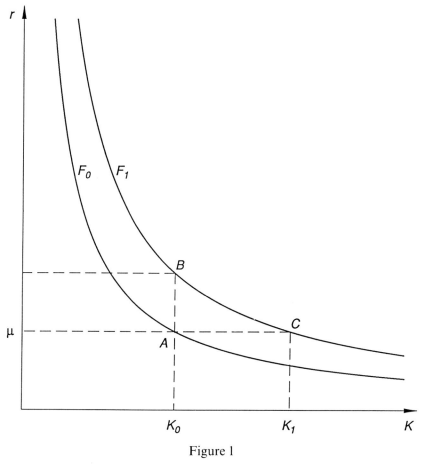

Figure 1

K_0 is the stationary value of K corresponding to the common rate of time discount μ, with the initial technology. Rae treated most societies as being already at this point, though he seems to have made an exception for North America, which was accumulating fast with $r > \mu$.[10] According to Smith, and the other classics, most Western societies were well to the left of K_0, and proceeding slowly towards it, at a rate that made the stationary state a very distant prospect. According to Rae, the only way the economy can grow (apart from a fall in μ) is through invention, shifting the equilibrium from A to C, along a path like ABC. He discussed the temporary increase in the profit rate following an invention (*NP*, p 263), distinguishing it from the (permanently) high profit rate in societies with a 'deficiency' in the effective desire of accumulation. The first is a sign of progress, the second a cause of poverty.

Rae dramatised his difference with Smith by making fun of Smith's triumphant account of capital accumulation in England, and of the scope for further accumulation. According to Smith, 'The annual produce of the land and labour of England is certainly much greater than it was more than a century ago . . .' but if the revenue squandered in wars had been saved instead, 'to what height the real wealth . . . of the country might by this time have been raised it is not perhaps very easy even to imagine' (Smith, 1776, pp 334–5, quoted in *NP*, pp 25–6). The point is that Smith thought that there was almost unlimited scope for accumulation without any need for 'invention'. Rae drew a parallel with population; 'Before the time of the Essay on Population, arguments and conclusions very similar to these were brought forward concerning the waste of human life in wars . . .' (*NP*, p 26), and launched into a parody of Smith, imagining how large the population might be if those killed in wars had lived and had children. Smith would, of course, have rejected this argument as applied to population, as did Rae, on the grounds that population is limited by employment. Rae rejected Smith's treatment of accumulation for the same reason.

> There must be some strong inherent vice in any community, where the certain prospect of plentiful subsistence does not produce an abundant population. It can only be, also, from the effects of some great inherent vice, that, in any community, a very profitable investment for capital can be held out, and yet capital not accumulate with great rapidity.
>
> (*NP*, p 29)

In other words, both capital and labour are in relatively elastic supply. The size of the capital stock is determined by the demand for capital, and growth in this demand is governed by 'invention'.

> Before population can advance, there must be something on which it can subsist; before capital can increase, there must be something in which it can be embodied . . . It is invention, which showing how profitable returns can be got from the one, and how subsistence procured from the other, that may most fitly be esteemed that cause of the existence of both.
>
> (*NP*, p 31)

Rae accused Smith of a fallacy of composition. An individual farmer, for example, can grow rich by buying more land. A nation cannot; it can only add to the capital stock by simultaneously changing its composition (*NP*, p 9), which drives down the rate of return quickly unless invention provides new uses for capital. A farmer who uses flails to thresh grain needs a certain number of them, and has no use for more, as long as he works the same land. It only became possible to invest more in this particular activity when the threshing machine was invented, directly increasing the capital employed, and reducing costs, allowing expansion of cultivation at both the intensive and extensive margins (*NP*, pp19–20).

ECONOMIC POLICY

Inventors and innovators are typically not well rewarded (*NP*, p 217), because the benefits they produce are shared with others; 'the fruits of the labors of genius, are the property of the whole human race' (*NP*, p 222). Rae, in other words, recognised that knowledge is a public good, and that this causes a problem of incentives. He thought that most invention was the result of substituting new materials for old, or of applying accepted principles in new circumstances or to different materials. Necessity is frequently the mother of invention; Britain, for example, was forced to turn to coal when wood became scarce (*NP*, p 245). Wars and other events which disrupt existing patterns of trade stimulate invention (*NP*, p 222). Transferring techniques to a new place or set of circumstances is difficult, but Rae also regarded it as a major source of invention and thus of economic progress.

Taken together, these arguments formed the basis of Rae's case for protection of infant industries, as well as for other forms of government intervention to promote invention (*NP*, pp 15–16). He was well aware of Smith's case for *laissez-faire*, and understood that he had to show that there was some form of market failure if he was to justify intervention. He found it in the divergence of private and social benefits when innovations are copied.

> . . . to transfer a manufacture from one country to another, must always be a very tedious and expensive operation, for any individual to perform . . . To balance the extraordinary outlay, [the innovator] must have extraordinary returns.
>
> (*NP*, pp 51–2)

But any extra profits will soon be competed away by free riding rivals, who can gain access to the technology by tempting away skilled workers. As a result, innovators usually fail. Rae charged Smith with wanting to wait until 'the miscalculations of some unfortunate projector confer on us a public benefit' (*NP*, p 53). Profits may sometimes be high enough for an individual to introduce an import substituting industry and still benefit, for example if the inputs required are particularly cheap locally. If so it would have been optimal to have introduced the industry at an even earlier date if social benfits had been taken into account (*NP*, p 54).

> . . . the introduction of an art into any country . . . is a great good to all, . . . but it is maintained, that it is impossible for all the members of the community advantageously to unite in bringing about this common benefit . . . a new channel might be opened from the exhaustless river of human power, springing from the mingled sources of nature and art . . . [but] there is an obstruction . . . No individual will open up the channel, because, were he to do so, he could derive no

more benefit from the labor than others who had not labored . . . the legislator, the power acting for the whole society, might do so (*NP*, pp 55–6).

For its date, this is a surprisingly explicit exposition of the case for public provision of public goods.

Rae's influence

The *New Principles* were not very well received; most reviews were hostile, and Rae retreated to Canada as a school teacher. On the other hand, Nassau Senior appreciated its quality, and recommended it to John Stuart Mill, who referred to it warmly in his *Principles* of 1848. An Italian translation was published in the 1850s. Over the years the *New Principles* has had a considerable influence on a rather diverse set of writers; perhaps the diversity of its influence explains its relative neglect by historians and economists.

Rae's influence has been most direct, and most often noticed, in the theory of capital, saving, and intertemporal choice. Böhm-Bawerk, it is true, rediscovered (and advanced on) Rae's ideas quite independently, though he acknowledged them generously when the omission was pointed out to him. Irving Fisher, the other great founding father of the modern theory of captial and interest, dedicated his *Theory of Interest* (1930) to John Rae and Eugen von Böhm-Bawerk, 'who laid the foundations upon which I have attempted to build', and stated in the preface that every essential part of his theory had been 'at least foreshadowed by John Rae in 1834'. A count of references in the index show more to Rae than to any other writer, Böhm-Bawerk included (though references to Böhm-Bawerk tend to involve more substantial discussion).

Mair (1990)[11] points out some less obvious channels through which Rae influenced subsequent work. There is reason to think that Veblen drew quite heavily on Rae (it is difficult to be sure, since Veblen rarely acknowledged his intellectual debts). Both discussed conspicuous consumption (as Spengler, 1959b, noted), but Mair picks out the common emphasis on technical change as a more substantial link.[12] Rae's emphasis on technical change also suggests the possibility that he may have influenced Schumpeter. Again one finds many points in common. Schumpeter (1911), like Rae, argued that an economy will settle into a static equilibrium unless the equilibrium is disturbed by 'innovations' (Rae's 'inventions'), and he referred approvingly to Rae ('the powerful penetration and originality of this work may still repay perusal by the modern reader'; p 11). Schumpeter's analytical framework differed from Rae's in many ways, as one would expect of a work written nearly eighty years later, but the basic insights are remarkably similar.

Conclusion

To treat Rae simply as a precursor of Austrian or neoclassical capital theory, while true, would be inadequate. To regard him as no more than a 'sociological' or methodological critic of Smith would be equally limited. He certainly did emphasise social and moral factors as determinants of saving and of inventive activity, but he embedded these insights in an analytical framework every bit as rigorous as any writer of his time. His main concerns were squarely in the classical tradition; he aimed to rival Adam Smith, by producing an alternative explanation of the causes of the wealth of a nation and of the policies best calculated to advance it. He assumed subsistence wages and an endogenous population, which might be regarded as the hallmark of classical economics. Indeed one might almost argue that his theory is a variant of Ricardo's. Both assumed subsistence wages, and deduced a falling profit rate caused by land scarcity, with a stationary state staved off by technical change. He differed from Smith and Ricardo over the rate of convergence to the stationary state in the absence of technical change, taking a very pessimistic view of the scope for growth without technical change. At the same time, he consistently took the rational pursuit of subjective (but not necessarily selfish) aims as his basis, and analysed production in terms of choices between more and less 'capital intensive' techniques, but these 'neoclassical' features were embedded in an essentially classical framework. Above all, he was the first (as far as I know) to place technical change, not capital accumulation, at the centre of a theory of growth and development, and to work out its implications rigorously.

NOTES

1   Not to be confused with the biographer of Adam Smith. For a biography and further discussion of his very varied writings, see James (1965).
2   The edition cited has identical pagination to the original edition and the Kelley reprint.
3   The capacity of the instrument is presumably only defined for a specific user, the one who 'esteems' its benefit equivalent to a certain amount of labour. Rae's examples, at this stage in his argument, are mainly of isolated individuals (pioneers in the Canadian backwoods and the like) who consume the resulting benefits themselves, but he was not entirely consistent. The argument is extended to a market system later.
4   Despite the importance of 'materials' (land) in the analysis, Rae said nothing about rent.
5   Note the shift in assumptions; previously, the discussion was based on an individual doing the work himself, while here the assumption is that workers are hired to do the job and paid a wage. Note also that Rae deliberately adopted the assumption of fixed wages as a simplification: 'it is not intended to enter into any investigation of the principles determining the amount of the wages of labor'(NP, p 97).
6   Incidentally, many of Rae's examples derive from his experiences in the backwoods (literally) of Canada; pioneers construct houses of less durable materials than those used in Britain because there are more urgent claims on their time.
7   Rae can perhaps be excused, since many Keynesian writings as recently as the 1960s dealt with investment in much the same way; calculate the internal rate of return for each potential investment separately, then compare it with the cost of capital. Since he worked with numerical examples, it is hardly surprising that Rae failed to

notice that internal rate of return calculations can yield multiple solutions, so that it may not be possible to order instruments uniquely.

8   The *New Principles* were republished in 1905 (in a somewhat mangled version) by one Charles Mixter under the title *The Sociological Theory of Capital*. On the sociological component in Rae's work, *Cf.* Mair (1990).

9   Spengler (1959a, p 397) claims that Rae did not 'make use of the stationary state'. Rae expected continued invention to stave off stagnation, but it is very clear that he thought growth would soon stop without invention.

10   Even for North America, though, he stressed the need to adapt and import technology: see below.

11   Mair argues that Rae was an important figure in the Scottish tradition of political economy. It is clear that Rae's overall intellectual framework was formed in Scotland, under the influence of the Scottish Enlightenment, though his main interests at that time were scientific and he did not turn to economics until after he had left Scotland for good. At the same time, many of the distinctive features of his ecnomics seem to have been suggested by his experiences in Canada. His choice of examples suggests that his concern with the choices between more or less capital intensive techniques may have been prompted by the contrast between the methods used in pioneer communities in Canada and those used in Britain. Rae himself stressed the creative possibilities unleashed by the establishment of industries in new circumstances and locations; his own work could be seen in those terms, as the result of transplanting a Scottish tradition to the New World.

12   Mair also associates Rae with Veblen's account of the potentially disruptive effects of technical change, though here I must disagree; as I read him, Rae argued that disruption stimulates technical innovation, rather than the reverse.

REFERENCES

Fisher, I (1930). *The Theory of Interest*. Reprinted 1977, Philadelphia: Porcupine Press

James, R W (1965). *John Rae, Political Economist* (2 vols). University of Toronto Press

Mair, D (1990). 'John Rae: Ugly Duckling or Black Swan?', forthcoming, *Scottish Journal of Political Economy*

Rae, J (1834). *Statement of Some New Principles on the Subject of Political Economy*. In James (1965), vol II

Smith, A (1776). *An Inquiry into the Nature and Causes of the Wealth of Nations*. Edition cited: R H Campbell, A S Skinner and W B Todd (eds), Oxford University Press, 1976

Schumpeter, J (1911). *The Theory of Economic Development*. English translation by R Opie, New York: Oxford University Press, 1961.

Spengler, J J (1959a). 'John Rae on Economic Development: a Note', *Quarterly Journal of Economics*, 73, pp 393–406

——— (1959b) 'Veblen and Mandeville Contrasted', *Weltwirtschaftliches Archiv*, 82, pp 35–67